THE AGE
OF TELEVISION

THE AGE
OF TELEVISION

A study of viewing habits
and the impact of television
on American life

LEO BOGART

Third edition
Incorporating the original text with
added new introduction, notes, and
bibliography

FREDERICK UNGAR PUBLISHING CO.
NEW YORK

This volume comprises the original text of the 1958 edition with a new Introduction, revised Appendix, extensive notes updating the text and presenting new research material, and a supplemental bibliography. The index covers the entire volume.

Acknowledgments

In preparing this new edition I have received valuable assistance from a number of my associates, including Mary Lehr, Julia Walter, Ann Brady, and Joseph Wallis. My special appreciation goes to Marie Thornton, for digging, assembling, typing, and keeping me more or less under control.

CONTENTS

TABLES

NEW TABLES WITHIN THE NOTES

INTRODUCTION
TO THE 1972 EDITION

This is a book about a bygone era. Already the age of television as we have known it can be seen as an episode in the history of mass communication, in which an ever-evolving technology will produce new "ages" at an accelerating pace. "The Age of Television," as described in this volume, was the period of television's brilliant burst into the main line of American culture. I wrote this book in the mid-1950's; the first edition covered TV's first dozen years. During this time, TV ceased to be a novelty and became the entertainment center of four out of every five homes in the nation. Another dozen years have passed since then; in that time ownership of TV sets has become virtually universal and television has matured and consolidated its hold on the public's leisure time. The main features of TV's development were already clearly in evidence when this book first appeared, so that it is interesting to note in retrospect how few are the significant changes that have taken place since then in the pattern of viewing. But television is on the threshold of major changes that will make it a qualitatively different medium a dozen years from now. Essentially, television appears to be headed along the same path that radio took before it; viewing, which has always been a group experience, is becoming personal and individual. This impending transformation will carry with it great implications for television's programming structure, its economic support, and its social impact.

The fact that television is about to undergo important qualitative changes makes it particularly appropriate to reissue this review of its effects on the life of the nation in its first and halcyon years. In considering this new edition I concluded that the original book, though dated, was in no sense obsolete, and that the additional perspective of the intervening years gave me no reason to modify the record, though it was obviously essential to update it.

When this book was first in preparation, it was still possible to do a thorough and conscientious job of summarizing all the available evidence on what television was doing to the American people and the American scene. Today an exhaustive bibliography of the literature on TV would fill a thicker volume than this book. To summarize all the research would not only be impossible; it would be pointless. A great deal of what has been researched and written is redundant; much of it applies to specific programs or to other transient phenomena in TV's history; and, since television as a field of endeavor has produced its own new subspecialties, much of it is of very specialized interest.

Rather than write a new book or rewrite the old one, I have chosen to provide the reader with a set of notes that tell him what he must know in order to read the earlier text from the vantage point of 1972. That is, in the notes at the end of the book I have included the latest statistics available, and where appropriate, have cited significant recent studies that bear on the subject matter of each chapter. (I have kept within the book's original frame of reference to the American scene and have not attempted any thorough review of what has happened in other countries.) The appendix on broadcast research has been rewritten, and the bibliography has been supplemented. But the body of the text has been left intact. When the text says "today," it is referring to the present tense of the 1958 edition.

What essentially is different now than it was then? In 1958 one American family in five was still without television, and an interesting theme in television research was the periodic measurement of the medium's growing level of penetration. Those who were best able to afford it were the first to acquire TV sets, and those with the lowest incomes were the last. The propensity to view television, however, is in inverse proportion to income, education, and other indicators of social status. People of higher means and schooling simply have more alternative ways of spending their time; they can better afford baby-sitters, nights on the town, and paid entertainment; and they are generally more oriented to the printed word. Thus, for the first part of TV's history, the characteristics of the measured audience represented a mixture of the social differences in the distribution of set ownership and the social differences in viewing tastes and viewing time.

Today only one household in twenty is without a TV set. These non-TV households are characterized mainly by their marginal status. They tend to be composed of old, poor, and rural people. A disproportionate number live alone or are people on the move, with a minimum of belongings. Many of them are individuals who live almost outside the media system — they read little, even listen to radio rarely. Mixed in with this low-status group is a handful of eccentrics from the higher end of the social scale — the intellectuals who "won't have a set in the house."

What all this means is that in today's era of near-saturation ownership, differences in viewing habits reflect personal preference rather than access to TV itself. Except for a few sheepherders in isolated regions of the mountain states, everyone in America is within range of a TV signal — and this is a far cry from the early days. For years TV aerials have sprouted from the roofs of the humblest sharecroppers' shacks and of the most miserable urban tenements. Television is a necessity of life for those who live in poverty, and all but a small proportion of those at this level own sets. The stabilization of the size and character of the TV audience has had its repercussions in the domain of programming content. In TV's period of growth, the commercial broadcasters were receptive to innovation and experiment. They continually sought new ways to expand the audience by extending the hours of the broadcast day and by searching for new formats and fields of achievement. The decade of the 1960's was one in which the universal mass audience, already established, was incapable of expansion. Viewing as a pastime had already found its upper limits, subject to the inevitable competition from other alternative activities. At the same time, the television industry itself became steadily more competitive, as the number of commercial stations (and particularly of nonnetwork independent stations) continued to grow, as the UHF audience increased with the aid of a Federal requirement that TV-set manufacturers provide a UHF tuner as standard equipment, and as public television and cable television became significant new forces on the scene.

At this writing, the average American household is within viewing range of nearly seven different television stations, and it will have even more choices available as the years go by.

The growth in the number of stations on the air (from 562 in 1960 to 878 today) and the rise of cable systems have widened the range of choices for the television viewer. (The National Cable Television Assn. estimates that the proportion of homes in areas served by cable TV will rise from 18% in 1970 to 80% in 1980 and that the proportion of all U.S. homes tied into cable TV will rise from 7% in 1970 to 32% in 1980.) The lifting of the legal barriers to pay TV will also introduce new attractions. The available audience inevitably must be divided as the number of program choices continues to grow, and it will be further divided as the number of TV sets in each home increases, giving individual tastes a freer rein. Total size of the television audience at any given time period, however, is generally inelastic (except on such occasions as a moon landing or a Presidential address). Televiewing is limited by competition from other activities and does not go up when people have access to a greater number of channels. Nor does it appear responsive to the quality of programming.

The most important change taking place in television is its transformation from a medium of generalized family entertainment into one of more intimate, personal viewing.

Many of us remember radio in its prime, the set in the center of the living room with the family gathered around it listening to "Amos & Andy" or to the squeaking door of "Inner Sanctum." Radio commanded great attention. People participated; it held them together in the family living room. Contrast that with radio today — still a great communications medium, but totally changed in character, both in content and in the nature of the listening experience. Today we can see television going the same route, from a family entertainment center to an intimate, personalized, individual medium of viewing. When the TV set goes from the living room to the bedroom or den, the family audience spreads out. As that happens, the broadcaster whose program is being tuned within a household no longer has the same chances as in the past to get the attention of most persons in that home.

Although the total number of hours of TV-set usage per household has remained steady in recent years (an average of almost 6 hours in 1970, according to the widely used A. C. Nielsen estimates), the size and composition of the audience viewing TV has already undergone some significant changes. Not only on the part of the general public but even within the television industry itself the extent of these changes is obscured by the widespread confusion of "ratings" based on a mechanical measurement of TV-set tuning with the reality of communication with individuals.

About a third of all U.S. households now have more than one TV set, and these households include 40% of the nation's adults. The number of multiset households grows steadily. Miniaturization of components has made possible smaller portable TV sets available at comparatively low prices. Color has brought new dimensions to TV. When a family acquires a color TV set, the old black-and-white set is commonly retained rather than discarded or traded in, and we have a two-TV family.

For every 100 hours an adult spends in front of the TV set in a one-TV home, he spends only 44 hours per set in a multi-TV home, although he watches about the same number of hours altogether. This sharp difference is easily obscured when TV statistics are expressed in terms of sets in use and homes using television, as though these ratings could be translated into the same number of *people* watching as in the past.

By 1975 a majority of households will have several sets. If the most TV-oriented within any family size or income bracket were the first ones on the block to get color or the second set, this would suggest that the total time people spend watching television will drop as time goes on and the lighter TV viewers follow the crowd. Women's daytime viewing will be affected by the steady increase in the proportion who work, which now represents 36% of all married women. Simmons' data indicate that audiences for prime-time network programs fell by 13% between 1967 and 1970, reflecting increased competition from independent stations.

Apart from short-run fluctuations influenced by the unemployment rate, the total time spent viewing television is unlikely to show any increase as long as it must compete with other household and personal activities. It is, moreover, limited by the apparent stability of the average work week, which the NICB (National Industrial Conference Board) estimates to be diminishing at the rate of 0.3% a year between 1947 and 1980, or about one hour weekly every eight years. Leisure time is not growing at a pace that is likely to swell TV viewing significantly.

The growth in the number of active channels, along with the lengthening of the broadcast day, has vastly sharpended TV's already prodigious appetite for programming material. The development of video-tape recording brought about the virtual elimination of live programming. (Tape provided substantial advantages in flexibility, economy, and image fidelity, over the filmed kinescopes of the 1950s.) Reruns of past programs became a standard part of television fare, and not only in the dog days of midsummer. The rise in TV's demands for content coincided with changes in the structure and economics of the motion-picture business and overcame the last resistance to the release and sale of Hollywood's film libraries for TV use. Feature-film showings became a part of the regular prime-time network lineups as well as a stock feature of local station fare in daytime and late evening hours.

The production of programs especially for television also underwent a significant transformation as a result of rising costs and of advertisers' desires to scatter their messages widely over a broad cross-section of the viewing public. These two factors produced a steady attrition in the institution of exclusive program sponsorship by a single advertiser. (By 1971 only 7% of network programming fell under this heading.) Instead, network advertisers increasingly spread their messages across an array of programs in "scatter plans" designed to broaden their coverage, and a larger share of all national advertising was placed on local stations on a "spot" basis rather than on the networks. The effect of this was to do away with program production as a function of the advertising agency and to reduce sharply the production activities of the networks. The creation of TV's basic product for the evening hours of maximum viewing became the domain of the "packagers" — essentially Hollywood entrepreneurs who operated independently with the network program departments as their principal clients.

The networks' programming philosophy was founded on two principles discussed in this book: (1) The total size of the viewing audience is remarkably inelastic at any particular time, because viewing is essentially a pastime activity indulged in for its own sake rather than for its content. As already noted, increasing choice merely divides the audience, which selects among the available alternatives; improving the quality of a program may add to its competitive strength but will not add to the overall number of people watching TV. (2) Inertia is a powerful force in establishing the pattern of viewing; a high proportion of those tuned to any given program will remain automatically with the same station for the next program, provided there is no sharp discontinuity in the basic audience appeal. As a result, network programming specialists think in terms of the attraction and holding power of their program *lineup* over the course of an evening, rather than in terms of *individual* programs regarded in isolation. Furthermore, they plan their own schedules on the basis of their shrewd expectations of what the competing networks have up their sleeves, and ruthlessly realign them when programs fail to show the strength required to stand up to the competition. This can be done all the more readily because at any given moment there is always any number of program "packages" available for sale and already "in the can," at least in pilot form. (A script for a half-hour pilot program costs between $15,000 and $20,000, and production of the prototype costs around $250,000. NBC reports that it reviews over a hundred new program ideas each year, orders between 30 and 50 scripts, and commissions between 10 and 20 completed pilot programs. There is sometimes a lead time of 18 months between the first program ideas and the screening of a program for prospective advertisers.)

The cumulative effect of all this has been to give a growing proportion of commercial television entertainment a canned or prepackaged character that has only accentuated features already firmly established when this book first appeared: adherence to tried and true formulas in dramatic plots and characterizations, blandness and superficiality in the treatment of serious themes, avoidance of social and political controversies except insofar as these can be dealt with in stereotyped form. The real reasons for this insipidity are the inexorable economic demands to go after the broad mass audience and the limitations in the size of the available pool of talent. (The typical program director of a local TV station earns between $10,000 and $20,000 in 1971 — certainly a living wage, but hardly one munificent enough to provide an irresistible attraction to creative geniuses.) Overall, there seems to have been a diminution, or at least reduced visibility, in the innovative and experimental approaches to programming content and format that were evident in television's earlier, yeastier days.

Effective in the fall of 1971, the Federal Communications Commission had ordered a reduction in network time from 3½ to 3 hours nightly, with the ostensible purpose of encouraging local production efforts when the audience is at its peak. There was every initial evidence that this time would in most cases be filled by syndicated packaged programming emanating from the same Hollywood sources as the network shows, but with different, indirect formulas for sponsorship and financing.

While the American broadcasting system, commercial and noncommercial, continues to give forth, predictably, some entertainment programs that rise far above the general level and, on rare occasions, to brilliance, there is no reason to revise the judgment rendered in the first edition of this book, when I voiced skepticism that TV could in any sense be considered a major new art form. Its most outstanding drama has been produced on film or tape, with the aid of all the devices of editing and montage that make film a different medium than live performance, with its theatrical constraints and uncertainties.

On the other hand, television news has indeed come into its own as a unique, new form of communication, far transcending both the radio newscast and the film newsreel, which were its original ancestors. Because of its capacity to expose enormous audiences to events as they happen or to statements as they are actually made, television, unlike newspapers, radio, or magazines, makes news and *is* news. This is true when television projects live coverage of dramatic events in war, public ceremony, civil disorder, or the political process. It is perhaps even more striking when public officials use television as a forum to reveal new policies or to debate established ones.

The past fifteen years have seen a steady rise in the American people's acknowledged dependence upon television as a major source of information about public affairs. Curiously enough, the willingness of a comfortable majority to say that they get most of their news about what is going on in the world today from TV does not jibe with the actually

limited size of the daily audience for the typical straight
news broadcast. (In New York City an average of 23% of
the adult public watch the sum total of all three network
early evening newscasts.) The readership of newspapers and
of news magazines is as great as it has ever been. A number of
radio stations have successfully gone to an all-news format,
and most AM radio stations now offer a continual succession
of hourly newscasts throughout the day. It is evident that
when people say they get most of their world news from
television, they have something more in mind than the bulletins and probably more than the accompanying film footage. It is more likely that they respond to the total experience
that TV provides them through newscasts, documentaries,
interviews, discussions, and debates — but most of all, through
its direct and immediate presentation of those rare historical
moments in which every man can now feel himself to be a
participant: a riot, a coronation, a political convention, an
Olympic match, a landing on the moon. (The telecasts of
Apollo 14 were watched by an estimated 600,000,000
people.)

It is on such extraordinary occasions that television
sometimes seems to approach the function assigned to it in
Marshall McLuhan's vision of the "global village" — a world
bound together in the common experience of instantaneous
communication.

Since the age of television came to America, it has
come, in one form or another, to most parts of the world.
While nowhere else has it achieved as yet quite the universality of penetration that it has in the United States, the
high levels of TV-set ownership in Canada, Western Europe,
Australia, and Japan have already established its preeminent
position in the leisure time of those countries. In East
Europe, Latin America, and the Soviet Union, television is
a major force in the urban culture. Even in parts of the
underdeveloped world, like the Middle East, where the number of TV sets is still low relative to the population, the
influence of television radiates far out from the small minor-

ity of TV owners, through sets displayed in cafés and other public places. India and Israel belatedly abandoned their longstanding resistance (on economic grounds) to the introduction of TV. Only South Africa has, for political reasons, remained as a major holdout. When South Africans were forced to get their coverage of the moon landings on radio while the rest of the world watched it on television, a great public clamor went up. In 1971 the government announced plans to introduce TV.

In bilingual societies such as South Africa, Canada, and Belgium, the approach of television has provoked anxiety about a shift in linguistic identity toward the culturally dominant group. This possibility is not merely imaginary; a C.B.C. study in 1965 found that in areas within reception range of both French and English language broadcasts, one out of every nine French-speaking households viewing evening TV watched an English channel, but only about one English family out of fifty was watching a French channel. In warring Jordan and Israel, by contrast, it is common practice to "eavesdrop" on the enemy's television programs, for a change in pace.

Wherever it has gone, television has broadened perspectives, made the remote familiar, and raised aspirations. Thus it has become a revolutionary force in a world in which people coexist on many different levels of technology and income.

The *Economist* (March 28, 1964) observes: "Today, hardly a child in the whole of Italy has not seen close-ups of beautiful boys and girls industriously brushing their teeth. Yet how many of these children actually possess a toothbrush or can reasonably expect to own one when they grow up? Two years ago at Ferrandina, a town of 10,000 inhabitants in Lucania, the average sale of toothbrushes was forty a year. Can modern Italy provide fifty million Italians with toothbrushes and all the other things that belong to a modern industrial standard of living?"

The importance of American-produced programming

in the broadcast output of television stations around the world has in many cases evoked nationalistic concern about the spread of U.S. "cultural imperialism," and in a number of cases has produced arbitrary limitations on the amount of foreign programming permitted.

The success formulas of American commercial entertainment have worked well around the world because they seem to correspond to certain human universals. In this respect the widespread adoption and imitation of American TV programs follows (and perhaps reflects) the historical appeal of Hollywood films. Whenever European viewers have had a choice between commercial television (with programming along the lines of the American model) and uplifting noncommercial television, the former has captured the lion's share of the audience. BBC2, introduced as a "culture channel," had only 6% of the TV audience two months after it came on the air, when it was still a novelty.

After TV finally came to Saudi Arabia in 1965, the daily programs began with 20 minutes of readings from the Koran and proceeded with "Peyton Place." The New York *Times* of March 11, 1968 reports that "when the outlaw in a Western strides to the bar the soundtrack may say: 'Gimme a slug of whiskey!' But the Arabic subtitle will read: 'Give me a glass of orange juice.'"

Although American television programs have not become staple fare in the Soviet Union, the tube's insatiable demand for new material has caused East-European broadcasters to turn to Hollywood for help. Jackie Gleason, Dick Powell, Dinah Shore, and an assortment of other American television personalities, as well as such programs as "Perry Mason" and "The Defenders," have been syndicated on East-European TV.

In country after country, research into viewing habits shows patterns similar to those described for the United States in this volume. In Italy and Japan, Argentina and Iran, viewer surveys find that peak TV usage is between 8:00 and 10:00 P. M. In Iran, a 1963 survey found TV-set ownership concentrated among the elite: half the men in TV families worked for "the government, private companies, or the security forces." Half named television as "the best source of news and means of pleasure and fun for you."

But the "global village" is, alas, still only a vision. Although international telecasting, especially of sport events, has become a common reality, especially in Europe, the overall effect of television, as of all other mass media, has been to strengthen the sense of *national* cultural and political identity. In the United States, TV has weakened regional and parochial orientations, accentuating a trend already set in motion by the vastly increased mobility of the population. But while it has certainly improved the average American's level of familiarity with the world at large, the overall effect has probably been to heighten his sense of nationalism rather than to give him a feeling of world citizenship.

Another of McLuhan's provocative theses appears to lack support from the evidence. He has argued that television, with its constantly changing succession of light impulses upon the picture tube, demands greater activity and involvement on the part of the audience than does print, with its orderly progression of characters in sequence across the page. As I said in the first edition of this book, televiewing is passive if for no other reason than that the viewer must accept the broadcaster's sequence and pacing, while the reader is engaged in an active search for information, and the flow of messages is under *his* control. This proposition seems to be somewhat supported by a recent comparative study by Herbert Krugman of brain-wave activity while viewing and while reading.

McLuhan has proclaimed that the "Gutenberg Galaxy" of print communication is obsolete and that the children of the television era have gravitated to the newer forms of communication — film and the electronic media. Their knowledge of the world, he claims, is founded in new forms of sensory experience through the rapid juxtaposition of incongruous and unrelated images, such as the sharp, brief cuts of contrasting footage in a film by Truffaut or Antonioni or the succession of television commercials for toothpaste, dog food, and banking services. For example, on June 5, 1968, the Huntley-Brinkley report followed its bulletins and film clips on the assassination of Robert Kennedy with commercials for Newport, "the smoothest tasting menthol cigarette," and then for Phillips 66 tires.

But in fact such fast switches of stimuli are not unique to the newer media; they are evident in any newspaper or magazine, or on the shelves of any library. (Collage as a static art form preceded the invention of montage by Eisenstein and Pudovkin.)

Empirical research fails to support the theory that children raised in the electronic era have abandoned the traditional forms of communication. During the same period that the first TV generation has grown to maturity, there has been a spectacular increase in educational achievement levels. Since education is linked to a greater reliance on print and less on broadcasting, causes and effects are hard to disentangle. Young people have clearly *not* stopped reading. The 18–24 age group, which was 16½% of the entire population over 18 in 1970, accounted for 24% of the books purchased in the United States that year. A Gilbert youth study found that newspapers are read every day by 73% of the young people aged 14–25, and by 86% of the married people of 25 or less who had already embarked on their independent lives.

The continuing appeal of print to young people does not of course change the fact that they are offspring of the electronic era. 82% listen to radio on the average day, but the extent of daily TV viewing shows interesting differences: 74% of the high-school youth, and 60 % of those in college, with a vastly expanded variety of demands on their time. Among those in the 14–25 age group who are out of school, 70% watched TV "yesterday."

There are also striking differences in the median

amount of daily time spent viewing: 2 hours and 13 minutes for the high schoolers, 1 hour and 2 minutes for those in college, and (among those out of school) 1 hour and 25 minutes for the college graduates, and 2 hours and 39 minutes for the others.

Moreover, the perception that young people have of their own viewing habits leads to the conclusion that they tend to regard TV as something they outgrow as they get older. Among high-school students 65% say they are watching less than they used to, and 16% say they are watching more; among those in college 71% say they are watching TV less, and 20% say more (their perception of their newspaper reading, incidentally, shows the opposite tendency). These data are merely a subjective expression of what viewing figures have persistently shown — that time spent with TV is at its peak among children at about the eighth-grade level and then declines as they become more independent, discover the opposite sex, and enter the pattern of dating and going out as a substitute for home-oriented evenings. It is clear that the presence of the television set in the home since infancy has not brought about any total dependence on TV at the expense of print media.

In short, the main effects of television in redistributing leisure time had already been felt by 1958. Television has continued to develop as a powerful and effective marketing force, attracting an increasing percentage of advertising expenditures, which have continued to grow along with the economy. As this has happened, other media have been forced to adapt and to change character to some degree. Great magazines (notably *Look, Collier's* and the *Saturday Evening Post*), Sunday supplements (*The American Weekly, This Week*), and large metropolitan newspapers (most notably in New York) have disappeared from the scene, though in every case the reasons for their demise have been highly complex and not attributable to television alone. Fiction has virtually disappeared from general magazines, but this is as much due to the spectacular rise of paperback books as it is to the attractions of television entertainment as an alternative form of fantasy experience. Specialized magazines have continued to grow in number and in circulation, maintaining the trend described years ago in the first edition of this book, while general magazines (including those of the highbrow variety) have lost ground. *Life* and its now defunct competitor, *Look*, have had a particularly difficult time in attracting advertisers, and television competition has forced them and many other large periodicals to subdivide their circulation into regional editions as a way of getting new business. The shifting of advertising budgets has reflected changes in advertisers' subjective judgments about the intensity of attention and interest that magazines arouse for their readers, rather than changing measurements of the *number* of readers. Many a big magazine and newspaper has gone under, or is in trouble today, in spite of its high level of circulation and readership. TV has helped cause their abandonment not by their audiences, but by their advertisers.

It is hard to blame television, though, for the death of big-city newspapers plagued by the movement of affluent readers and department stores to the suburbs, by acute problems of afternoon deliveries through increasingly clogged traffic arteries, and by labor contracts that have restricted their ability to automate their plants and to operate economically. To the degree that television contributed to the failure of individual dailies, it did so as part of an amalgam of forces, most of which would have come into play even if there were no TV at all. Overall, the number of dailies is no less than it was a quarter century ago; the number of weeklies grows steadily, and the press remains prosperous and influential.

A dozen years ago, there were still enough non-TV households in the United States to make network radio a continuing and economically viable reality, persisting with the same format of drama, variety, and comedy shows that had been established in its heyday. By 1972, however, these vestiges of the past have died out completely. There are still four radio networks, but they are primarily a channel for news and special events. With a vastly increased number of stations offering the listener more choices, radio has settled into a pattern of output that stresses its own unique aural qualities and its transistorized omnipresence: music, news, sportscasting, and conversation. As the direct progenitor of television, radio was more strongly affected by television's presence than any other medium, and yet it flourishes at least as a business and as a public convenience, if no longer as a form of creative expression.

The motion-picture medium responded to the competition of television by changing its format first, and later its content. The film industry's initial reaction was to move to color and the wide screen in order to differentiate its product as much as possible from the televised image. In more recent years it has proceeded to concentrate on subjects, themes, and visual and verbal expressions that have until now been impossible to present on television. The easing of censorship of films from the prudish standards set by the Hays Office reflected self-interest as well as the broader change in society's standards, which liberalized court rulings have underpinned.

While television continues to emphasize "family" entertainment, the film industry has moved from permissiveness to exploitation of nudity, sex, profanity, and other ingredients of content in which television cannot compete. (There is no reason to assume, however, that with TV's unabating demand for film programming, and with the advent of pay TV via the cable, a late-night market will not soon be found for "adult" movies.) The motion picture, which for decades was the great mass-entertainment medium, has in the television era taken on many of the attributes of an elite art form. To the young intellectuals of a generation reared on TV, moviegoing is an "intimate" rather than a mass experience, and the film cult of today stands in ironical apposition to the lowbrow movie fan clubs and magazines of the 1930's and 1940's, which today have

their counterparts in the world of television. The movies
have been transformed by television and, in some measure,
have been taken over by television, but they have hardly
been destroyed.

The decline in movie attendance has darkened thousands of downtown movie theaters in cities throughout the
country, with accompanying effects on restaurants, night
clubs, newsstands, ice-cream parlors, florist shops, and other
small-service businesses that catered to the needs of movie-
goers in an era when motion pictures were a major means
of evening entertainment and a common occasion for going
out. The pedestrian traffic of moviegoers provided a stimulus to casual strolling, and the disappearance of the downtown movie crowds helped to hasten the disappearance of
the casual walkers in the evening, which once made American urban centers far livelier than they are today. Thus
television has been part of the array of intermeshed causes
that have brought about the decay of central business districts, increases in street crime, and even changes in the
racial composition of cities. While it would be fatuous to
assign television any significant responsibility for these symptoms of far-reaching social change, it is also a mistake to
ignore its contribution to the process.

Since the age of television has also been an age of
growing affluence, it is hard to single out the specific influence of TV upon the American way of life. The high culture has had an expanded participation, as measured by
book sales, museum attendance, and exposure to the live
performing arts. But this is paralleled by the growth of
popular pastimes as measured by travel and expenditures
on recreation.

The years of television's growing presentation of live
sportscasts have also been years of increased attendance at
sporting events. But while the number of active sports fans
is larger than ever, attendance at different types of matches
has shifted in relative popularity. Such formerly exotic
sports as golf, tennis, ice hockey, and soccer became famil-

iar to the mass audience through telecasts and enlarged their publics. Professional baseball has dropped behind horse racing, auto racing, and football in paid admissions, and wrestling and basketball have also shown comparative losses relative to other sports. In 1960 a total of some 25,000,000 persons paid to attend professional and amateur football games. In 1969 the figure was nearly 37,000,000. Professional football's star performers, like Joe Namath, had become glamorized and familiar TV personalities.

Participation in sports and other activities is an indication of higher income and prosperity, of better education, of increased personal mobility, of a population more concentrated in metropolitan areas. But television's impact has been an integral part of the forces that have made for change. TV has given, and gives, massive exposure to aspects of the culture that were formerly the province of the few. People want to see for themselves, and to enjoy for themselves, the things they have seen on the picture tube.

With no part of the population has television's acculturating role been more powerful than with the Negro minority. The incongruity between the idealized upper-middle-class life of the television world and the reality of the slum has undoubtedly sharpened frustrations, and the endless display of consumer goods in TV commercials surely makes them seem both desirable and accessible to people with limited purchasing power. While it is nonsense to blame television for disorder and looting, television provides an important source of the ghetto Negro's perceptions of what the white world looks like from the inside. In a 1967 survey made by Opinion Research Corporation for the Bureau of Advertising, only 22% of the whites said they "looked forward" to the commercials on TV, but the figure among Negroes was 48%.

Various television programs may have significantly different appeal to Negroes than to whites. A 1963 SRDS Data Inc. study found that "The Defenders," a program that ranked 30th in popularity with the general public, had nearly twice as many Negro viewers as the number-one general favorite, "Beverly Hillbillies," with whose "cracker" protagonists Negroes must find it especially hard to identify. Jackie Gleason, a comedian who projected an urban working-class characterization, ranked number one with Negroes, and 13 with the general public. Red Skelton, whose program ranked 6th overall, and first among comic shows, had only 10% Negroes among his viewers, while 18% of Gleason's viewers were Negroes.

Differences in viewing habits between Negroes and whites are largely a reflection of their typically different incomes and social positions. The O.R.C. survey found that 75% of Negroes watched television "yesterday," compared with 83% of whites. (The difference can be explained by the higher proportion of Negroes, especially in the South, who do not own television sets: at the time of the survey, it was 12% for Negroes, 5% for whites.) Negroes and whites report similarly on their exposure to morning and afternoon TV, but while 76% of the whites report viewing "yesterday" evening, only 67% of the Negroes do. The proportion of heavy viewing (for two hours or more) was identical for Negroes and whites, but whereas for whites the proportion became less with increased education, among Negroes it was higher among those with a high-school education than among those without one. (This almost suggests that the lower-middle-brow common denominator of most TV programming may actually repel some of the less-educated members of the Negro audience.)

Broadcasting's longstanding discrimination against Negro performers did not begin to break down until the 1960's. When Harry Belafonte appeared on network specials in the late 1950's, hate mail from the South intimidated the sponsors. As late as March, 1968, a monitoring study of 8,920 television commercials, made for the New York City Commission on Human Rights, found only 190 that included any minority-group performer, and 49 of these were public-service announcements. The very hearings at which this study was presented gave rise to major changes in broadcasting practices in the use of Negro performers both in programming and in advertising.

Just as television in its first decade unwittingly helped to maintain racial stereotypes by simply never portraying Negroes as members of its fictional fantasy world, so it now appears to be operating as a significant force to make Negroes a visible and acceptable part of the national scenery to which white children become accustomed at an early age. Through its portrayal of Negroes in middle-class roles, the long-term positive influence of television, both upon white attitudes and upon Negro self-perception, will inevitably far outweigh the disturbing and disrupting effects of televised portrayals of racial violence. Television's intelligent and sympathetic portrayal of the civil-rights struggle of the mid-1960's played an important part in the transformation of white public opinion, North and South, and discredited the diehard defenders of segregation.

The political power of television has, of course, been felt in many fields besides that of race relations. Television welded the nation together at the time of President Kennedy's assassination and wrenched it apart through its relentless exposition of the agonies of the war in Vietnam. In the past decade television has become the principal medium of political campaigning. It has changed American politics through its emphasis on the candidate's personality, appearance, and style, and through its progressive reduction of his policy positions to the confines of a 30-second spot announcement. The machinery of nominating and electing a presidential candidate has become a gigantic spectacle, the biggest show in TV's show business. And because TV, most notably in the 1960 Kennedy-Nixon debates and in its coverage of the 1968 Democratic Convention demonstrations, may have provided a decisive push to particular candidates, it has changed the course of American history.

In a world in which the daily news is perennially full of war, mayhem, and disaster, it makes little sense to blame television for the social violence it symbolically reflects and perhaps in some small measure deflects. Since the first edition of this book was written, a substantial amount of research has accumulated on the subject of TV violence and its effects on the young. The evidence remains ambiguous in its implications. Much of the laboratory research demonstrates that children become more aggressive after they have been exposed to filmed representations of violence. Some studies suggest that such exposure may also siphon off hostile impulses so that they are expressed vicariously and not vented against real people. Perhaps the best conclusion that can be drawn is that of common sense. Regardless of whether or not the events that take place in the psychological laboratory are accurate reflections of the real-life effects of communication, it is difficult to assume that the content, characterizations, and values depicted in television programming are *not* a significant influence upon the viewers. This influence may be subtle and slow; it may be more intense for some kinds of people than for others, and it may even produce reactions of an opposite nature among different sectors of the viewing public. But when one once admits that television programs, like television commercials, have a persuasive effect, mere logic leads to the conclusion that there is harm, and perhaps even danger, in the persistence of violence as an important ingredient in programming content. The exploitation of the violent and sensational is merely an aspect of television's influence as the mightiest expression of commercialized mass culture.

To the degree that television presents a simplified, trivialized, sanitized version of the passions and struggles in the real world, the vast amounts of time dedicated to it by its audience have led to a deadening of perception and a conformism in outlook and style. But the cultural effects of television have been a paradox from the start. TV has been a force of great enlightenment, bringing exposure to high culture to millions of people who would never seek it out on their own. It has been a powerful force for political liberalism. The news and public-affairs departments of the networks have been run by newsmen of the highest professional caliber, who have brought both greater expertise and a more cosmopolitan outlook to the treatment of national and world news than can be found among the telegraph editors of most daily newspapers. But because television aims its programming directly at the modal points in the society, at the middle-aged, middle-income, average American with an I.Q. of exactly 100, it remains, as was originally described in the first edition of this book, a force for homogeneity.

The changes that seem in store for television in the decades to come are bound to reduce this homogeneous effect, for they inevitably suggest that viewing will become a steadily more individual affair, with a greatly expanded range of choice. At the close of the 1950's, the unanswered questions in television's future were related to the growth of UHF and to the fate of pay TV and educational and public television. These questions still remain largely unanswered. Although since 1964, all new TV sets have been manufactured with UHF tuners, there is still more effort involved than the simple click of the VHF-station selector, and audiences continue small. Few UHF stations are affiliated with either of the two leading networks, and few have been profitable.

Educational and public television have continued to grow, both in the number of stations and in audience size. About eight out of ten U.S. TV sets are within signal range of one or more of the roughly 200 public- and educational-TV stations. Some 20% of the households tune in to ETV at least every week. The American Research Bureau found that in nineteen of the biggest cities, ETV's audiences increased by 75% between 1966 and 1970.

The report of the Carnegie Commission led to the formation of the Corporation for Public Broadcasting, which represented the first recognition by the Federal government of its responsibility for financing programming in the public interest. In spite of its gains, however, noncommercial television has not yet shown a capacity to make any substantial inroads into the large audiences of the entertainment broadcasters, and it seems destined to meet the interest of no more than an elite minority. The Public Broadcasting Laboratory, which attracted wide attention because of its sponsorship by the Ford Foundation in 1967, had an audience share in New York that sometimes fell to 0.2%, though it generally averaged between 1% and 2%

Pay television was a center of controversy at a time when it had substantial backing and encountered the determined opposition of both the TV networks and the motion-picture-theater owners. In 1964, their successful lobbying outlawed pay TV in California, where it seemed to be headed for an important test. Although the California ban was subsequently invalidated by the Supreme Court, interest in pay TV waned as a result of its unsuccessful performance in several test markets. But it seems likely that more will be heard on this front, for the advent of cable television will accustom a growing number of householders to the payment of a monthly television bill, and the inclusion of a few occasional extra charges for "special" programs will seem like a comparatively easy burden to bear (especially in comparison with the more complex and unusual arrangements required in a wireless pay-TV system). Although cable television began as a means of bringing signals to areas cut off from normal reception by mountains or other topographic features, CATV systems have successfully been introduced into urban areas such as New York as a means of improving already good reception, especially color reception. Eventually CATV's main sales argument may be in its ability to feed in remote stations and thereby add greatly to the number of available choices. Industry optimists have predicted that the cable-connected TV set will inevitably be replaced by a home-communications system, including a unit for the facsimile display of newspaper pages and other "printed" information, and a console to permit computerized banking and shopping.

Be that as it may, the spread of the cable-TV hookup will indeed create vast potential audiences for pay television. If even a tiny fraction of the viewers are willing to have a dollar or two added to their monthly cable bill in order to see a first-run feature film, the income (and profit) might be substantially greater than that from advertisers on a commercially sponsored network show with one fifth of the country watching it. This could bring about sharp changes in the balance of economic forces that have sustained television up to this point, with a train of attendant effects on the structure of programming.

The development of cassettes and other forms of video recordings represents yet another intrusion into the established pattern of TV entertainment. As with color television, the cost of the player unit will come down as a mass market is created, but the cost itself is the chief obstacle to the growth of this mass market. It takes no seer to predict that the cassette player will eventually find the same degree of universality as the record player (which is present in 82% of U.S. households). The market for video cassettes will undoubtedly come to resemble the phonograph-record market in character if not in size, with "classical" recordings of great plays and documentaries of historic events, and a much larger number of "popular" recordings ranging from rock-and-roll concerts to the complete library of Ed Sullivan shows. Just as listening to phonograph records takes away from radio-listening time and from other leisure hours, so watching video-cassette performances may be expected to produce some incursions, though probably rather small, into TV viewing. (A 1971 survey commissioned by CBS for its own use led the company to conclude that cassette viewing would not take place at the expense of regular TV watching, but would create its own new demand.) Cassettes will not only be bought but rented and borrowed from libraries. They lend themselves readily, moreover, to the demands of a pay-TV system, and thereby could greatly expand pay TV's array of program selections.

Eventually, the development of satellite broadcasting will make it possible to receive, on sets equipped with the necessary adapters and amplifier units, signals at home from any TV transmitter in the world. The history of worldwide shortwave broadcasting suggests that the audience for such international telecasts will be small, except on extraordinary occasions. But the possibility carries with it the intriguing promise of TV's growing capacity to satisfy ever more varied, and therefore higher, interests, and to become a more powerful force for communication and empathy among the peoples of the world.

October, 1971   Leo Bogart

ADDENDUM: The most ambitious and costly study ever conducted on television's effects was completed just as *The Age of Television* went to press. This was the report of the Surgeon General's Scientific Advisory Committee on Television and Social Behavior, summarizing a $1 million crash-research program on the effects of TV violence on children. (Many of the 43 individual studies had already been reported piecemeal and are reviewed in the notes to Chapter 12.)

The Commission voiced its findings unanimously, and hence cautiously, in terms compatible with my own independent reading of the available evidence: "There is a convergence of the fairly substantial experimental evidence for short-run causation of aggression among some children by viewing violence on the screen and the much less certain evidence from field studies that extensive violence viewing precedes some long-run manifestations of aggressive behavior. This convergence of the two types of evidence constitutes some preliminary *evidence of a causal relationship* [Italics mine]. But a good deal of research remains to be done before we can have confidence in these conclusions." (The final statement is an almost obligatory one in any social research report based on statistically limited samples.)

More specifically, the report concluded that "violence depicted on television can immediately or shortly thereafter induce mimicking or copying by children" and that "under certain circumstances television violence can instigate an increase in aggressive acts." It could not be concluded by the Commission that the children thus affected were a majority;

there was no way of estimating, from the nonrepresentative population samples studied, how large a fraction of the juvenile population was actually affected. Among very young children those most responsive to violence were the ones most aggressive to begin with. But although aggressive children watched more television, there was no clear-cut indication that they watched more violent programs.

In spite of the fact that the Commission found "evidence of a causal relationship," the failure to produce a cleancut assertion aroused considerable confusion. In the *New York Times,* the story was headlined, "U.S. Report Says TV Violence Has No Harmful Effect on Youth," and the story in *Broadcasting* magazine, in a curious reversal of the Commission's own language, said, "A blue-ribbon committee of social scientists has concluded that there is no causal relationship between television programs that depict violence and aggressive behavior by the majority of children."

But any serious attempt to disentangle the effects of television from those of other forces in the surrounding society was predestined to leave room for ambiguity and for further investigation. The big unanswered question about television violence is not what it does directly to evoke antisocial or aggressive impulses in specific instances, but what it does to the character of those who grow up to accept it as a normal symbolic expression of the culture.

February, 1972   L.B.

NOTE TO THE READER

The notes for each chapter have been lettered consecutively. Where a note refers to a specific sentence, paragraph, or table in the text, the corresponding letter appears in the margin of the text close to the particular reference. It is suggested that the reader refer to the note along with the text material.

Where a note has only general reference to an entire section, however, the corresponding letter appears in the margin of the first line of that section. It is suggested that the reader refer to this note after he has read the entire section in the text. It can generally be assumed that any letter appearing in the margin of the first line of any section indicates such a note.

FOREWORD

The readers of this book will approach it with very different ends in mind. As viewers or as citizens, some will have a general interest in learning about the impact of television on American life. Others, as working members of the television industry, have a direct professional need for information about the audience and its viewing habits. Still other readers, as students of human behavior, will be primarily interested in television as a form of communication or as an instrument of social change. Regardless of the perspective from which the reader approaches the following pages, we can assume that he is concerned with television's effects on people rather than with the technical aspects of television broadcasting or production.

Most of the source material for this book comes from studies which have used the interview method of asking people what television has meant in their lives. This book is not a report on any one survey. Instead it puts together the results of many individual pieces of research undertaken for different purposes in different places and at different times. There is no common thread of interest in these studies other than television itself, and the author's task has been one of putting the findings together in meaningful sequence, with such interpretations as are necessary to make them consistent and understandable.

While the author has also included some observations of his own, and reviewed the opinions of other writers, this is primarily an attempt to create order out of the evidence, without any pretension to render judgments on the medium. Although the raw material for this book comes from the research which has been done on television and other media, this is not a treatise *on* television research. That topic is discussed in broad outline, in an appendix. The emphasis in the text is wholly on the findings of research, and methodology is discussed only insofar as this is sometimes necessary to assess the validity of the studies reported.

The writer of a work like this one, which summarizes evidence accumulated from diverse sources, necessarily labors under inhibitions which do not face the essayist or critic. His imagination is hemmed in by the facts before him; his tone must be sober and constrained. If he has an axe to grind he should keep it out of sight; better still, he should bury the hatchet altogether.

In less than a decade of active life, television has become the principal leisure-time companion of the American people, and as such is a major source of the ideas they hold of the world around them. In assuming this position of triumphant dominance, television has altered the pattern of other activities. It has not, however, transformed the values which Americans hold dear. It has taken the features already most expressive of our culture and has heightened and intensified their impact upon the daily life of the average person. There is nothing in the content of television programming which is not already vividly apparent in the motion pictures, radio, magazines or the press; TV is saying the same things, but in a much louder and more insistent voice—a voice to which we will all be listening for a long time to come.

If there is any one particular assumption which has guided the selection and discussion of material, it is simply this: television is a wholly neutral instrument in human hands. It is and does what people want. The effects it has wrought in the lives of the audience arise from the psychological needs and social expectations of human beings in modern society. Television is not a monster uprooting established patterns of interest and activity; it is a catalyst, creating changes where the elements of change are already present below the surface. Many Americans who were last minute holdouts against TV expressed a fear that the set would "take over" in their lives. Perhaps for some this anxious prediction has proven true, but it only means that the viewer has relinquished his control of the tuning knob. Such a loss of control cannot be blamed on TV. It reflects a condition of self-hypnosis which is in itself a response to the demands of contemporary life.

In a world in which the average person finds himself with more and more leisure on his hands, the continuous flow of television entertainment represents to most people an innocuous way of passing the time. But television is not merely a diversion; it is an endless source of ideas and information and a powerful influence on values. In studying television we cannot avoid important social implications, no matter in what direction we face.

We will look at television first from the standpoint of the audience and its viewing habits, then by examining TV's impact on American life, and finally in terms of the unresolved issues in its future.

What is the historical setting within which television has risen? The book opens by considering television as one of the mass media which are the peculiar product of modern technology and of our complex society. The great audiences which television has attracted can only be understood in relation to the continuing growth of leisure time and the need for new pastimes to fill it. In tracing TV's growth pattern, we can see how it has spread from a small segment of the population to every social level. Noticeable differences exist between the television-owning majority and the minority which is still without TV.

What is the nature of TV's appeal to its audience? To understand why and how people watch television we must examine the viewing experience as a psychological phenomenon. The classic explanations of how art is experienced by its audience must be modified in the case of the popular arts, of which television is the newest. The broadcast media, radio and television, can be distinguished from the popular arts generally. To be even more specific, we can also describe the features which make TV a unique medium.

What can people see on television? Having discussed television viewing in terms of the motivations of the audience, we are better prepared to look at the actual content of television programming. The first question to answer is where this programming originates. Next we must see how broadcast time is allocated among programs of various types, and to describe the kinds of characters and situations depicted in television drama.

How do people watch television? To find out how different kinds of people watch television, we must examine how much they view, when they view and what they view. It is also important to look at the over-all trends in audience size and composition, by time of day and season of year, and to see whether the nature of TV viewing has changed since the early days of the medium.

Viewing is characteristically a social, rather than an individual activity. We investigate this social aspect by considering the reasons why the set was bought in the first place, and then follow the stages of TV's growth. Further, we trace the effects wrought by the advent of television on the routine of family life, on conversation, visiting and going out.

What effects has television had on the other media? The effects of television can be discerned not only in the general pattern of sociability, but in exposure to the other mass media. Among these, radio, as TV's closest relation, has been most directly influenced; in fact it has been virtually transformed into a different medium. TV's effects can also be traced in detail on the reading of books, magazines and newspapers, and on attendance at motion pictures and sports events.

What problems and opportunities does television present to the advertiser? Since television in the United States is supported by commercial sponsors, its growth has had profound repercussions on the size and distribution of advertising budgets. Television's values for the advertiser can be compared in the light of differences in practice for various types of companies and differences of performance for various types of programs. We also contrast the qualitative advantages of TV with those of other media. Television's sales effectiveness is difficult to measure, but it has been the subject of intensive research. In a narrower sphere, a great deal of study has centered on what makes a television commercial more or less effective.

What is TV's impact on politics? Television has demonstrated its capacity to modify political opinions as well as brand choices and consumption habits. It plays an increasingly important role in the flow of news and information. It has become a particularly crucial influence in forming the popular image of public personalities, particularly candidates for election. It is therefore pertinent to describe the part which television has come to play in the political process.

How does television influence youth? While the political consequences of television are obviously of great social importance, the greatest demonstration of public concern has centered on TV's influence on children. The amount and kind of viewing done by children varies from one age level to the next, and there are also noticeable changes in the kinds of programs preferred. Parents differ in their attitude toward children's viewing, and in the kinds of controls they exercise over it. Strong controversy has been aroused, not only among parents, but among psychiatrists and child psychologists, over the question of whether TV programs are a disturbing influence on children. There is more opinion than evidence on this point.

What are the questions in TV's future? Television will change in the years to come, as color replaces black-and-white, and as TV spreads around the world. While there is general agreement that the educational potentialities of television are considerable, there is no commonly accepted policy of how these potentialities can best be fulfilled. Two unresolved problems facing the broadcasters and the Federal Communications Commission are ultra-high-frequency television and pay television, both of which represent possible changes in the present structure of the industry. The biggest question that confronts television's policymakers concerns the responsibility of the broadcasters. Should they be responsive to existing public tastes or do they have the mission of shaping and altering those tastes? This book makes no attempt to answer this crucial question, but it seeks to present a thoughtful review of the evidence on which a considered judgment can be formed by the reader.

While the facts collected here are the results of studies by many individuals and organizations, I am solely responsible for the manner of presenting and interpreting them. Any opinions expressed in these pages are my personal ones, and in no way reflect the views or policies of the company with which I am associated.

Thousands of articles and reports have been written on the social aspects of television, and many of them include research findings or intelligent commentaries which are worth reference. In writing this book, I have tried conscientiously to track down every study, major or minor, which seemed likely to contribute to its general objectives. No such attempt at comprehensiveness could be altogether successful, and I regret the inevitable omissions.

I have tried to say what there is to say without lapsing too often into sociological jargon; at the same time I assume that the non-scientific reader can read a table of simple percentages and that he knows something about the rudiments of sampling (e.g., that a small group, selected by chance from a large population, can be said to represent it, with a degree of accuracy that varies with the size of the sample).

There are no footnotes in this book. To the scholarly reader this will seem unorthodox, but there is no reason why it should impede him from further exploration of the sources. These are listed in the bibliography, and they can be easily identified from the authors' names or from other references in the text itself. A great many of the studies described in this book can be tracked down only to short manuscript or mimeographed reports, or to accounts in the broadcasting trade press. Footnoting such items seems to me to serve no serious scientific purpose, so I would rather be consistent and leave out the footnotes altogether. The reader with specialized interests can use the bibliography to locate the articles, books and reports that touch on a subject important to him, and he would hardly ever want to stop with the particular pages to which a footnote might refer. As for the general reader—his attention will be diverted often enough by the text itself, and I would rather not present him with any further menaces to navigation.

If I have defied scholarship by avoiding footnotes, I may have deferred to it excessively by my attentiveness to detail. Particularly in the chapters on TV's effects on other media I have included mentions of all available existing studies, even when their findings duplicate each other. The specialist will find these statistics pertinent, though the more general reader may want to skim over them, and concentrate on the discussion of what the numbers mean.

I should like to express my appreciation to the research services, authors and publishers whose reports, articles and books I have used as source material, and particularly to those who have given me permission to make extensive use of quotations or tables.

This book would not have been launched except for the initiative of Hans Zeisel, who pioneered brilliantly in media research at McCann-Erickson, Inc. I have called frequently for help on my colleagues at McCann-Erickson, all walking treasurehouses of information: Seymour Bernstein, Robert J. Coen, Katherine Dodge, Coral Eaton, William Horn, Delphine Humphrey, and Charles M. Kinsolving, Jr. Without the aid of my most efficient secretary, Joan Walters, not one line of the manuscript could ever have taken shape. I owe her my special thanks. A word of commiseration is due to my wife and daughter, for they have had to watch television by themselves on the evenings and weekends in which this book was written.

L. B.

1. MID-CENTURY AMERICA AND THE GROWTH OF TELEVISION

On the evening of March 7, 1955, one out of every two Americans was watching Mary Martin play "Peter Pan" before the television cameras. Never before in history had a single person been seen and heard by so many others at the same time. The vast size of the audience was a phenomenon in itself as fantastic as any fairy tale. **(A)** The age of television had arrived.

In the stream of history, a great invention is always both effect and cause. It arises from the existing base of knowledge and technology, and from the kinds of questions which the challenges of life in his place and time suggest to the curious mind of the inventor. Once it has come into being, the invention acquires a dynamism of its own, merging with a thousand other forces and events to set in motion new ways of action and thought.

Television broadcasting as it exists in America today is not merely the product of a science which has mastered mysteries of light and sound and electronics. It is also the creature of an economy capable of producing and distributing goods on a massive scale and of a society so complex that its business cannot be handled by face-to-face communication.

The Mass Media and the Great Society

America in the mid-twentieth century is the supreme embodiment of what social philosophers since Adam Smith have characterized as the Great Society, and which they have contrasted with the simpler life of our ancestors or "primitive" contemporaries. This is a society in which people assemble in large aggregations, in which wealth grows through the increased productivity made possible by a division of labor. But as work becomes specialized, and as the tempo of life is speeded, the relations between human beings change their character.

1

It is no accident that the invention of the printing press and the discovery of America were products of the same half-century. There is also no cause for surprise in the fact that television and controlled atomic fission came as parallel discoveries. As the world acquires new vistas it becomes more intricate. There is more being done and a consciousness of more to be done: more information needed and more information to communicate. Modern industrial technology has made possible the reproduction of communications on a massive scale. The linotype, the rotary press, the motion picture camera and the vacuum tube all provide a basis for reaching vast audiences.

In a more complex world of specialized tasks and lessening distances, the ties between a man and his next-door neighbors may be less important than those which bind him to fellows of his own profession or hobby or taste. As the social bonds of traditional community living have weakened, the mass media have created a new set of common interests and loyalties. They offer a new kind of shared experience, in which millions can laugh at the same jokes, feel the same thrills and anxieties, and respond to the same heroes.

Mass media are possible only where mass-produced symbols are meaningful. In a world of standardized goods, it is to be expected that entertainment should be dispensed through impersonal commercial agencies rather than through the intimate channels of conversation and play that prevail in more simple communities. With no other form of impersonal communication has the sharing of experience been possible on so universal a scale and to so intense a degree as with television.

Toward a Middle-Class Society

In the last century, technological growth has brought about far-reaching changes in the American economy and in the American style of life. The United States is today a "middle-class" country not only in its income but in its values.

(B)   While the 1930 census showed 30% of the population in white-collar jobs, the figure had grown to 37% in 1950. In the last twenty-five years the number of professional men has more than doubled; managers and proprietors have increased by 50%. Proportionately fewer people run small family businesses; more work for big companies. Less than half the work force is engaged in making or growing things.

Whereas only one person in five had a middle-class standard of life or better in 1929, one in two had achieved this by 1952. *(Fortune* magazine estimates 20% of all U. S. families had an income of $4000 or over after taxes in 1929; 49% were in this bracket in 1952— using constant 1952 dollar values.) Real income—in purchasing power—is about 50% higher per person today than it was just before World War II. Between 1929 and 1957, real disposable income per household grew from $3820 to $4900 (in 1947 dollars), while households grew smaller (from 4.1 to 3.3 persons apiece). Women in ever-increasing numbers have entered the labor force, raising the total income of millions of families.

Americans today are better educated than their parents. Children stay in school longer, and succeeding generations have become constantly better educated. By 1950, 52% of the adult population had been to high school or college; before the war only 39% had gone this far in their education. Today, of every three persons of college age, one is actually attending college.

Improved education, like higher income, carries the implication of a change in outlook. So does the changing distribution of the population. Americans are more heavily concentrated in large metropolitan areas than they ever were in the past, but increasingly they move to the suburbs rather than the central cities. By 1956, a fifth of the total population was living in the suburbs of metropolitan areas, with an additional 8% in semi-suburban communities. Between 1940 and 1950, the proportion of families who owned their own homes went from 44% to 55%. While population grew by one-fourth in the last quarter-century, the number of households grew by one-half.   (C)

To a greater extent than ever before, the distinctions in income between white-collar and manual workers have been diminishing under labor union pressure, and the distinctions in style of life are also tending to disappear. Studies made by Macfadden Publications show few differences in the buying patterns of wage-earner and white-collar households in the same neighborhoods. This point has been well described by Frederic Dewhurst and his associates of the Twentieth Century Fund:

"The banker or well-to-do businessman of the 1890s dressed and acted the part. He rode in his own carriage, driven by a hired coachman. The man of modest income, whether farmer or mechanic, also dressed and acted the part. Although the farmer drove to town with his own horse and buggy, the bicycle was the only form of personal transportation the city worker could afford—as it is today even in the more advanced European countries. Today American farmers and city dwellers, those well-off and those in modest circumstances, drive their own cars. The debutante of half a century ago was distinguishable at a distance from her unfortunate sister who had to work for a living. Today they both wear nylon stockings and fur coats and although there may still be a big difference in the cost of their wardrobes, it takes a discerning feminine eye to tell them apart.

"As to the typical products that have transformed the household during the past half-century, the upper and lower income groups both use the same vacuum cleaners, refrigerators, deep-freezers, oil burners, gas and electric stoves, radios and television sets. Their homes may have much the same kind of bathroom equipment and plumbing and lighting fixtures. They read the same newspapers and magazines, go to the same movies, listen to the same radio and television programs. They smoke the same brands of cigarettes, drink the same frozen orange juice, eat the same canned, frozen or out-of-season fresh food, bought at the same supermarket."

The far-reaching changes which have taken place on the American scene have prepared the way for the growth of television:

1. The expansion of purchasing power, and the creation of a vast demand for the amenities of life made it possible for people to acquire television sets rapidly and on an enormous scale—41,000,000 in a dozen years.

2. The vast growth of the American economy also made possible a huge advertising investment in the new medium, and provided commercial backing for its high programming costs.

3. The concentration of population into metropolitan areas made it economically possible to bring television quickly to great numbers of people, in spite of the short range of TV signals (com-

pared to radio) and in spite of the financial and legal obstacles to the rapid construction of stations in outlying smaller towns.

4. The levelling of social differences is part of a standardization of tastes and interests to which the mass media give expression, and to which they also contribute. The ubiquitous TV antenna is a symbol of people seeking—and getting—the identical message.

The Growth of Leisure

The increased fruitfulness of the American economy has made life more pleasant by bringing more of its comforts within the budgetary reach of the average man; it has also given people more time to spend at their own discretion. Until relatively most recent times, life for most people in Europe and America was a steady alternation of work and sleep, with little time for the luxuries of art or entertainment.

Over the last century, both the conditions and philosophy of work have changed. "Honest toil" is no longer accepted as the principal mission of man on earth. A hundred years ago, woman's work was never done and men sweated in farm, factory and office virtually from dawn till dusk. Today leisure gives signs of replacing work as the main focus of living. The great growth in leisure has meant a rising demand and an increasing opportunity for the mass media. It has given Americans the many hours which they now spend watching television.

There are two principal reasons why people today have more free time on their hands:

1. They are spending fewer and fewer hours at work, because of a steady decline in the average length of the work week and a constant increase in vacation and holiday time. A century ago the average work week was 70 hours. It will be 37½ hours by 1960. For (D) every waking hour the average American worker spends at his job each week he has two to spend at his discretion. Part of this must go for transportation, eating and life's necessary tasks, but the bulk of it is free for him to follow his own bent.

2. Apart from work, life in mid-twentieth century America is more convenient for most people than it ever was in most other times

and places. Labor-saving gadgets and devices have reduced the modern housewife's burdens. Her chores are more quickly done, even though she is less likely to have the aid of a domestic servant than was her mother or grandmother.

A few examples will illustrate the extent of the transformation: By 1950 four American homes in every five had mechanical refrigerators; seven in ten had a gas or electric range; seven in ten had electric washing machines (and an additional 12% used self-service laundries); three in five had vacuum cleaners. These proportions are greater now, and are still growing.

(E)

Thermostats and automatic stokers make furnace-tending less painful (and time-consuming) for the head of the household. The power lawnmower and the automatic dishwasher have lightened even the children's chores.

Fashions in eating have changed, as popular recipes stress rapid preparation, and as prepackaged and frozen foods have made cooking easier and more efficient. And actually, more meals are being eaten in restaurants. Self-service stores now account for nine dollars of every ten spent for groceries. (They represented three dollars in five in 1946, three in ten in 1939.) Shopping in supermarkets is quicker than the old style of personal service, and the self-service principle is being constantly extended beyond the grocery field. The development of suburban shopping centers has saved still more time for millions of families.

(F)

One woman in every five is working today—and the majority of the women who work are married. A study made by the General Electric Company shows that these working housewives manage to spend nearly three-fourths as much time on their household chores as the full-time housewives do, and they spend nearly as much time in social activity. However, they spend only half as much time on personal maintenance and in relaxation.

The increase of leisure, it should be noted, has not set limits for the growth of the media. Radio, and to some extent television, can claim more than free time; they get into the hours of work. Radio follows the housewife as she does her chores and brightens the hours of the worker or shop clerk at his job.

The rise of the mass media cannot be explained merely as

an effect of the growth of leisure time. There has also been a reciprocal effect. The mass media have themselves spread popular awareness of what constitutes a good life. By making the good life familiar, they have made it seem possible (as well as desirable) for the great masses of people. They have offered glimpses of a life apart from work, a life more genteel or interesting than most of the audience knows first-hand, but one into which it can readily project its imagination. To varying degrees, people model themselves after the idealized characters who figure in TV or film dramas, in magazine short stories and in cigarette ads. The mass media have thus supported a system of values which encourages striving for greater achievement, which is expressed in more wealth and more leisure.

With more people, more money to spend and more free time, all the media have shown a phenomenal growth, and this growth has continued for a generation, apart from a setback during the Depression years. Today four Americans in five read magazines and daily newspapers, and they read more copies of both than were ever before published. The number of newspapers sold every day is greater than the number of households. In total, magazines sell almost as many copies per issue as there are people to read them.

TABLE 1

Post-War Growth of Magazines and Daily Newspapers

	1946	1956
Magazines (A.B.C., including Reader's Digest)		
Number	240	282
Circulation	139,000,000	185,731,000
Daily Newspapers		
Number	1,763	1,761
Circulation	50,927,000	57,101,000

(G)

Radio is now in virtually every home in America, in two-thirds of the 54,000,000 passenger cars on the road, and in 10,000,000 public places. Television, when it first arrived, rode in on the crest of a rising wave of interest in the existing media.

(H)

The Growth of Television

(I)

Television today is a firmly established feature of American life. It is present in four out of five U.S. homes, and within reception range of all but 3%. Because of the increase in population, there are actually more homes with television sets today than there were homes with radios just before the beginning of World War II. This entire growth has taken place in less than a decade.

Television's history goes back much further than the post-war era. It was first developed in the '20s and '30s. Its real development did not begin until the perfection of an electronic scanning device and picture tube by Vladimir Zworykin in 1931 eliminated the need for a cumbersome scanning disc. In an address before the Radio Manufacturer's Association in October, 1938, David Sarnoff declared that "television in the home is now technically feasible."

Not everyone agreed. The magazine *Radio Guide* sent its friends a century plant seed wrapped in cellophane, with a note that read: "Plant it in a pot, water it carefully, expose it to the sunlight. When it blossoms, throw the switch on the new television cabinet that your grandson will have bought and you may expect to see telecasts offering program quality and network coverage comparable to that of our broadcasts of today."

The following year the National Broadcasting Company began telecasting from the New York World's Fair, and the Columbia Broadcasting System and Allen B. DuMont laboratories went on the air soon afterwards. The Federal Communications Commission approved commercial television for July 1, 1941. By the end of the year there were half a dozen commercial television stations in the United States (three in New York) and approximately 10,000 television sets, half of them in New York. Department stores began to advertise sets and assembly kits were on sale to radio enthusiasts who wanted to put them together themselves.

Development of television was interrupted by the war, with the heavy diversion of electronic parts and equipment to military use. During this period no new television sets were sold, and production got off to a slow start after hostilities ended. By January, 1948, there were 102,000 sets in the nation, two-thirds of them in

New York. By April the number of sets had more than doubled. During that year nearly a million television sets were manufactured, compared with 179,000 in 1947, and 6500 in 1946.

Television broadcasting developed swiftly under the aegis of the major radio networks who invested millions of dollars in what was destined to be an unprofitable enterprise for its first few years. There were 24 stations on the air in 15 cities. The first television network linked New York, Schenectady and Philadelphia for nightly sponsored shows.

The expansion of television was interrupted in September, 1948, by the Federal Communications Commission, which ordered a "freeze" on new station permits. The purpose of this move was to allow time to study and work out the problems of allocating enough channel assignments to make the medium truly national in scope. To avoid interference in transmission, F.C.C. rules permitted no two stations closer than 190 miles apart to broadcast on the same channel. With only 12 channels available, this set very tight limits on the number of possible stations. During the period of the "freeze," which lasted until July, 1952, television was confined to 63 major metropolitan areas, and was within reception range of nearly three-fifths of the U.S. population. In these areas the number of sets grew steadily as mass production brought prices down and as program quality improved. This improvement in turn reflected the growth of the audience, which made the medium more attractive to advertisers. It also was helped by the spreading system of coaxial telephone cables linking stations in different cities and thus bringing entertainment of national network caliber directly to local stations.

The lifting of the "freeze" brought about a new boom in television as seventy new channels in the ultra-high-frequency (U.H.F.) band were added to the original twelve in the very-high frequency (V.H.F.) range. Movies, newspapers, magazines and radio had made television familiar even to those parts of the country which had never seen it. As a result, television did not have to go through the slow stages of growth it had undergone in the areas where it had first been introduced. Cities caught "TV fever" as new stations opened up. Elaborate promotional efforts stimulated a high degree of popular excitement and enthusiasm, and many sets were sold even before the stations came on the air.

Unlike AM radio signals, which can be received over considerable distances, television coverage is limited to a radius of somewhere between thirty and one hundred miles of the transmitting antenna. The reception range is affected by such things as the height of the antenna, the power of the transmitter, the channel on which the signal is broadcast, and the character of the terrain. Since a station can only service a limited territory in the vicinity of the city in which it is located, the smaller cities and more sparsely populated areas had no television long after the major metropolitan centers had a number of stations.

The equipment required to set up a station is expensive. Operation and programming are far more costly for television than for radio. A station supported by advertising must necessarily have a substantial number of potential viewers within range of its transmitter in order to produce sufficient revenues to pay for its high construction and operating costs. Nonetheless, the number of stations has continued to grow, though the growth has shown signs of tapering off.

TABLE 2

Growth of Homes Owning Radio and Television

(Source: A. C. Nielsen Co., NBC, CBS)

(In Millions)

	Total U.S. Homes	Radio Homes	TV Homes	Per Cent in TV Coverage Area	Per Cent Owning Radio	Per Cent Owning TV
1925	27.4	2.7	–	–	10%	–
1930	30.0	13.8	–	–	46	–
1935	31.9	21.5	–	–	67	–
1940	34.8	28.5	–	–	82	–
1945	37.6	33.1	–	–	88	–
1950	42.9	40.8	3.1	56%	95	7%
1951	44.2	41.9	10.0	60	95	23
1952	44.7	43.3	16.0	62	97	37
1953	45.6	45.2	21.2	67	99	46
1954	47.6	46.6	27.7	95	98	58
1955	47.8	47.0	32.0	97	98	67
1956	48.0	47.0	35.1	97	98	73
1957	50.0	48.5	41.0	97	98	82

In its short life, commercial television has risen to about the same dimensions (in number of homes) that radio had achieved by the end of World War II. About fifteen years after the beginning of commercial radio broadcasting, three-fourths of the homes in the United States were radio-equipped. Television has reached the same proportion in less than a decade. By 1950, radio had reached a virtual saturation point; it was present in 95 homes out of a hundred. But television will probably arrive at this level long before another fifteen years have past.

Television's growth in the near future will not continue as rapidly as in the recent past. There are two reasons for this:

1. Television grew fast as it came to new parts of the country. But the stations just starting up, and those which will start in the future, are mostly in smaller cities already within range of TV transmitters in other places.

2. The initial growth of television took place most slowly among families who were least able to afford it, and also in very small families, especially childless ones, where there was least demand for it. Many of these families will continue to get along without TV for a while.

In the dozen years since the end of World War II, 51,000,000 television sets were manufactured in the United States, according to estimates made by the Sylvania Electric Company. Of these, all but 9,000,000 scrapped or discarded units were in use in the middle of 1957. (J)

By 1956, the U. S. public had invested $15.6 billions in its television sets—$10.4 billions for the sets themselves, $2.4 billions for servicing, $1.7 billions for antennas and other components, and $1.1 billions for replacement tubes. (The cost of electric power consumption is not included in this estimate.)

Of the 42,000,000 sets in use, the great majority are large-screen sets of relatively recent vintage. 55% have 19-21 inch-wide tubes (4% are even wider), 29% are 16-18 inch models, and only 12% have screens 15 inches or smaller in width. 2,250,000 are portables. (K)

A necessary prerequisite to the growth in the number of television sets has been the expansion of the television coverage area. Before the lifting of the TV "freeze," about 56% of the nation's homes were within reception range of a TV station; today the figure is 97%.

This expansion of coverage in turn reflects the soaring number of television stations, located in an increasingly large number of viewing areas (see Table 3).

TABLE 3

Growth of U. S. Television Reception

(Source: Television Bureau of Advertising)

		Number of Television Areas	Number of Television Stations
January	1949	28	48
	1950	56	96
	1951	61	106
	1952	62	108
	1953	73	120
	1954	192	309
	1955	239	395
	1956	243	459
	1957	251	502

(L)

More stations have not only brought more new people within range of television; they have also broadened the range of choice of the television owner, bringing more channels within his reach. Only 4% of the viewers are within range of only a single station. 72% of television homes can today receive four stations or more; even though only eighteen cities have four or more channels operating, stations located in other nearby cities are often within viewing range.

(M) The increased opportunity for programming choice on the part of the viewer was spurred also by the beginnings of multiple set ownership (which included 6% of all TV homes by mid-1957). As the early, small-screen sets became obsolescent, many of the original TV owners acquired new sets with wider screens. In many cases the old set was neither discarded nor traded in, but moved out of the living room and into some other part of the house, giving the individual viewer even greater freedom to select what he wants to see.

By January, 1958, there were 521 stations on the air in the (N)
United States, and forty in Canada. Thus television has gradually
come to approach some of the potentialities for individual choice
and selectivity that existed in radio. As smaller cities acquired their
own TV transmitters, wider areas were brought within reach of stations in nearby cities as well as of those in their own. Nearly four
hundred community antenna systems, operating on a subscription
basis, provide television service to many homes whose reception
might otherwise be faulty because of unfavorable terrain.

TV and Non-TV Homes: The Changing Pattern

In television's early days, or in its early days in a new tele- (O)
vision area, sets were acquired first by those of above-average income,
like any other expensive consumer goods. Unlike many other similarly expensive commodities, television quickly spread to the lower
income levels.

An early TV survey in New Brunswick, New Jersey, conducted by Rutgers University under CBS sponsorship, found that the
pioneer set owners who had acquired TV before July 1947 were
considerably higher in social status than those who bought sets during the year 1947-48. Of the pioneer owners, 19% were semi-skilled
or unskilled, 36% were white-collar or skilled workers, and 45% were
proprietors and professionals. Of the later purchasers, 37% were semi-
skilled and unskilled, 45% white collar and skilled workers, but only
18% proprietors and professionals.

The broadened base of television ownership may be clearly
seen by a reanalysis of data collected annually, since 1949, by the
Market Research Corporation. Their sample may be divided into
equal quarters on the basis of income. If television ownership were
evenly distributed regardless of income, it too would naturally be
divided into four equal parts. In 1949, the bottom fourth of the
sample population owned only 13% of the sets, while the two top
quarters owned a disproportionately heavy 30% apiece. Today the
bottom quarter is up to 19% of the sets, and the two top quarters
have dropped correspondingly in their share of the total.

TABLE 4

The Changing Distribution of TV Ownership

(Adapted from reports of the Market Research Corporation)

Per Cent of All TV Sets

Income Level	1949	1951	1953	1955	1957
Upper Fourth	30%	30%	30%	29%	29%
Second Fourth	30	29	28	28	27
Next Fourth	27	25	26	25	25
Lower Fourth	13	16	16	18	19
	100%	100%	100%	100%	100%

A number of surveys made throughout television's history could document the change in the composition of the TV-owning public. Because the Market Research Corporation has maintained the same methods of measurement year after year, its findings show the trends much more clearly than would be the case if unrelated surveys were compared.

Table 5 shows the percentage of TV ownership in households of differing characteristics, for the years 1949-1955. Each figure shown under a given year represents the proportion of television-owning households in the particular category.

The most striking feature of the trend figures shown in Table 5 is the steady narrowing of the differences in the proportion of TV ownership among various sub-groups of the population. This is an inevitable by-product of the fact that more and more people have acquired TV, and that the rate of growth has been most rapid where the opportunities for growth were greatest—namely, in groups where ownership has been below average.

For a long while, the college-educated lagged behind the high-school educated in TV ownership, though the gap has now virtually disappeared. The least-educated (those who have been only to grade school) are still behind in ownership.

In the last four years alone, TV ownership has spread from one farm family in four to over half. Of the rural non-farm families, two-thirds now have sets. Small families, childless families, and families where the housewife is older, have been, from the start, below average in TV ownership. They, too, are edging up to the average.

TABLE 5

Growth of TV Penetration in Different Segments of the U. S. Market

1949-1956

(Source: Market Research Corporation reports)

	September 1949	October 1950	July 1951	July 1952	July 1953	July 1954	July 1955	July 1956
U. S. Total	6%	18%	27%	37%	49%	58%	68%	76%
Region								
Northeast	13%	35%	45%	59%	69%	77%	85%	88%
South	1	4	13	17	30	37	54	64
North Central	4	15	27	39	50	61	70	79
Mtn., S.W.	*	3	10	16	31	40	52	62
Pacific	5	19	26	34	47	56	66	76
City Size								
Farm	*	3%	7%	12%	23%	28%	43%	54%
Under 2,500	*	5	9	16	26	41	56	67
2,500 to 50,000	*	9	16	18	31	39	53	65
50,000 to 500,000	*	17	28	37	51	64	75	82
500,000 & over	14%	40	53	69	77	81	87	89
Income								
Upper Fourth	7%	24%	33%	45%	58%	70%	81%	87%
Next Fourth	7	19	32	41	55	63	76	85
Next Fourth	6	18	28	40	50	59	69	76
Lowest Fourth	3	12	18	23	32	41	48	58
Education								
Grade School	4%	16%	23%	31%	43%	51%	62%	70%
High School	7	22	34	45	57	65	75	83
College	6	17	24	38	48	61	73	79
Family Size								
1 & 2 Members	4%	12%	19%	28%	38%	48%	59%	69%
3 Members	6	18	30	41	52	65	73	81
4 & 5 Members	7	22	35	45	58	69	78	85
6 & More Members	6	19	27	39	53	55	66	74
Age of Housewife								
Under 35	8%	23%	36%	44%	58%	65%	75%	82%
35 through 44 Years	8	23	37	48	60	68	74	82
45 Years & Over	3	12	19	28	40	49	61	70
Presence of Children								
5 Years & Under	7%	23%	36%	48%	54%	65%	75%	81%
6 to 12 Years	7	22	35	46	56	65	76	83
13 to 20 Years	6	18	28	39	49	58	71	78
No Children	4	13	21	29	37	50	61	70

*No Data.

TV and Non-TV Homes: A Comparison

(P)   Although the differences are diminishing, as TV penetration grows, the four homes in five which have television are still not identical with their non-television neighbors. The most accurate recent information on the subject is provided by a survey made in June, 1955, by the U.S. Bureau of the Census. At a time when 76% of U.S. households owned at least one television set (and 7% of the total had two or more sets), substantial differences (shown in Table 6) were found to exist in set ownership, by region, size of family, and city size.

Television ownership is heavily concentrated in urban areas, and particularly in the large metropolitan centers. There are several reasons for this. It is in these areas that television was first established; they still enjoy a better quality of reception and, typically, can receive a larger number of stations than most rural areas. They are better able to afford television, since their family income is above the national average. Cities of a quarter-million or more inhabitants have the highest concentration of households with television—about four in every five.

Farm dwellers, last to come within range of television, and below average in income, are lowest in ownership. Accessibility is one explanation. In December, 1952, a mail survey conducted among 300 farm families subscribing to *Successful Farming* magazine found that among the 22% who then owned television sets, the average distance from the nearest TV station was 43 miles. Of every ten farmers who were television owners, four lived over fifty miles from the nearest television station.

Families with children were from the start under especially heavy pressure to acquire television. In families of three, four and five persons, television ownership is substantially higher than in two-person households. It is also higher than in households of six or more persons—probably because these are more often found in rural areas than anywhere else. People who live alone are least apt to own a television set (though paradoxically, they might be able to profit most from its companionship). This may be because their income is lower, or because they spend less time at home and generally lead more mobile lives.

Urban areas—and TV ownership—are geographically concentrated most heavily in the Northeastern States. The Rocky Mountain and Midwestern States, with their relatively sparse distribution of population, and the South, with its lower income level, lag behind the rest of the country in TV penetration.

TABLE 6

Penetration of Television, June 1955

(Source: U. S. Bureau of the Census)

	% of Households Owning TV
By Urban and Rural Location	
Total Urban	74%
Inside urbanized areas of:	
3,000,000 inhabitants or more	81
1,000,000 to 3,000,000 inhabitants	82
250,000 to 1,000,000 inhabitants	79
50,000 to 250,000 inhabitants	74
Outside urbanized areas, in urban places of:	
10,000 inhabitants or more	62
2,500 to 10,000 inhabitants	52
Rural Non-Farm, Total	61
Rural Farm, Total	42
By Size of Household	
1 person	36
2 persons	64
3 persons	73
4 persons	79
5 persons	78
6 persons or more	66
By Census Regions	
Northeast	80
North Central	72
South	53
West	62
U. S. Total	67%

The characteristic differences, in family size and city-size location, were also found when television and non-television homes were compared by the National Broadcasting Company in a survey of women's daytime television viewing habits. (This study was made by Willard R. Simmons and Associates in January, 1954, at a time when 57% of the households had TV.)

As Table 7 shows, this study also confirmed that television is more often found in homes where there are children under 18, where family income is higher, where the head of the house has an occupation of higher status, and where the housewife herself is younger and better educated. The television families are more apt to own a car, and to be home-owners. In the television home, the woman of the house is more apt to be married, and to be employed outside the home. Because Negroes enjoy a lower average income than whites, and because a sizable proportion of them are rural Southerners, relatively fewer Negroes than whites are television owners.

TABLE 7

A Comparison of Women in TV and Non-TV Homes

(Source: NBC-Simmons "Daytime TV" 1954 Study)

Per cent of homes in each category	TV Homes	Non-TV Homes
Children under 18 years	60%	48%
Under $3,000 Income	20	53
Professional, semi-professional, managerial occupation (head of house)	23	14
Grade school education or less (housewife)	24	39
Own automobile	77	63
Own home	58	51
Live in single-family dwelling	63	72
Metropolitan areas	77	37
55 and older (housewife)	18	28
Married (housewife)	80	71
Employed outside the home (housewife)	35	28
White	93	84

The study points to some differences in the interests of housewives in TV and in non-TV homes—differences which follow from the less educated and urbanized character of the latter group. The non-TV owners have fewer interests. In particular, they are less interested in wordly subjects like fashion and clothes, diet and health, home decoration, news and current events, make-up and personal appearance (see Table 8). In short, they appear to lead narrower, more restricted lives than do the television owners.

TABLE 8

Topics of Interest Selected by Housewives
in TV and Non-TV Homes

(Per Cent Selecting Each Topic, From the List of 11,
as Being "Especially Interesting")

(Source: NBC-Simmons "Daytime TV" 1954 Study)

	TV Homes	Non-TV Homes
Clubs and organizations	14%	13%
Cooking and baking	55	56
Diet, nutrition and health	26	20
Fashion and clothes	43	35
Gardening	22	30
Home decoration	38	31
Make-up and personal appearance	33	23
New housekeeping aids	28	26
News and current events	48	40
Parties and entertaining	15	11
Sewing and needlework	41	45

An analysis by Daniel Starch shows that among families without children, 19% purchased new television sets in the years 1952-1954.
Among families with children aged 14-17, 23% purchased a set in
this period. The proportion increased as the age of the children
decreased, with the heaviest proportion of new purchasers (32%)
found among parents of children under 2.

In a study of religious broadcasting in New Haven (1952),
Everett Parker and his associates found that religion (and presumably ethnicity) were strongly related to television set ownership,
independently of social class (which by itself is related to religious
affiliation). In a cross-section of 3559 interviews, it was found that
at every social class level, TV ownership was lower among Protestants
than among Catholics or Jews. The difference was particularly noticeable at the upper and upper-middle social level. Thus in the highest
social category (the wealthy families whose heads were leaders in
the community) TV was owned by 82% of the Catholics, by 82% of
the Jews, but by only 34% of the Protestants. At the next level, the
"well-to-do" who lack inherited wealth, 75% of the Catholics, 78%

of the Jews, but only 51% of the Protestants, had TV. By contrast at the lowest level, among the tenement dwellers, TV was found in 81% of the Catholic homes, in 63% of the Jewish homes, and in 61% of the Protestant homes. In the words of the authors, "something in the nature of a 'Protestant culture,' vague as it might be, influenced Protestant families in New Haven against the purchase of television sets and this made the proportion of Protestants in the general television audience smaller than the proportion of Protestants in the total population." There is no evidence as to whether this fascinating observation applies to other places than New Haven. In any case, as television ownership approaches saturation, such differences among different population groups have naturally tended to disappear.

Charles Swanson and Robert Jones, interviewing a probability sample of 202 Minneapolis adults in the spring of 1950, found that the TV owners did not differ from non-owners in income, education, social activity, or average intelligence level; however they showed greater variability in intelligence, and tended to know less about government affairs.

As television grew to its present stature as the most powerful medium of communication on the American scene, the life of its viewing public was influenced in many ways. Later chapters will trace changes in the pattern of TV viewing and in the other activities which have been affected. These changes can best be described if we first examine the nature of television's appeal to its great audience and the character of the programming content it offers for popular consumption.

2. POPULAR CULTURE
AND THE APPEALS OF TELEVISION

To understand why and how television exercises its profound fascination for millions of viewers, we must see it first in broad perspective as one of the popular arts, and then in the more limited context of broadcasting. A substantial amount of reflection, research and discussion on radio has taken place in the past thirty years. Much of it, though not all, can add to our understanding of television and its appeals. But we must also define and examine those characteristics unique to television which differentiate it from radio as well as from the other mass media.

Television as One of the Popular Arts

Many of the most important things which can be said about television apply equally well to other contemporary forms of mass communication. The media may be seen as vehicles by which information and ideas are communicated to the masses of people. Discussion of the popular arts usually refers to the content or subject matter which the media offer their audiences.

It is useful to distinguish the popular arts, of which television is an example, from the elite art which has been accepted, admired and transmitted through history. (By "elite art" we refer to the fine arts as they have traditionally been described, with the concept of "beauty" usually at the heart of the description.) To be sure, a large twilight area lies between the two categories. A great motion picture, a great television drama or a great short story in a magazine is "art" by any definition, though it is not necesssarily typical of the bulk of output in these media.

The following description exaggerates the differences between popular and elite art, for the purpose of making the contrast clearer. There are obviously many exceptions which can be found on any of these points.

21

1. *The Audience.* The outstanding characteristic of the popular arts, compared with the elite arts, is that they reach vast numbers of people. By contrast, the taste for elite art has usually been
centered in a very small part of the public. A case in point might
be the comparative circulations of *TV Guide* and of the *Art Bulletin.*

The audience for the popular arts is not only much larger
than the elite art audience; it is also far more heterogeneous. Whereas the elite audience tends to be heavily concentrated in an urban,
well educated, upper-income milieu, the popular art audience is widely
distributed and is characterized by considerable diversity of life styles,
beliefs and tastes.

Because it has this diversified character, the public for popular
art is relatively unconscious of itself as an audience. It lacks a common intellectual idiom by which a given art form may be experienced or judged. Its standards of value are less constant, less definite,
less integrated, less vocal and less critical than those of the elite art
audience. Here again, our categories are not mutually exclusive. The
same people may participate in both spheres, but a given individual
responds appropriately as the occasion requires. He is apt to apply
a different standard of value when he looks at pictures in an art
exhibition than when he looks at magazine covers on a newsstand.

2. *Artist and Audience.* There is more meaningful two-
way communication between artist and public in elite art than in
popular art. The elite audience is more self-confident, more likely to
express its preferences. Its judgments are supported by critical canons,
and are expressed through its spokesmen, the critics. Thus the elite
artist is continually stimulated through reproof or praise expressed
in rational or esthetic terms and addressed to him directly in his
creative role.

The success or failure of a popular artist is more often directly
indicated by his changing record on the cash register. Obviously,
motivations overlap. The elite artist today is as concerned as were
his historical predecessors with problems of material well-being, and
the successful creators of popular art are talented and conscientious
technicians who take a genuine craftsmanlike delight in their work.

We may think of the elite artist's primary concern as the expression of a strongly felt personal experience. Whatever may be
his original or underlying motivations, his creative activity emerges

out of an emotional involvement with his subject and a need to give it individual expression. By contrast we may think of the popular artist as one who sets forth deliberately to conform to the tastes and wishes of his public, as these tastes and wishes are interpreted by the operators of the mass media — publishers, editors, producers, directors or sponsors.

It is only in relatively recent years that the popular arts themselves have acquired a body of critics and commentators. These critics do not generally influence the production of popular art to the same extent that this is true in elite art. To this statement there are exceptions: the views of the New York motion picture critics affect box office attendance; popular music has its highly vocal and influential devotees.

The television critic is not in a position to influence the audience for any particular performance of a program because he watches that program at the same time that they do. He cannot even begin to cover and report on the full range of weekly output in his medium. **(A)** However, over a period of time, his judgments may influence tastes and viewing habits. Most important, he helps to form the opinion held by people in the broadcasting industry of a program, its stars or producers. The critics for the New York *Times* and *Herald Tribune* and for *Variety* help to fix the level of esteem in which the producers of a television program are viewed by the people they consider significant. In this way their role resembles that of the traditional critics of elite art.

3. *The Institutions of Art.* Elite art, as we have just noted, is guided by a prevailing set of esthetic principles (or in a time of differing standards, like the present, by one of several sets of principles). The objectives of the artist are therefore set by the work itself. He seeks to achieve a quality of expression adequate to the problem he has chosen. He can strive only to outdo himself.

Of course this is not completely or always true. To secure material success or critical acclaim, artists accept conventions of technique or genre, and still produce works of merit. (One thinks of Haydn, or of contemporary Soviet composers.) But once the limits of subject and style are set (regardless of how much the artist has to do with their selection), it is the artist's task to realize the work as he conceives it.

By contrast, popular art is designed first of all as a commodity subject to the rules of supply and demand. Its success must be measured on a comparative or competitive basis. The wide audience of the popular arts demands a much more elaborate structure of production and distribution than is true in elite art with its restricted institutions: the art galleries and academies, the concert societies, the little magazines.

Within the intricate apparatus of popular art, geared to the needs of the market, there occurs an inevitable specialization of functions. Every individual involved in the creation of popular art is merely one worker on a long intellectual assembly line through which it passes on its way to the final consumer. This means, as has just been said, that the artist's contact with his audience is attenuated. It also means that he no longer controls his product. The ends of his activity are fixed: to win the largest possible audience. Often the means are also restricted by formula and convention.

4. *Content.* Because its audience is larger and more heterogeneous, popular art employs themes and symbols which are less complex than those of elite art. They must be intelligible to a less sophisticated public. They must assume a less specialized universe of discourse and a lower level of interest than that which is offered by the elite audience.

The commercial incentives of popular art make it essential to attract and to hold as large an audience as possible regardless of the means employed. The popular artist therefore uses those techniques which assure the public's patronage, and these are not always the ones which promise the most adequate attainment of esthetic goals. Thus the popular arts tend, in at least two ways, to be conservative.

a. They usually cannot afford to use any but tried and tested devices and forms. They tend to avoid the bizarre or the experimental. even to the point of stereotype. They are generally realistic, literal, and easily grasped, and they shy away from symbolism.

b. They also tend to be conservative in their overt political and social contents, since it is dangerous to offend any sizable portion of the audience by questioning its established values or beliefs.

Another reason for the conservatism of the mass media is that as commercial institutions they are part of a business community whose predominantly conservative thinking very often contrasts with the traditional role of the artist as critic of the social order.

5. *The Art Experience.* Elite art is created with the expectation that the audience will give it concentrated attention. Attention is necessary to perceive and enjoy the many subtle skills employed in its achievement. Because it expresses thoughts which are profound and intensely felt by the artist, elite art also has the power to marshal the complete interest of its audience. Moreover, it is surrounded by a social ritual in which devoted silence has an important place.

By contrast, popular art is typically absorbed at a rather low level of attention. This is possible because it is relatively simple and easy to absorb, in keeping with the nature and tastes of its broad audience. Moreover, exposure to the popular arts often takes place under circumstances when the audience is tired or when its interest is at least partly diverted in other directions. This is as it should be, since the audience turns to the popular arts in search of recreation. The great volume of output in the popular arts also tends to diminish the intensity of experience it represents for the audience, since any one item loses its unique interest in relation to a multitude of similar items.

Characteristics of the Broadcast Media

So far, what has been said of the popular arts applies equally well to all the contemporary mass media. When we turn to broadcasting we can carry our description even farther. What are the special characteristics of television, in relation to its audience, which it shares with radio?

1. *Universality of Symbols.* The broadcast media in the United States reach and speak to vast numbers of the population. Because they cut across all lines of geography and social class, they must deal in universal symbols rather than with those which are peculiar to any region (as newspapers do) or to any social group (as most magazines do). Throughout the country, millions of people hear the same broadcast programs, with the same stars in the same situations, and the same topical references to personalities and places. All this produces a measure of shared cultural experience which no other society has ever known.

This has both a positive and a negative aspect. It helps to create a community of thought and knowledge and thereby prepares the way for the consensus on which a civilized democratic society must ultimately rest. On the other hand, it reduces individuality of experience and opinion. To the very extent that it makes for standized values it tends to produce an atmosphere of conformity.

2. *"Official" Character.* Precisely because television and radio are universal in their symbolism and penetration, they have a sacrosanct and "official" aura, to an even greater extent than other mass media like magazines and newspapers.

By bringing the voices of the President and other officials to the public, broadcasting has established itself as the most direct and vital medium by which the government communicates its decisions and pronouncements to the world. Far more than in the United States, where the broadcast media are privately operated (though under federal control), this is true in countries where radio and television facilities are actually operated by the government.

Maurice Gorham has described dramatically how important and comforting a force radio became in wartime Britain. It gave the individual isolated listener a feeling that higher powers were operating in his interest and that, no matter how badly things were going immediately and locally, on the whole they were well under control.

> "The very familiarity of radio had a reassuring effect. The well known voices of the news-readers and announcers became symbols of reality in a topsy-turvy world. If you were waiting in a firestation for the bells to go down, if you had lost your home that morning, if your place of work had turned into a pile of rubble overnight, still nine o'clock would bring the strokes of Big Ben and the unfailing news.
>
> "The news readers and announcers carried much of the burden of broadcasting in those years. They were constantly faced with news of all sorts of gravity, with mentions of foreign places and foreign names that nobody knew how to pronounce, with crises when programmes could not be broadcast and broadcasters failed to appear. They had to sound unruffled whatever happened at their end of the microphone, for nothing would have been more apt to spread panic than any sign of it on their part; and they always did."

A recognition of this public dependence on broadcasting's

familiar voices was recently incorporated into plans for U. S. civil defense. It was decided that, in the event of a national emergency, well-known voices like those of Arthur Godfrey and Edward R. Murrow were to sound the alarm over the radio.

The very fact that the audience considers broadcast information "official" made possible the few great hoaxes which radio perpetrated in the course of its active period. The first of these took place in England shortly before the general strike of 1926. A burlesque account was given of a riot of unemployed led by the "Secretary of the National Movement for Abolishing Theater Queues." Because the broadcast was handled in the manner characteristic of BBC news, it was taken seriously by people all over the country in spite of the fact that it was an obvious parody.

Years later in the United States, even greater alarm was caused, and in part for the very same reasons, by Orson Welles' Mercury Theater radio dramatization of H. G. Wells' "War of the Worlds." In a study by Herta Herzog, people interviewed in New Jersey (the area "invaded" by the Martians) explained their terror by saying, "the announcer would not say it if it were not true."

> "We have so much faith in broadcasting. In a crisis it has to reach all the people. That's what radio is here for."

3. *Glamor.* Because the personalities of the broadcast media are universally known, they are thought of as famous, important, and powerful. This gives the entire industry a special aura of glamor in the eyes of the audience. Like the world of film and, to a lesser extent, the world of the big magazines and newspapers, the world of broadcasting is part of the domain of public interest, and it carries implications of glitter and romance. It is an idealized world in which life is more interesting, varied and full than it is in everyday reality. Its people are thought to move fast and dramatically, to be on the inside of great events. They are themselves more handsome and rich than the average person and are therefore objects of envy or identification. The fact that broadcasting performers are highly talented and highly paid is never absent from the consciousness of the audience. The very knowledge that a famous comedian earns many thousands of dollars for a performance makes that performance seem

more interesting or more important. It is "proof" that the entertainer is good and deserves to be watched.

4. *The Illusion of Realism.* The broadcast media carry a special illusion of reality. The viewer of a television program or the listener to a radio broadcast is hearing and seeing something which is actually taking place. At a dramatic spectacle, at the movies, or in reading, the audience is in some measure aware of the conventions of the craft. It knows that the film was made at some time in the past and that it was spliced and put together under careful direction. It knows that the writer's words have been edited and set in print. It knows that the spectacle on the stage is not real life. But in the broadcast media the things taking place seem like "the real thing," even though the viewer or listener alters what he hears or sees in terms of the expectations he carries within himself.

(B)   5. *The Audience Shapes Content to Fit Its Own Expectations.* The psychological phenomenon of projection is a familiar feature of everyday life. It comes into play in the response which people make to the popular arts, perceiving and interpreting content to fit their own unconscious motives, expectations and wishes.

This is more true of radio than for any other mass medium, because it offers the greatest play for the imagination. The only stimulus is aural. There is no record to which repeated reference can be made. It is relatively easy for the listener to make what he wills of what he hears. Three illustrations of this point may be cited:

a. Theodor Geiger, studying listener attitudes toward classical music in Denmark, announced a recorded symphony concert as "popular gramophone music" on one occasion. On anther occasion it was announced as classical music and all the musical terms were fully explained. Although the content of the program was essentially the same, it drew twice the audience when it was described as "popular."

b. In a study of fan mail addressed to Deems Taylor, commentator for the New York Philharmonic Orchestra broadcasts, the present writer found that even listeners who were critical of the program preferred to think that Taylor secretly shared their views.

"Aren't you ashamed to deliver that drivel handed to you by your sponsor . . . but, please, oh please tell me you do not believe a word of it."

c. In his study of "The Invasion from Mars," Hadley Cantril (1940) points out that among the persons who took the program at face value were some who heard it from the beginning (at which time it was clearly announced as a dramatization of H. G. Wells' fantastic novel). Many people who actually heard this opening announcement chose to believe that the earth was really being invaded by creatures from another planet. As Herzog comments, "the idea that everyone today is prepared to believe unusual and gruesome events is the theme which, in many variations, runs through the interviews." Here, again, the predispositions of the audience governed the way in which the broadcast was perceived.

In television, the presence of the visual element reduces the amount of unstructured stimulation of the sort which radio offers its audience. Yet there is still much that the viewer can adapt to suit his fancy.

Dallas Smythe (1954) points to the number of different ways in which a televised wrestling match may be interpreted by different segments of the audience, and observes that each of these interpretations may correspond to a different "reality."

"A televised wrestling program is an ambiguous stimulus field. Superficially it is often thought of as a sport. If it is perceived as a sport, what representation of the human condition does it provide? An image of skillful use of trained bodies? an image of resplendent or gross sex aggression in a sexually deviant context, e.g., against a person of the same sex? An image of 'natural man' competing for survival without the benefit of accepted law? Or 'n' other interpretations of reality? But wrestling may also be perceived as a form of folk-drama. As such does it provide the material from which an audience member fills his need for a sardonic morality story in which virtue is cruelly mistreated by evil cunning until finally by superior skill virtue wins in the end? Or an image of a more cynical kind of how 'you can't win by being honest' —where as more frequently happens, the villain who has 'got by' with unfair practices in the end wins over the stubbornly honest hero? Still others in the audience perceive wrestling from yet another dimension of meaning. These embittered souls 'know' wrestling is 'fixed'. They watch it as if to repeatedly build up their damaged self-respect by observing that the ringside audience and presumably that 'they' who watch the match on television are inferior beings who believe wrestling to be 'on the level'."

In a study reported in more detail in Chapter XI, Kurt and Gladys Lang make a similar point. They note that viewers of political broadcasts tend to look on public personalities in terms of their own party loyalties and their interpretations of campaign issues.

6. *The Illusion of Intimacy.* Because the audience projects itself and its wishes into what it hears and sees, the broadcast media can create the illusion that their performers or announcers communicate directly to the people on the receiving end. This illusion is achieved because radio and television have a quality of immediacy. The listener or viewer feels that the person he hears is a real individual talking to him "right here and now."

Moreover, because the receiver is located in the home, the act of communication takes place in familiar surroundings. This helps to create an intimate situation which contrasts with the more formal atmosphere of the theater or with the impersonal symbolism of the printed word.

Broadcasting is farthest, perhaps, from the illusion of intimacy in the television spectacular. It is closest in the radio disc jockey whose "relaxed" style seeks to create the impression that he is speaking only to each individual listener, as an old and dear friend. No one has described this better than Rudolf Arnheim did in 1936:

"At the Katowice station there is a man who, in the evening after the programme is finished, runs a French post-box. It deals with private letters whose contents are read out for foreign countries. This broadcast goes on for hours. In the quiet of the night the man comfortably reads out his letters. He makes little pauses to acquaint himself with the contents, murmurs to himself, bursts out into cheery laughter when something amuses him, gabbles hurriedly through unimportant passages, stutters over some difficult name, reads it again, spells it out, growls with annoyance, falls silent and starts happily all over again. Perhaps it is too much of a good thing, and this sort of shirt-sleeve business would scarcely do as a regular item, but he too charms directly by the intimacy of his way of speaking. One feels like the guest of an old friend who is looking through some dusty old correspondence by the fireside."

The quality of direct and intimate contact so delightfully described in the preceding quotation is carefully nurtured by skillful performers. This very illusion of personal communication with a glamorous, famous personality gives the broadcast media much of their appeal. (In the previously mentioned study of Philharmonic fan mail it was apparent that the intermission commentator, who seemed warm and easy to know, provided the audience with a point of direct contact through which it could come to grips with the content of a "high-brow" program.)

One day during World War II, Kate Smith, the singer, appeared on the radio at repeated intervals to make brief one-minute announcements asking listeners to pledge funds for war bonds. In his study of this marathon appeal, Robert Merton notes that many listeners were particularly impressed by the idea that such a famous star would sacrifice herself for the public good. Listeners who "knew" Kate Smith in a different context (that is, in her regular formal program) felt that they were watching her go through a critical personal experience. They became personally involved because they felt that they were actually witnesses to her ordeal. A respondent compared people listening to Kate Smith in a saloon to "a crowd watching a weight lifter, a toreador, or a tightrope walker."

"After each announcement there was a sort of tension in the place to see whether she would come on again."

"One fellow wanted to have the radio turned off. Well, the reaction was that he was going to be thrown out. Nobody wanted it turned off."

These listeners were not merely anonymous members of a vast impersonal audience. They were obviously deeply involved with the affairs of an individual to whom they felt very close.   (C)

7. *The Illusion of Drama.* The broadcast media are peculiarly able to create in the audience both a feeling of intimacy and a sense of being present at actual events. This means that these media can manipulate the audience's view of reality, making events seem more dramatic than they actually are. Merton points out, for example, that

an extraordinary impression can be created by interrupting the normally sacrosanct schedule of the broadcast day:

> "When the day's broadcasts began, Smith explained that this was no ordinary event . . . And not only Smith, but the whole vast mysterious machinery of a radio network must be recognized as animated by this extraordinary occasion . . . There was little possibility of escaping the atmosphere of excited anticipation . . . Listeners clearly felt that they were witnessing or even participating in a special event . . . Spot announcements at odd moments during the radio day are usually discrete. Each is complete in itself. Listeners who hear several such announcements do not respond to them as a series or unity. In contrast, the Smith war bond drive was experienced by most informants not as a procession of unrelated parts, but as a integral event enduring all day and into the night . . . One immediate consequence of this time-binding structure was a frequent compulsion to continue listening. Fully half of the hundred informants had listened to Smith more than ten times that day."

Earlier, Arnheim had set forth the thesis that radio has a unique capacity for creating an illusion of drama because dramatic action is more vividly expressed through sound than through sight. Visual phenomena may be active, he notes, but they may also be static, in that they represent what exists in spite of the passage of time. However, most sounds imply that something is actually happening and activity is the essence of drama.

Yet radio is not unique in its capacity to create the illusion of drama. Television also has demonstrated its ability to create by artifice the impression that important things are taking place.

Considerable popular excitement and front page newspaper headlines have been generated by television quiz programs like the "$64,000 Question" and its imitators, "The Big Surprise," and "Twenty One." The stakes are high, and the questioning process is spun out by design from week to week, in order to heighten tension and raise audience interest to fever pitch.

The contestants in these programs are as carefully screened and selected for their talent and audience appeal as are the star entertainers of any television variety show. Yet the viewers are drawn powerfully to the program by their belief that the quiz represents a real life drama being played before their eyes. The protagonists are individuals whom they envy and admire and with whom they identify their own hopes and dreams. The events taking place are considered as though they are altogether unexpected, like the surprising turns of a plot in a mystery novel. Attention is mobilized and held because the viewers feel that they are witnessing great moments of decision.

8. *The Creation of Fantasy.* Like the other popular arts, radio and television are vehicles of fantasy. They help to create the symbols through which the wishes of the audience may be expressed and released. They provide readymade daydreams in which the audience is invited to participate. A good deal of controversy in connection with the popular arts centers on the importance and function of the fantasy which is generated in this way. Three schools of thought may be distinguished:

a. The critics argue along these lines: Broadcasting, and the popular arts generally, represent a make-believe world in which the audience is invited to act out its unconscious and often anti-social desires. This not only provides an outlet for aggressive impulses; it actually stimulates them.

The audience is diverted from the solution of its own real-life problems to participate vicariously in the imaginary problems of the personalities depicted on their television screens or over their radio loudspeakers. In their search for an "escape" they lose their capacity to grapple effectively with the real world around them.

b. Another body of opinion holds that the fantasy experience afforded by broadcasting enables the audience to cope more successfully with everyday life. Lloyd Warner and William Henry sum up this view in their study of a radio soap opera, "Big Sister":

> "The representative programs we selected function very much like a folktale, expressing the hopes and fears of its female audience, and on the whole contributed to the integration of their lives in the world in which they live."

The characters and actions "expressed the values and ideas common to the restrictive confines of the family where the women who listened lived their lives."

"The effect of the 'Big Sister' program is to direct their hopes into confident and optimistic channels . . . The petty difficulties of the women, seemingly insignificant, are now dramatized and become significant and important; and the women who experience these difficulties feel themselves to be significant people . . . The 'Big Sister' program thus acts constructively in the lives of the women and functions for them very much as did the morality plays of former times. The dramatis personae, in act and symbol, express the conflicting forces of good and evil . . . Emotions are released adaptively, beliefs are socially oriented, and the values of the groups are reaffirmed in the experiences of the audience."

Seen in this light, the soap opera provides useful instruction for its listeners on the techniques of handling real life problems, and enables them to make a happier adjustment to what seems, as the authors describe it, a rather dismal existence.

Though this interpretation appears to be directly at variance with the preceding one, there is a common element to these two schools of thought. Both rest on the assumption that the content of broadcast programs affords a means of identification by which the audience can express its own feelings and rehearse its own problems on a symbolic or vicarious level. That is, both the critics and the proponents start with the assumption that program content represents a psychologically meaningful experience for the viewers or listeners. However, there is an alternative to this assumption.

c. It can also be argued that the popular arts are neither "escapist" nor "adaptive" in function, but merely recreational. This viewpoint assumes that much listening and viewing represents a merely superficial experience for the audience, not one which is meaningful enough to make for subconscious identification or fantasy. Listening or viewing is primarily a pastime, rather than the expression of deepseated psychological needs. To be sure, the psychological predispositions of the audience influence the selection of programs from among available alternatives, but it is the *activity* of viewing or listening — as a form of relaxing or "killing time" —
(D)   which provides the principal motivation.

In an age of abundant leisure, the broadcast media provide a semblance of occupation and a focus of attention for people with time on their hands and no strong interests to pursue. Radio and television can do this more easily than print because they provide a feeling of human companionship and contact.

The radio-TV columnist of the New York *Herald Tribune,* John Crosby, relates that he once asked a housewife why she listened to soap operas. He received the answer that soap operas were all she could get on the radio. "Then why not turn off the radio?", he asked. "It's a voice in the house," she said.

9. *Listening and Viewing Are Passive.* To consider radio listening or television viewing a pastime is to imply that it requires little effort on the part of the audience, compared with reading. Its meanings are manifest and easily absorbed.

This is reflected in the receptiveness with which the audience takes in the broadcast message. Hadley Cantril and Gordon Allport note that "the listener seems as a rule to be friendly, uncritical and well-disposed toward what he hears . . . The plethora of platitudes reaching our ears during the day would be unbearable if we encountered them in print."

The viewer is limited to the available programming fare, to schedules which are not set to his personal convenience, and to the room of his home where his set is located. By contrast the reader controls what he reads and where and when he reads it. He can vary the pace and intensity of his attention by skimming or studying; he can pick up his book or magazine as often as he likes.   (E)

David Riesman has raised the question of whether television represents an opportunity to avoid decision-making in the sense of other media experiences:

"Does the fact that one sees something in one's living room with no real decision made, such as is involved in going out or being some place at a particular time, imply a loss of variety or change of pace? Does one dress down before looking at television instead of dressing up as one might to go to the theater? Is the fact that one can switch the channel any time alter the character of the event itself by requiring a constant decision or redecision to keep looking as against switching the channel or wandering off to the kitchen or looking around or chatting with people in the living room?"

10. *The Absence of Social Participation.* The broadcast audience has the feeling of direct contact with a performer because communication is immediate in time and because it hears the actual voice or sees the face of the speaker. But this sensation is an illusion, for the communication is one-sided, however direct and immediate it may be. The listener-viewer still has the option of turning off the set. He can make a disparaging remark, leave the room, or otherwise express his indifference, annoyance or remoteness from what is being said to him.

The broadcast audience is free from what Cantril and Allport call the "conventions of the rostrum." It can behave toward the speaker with an irreverence and discourtesy which would be totally out of place in a theater or lecture hall. The broadcasting performer's hold over his audience is in fact no greater than the writer's control over the reader, though it seems much greater.

Since its early days, the broadcasting industry has encouraged the illusion of two-way communication by putting on shows before live studio audiences. This gives the entertainers the feeling that they are facing real people, thereby presumably heightening their art as well as their morale. The applause and laughter of the studio audience also stimulates the remote public and creates a sense of participation. At the end of many shows, the television camera roams up and down the studio aisles to heighten the feeling of communion between the waving, smiling people on the screen and the invisible spectators.

In the case of many filmed comedy and variety programs, whether or not performed before a studio audience, audience reaction is dubbed in after the performance to suit the intentions of the directors. A newly developed machine facilitates this process, permitting applause or laughter of appropriate dimensions to be introduced.

In radio it is easier than in television to sustain the illusion of direct communication. The announcer, the comedian and the dramatic actor are invisible while they read from their scripts, and listeners may imagine that they are being spoken to directly or that they are actual witnesses to the scenes being played. In television it is harder for the audience's imagination to come into play. The presence of a script must as far as possible be disguised. It must always appear as though the speaker is talking directly to the viewers. The invention of the Teleprompter enables him to sustain the illusion that his eyes are looking into theirs, when he is actually reading his lines just outside the reach of the audience itself.

11. *The Limited Choice for the Audience.* Another singular characteristic of the broadcast media is the fact that they present the audience with a choice of content which is extremely limited. A television set can pick up only a handful of channels. Even though a sensitive radio receiver can bring in hundreds of stations on a clear summer night, the choice is still pathetically small, compared with the volume of print material on a vast diversity of subjects. The reader can pursue his most individual and special interests, and select from a wide range of nuances of experience. There is an incongruity in the fact that the media which are most accessible to the average person, which employ the most nearly universal symbols and attract the largest audiences, also limit the expression of individuality in taste and interest.

12. *The Neutral Character of Broadcasting.* Compared with newspapers, magazines and books, broadcasting tends to be non-controversial. There is less room for the expression of extreme or deviant opinion. Of course conflicting viewpoints on political and other subjects are aired on discussion and interview programs. But the over-all character of the medium encourages the adoption of conventional, conservative or popular views.

There are two major reasons why broadcasting content generally steers clear of sensitive or delicate subjects. The first explanation follows from the fact that a system of commercially sponsored broadcasting is primarily concerned with the acquisition of large audiences. Advertisers who use broadcasting to deliver messages about their products understandably shy away from the possibility of antagonizing any group of potential listeners — and customers. In print media, the writer or editor can appeal directly to the people who agree with his viewpoint or who are at least interested in reading what he has to say. He assumes that those who disagree with him will find their own organs of expression somewhere else. But the broadcaster is less likely to be satisfied with only a segment of the total audience. He must try to reach everybody and if possible to please everybody; at least he must avoid rubbing anyone the wrong way.

But there is another and perhaps more basic reason why broadcasting has a neutral character. Cantril and Allport, discussing "The Psychology of Radio," drew a fundamental distinction between visual and auditory presentation. They point out that any auditory presentation must proceed in steps and in sequence. (This could easily apply to television, which is governed by the same time-rules as radio.) A visual or print presentation can be "interlocking," in that a number of complex ideas can be grasped simultaneously.

This leads to the conclusion that print is more suitable for the presentation of analytical and complex ideas. As such it lends itself better to a critical approach. By contrast with the reader, the broadcast listener is relaxed and not in the mood for controversy. If his daily fare is without a strong ideological flavor, it is because he likes it bland.

Television as Distinct from Radio

Thus far, in discussing the principal characteristics of the broadcast media, most of the points mentioned are equally true of radio and television. Many of them first drew attention and comment before the advent of TV. In what respects does television significantly differ from radio, in its appeals and in its impact on the audience? There are real qualitative differences between the two broadcast media and the other mass media. By contrast, the differences between television and radio seem to be more a matter of degree than a matter of kind.

1. *TV Focuses Attention.* Television mobilizes a greater degree of attention than radio does. Its message is delivered with greater impact, because it mobilizes two senses rather than one. Since sight as well as hearing is focused, there is less possibility of distraction. While the radio listener may be reading, driving or working, the TV viewer is typically wholly absorbed in his viewing.

2. *TV is Concrete, Not Abstract.* Because it mobilizes the sense of sight as well as hearing, television presentations have a literal character. The viewer has less room than the listener in which to

exercise his imagination. There is a relatively narrow gap between what appears to his senses and the reality which he projects into it.

The listener is continually using his fantasy. He must set the stage in his own mind, produce faces to match the voices that he hears, and otherwise provide an imaginary visual accompaniment to whatever actually comes to his ear. The television viewer cannot sustain this kind of illusion. He is forced to associate voice and sound. It is harder for him to think abstractly. He must assume that what appears on his screen is exactly what he is supposed to see.

3. *The Performer as a "Whole Man."* Television calls for a new type of broadcaster. Twenty years ago the theorists of radio, like Arnheim, spoke of the "dehumanization of the announcer." For Arnheim, the broadcaster was an anonymous, impersonal creature, who existed only as a disembodied voice. In manner of inflection and delivery he sought to approximate as far as possible a standard style of speech (symbolized in England by the "BBC accent"), from which all traces of regional as well as personal individuality had been removed. This description, which may have been true of radio in the thirties, no longer necessarily applies to radio as it exists today, with the standardized announcer replaced by the disc jockey whose stock in trade is his individuality. However, even the individuality of the disc jockey can take on an institutional character. When WNEW, an independent station in New York City, lost its well-known disc jockey, Martin Block, to the American Broadcasting Company, it replaced him with another one who sounded very much like his predecessor.

In television the announcer can no longer be "dehumanized" except where he appears as an off-screen voice in filmed commercials. Even though television announcers and performers tend to be selected in terms of the standardized Hollywood conceptions of male beauty, their faces are not and cannot all be alike. This means that individuality cannot be suppressed as it could be on radio. The voice no longer forms the basis on which a judgment is made of the entire personality; instead the face offers the major cues.

4. *TV is More Powerful.* Because it mobilizes more attention (F) and attracts more time from its audience, television is a more im-

portant force than radio ever was in the cultural, social and economic
life of the nation. Television is more spectacular as a medium, because its productions are grander, supported by advertisers on a larger
scale than radio knew in its prime. TV provides its audience with
more bedazzlement, whether or not it offers more entertainment.
Like radio, television can make reality seem more dramatic than it
really is, but it can do so with stunning effectiveness.

In an unusual perceptive study on "The Unique Perspective
of Television and Its Effect," Kurt and Gladys Lang describe the
extraordinary capacity of the new medium to dramatize an event and
a public personality. The subject of their report is MacArthur Day in
Chicago, a triumphant homecoming arranged after the General's
dismissal by President Truman at the height of the Korean War.

The Langs employed 31 participant observers in this study.
Most of them mingled with the crowds at the airport, or along the
route of the official parade through the city, at the scene of the
General's dedication of the Bataan-Corregidor bridge, and at his evening speech in Soldier Field. Other observers watched the same
events over television. Thus it was possible to compare the impressions which the TV audience received of the day's happenings with
the impressions of those who witnessed them directly.

The research itself started from the assumption "that the effect
of exposure to TV broadcasting of public events cannot be measured
most successfully in isolation. For the influence on one person is
communicated to others, until the significance attached to the video
overshadows the 'true' picture of the event, namely the impression
obtained by someone physically present at the scene of the event."
This assumption was well supported by the evidence.

The crowd which turned out to see MacArthur was "in search
of adventure and excitement"; they were not a "casual collection of
individuals," but people who deliberately intended to be witnesses to
an unusual spectacle. For these spectators, the celebration proved a
disappointment. The observers reported "only a minor interest" in
the Loop offices on the parade's route, and no unusual crowding
along the way. " 'We should have stayed home and watched it on
TV,' was the almost universal form that the dissatisfaction took. In
relation to the spectatorship experience of extended boredom and

sore feet, alleviated only by a brief glimpse of the hero of the day, previous and similar experiences over television had been truly exciting ones which promised even greater 'sharing of excitement' *if only one were present*. These expectations were disappointed and favorable allusions to television in this respect were frequent."

In this respect, the crowd's instincts were altogether correct, for television was not only a more convenient way of observing the spectacle; it also permitted the viewer to retain his illusion of seeing history in the making. Instead of contradicting the expectations of its audience, cameras and announcers actually interpreted what happened in such a way as to bear out the initial expectations.

The camera was free to roam around at will, neglecting what seemed unimportant or undramatic, and concentrating on close-ups of the hero or the other principals, or on particularly enthusiastic members of the crowd. The presence of the camera was itself sufficient to arouse cheers and waving from the spectators, which the television audience interpreted as evidence that the excitement was generated by the parade itself.

"The idea of the magnitude of the event, in line with preparations announced in the newspapers, was emphasized by constant reference . . . In view of the selectivity of the coverage with its emphasis on close-ups, it was possible for each viewer to see himself in a *personal* relationship to the General . . . The cheering crowd, the 'seething mass of humanity', was fictionally endowed by the commentators with the same capacity for a direct and personal relationship to MacArthur as the one which television momentarily established for the TV viewer through its close-up shots."

In summary, the Langs point to three characteristics of a televised event which make it different from the original. First, the "technological bias" makes it possible for television personnel to focus attention on the elements they consider interesting or important. Secondly, the announcer's commentary bridges the transition from one camera view to another, providing a continuity of structure and mood. Finally, the event itself is made more dramatic because the participants (including the crowd at the scene) are conscious of being seen by the television audience.

Is Television a New Medium?

Some authors have questioned whether television really represents a "new medium of expression." Arnheim puts the point in this way:

"With the coming of the picture, broadcasting loses its peculiarity as a new medium of expression and becomes purely a medium of dissemination. It will be able to transmit films for us, and then film esthetics will apply to its presentations; it will give us theatre pieces and then the dramaturgy of the theatre will apply to it; and, by giving both, it will make even more distinct the impure mixture of the two forms of art in the talking films of today . . .

"The divorce between theatre and film which today depends largely on such external facts as that, in the one case, it is a matter of an actual flesh-and-blood performance and in the other of a merely projected representation, and that both sorts of performance are given in different buildings, will either vanish before the screen of the television apparatus, or will have to be founded on more essential and inner differences. The television apparatus will also be a lecturer's desk, a concert platform and a pulpit, and will be differentiated from these, not in the method of presentation but only in the method of dissemination . . .

"So television as a means of spiritual intercourse, proves to be a relative of the car and the aeroplane. It is merely a means of transmission, containing no such elements of a new mode of presenting reality as the film and non-pictorial wireless."

More recently (1953), Franklin Sweetser has argued similarly that "television offers very little that is new in the way of *content,* although it is selective in its emphasis as a result of its technical scope and limitation . . . The ideas and images communicated are largely those also presented through other media."

In both these quotations the underlying assumption is that television functions largely to project information or to communicate experience in a manner already well developed either by the traditional art forms or by the other popular arts. Certain qualifications immediately suggest themselves. Television drama, for example, uses techniques which are in some ways quite different from those of the legitimate theater or motion pictures. The actors have a highly restricted scope of movement. The amount and type of scenery permitted, and the frequency of scene change, are seriously different both from Broadway and from Hollywood. It must be acknowledged that the differences are far less drastic than those between radio drama and the drama of theater or motion pictures.

Roger Manvell describes one of TV drama's unique features as follows:

"The emphasis made by the television director . . . is all the time on the actor's body and face, which is most of the time seen in close-shot owing to the small size of the screen. The film, with its large screen and high degree of magnification, quite logically stresses the actor *in his environment,* and dramatizes places and objects along with the actor. Television drama, like stage production, stresses the actor rather than the details of environment; similarly it must do almost all its work through dialogue, rather than through the quickly observing eye of an ever-mobile camera in a film studio. . . . The logic of the television medium demands a much slower tempo of performance than the film."

T. W. Adorno argues that the inherent nature of the television medium makes its dramatic efforts pat and standardized, in contrast with literature.

"Readers could expect anything to happen. This no longer holds true. Every spectator of a television mystery knows with absolute certainty how it is going to end. Tension is but superficially maintained and is unlikely to have a serious effect any more. On the contrary, the spectator feels on safe ground all the time . . . The element of excitement is preserved only with tongue in cheek . . . Everything somehow appears predestined."

Theater, film and television are all branches of the same dramatic art. Television, like each of the other two, is unique as a medium because the conditions under which communication takes place in each case shape both the substance of the message and the way of expressing it.

3. THE CONTENT OF
TELEVISION PROGRAMMING

(A)   Unlike radio, which gradually developed program techniques and formats over a period of years of trial and error, television came into existence in a nearly full-blown state. As the offspring of radio, it immediately fell heir to many of the established programming patterns of that medium, to which was now added a new visual dimension.

Live television drama has also borrowed heavily from the well-tried formulas of Hollywood. From the very start television relied on standard feature motion pictures to fill a large proportion of its total air time. As time went on an increasing number of "package" programs developed especially for TV were put on film, to permit economies of production, more flexible scheduling and additional revenues from repeat broadcasts. 57% of evening network program
(B)   time is now on film.

The widespread use of Hollywood films helps to make the sum total of television fare remarkably uniform from coast to coast. Compared with the radio listener, the TV viewer's choices are limited even more than might be suggested by the fact that there are far fewer TV than radio stations among which to choose. There is also greater uniformity of television program content, compared to that of radio. A much higher percentage of TV than of radio programs come from the networks; correspondingly fewer are locally originated.

There has thus far been less room for independent stations, not affiliated with a network, in television than in radio. One reason why there are few unaffiliated TV stations is that there are comparatively few stations altogether. By contrast with the situation in radio, there are only a few cities where there are more TV stations than networks —and network affiliation is always limited to one station in any town. Television stations in one- and two-station markets are often affiliated with several networks so that they can actually pick and choose among top caliber national programming in the peak viewing hours. Many

44

small radio stations are operated on a shoe-string, but TV equipment is more expensive. It is harder for a small independent TV station to go into business and keep solvent.

It costs a great deal more to prepare a television show than to put an equivalent show on radio. This means that program support tends to come from the large national advertisers who have bigger resources than the local sponsor and who can spread their production costs over a number of stations. This fact also heightens the relative importance of network over local programs for TV as compared with radio.

In television's early years most stations confined their air time to the evening hours of peak listening, but more and more stations are broadcasting on a full daily schedule. This has heightened TV's appetite for additional programming material. Television faces a greater problem than radio in filling air time, because it requires programs which are visually as well as orally stimulating, while radio can easily fall back on recorded music.

The content of television programs is bounded within certain limits by the size and composition of the audience available at different times of the day and evening. Programs of a type which entails heavy production expenses are almost inevitably broadcast during the peak hours of evening and weekend viewing, when the size of the audience will justify the cost.

Early morning shows are usually designed to appeal to the entire family, which has not yet split up for school and work. After 8:30 or 9:00 A.M. (except for films and a few shows for pre-school children), the air waves are largely devoted to programs aimed at the housewife. These women's programs continue until late afternoon when the children are back from school and play. During the hours when children's programs are dominant, some stations continue to go after the women's or general adult audience. From the time of the dinner hour, programs assume a family character. Except for sports shows, they are not aimed strictly at one sex, nor are they usually aimed at one particular age group.

These elementary facts on the composition of the audience set the broad limits within which programming decisions are made.

They do not themselves determine what kinds of shows go on the air. The proven or estimated popularity or unpopularity of individual programs is an important consideration.

One essential characteristic of the viewing audience is its demand for variety. In this respect the audiences for all mass media appear alike. People approach them in different moods and with different expectations at various times, and they are quickly able to adapt their moods and expectations to fit what is being offered to them. We shall see in the next chapter that television programs of very different types tend to get audiences of about the same size, on the average. The reason is that the same viewers watch many programs that range over a wide variety of types. Hardly any part of the audience limits its viewing to programs of only one particular stripe, like mystery, drama or comedy.

The network broadcasters are strongly aware of the audience's demand for variety in programming, and they normally seek to provide some balance in their schedules. Their main concern is to maintain enough sequence, continuity and drawing power in their total line-up of programs to be able to hold their audience throughout the evening at maximum strength. In setting up a schedule they try to take into account the competitive programming for the same time period, but full information on the plans of the rival networks is not always available at the time when their own decisions are made. This accounts for the phenomenon, occasionally encountered, of two networks simultaneously offering programs of the same type. When this happens there is frustration both on the part of that segment of the audience which would enjoy the chance to watch *both* shows (at different times), and also on the part of those who do not care for this type of program at all and whose choice is limited accordingly.

While the networks control the timing and selection of programs, they do not necessarily control their content. *Sponsor* magazine of October 31, 1955, reports that the networks control only half of the 844 hours of weekly network programming. The remaining shows are the property either of advertisers and their agencies or of "package producers." Of twenty new shows scheduled to go on the networks in the 1957-8 broadcast season, only five were actually produced by network staffs.

From the standpoint of the audience the crucial distinction is not between network and non-network shows, but between "big time" and local ones. A telephone survey in fifteen cities, conducted by Qualitative Research, Inc. for the Katz Agency (1956), asked 400 TV set owners, "Of the television programs you watch regularly do you think you can tell the difference between those that are network-originated and those that are originated from local stations?" 55% felt they could distinguish the two types of shows. These people were then given the names of six programs (three network and three syndicated-film non-network) and asked to identify their origination. The network shows were identified as such by 65% on the average, but the non-network shows were identified as network-originated by 45%. Altogether then, 85% of the total sample were unable to distinguish between the two types of programming.

Big Stations and Little Stations

In TV as in radio, big stations and little stations do not usually follow the same programming format. Since the big stations tend to be in big cities, and the little stations in little cities, this means that people in large and small towns are not exposed to the same kinds of broadcasts in the same proportions.

"An Analysis of Radio's Programming" made by Kenneth Baker in 1946 found that half the programs broadcast by small stations (of 250 watts or less) were of a musical type. For the large stations (of 7500 watts and over) only a third of the programs were musical. Baker found that the small stations in his sample broadcast only 14% of their programs on a local live basis, compared with 33% of the large stations. Conversely, a larger percentage of the programs broadcast over the smaller stations were recorded or transcribed, or came from the network. The smaller stations were more apt to be considered expendable by national advertisers. They carried a lower percentage of commercially sponsored network programs (21%), compared with the large stations (34%). However, they carried about the same proportion of "sustaining" non-sponsored programs (37%).

A further distinction between large and small radio stations had been described earlier by Alvin Meyrowitz and Marjorie Fiske. They pointed out that the small station, which was less apt to have a network affiliation, carried a local appeal and tended to attract a less educated audience with relatively limited horizons. The large station, typically affiliated with a network, carried the "glamor" appeal of New York and Hollywood where its programs originated.

If this was so in the case of radio, it carries an interesting implication for television which, as we have noted, has thus far had much less room for independents. Since evening programming on TV is overwhelmingly supplied by the networks, the medium as a whole tends to present a highly uniform cultural influence, and one with a predominantly metropolitan, sophisticated "glamor" appeal.

A survey made by the National Association of Radio and Television Broadcasters in 1955 found that 51% of *all* TV station operating hours (day and evening) are devoted to network programs. Of the locally-originated broadcast time, approximately two-thirds
(C)   consisted of live programs and the remainder is on film. (To put this another way—of every hour broadcast by the average television station, about twenty minutes is locally produced, thirty minutes comes from the network and ten minutes is a film produced in Hollywood or New York.)

This survey revealed some interesting differences between television markets of different sizes in the proportion of network and locally-originated live programming. As Table 9 shows, the very smallest markets, in which there are proportionately the least number of television homes, have the highest percentage of their air time devoted to films, and the lowest percentage (only a third) to network programs. These newer or smaller markets represent less desirable territories for the advertiser, and the per capita cost of attracting an audience is higher than in the bigger TV cities. There is therefore less inclination among buyers of advertising time to add stations in the smaller markets to a network line-up.

Larger markets have a higher percentage of network hours, but the highest percentage of broadcast time devoted to network shows was found in the middle-sized markets ranging between 150,000 and half a million television homes. These markets are generally large enough to attract the interest of national advertisers, but not so large that they contain stations which lack network affiliations.

The very biggest markets, with over a million television families, have more independent stations, but their broadcasting day is longer—twice as long on the average as the stations in the very smallest TV markets. Because they have more air time to fill, network programming (which might be used up to the available limit) still represents a somewhat smaller proportion of the total than is true of the middle-sized markets.

TABLE 9

How Is TV Time Distributed?

(Source: NARTB 1955 Survey)

Number of TV Families in Station Area

	All Stations	Less than 50,000	50,000- 150,000	150,000- 500,000	500,000- 1,000,000	Over 1,000,000
Network hours	51%	33%	44%	56%	53%	48%
Local hours						
Live	19	26	15	17	21	20
Film	30	41	41	27	26	32
	100%	100%	100%	100%	100%	100%
Total Operating Hours	98:25	63:57	75:54	103:34	114:15	115:16

The distribution of total broadcast time, as just described, gives no accurate indication of the importance of network programming in determining the general character of TV. Network broadcasts typically come at the times when television has its largest audiences, so that their impact on the total viewing experience of the American public is proportionately far greater than the previous discussion indicates.

In those few cities where the number of television outlets exceeds the number of networks (three), individual non-affiliated stations may develop a specialized kind of programming character which resembles that of many independent radio stations. This is most apparent in New York City, which has seven working channels, and Los Angeles, which has eight (including one in San Diego).

In a study of all the programs on Los Angeles television during a week in 1951, Dallas Smythe and Angus Campbell discovered that the amount of air time devoted to "drama" ranges from 60% for KFI-TV to 25% for KTTV. This reflects the high percentage of time devoted by KFI-TV, an independent station, to broadcasts of feature films (which these researchers classified as "drama"). By contrast, children's programs represent only 1% of the time on KFI-TV, but 26% of the time on another station. Domestic programs dealing with cooking, shopping and personal care range between 43% and 3% of air time on different stations.

How Network Program Time Is Distributed

(D)   How is TV network time actually divided among programs of different types? One way to answer this question is to see how sponsored evening network programs break down into the categories defined by the A. C. Nielsen Company in connection with its audience measurement service. (Nielsen's program listings are not altogether complete; they do not include sustaining programs, or those carried on regional networks, or cooperative programs in which local sponsors participate, or nationally sponsored film shows broadcast on a "spot" basis, but they cover the great bulk of network shows.)

TABLE 10

Changes in Sponsored Evening Television
Network Program Content
(March)

(Based on A. C. Nielsen Program Categories)

	1950	1953	1955	1957
News	7%	9%	5%	5%
Quiz, Audience Participation	11	12	10	13
Mystery Drama	7	12	5	7
General Drama	20	17	19	28
Concert Music	2	1	2	1
Musical Variety, Popular Music	16	6	19	9
Situation Comedy	4	13	18	14
Sports Events	14	14	5	3
General Variety	19	16	17	20
	100%	100%	100%	100%

In Table 10 all the network programs listed by the Nielsen service have been classified and the total for each category has been computed as a percentage of the sum of network broadcast hours. This has been done for the month of March at four points during a recent seven-year period in which television underwent enormous growth. Between 1950 and 1957 television emerged from almost nothing to become a major force in American life. Yet it is apparent from the table that during this period there was no striking change in the way that the television networks distributed their time among programs of various types. Even though some individual types of shows rose or fell in their share of the total time, the general formula used by the broadcasters remained much the same.

Drama, comedy-variety, music and quiz shows are the staples of television's daily programming diet. Although the program categories are broadly defined, it is clearly apparent that they are virtually all in the realm of entertainment. With the exception of news shows, none of them are concerned with ideas or information.

The absence of major change jibes quite well with an observation made by Paul Lazarsfeld and Patricia Kendall in analyzing the results of two successive surveys on radio listening habits. These surveys showed a virtually identical pattern of programming likes and dislikes in 1945 and 1947. The authors conclude that the American public changes its entertainment tastes very gradually, when it changes them at all. The preferences of the audience influence the programming decisions of the broadcasters, and vice-versa. It is therefore not too surprising to find the same general consistency we find in examining audience opinion also reflected in the distribution of television air time.

The TV programming pattern has not been altogether static, however. Two big changes can be traced in the seven-year period studied here: (1) the rise of the situation comedy, which deals primarily with domestic situations, and (2) a decline in sponsored sports events.

While a rise was shown by situation comedy, perhaps because of the enormous success of "I Love Lucy," this does not appear to have taken place at the expense of other types of comedy programs. At least there was no change in the position of general variety programs which usually feature comedians among their "acts."

The decline in sports programs reflects a tendency for such events increasingly to be televised under local sponsorship rather than on the network. It does not necessarily mean that there are fewer sports programs on the air, though it certainly means that they have been shunted into less desirable viewing periods.

Mystery drama took a jump between 1950 and 1953 (the heyday of "Dragnet") but it has since declined, while general drama remained quite stable until after 1955, when it rose sharply.

Musical variety and popular music programs show noticeable shifts from year to year.

In spite of the relative stability of program types during the brief life of network television, and although certain favorite entertainers and shows remain from year to year, the programming schedule has undergone striking changes season after season. There is generally a substantial clearing of the decks during the summer months, and the new line-up each fall invariably shows many newcomers launched, as well as many gaps in the ranks of the surviving veterans.

An analysis presented in the January 19, 1957 issue of *Sponsor* magazine shows that of 110 network programs broadcast during the 1952-3 season, only 40 (36%) had survived into the season of 1956-7. There were striking variations in the survival rates of different types of shows. The three documentary programs on the air in 1952 were all continuing four years later. Eleven of the fourteen general drama shows also survived. In 1954 there were four news shows, four sport shows and four adventure dramas broadcast. In each case half survived into the 1956-7 season. Of the seven straight variety shows only three survived. The survivors also included four out of eleven comedy-variety shows, three out of eleven musical programs, five out of 18 situation comedies and four out of 18 quiz-panel shows. Of the 16 crime-mystery programs broadcast in 1952, only one was still on the air four years later.

The TV Spectacular

One important development in TV programming which is not fully mirrored in Table 10 is the emergence of the television "spectacular" since 1954. The spectacular may be defined as a program an hour or longer in duration which gathers together far more than the usual assemblage of stellar talent and therefore incurs far more than the usual production costs. A spectacular is not broadcast on a regular weekly basis like other programs, but is presented as a "special event," strongly promoted and advertised. The first spectaculars were produced as "one-shots" for highly special occasions like a company's major anniversary. After their first season a number of them have become regularly scheduled programs which differ from other shows in their infrequency—once a month rather than once a week.

Spectaculars have taken the form both of dramatic and variety presentations. In their initial phases they were closely related to the attempt on the part of the networks, particularly the National Broadcasting Company, to boost color television to popularity; most spectaculars have been broadcast in color as well as in black and white.

Spectaculars were sold to advertisers on the premise that viewers would appreciate an extraordinary spectacle. It was argued that the large audiences attracted would compensate for the high costs of production. As a matter of fact, a number of advertisers who were among the first sponsors of spectaculars have expressed disappointment and changed their strategy. Others have remained satisfied.

On the whole, viewers appear to have reacted favorably. Some individual spectaculars have attracted audiences of unusually large size, even for television. Others have done no better than many conventional variety shows which cost far less to produce. In a number of cases, spectaculars have not been able to outpull the regular program schedule offered by the competing network. Some spectaculars appear to represent a relatively less efficient advertising vehicle than can be obtained with conventional programs, and their audiences do not seem to have any higher an awareness of the sponsor or his products. For the viewers, on the other hand, spectaculars present an opportunity to see entertainment of exceptional quality. If there is a contradiction of interests in this, the audience thus far seems to have had the best of the bargain.

The advent of spectaculars may have had one interesting side-effect. Their audiences are in large measure attracted by display advertisements on the television pages of newspapers. The fact that their appearance is announced in this way has possibly encouraged the practice, on the part of viewers, of consulting program listings. This suggests that, over a period of time, it may be expected that viewers will become more selective and deliberate in their program choices, and that random tuning will decline in importance.

A Content Analysis of the Television Week

Thus far we have approached the subject of television content in terms of program types. We have looked at groups of programs which share certain major characteristics that lead broadcasters and advertisers to think of them as belonging in one category or another.

A different approach to the subject is exhibited in a group of studies which have gone beyond the general categories to look at the components of individual programs. This research attempts to describe what is perceived by the viewer rather than what is listed in the schedules or audience rating reports.

Between 1951 and 1953 a series of studies of TV output was made under the direction of Dallas W. Smythe for the National Association of Educational Broadcasters. Smythe and his associates approached the question of TV's content with the premise that any communication reflects and carries certain specific definable cultural and social values. They therefore were particularly concerned with the kinds of symbols which television broadcasters, consciously or unconsciously, used to depict reality.

In each city studied by Smythe, the total output of all the TV stations was monitored over a seven-day period. This period was assumed to offer an adequate sample of the output in that area. The monitoring was done by trained observers who coded and timed the content of what they saw, in terms of predesignated categories.

The first study, by Smythe and Campbell, has already been cited. In an analysis of Los Angeles television for the week of May 23-29, 1951, the authors found that a fourth of total TV program time was devoted to "general adult drama." Smythe did not separate feature films from other types of television drama because he was concerned with the character of what went out over the air rather than with the manner in which it originated.

About 16% of air time consisted of domestic (homemaking) programs; 12% was news, 10% children's programs and 6% music. Only 3% was devoted to programs of an informational type and 2% to programs featuring public institutions. Less than 1% each were spent on religion, weather and public events. Between 7 and 11 PM (when viewing was greatest) very little air time was devoted to public issues.

Network regulations give the sponsor six "commercial" minutes for a full-hour program, but one or two minutes are usually sold by local stations for "spot" announcements between shows. In Los Angeles Smythe and Campbell found that 18% of all the broadcast time involved advertising. About 12% of the time went for direct selling of the sort which jibes reasonably well with the regulations just cited. However, an additional 6% of the time represented another kind of exposure to advertising. In these instances the sponsor's name or slogan was part of the background against which the entertainment took place, or part of the show's opening and closing.

Smythe and Campbell also noted that over half of the program time during the children's hours between 5 and 7 PM was devoted to western dramas (largely film). Two-thirds represented either western crime or action drama.

The second study of the series is reported by Donald Horton, Hans Mauksch and Kurt Lang, who studied the broadcast output of four Chicago stations for the first week in August, 1951. In this case also it was found that 26% of the total broadcast time was devoted to drama. In a more refined breakdown, 6% was classified as adventure and action drama, 6% western and 5% crime and horror.

Sports accounted for 18% of air time, variety and vaudeville programs for 8%, "personality programs" for 6%. Quiz, stunt and talent programs represented 6% of broadcast hours, music 3%.

Programs dealing with social problems accounted for less than half of one per cent of the total. The proportion of informational shows appeared to be higher in Chicago for the week studied than it had been in Los Angeles a few months earlier. 12% of broadcast time was classified as being informational in character and 3% as "orientational."

There is no indication of whether this reflected an actual difference in programming policy between the Los Angeles and Chicago stations, or merely the fact that unsponsored shows of an informational character may have gone on the air in Chicago for the summer slack period. In Chicago a higher percentage of total air time appeared to be devoted to advertising (perhaps because there were fewer stations to share the burden). 15% of air time went into the primary or "direct-sell" type of advertising, and the total percentage was raised to 28% by advertising of the indirect or secondary type.

85% of the program time was found to be addressed to adults generally. Only 7% was aimed specifically at women and 8% at nursery or elementary school children. Practically none was directed at men or to teen-agers.

A year later Smythe analyzed TV broadcasting in a one-station market, New Haven, Connecticut. Here he found about the same proportion of total air time devoted to drama (29%) and to advertising (13% on "primary" advertising) as in his research in the larger markets. In New Haven, Smythe looked beyond the broad program categories to consider what the programs actually contained. His most interesting finding in this respect was that during the hours in which children's programs were broadcast (between 5 and 7 PM) violent acts were shown at twice the rate as at other hours of the week.

During the period that his other studies were being done and analyzed, Smythe was also embarked on a longer-range investigation of TV content in New York City. Since this was carried on over a four-year period, it permits a comparison of trends (shown in Table 11). The 1954 study was directed by H. H. Remmers.

Between the measurements made in 1951 and 1954, the total number of broadcast hours increased 18% in New York City, all on the network-owned stations. The largest increase, proportionately, took place during the children's hours and late evening hours. Smythe found 14% of air time devoted to advertising in 1951. By 1952 this had risen to 18% of the total and it remained at this level into 1954.

During this period, changes in daytime TV programming were more striking than those in the evening. More feature films were being aired, particularly to fill out the longer broadcast day. Smythe reports that filmed drama represented 46% of total air time in 1952, 53% in 1953, and 45% in 1954.

The biggest change was an increase in the percentage of time devoted to general drama (including films), from 25% to 43%. General variety programs fell from 14% to 7% of the total time. During the period studied, children's programming appeared to become dispersed over a broader time period. It became less concentrated in the conventional children's hours from five to seven.

TABLE 11

Breakdown of Total New York TV Air Time,
By Program Types

1951-1954

(Summarized from NAEB New York TV Content Studies)

	1951	1952	1953	1954
General Drama	25%	36%	43%	39%
Children's Drama	8	7	4	7
General Variety	14	6	4	7
Domestic Variety	3	2	5	—
Children's and Teen-Age Variety	2	2	3	3
Music	4	4	4	7
Personalities	4	2	3	5
Quiz, Stunts, Contests	7	7	6	5
Sports	9	7	6	3
News (General)	6	6	7	6
Other Information-Type	12	13	10	11
Orientation-Type	5	7	6	5
	100%	100%	100%	100%
Total Minutes	33,837	37,645	39,104	39,766

The Symbolic Content of TV Programming

In the New York studies Smythe went considerably beyond (E) his classification of general program types, by an actual examination of the symbols and characters involved in the programs. The description which comes out of this is one which must appear familiar to any student of the popular arts.

An act of violence or a threat of violence was found to occur about every ten minutes of broadcast TV time, with a slight (and probably not significant) increase between 1952 and 1953. Violence occurred mostly in crime, western action and comedy. In 1952 the fist or the foot appeared to be the chief agent of violence. In 1953 it was the gun.

Smythe presents a special analysis of 86 dramatic programs produced for television (as distinct from feature films). This gives some interesting indications of the kind of dramatic content which television offers its viewers. These programs represented 21% of total drama time on the air in 1953. They broke down about equally between domestic drama, crime, comedy and romance drama.

As the setting for these dramas, fictitious localities outnumbered real ones, three to one. In foreign settings, where it was often necessary or desirable for a city to be identified as Paris, Rome or London, real and fictitious locales occurred about equally often. In the United States, cities bore make-believe names or were left nameless in four cases out of five. This probably reflects the desire of the broadcasters to avoid offending any part of their audience. Since most television drama involves episodes of stress or trouble, the theory may be that any big American city where it takes place had best be left unidentified.

Television drama is set in the present, in four cases out of five. This is nearly always true when the scene is laid in the United States. Where the action takes place abroad it represents the past as often as the present.

There were 476 characters who appeared in the TV dramas that Smythe studied. They represented the protagonists whose fate the viewers were asked to follow and with whose concerns they were expected, in a sense, to identify their own. It therefore seemed particularly important to find out what kinds of people they were. In making this analysis Smythe followed in the tradition of earlier research which has demonstrated the wide disparity between the average man and the kinds of heroes depicted in the popular arts.

In the Payne Fund studies of the movies, made in the early 1930's, Edgar Dale found that 33% of the heroes, 44% of the heroines, 54% of the villains and 63% of the female villains were wealthy or "ultra-wealthy." Most of them appeared to have no occupation. Over 60% of the American population was married at this time, but in the films this was true of only 15% of the men and 21% of the women. Commenting on these findings, Henry Forman observes sardonically:

"Were the population of the United States, the population of the globe itself, so arranged and distributed, there would be no farming, no manufacturing, almost no industry; no vital statistics (excepting murders), almost no science, no economic problems and no economics. Such a world would speedily starve to death."

A somewhat similar comment might be made from Smythe's findings, though it could not be quite as caustic. While television characters in the 1950's also appear to be far from a typical cross-section of American life, they seem slightly less remote from reality than the film characters of the 1930's.

The daytime serials analyzed by Smythe had 6.7 characters each, whereas the dramatic programs which appeared only on a once-a-week basis, had an average of 5.4. Men outnumbered women, two to one. Their average age was 38. For the women it was 33. The world of television is largely populated by mature adults. Three-fourths of the characters depicted were somewhere within the age range of 20-49, which actually includes about half of the total U. S. population.

In four cases out of five the TV characters were white Americans. Only 2% were Negroes. 5% were identifiable as English, 3% as Italian, 2% as French and 1% as Russians. No Jews were identified as such. Television apparently has followed in one unfortunate tradition of the American film and stage by stereotyping Italians as a criminal element: only 44% of those depicted were shown to be law abiding, although other minority or foreign groups were not singled out in this way.

Nearly three-fourths of the characters in TV drama were shown to be employed or employable, compared with two out of every five persons in the population of the United States. Somewhat surprisingly, the TV villains were apt to be members of the labor force—in six cases out of seven, while one hero out of three had no discernible job or profession. While the movie heroes of an earlier day were apparently drawn in large measure from a leisure class whose source of income was uncertain, a majority of today's television heroes are *employed*—at jobs which tend to represent the American ideal. (This suggests a shift from the Depression epoch in which the subject of work was perhaps too sensitive to intrude into entertainment, to a boom period of full employment and idealization of the successful career man.)

According to Smythe:

> "TV reflects a culture which values highly managerial and service activities and rates low physical production work. Professionals, managers, officials and proprietors, service workers and private household workers were 51% of the TV population, but only 11% of the United States population."

It is interesting to note that television depicts women's roles much more realistically than men's. About the same proportion of female characters in TV drama were housewives (two in five) as was true of the population. It is principally the children, the aged, the institutionalized who are underrepresented among TV characters. Television drama focusses on healthy people. Only 3% of those shown were unhealthy and an additional 2% mentally ill or "insane."

The frequent depiction of violence on television raises questions about the place of the criminal in TV drama. According to Smythe, one TV character in five is a lawbreaker. About four out of every five are law-abiding, men more so than women.

Women in TV drama were on the side of the angels more than men were. The TV villain was a man, rather than a woman, in four cases out of five, while among heroes the proportion of men was two out of three. Villains were older than heroes, on the whole, and when the villain was female she was distinctly older than the heroine—a threatening or obstructive matron or spinster. Their average was 43 for men and 47 for women while the heroes averaged 32 and the heroines 29.

Like other mass media in the U. S., television tends to present its more sinister characters in alien garb. Smythe found that Europeans accounted for 24% of the villains in TV drama but for only 10% of the heroes. On the other hand white Americans represented 83% of the heroes but only 69% of the villains.

Apparently it is only male foreigners who are apt to represent the forces of evil. Where the main hero was an American, he was a man in three cases out of four. Where the main hero was *not* an American, she was a woman in two cases out of three. In their personality traits, villains were generally depicted as antithetical to American cultural values, while heroes were, of course, well in tune. However, the villains were presented as being just as active and potent as the heroes were. The difference between the groups was one of morality rather than ability.

In terms of the commonly accepted standards of the American community, journalists were portrayed as most nearly ideal in their attributes of character, and scientists as most unlike the ideal. Policemen and other public officers were generally portrayed in a sympathetic light. Teachers were typically shown to be the most clean, kind and fair of the professional groups, and journalists the most honest. Scientists were least honest, kind and fair, and lawyers generally the "dirtiest" characters. Journalists, lawyers, teachers and law-enforcement officers were most apt to conform to a narrow stereotype of character whereas doctors were least apt to be portrayed in a stereotyped manner.

In general, Smythe's description of television's characters is congruent with other studies of the way in which American popular art presents reality—a simplified and idealized picture. An objection to these findings may be made on this score: Smythe and his collaborators base their analysis of TV's dramatic content on the sum total of *all* television programming, including a substantial amount of time devoted to local or package shows and to daytime serials with highly predictable plots. The effect of this procedure is that a televised act of violence, or an ethnic stereotype, carries the same weight, in Smythe's analysis, whether it occurs in a program broadcast in the early afternoon on a minor station (with an audience of a few tens of thousands) or on one of television's top dramatic programs, broadcast at a peak viewing hour on a major network outlet, with a million people watching.

Findings parallel to those of the Smythe studies were obtained from a content analysis of dramatic programs made by Sydney W. Head in New York City for the thirteen weeks of March, April and May, 1952. Head confined himself to 209 network-distributed programs prepared specifically for television. These shows were all of the type which are complete in a single episode, so that in a series with "running characters," every episode was tabulated as though it were unique. The observations were confined to a single coder, although his decisions were checked against independent judgments on a test basis.

Most of these plays especially studied for television are found to take place in the present (82%), in the United States (88%) and in a city (76%). 37% were of the crime-detection-adventure type, 22% were situation comedies, 20% general dramas, and 11% children's drama. Two-thirds of the major characters in the plays were men. Three out of four had identifiable occupations, and of these 17% were policemen (or the like)and a similar proportion were professional criminals. 62% of all the plays had criminal characters. Ranked by social level, the vast majority of the characters appeared to fall in the upper or middle classes, with lower class members infrequently represented. Head notes that "a relatively large number of salient characters are either *declassé* or ambiguous as to class." Three-fourths of the major characters are good, a similar number sympathetic. The two traits usually go together, except in those deviant cases where "a sympathetic character commits a moral transgression under the pressure of extraordinary emotional drive."

Head distinguishes between personalized antagonists—actual villains, and nonpersonalized antagonists, which occur in two plays out of five. Most of the latter represent aspects of the protagonist's self.

Head finds 3.7 acts of aggression or moral transgression per play—even more in children's plays. (7.6) than in crime-detection plays (5.1). Firing and pointing deadly weapons, and battery were the "most approved" aggressive acts (in that they are most often associated with good characters), whereas the least approved acts include drug and sex offenses, theft and homicide.

Minority ethnic groups are found to be strongly underrepresented, accounting for only one-tenth of the major characters. But these minority characters are not depicted as unsympathetic any more often than are the rest of the major characters. In fact only two out of 56 Negroes are depicted as bad.

Head notes that television drama differs from real life in several notable respects: its characters are overwhelmingly concentrated in big cities, in the middle part of the age range, and they are higher in social class and occupation. They have virtually no religious life, are almost never sick, rarely die natural deaths, and (as distinct from reality) commit homicide more often than rape. In all these respects, Head points out, television reflects the value-orientation of contemporary American society, as expressed also in prior studies of film, Broadway theater and magazine fiction content.

In commenting on the frequency of violent and aggressive actions in TV drama, Head refers to their possible function in supplying "sadistic and masochistic satisfactions." He notes that in crime-detection dramas, the audience's attention is focused first on the criminal and later on the hero who "often takes over the same kind of aggressive behavior previously associated with the criminal." The classical hero is the outsider (on the model of the Lone Ranger) who comes from nowhere to right wrong, and in the process, replaces (in audience interest) the original protagonist who is "helpless before the machinations of villainy."

Censorship

By and large, the content of television programming may be said to reflect the spontaneous and uncoordinated effort of different groups and individuals in the television industry to produce programs that will attract large audiences. The only centralized control is exercised by the networks, and it is largely negative—with the intention of eliminating undesired content—rather than positive. John Cogley, in his investigation of blacklisting in the broadcasting industry, uncovered considerable evidence to show that individual entertainers and writers suspected of Communist connections found it impossible to get assignments. There was however no indication that program content had been noticeably influenced as a result.

On the whole, the censorship imposed within the television industry concerns taste rather than politics. A study by Charles Winick has examined the script changes decreed by the internal censors of a major network during the period 1954-6. Winick had three judges analyze the changes in terms of fourteen categories. In the order of their importance (as determined by the number of changes) the

categories were: Sex, Violence, Advertising, Racial-Ethnic, Anti-
Social, Spoofing the Serious, Special Interests, Religion, Crudity,
Liquor, Medical, Animals, Legal and Political. The changes made
(F)   tended to be minor ones.

The character of what goes out over the airwaves is probably less important than the character of what the audience chooses
to see. Television programming ranges over a wide variety of subjects and fits in with a diversity of moods and tastes. It is in the
patterning of actual viewing habits, to be discussed in the next chapter, that we can best trace the impact of television on the temper
and outlook of the American public.

4. PATTERNS OF TELEVISION VIEWING

(A)

The appeal of television—as measured by the size of its audiences, night after night, and the amount of time spent viewing—is far greater than that achieved by any other medium of mass communication. With its dual impact on eye and ear television has an extraordinary capacity to entertain, inform and impress its audience, and to do so with a minimum demand for effort or concentration on the part of the viewers.

Television has claimed its vast audience in two very different ways: (1) It has diverted people from other media activities, like radio listening, movie-going and reading; and (2) it has tapped new reserves of the public's leisure. It has "made" new free time by cutting into other, non-media activities, or by combining them with TV viewing. It seems to be taking some time that was not really spent in activity at all, like sleeping, resting, or "sitting around"; it may be hastening the performance of household chores or personal tasks which were formerly stretched out to occupy empty hours.

By the spring of 1956, television had achieved indisputable ascendancy over the other mass media. A cross section of 2,000 persons in the New York Metropolitan area were asked by McCann-Erickson, Inc., "If you could have only one of these four, which would you prefer?" 50% chose television, 32% newspapers, 15% radio, and 3% magazines. Similar findings were obtained in Philadelphia. In Charlotte, North Carolina, a city dominated by a single station and with a lower percentage of television homes (75% compared with 90% in the other two cities), 40% preferred TV, 34% newspapers, 23% radio, and 3% magazines.

In television households, the total amount of time spent on all four major media is substantially greater than in non-television households. This finding emerges from a survey of the Metropolitan New York area made in 1951 for the National Broadcasting Company in cooperation with Hofstra College. In this study set-owners and non-owners were carefully matched to control for differences in their characteristics. Similar results emerged from a 1953 statewide

TABLE 12

Total Daily Time Spent with Four Media
(newspapers, magazines, radio, television)

	TV Owners	Non-TV Owners
Metropolitan New York, 1951 (NBC-Hofstra survey)	4 hours 14 minutes	2 hours 58 minutes
Kansas, 1953 (Whan survey)		
Men	5 hours 24 minutes	3 hours 38 minutes
Women	6 hours 13 minutes	4 hours 26 minutes
	After TV	*Before TV*
Fort Wayne, 1953-4 (NBC-Simmons survey: New Set Buyers)	4 hours 27 minutes	3 hours 10 minutes

survey made in Kansas by Forest Whan (who did not match the owners and non-owners in his sample.)

A study made in Fort Wayne for NBC by Willard Simmons in 1953-54 compared the total time spent with four media by the same individuals, both before and after they acquired television.

In every case, as is made clear in Table 12, it was found that television considerably increases the total amount of time spent with the media.

The Fort Wayne survey found that people were spending almost as much time with television after they acquired their sets as they had formerly spent with radio, magazines and newspapers put together. These were, to be sure, new television owners for whom the novelty of the new medium was especially great.

Media-Mindedness

Long before television, studies had shown that there are certain people who tend to expose themselves heavily to *all* the media. This can be understood in the light of the probability that all of the popular media reflect rather similar subject interests and (with all the exceptions that prove the rule) a common denominator of taste. In large measure, "media-mindedness" reflects differences in education and in socio-economic status. The college-educated upper-income group does the most reading, while the high school-educated middle-class group tends to include the greatest fans for movies, radio, and now, for television.

There are two reasons why the heaviest listening and viewing is found at the middle rather than at the top or bottom of the social and educational ladder.

1. Television and radio programs are for the most part directed to the psychological and cultural interests of the average, middle segment of the population, since this approach presents the greatest promise of attracting the largest number of people to the audience.

2. People of above-average education and income have a greater diversity of resources for spending their leisure. They have greater mobility and are less apt to be dependent on home amusements. They are more in the habit of reading, and have correspondingly less time and inclination for viewing or listening. At the opposite extreme, the people of lowest education and income are least apt to turn to the mass media for recreation or information. This may reflect a more constricted range of interests or a less developed capacity for sustained attention. In this group, the family and the home are not as much a focus of evening activity as they are in the middle class, and a greater proportion of the housewives are apt to be working during the day; this too means less opportunity to view and to listen.

Interest in the media is not simply a by-product of an individual's schooling and style of life. It also appears to reflect characteristics of his personality, though these are not necessarily all of a single kind. We can list several distinct hypotheses:

1. The "media-minded" person may have wider horizons, be interested in more things, have greater energy applied to all the spheres of life.

2. He may be a more insecure person, who requires a greater measure of distraction from his frustrations, who continually has to be diverted from the real world of people and problems to the fantasy world of the media.

3. He may have a richer imagination, which demands constant stimulation to feed his fantasy life.

4. He may be a more rigid and conformist sort of person, who welcomes the stereotyped images which are offered by the mass media.

Paul Lazarsfeld and Patricia Kendall, in analyzing two studies made by the National Opinion Research Center in 1945 and in 1947, found that people who listened to the radio most were also the ones who went to the movies most often and who read the most newspapers, magazines and books. Similarly, the heaviest radio listeners were the first to buy television sets, and they have become the heaviest viewers.

"Media-mindedness" was clearly demonstrated in a 1952 study directed by Thomas Coffin for the National Broadcasting Company. Coffin divided the television audience into "heavy" and "light" viewers and made a similar division for radio, magazines, newspapers and motion pictures. As Table 13 shows, the heaviest TV viewers were most often the ones who were also the most avid fans of the other media.

TABLE 13

Heavy Interest in Television Reflects Heavy Interest in All Media

(Source: NBC Metropolitan New York Survey, 1952)

Number of Non-TV Media to Which There Is Heavy Exposure	Per Cent of TV Owners in Each Group Who Are Heavy Viewers
None	35%
One	40
Two	43
Three	46

The "media-minded" people who were the pioneer owners of television sets also proved to be the greatest TV users. Studies made in "Videotown" (New Brunswick, New Jersey) by the advertising firm of Cunningham and Walsh compare the 1955 viewing habits of people who have owned their sets for varying lengths of time. In general, families who acquired their sets in 1951 or earlier spend con-

TABLE 14

The First to Buy TV Are the Greatest TV Fans

(Source: Cunningham and Walsh 1955 "Videotown" Survey)

When TV Set Was Purchased	Total Weekly Viewing Hours Per Person on Evenings (1955) Monday through Friday
Before 1951	12.2
1951	13.2
1952	10.9
1953	9.9
1954	5.7

siderably more time watching television now than do the more recent purchasers (see Table 14).

An analysis of television habits, made by the American Research Bureau in March, 1955, finds that half the television families account for two-thirds of all viewing. A fourth of the television families do two-fifths of the viewing. This heaviest viewing fourth are also the people who were first to get television. They have had their sets longest — 43 months on the average, compared with 31 months for the low-viewing fourth. They have the most children (two under 20 in the average family). By contrast, half the families in the bottom quarter (who do least viewing) have no children at all.

TABLE 15

How TV Viewing Varies from High to Low Interest Households

(Source: A. C. Nielsen data, April, 1955)

TV Interest Groups	Hours Viewed Daily
Top 20% of households	8 hours 59 minutes
Next 20%	6 hours 11 minutes
Middle 20%	4 hours 44 minutes
Next 20%	3 hours 28 minutes
Bottom 20%	1 hour 22 minutes
Total	4 hours 57 minutes

A similar analysis made at the same time by the A. C. Nielsen Company shows a closely similar pattern when TV homes are divided into five groups of equal size but differing viewing habits. Table 15 (B) indicates that the top fifth of the families in interest do 36% of all television viewing. One TV household in five has its set turned on nine hours a day.

In a study in New Haven by Everett Parker and associates (1952), 1.4% of the households were found to leave the television set tuned on continuously from early in the morning until bed-time.

How Much Time for TV?

The purchase of a television set did not automatically transform all the accumulated habits and life experiences of the average American. Its arrival in the house was apt to be an exciting event, much discussed in advance, and followed by a period of fascinated absorption.

During its first few weeks in the household, the TV set became the focus of attention and interest, with all the members of the household sampling all the available programs and neglecting other activities.

The novelty of television wore off swiftly. Though the family spent less time with it after the initial period of enchantment and experimentation, they did not return to their previous routine. Television had established its place as the most important single form of entertainment and of passing the time.

As the TV viewing habit became firmly established, its strength showed no signs of waning. If anything, the contrary took place. Daily viewing time actually appears to have shown a slight increase in the past few years, according to the measurements of the A. C. Nielsen Company (shown in Table 16).

TABLE 16

Average Hours of Daily TV Viewing, per TV Home

(Source: A. C. Nielsen Co.)

1950	4.5
1951	4.7
1952	4.8
1953	4.7
1954	4.8
1955	4.9
1956	5.0
1957	5.1

Different findings emerge from the "Videotown" surveys, which have been conducted since 1948 and therefore offer a particularly good means of tracing changes in the viewing patterns of a test community. Table 17 shows an upward trend in average weekday evening viewing until 1955, and a decline in the following year. However the "Videotown" findings, limited as they are to a single city, are less reliable as indications of what is happening in general than are the Nielsen figures which are based on a national sampling.

(C)   The A. C. Nielsen organization finds that the average TV home has its set on five hours a day, and this rises to six hours in

January. Sindlinger and Company, on the basis of a national sample of 7,000 interviews among persons 12 years or older, estimated that 71% of the (122,378,000) people aged 12 or older spent a grand total of 1,853,600,000 hours watching television during the week of March 17, 1957. On the same basis Sindlinger calculated that 56% of the public spent 969,800,000 hours listening to radio; 82% spent 401,700,000 hours reading newspapers; 29% spent 164,300,000 hours reading magazines.

A study of 3,000 U. S. households conducted by the Pulse for the Television Bureau of Advertising in September, 1956, found 73% of the American public watch television an average of 105 minutes apiece on the average day, while 65% read newspapers an average of 34 minutes.   (D)

TABLE 17

Increase in TV Viewing on Average Weekday Evening

(Source: Cunningham and Walsh "Videotown" Surveys)

	% of People Viewing in All TV Homes	Average Hours of Viewing for All People
1951	68%	2.2
1952	70	2.3
1953	73	2.4
1954	74	2.3
1955	85	2.6
1956	75	2.2
1957	78	2.3

Differences in Amount of Viewing

Where television is most accessible, people are not only most   (E) likely to own sets, but most likely to do some viewing outside the home, even if they do not have a set themselves. A survey of viewing habits in Kansas (made in 1953 by Forest Whan and summarized in Table 18) shows that 17% of the urban families regularly viewed TV outside their homes, compared with 14% of the village families and 11% of the farm families. The viewing reported was generally at the homes of neighbors, friends or relatives.

TABLE 18

Out-of-Home Television Viewing

(Source: Whan Kansas TV Survey)

	All Families	Farm Families	Village Families	Urban Families
View TV outside home	14%	11%	14%	17%
Where TV is viewed outside home				
Neighbor's home	30%	37%	41%	23%
Other friend's home	24	14	19	31
Relative's home	34	38	30	35
At some other town	3	6	1	3
Elsewhere	9	5	9	8
	100%	100%	100%	100%

Nielsen's audience measurements (Table 19) indicate that TV owners in big cities spend about the same amount of time with their sets on weekdays as do those in smaller cities and towns, and slightly more on Sundays.

The big-city viewers typically start viewing somewhat later in the evening than do the small-city residents, and they keep their sets on far later in the evening. In the Pulse study just mentioned, viewing remained at about the same level regardless of city size, except in rural areas.

TABLE 19

TV Viewing in Big Cities and Small Towns

(Source: A. C. Nielsen Co.)

	Counties Where Main City Has:		
	500,000 or More	*50,000-500,000*	*Less than 50,000*
TV hours per day per TV home	5 hrs. 8 min.	5 hrs. 4 min.	5 hrs. 2 min.
TV hours per Sunday	5 hrs. 24 min.	5 hrs.	4 hrs. 52 min.
Monday Evening			
6-7	33%	39%	39%
7-8	42	49	51
8-9	59	63	67
9-10	63	69	69
10-11	55	53	47
11-Midnight	36	26	18

Though they may go to bed earlier, TV owners on Iowa farms spend more time watching television than do either village or urban viewers, according to a statewide survey directed in 1954 by Forest Whan. This finding holds true, at least, for adults and teen-agers, though not for children, who spend more time watching TV if they live in villages than if they live on farms or in towns. (Table 20.)

TABLE 20

Weekday Time Spent with TV in Set-Owning Families

(Source: Whan 1954 Iowa Survey)

	Average Time Spent Daily (in hours)		
	Urban	Village	Farm
Total (average home)	11.25	11.70	13.20
Men over 18	2.96	3.00	3.64
Women over 18	4.41	5.03	5.13
Teen-Agers 12-18	2.95	3.02	3.41
Children 4-11	3.15	3.95	3.44

One possible explanation for the discrepancy between the Iowa findings and Nielsen's more reliable national measurements lies in the fact that Nielsen reports on homes, Whan on individuals. It may be that people in big cities are more apt to watch TV as individuals rather than as part of a family group, so that their viewing is spread over a longer span of time.

Common sense would indicate that women, since they spend more waking time at home than either men or children, would be the heaviest viewers, as a group. This is borne out by audience measurements such as those of the American Research Bureau, shown in Table 21.

The Iowa study shows, of course, that women spend substantially more time watching TV than men do. (See Table 20). Surprisingly, however, teen-agers and children, who presumably have more daily leisure time than adult men, do not spend substantially more time in front of the set (except in the villages, where children have fewer chores than on the farm, and where there are fewer outside attractions than in town).

According to Whan's Iowa survey, though women spend more time watching television than do other members of the family, they actually spend a smaller share of the time that they are at home and

TABLE 21

Weekly Television Viewing Hours, for Men, Women and Children

(Source: American Research Bureau, 1955)

Time Period	Set Hours	Men Hours	Women Hours	Children Hours
7 AM-Noon, Mon. thru Fri.	3.38	.88	2.86	2.39
Noon-3 PM, Mon. thru Fri.	2.33	.61	2.31	1.39
3-5 PM, Mon. thru Fri.	1.76	.41	1.49	1.68
5-7 PM, Mon. thru Fri.	3.53	1.66	2.19	4.66
7-10 PM, Sun. thru Sat.	14.15	11.81	15.98	10.81
10 PM-Midn., Sun. thru Sat.	4.56	3.88	4.76	.80
Midn.-2 AM, Sun. thru Sat.	.51	.37	.49	.06
Total*	30.22	19.62	30.08	21.79

*Note: This does not include daytime viewing on Saturday and Sunday.

awake. Women spend proportionately less of their available home time watching TV on Saturday than on weekdays or Sundays. Although men do a lot of TV viewing on Sunday, they spend relatively far more time on other activities around the home on that day than during the week or on Saturday.

Television's hold over young people is forcefully documented in this study (Table 22). During the week, of every five hours Iowa

TABLE 22

Television's Share of Available Time

(Source: Whan 1954 Iowa Survey)

	Percentage of "In-Home and Awake" Time Average TV Set Owner Spends with TV		
	Weekdays	Saturday	Sunday
Men, over 18	34%	30%	17%
Women, over 18	29	24	32
Teen-Agers, 12-18	43	40	55
Children, 4-11	43	33	51

children and teen-agers spend at home and awake in TV households, two are spent in front of the television set. On Sunday over half their available time is spent watching TV.

The Pulse 1956 TVB study showed that average daily viewing totaled 72 minutes apiece for children under six, rose to a high of 117 minutes both for children 6-11 and for teenagers 12-17, fell to 103 minutes for those 18-34, and then stayed fairly level (105 minutes for those 35-49, 108 minutes for those 50 and over). The average household whose head had not gone beyond grade school viewed television for a total of 301 minutes on the average day. Among the high-school-educated viewing is at a peak: 375 minutes a day per household. At the college level viewing drops to 336 minutes a day.

The Effects of Timing on Audience Size and Composition

The composition of the television audience varies at different hours of the day and the total size of the audience also varies. This is shown by a number of audience measurement services, like Videodex, Pulse and the American Research Bureau. These services differ somewhat in their survey methods, so that the figures they produce are not identical, but they all show a similar pattern of findings. This can be seen in Table 23.

TV viewing, like radio listening in its heyday, is preponderantly an activity of the evening hours, when the whole family is at home. However, there is now a substantial audience at all times of the day, and more and more stations are on a full daily schedule.

The television audience rises steadily through the morning and then remains fairly level until late afternoon. At this point, with the children home from school and play, set usage starts to rise again. It reaches a peak between 8 and 11 PM, then drops sharply.

By contrast, radio (at its present stage of competition with television) reaches its largest audience in the mid-morning, holds it through lunch, and then slips somewhat. It maintains an audience of fairly constant size until evening. From then on it declines as people switch their attention to the TV set. Table 24, based on the

TABLE 23

Size and Composition of the TV Audience, by Time of Day,
as Measured by Three Rating Services

A

(Source: Videodex)

	Men	Women	Children	Teen-Agers	*Viewers Per Set*
Weekday Evenings	34%	42%	17%	7%	2.7
Saturday Evenings	32	36	23	9	3.0
Sunday Evenings	35	41	16	8	2.8

B

(Source: American Research Bureau, Fall, 1954)

	Men	Women	Children	*Total Viewers Per Set*
Weekdays				
Sign-on—Noon	15%	49%	36%	1.8
Noon—6 PM	12	55	33	1.8
6 PM—Sign-off	34	45	21	2.5
Saturday				
Sign-on—Noon	13%	13%	74%	2.3
Noon—6 PM	46	25	29	2.3
6 PM—Sign-off	34	38	38	2.7
Sunday				
Noon—6 PM	42%	32%	26%	2.4
6 PM—Sign-off	33	39	18	2.4

C

(Source: New York Telepulse)

Time Period	Men	Women	*Children and Teen-Agers*	*Total Audience (100%)*
7-8 AM	25%	40%	35%	376,000
10-11	7	46	47	1,101,000
4-5 PM	17	30	53	1,895,000
5-6	13	20	63	2,751,000
8-9	33	38	29	5,672,000
11-12	47	47	6	1,538,000

audience rating measurements of the A. C. Nielsen Company, shows the percentage of homes watching television and listening to the radio at various hours of the day.

TABLE 24

How Television Viewing and Radio Listening Vary by Season and Hour, (Average Minute) 1957

(Source: A. C. Nielsen Co.)

| | *Per Cent of Total Homes in U. S.* | | | |
| | *Watching Television* | | *Listening to Radio* | |
Hour	*January*	*July*	*January*	*July*
7-8 AM	2%	1%	12%	7%
8-9	7	3	16	10
9-10	9	6	15	11
10-11	11	8	16	12
11-12	16	13	14	12
Noon-1 PM	21	14	15	14
1-2	19	14	15	14
2-3	18	16	12	12
3-4	21	16	11	11
4-5	25	17	11	10
5-6	31	17	11	10
6-7	39	19	11	10
7-8	45	22	10	9
8-9	53	29	8	7
9-10	54	35	7	6
10-11	48	38	7	6
11-Midnight	30	30	6	6

On the typical weekday, women make up about half the total television audience, morning, afternoon and evening; teen-agers and children represent about a third of the viewers in the morning and afternoon, and men constitute a third in the evening. Women viewers outnumber men at every hour of the day except after 11 PM. Even during the hours when they are most likely to be at home, it appears as though men are more likely than women to have other things to do, away from the TV set. A "pilot study" made in Detroit in 1955 by the American Broadcasting Company found that, while women viewed evening television 28% more than men, they exhibited proportionately even "greater interest"—46% more than men.

Between 4 and 6 PM over half the television audience is made up of children and teen-agers (nearly two-thirds between 5 and 6 PM). On weekends the viewing pattern changes. Children represent three-fourths of the Saturday morning viewers, and men (many watching sports events) outnumber women among the Saturday and Sunday afternoon viewers. Saturday evening audiences are somewhat larger than on other nights, because children are permitted to stay up longer.

The viewing habits of the television audience are influenced not only by the time of day, but by the timing of the major network programs emanating from New York or Hollywood. In the Central time zone, the top evening listening period starts, reaches a peak, and finishes about an hour earlier than in the Eastern states. This also tends to be true in the Far West, although many network programs are broadcast there on a delayed basis.

The size of the audience depends not only on the time of day but on the time of year, as Table 24 indicates. Viewing and listening are at their height in the winter months, and drop down in the summer, when outdoor activities beckon. Evening television, in particular, suffers during the summer months, even though the potential audience is not cut as badly as might be supposed. The youngest families, understandably, show the greatest differences between summer and winter viewing.

In Canada, where the climatic contrast between seasons is perhaps greater than in the United States, summer viewing is only at about half the level achieved in the winter peak. Studies by International Surveys show the average Canadian TV home has its set on for 2 hours and 18 minutes in July, for 4 hours and 18 minutes in March.

(F)

A survey conducted by Willard Simmons and directed by Thomas Coffin for the National Broadcasting Company found (in 1951) that in 95% of metropolitan New York TV families someone was at home on the average summer (June, July, August) night. As many as 56% of the families took no summer vacation away from home. And of the television families who went away, 29% watched television at some time while they were on vacation.

Summer is typically a season of "replacement" programs on the air. The viewer's dissatisfaction with unfamiliar or unappealing entertainment fare may deter him from watching, as much as the lure of the front porch, the beach, or the drive-in movie. In the later evening hours, as the family returns home before bedtime, summertime viewing comes closer to winter levels.

Daytime Television and the Housewife Audience

Television today operates, and is viewed, around the clock. The growth of the daytime television audience came about in the face of all the original prognostications. In *Advertising and Selling* of November 1938, one writer referred to the pioneer British experience: "They have found in London, that people want an hour of television in the afternoon and an hour at night, and will complain vehemently if they don't get it. But evidently, that's enough."

That same month, Eldridge Peterson, writing in *Printers Ink* (November 10, 1938), predicted:

"The number of hours during the day when television appears as an advertising weapon will be limited. Television will demand concentrated attention, both visually and aurally, from the consumer. Whereas many radios are tuned on at breakfast time, it is difficult to conceive a housewife, or a husband in a hurry to be off to business, stopping to concentrate his visual and aural attention at breakfast time on a television program, even were it in the dining room. Nor is the housewife during the early morning hours of the day, when she is preparing breakfast, getting the kids off to school, or doing the household marketing, readily available for television programs."

As recently as 1951, only 2% of the TV-owning housewives in "Videotown" watched television on the average weekday morning, —only 10% in the afternoon. By 1955, 17% were watching in the average morning, 27% in the afternoon. In 1956 the proportions dropped to 11% and 20% respectively. (The proportion of all people in TV homes who watched their sets at some time in the average day rose from 70% in 1951 to 87% in 1955, fell to 79% in 1956.)

Daytime TV audiences have climbed to a respectable level as more and more stations have programmed throughout the morning and afternoon, and as the quality of these programs has improved. But daytime viewing is still far below evening levels. At the same time, daytime radio has continued to hold its own reasonably well against the competition of television.

Before television entered the picture, a study by Paul Lazarsfeld and Helen Dinerman sought to distinguish women who listened to morning radio from those who did not, though they were physically able to do so. The listeners were divided into the "story audience" for daytime serials and the other listeners, who disliked the suspense and tension of domestic drama and wanted to be soothed and diverted from their troubles.

Four types of non-listeners are distinguished in this study: the "radio resisters," the "program resisters" (whose dislikes are less generalized), the "radio-restricted" (whose work did not bring them within easy reach of a radio set), and the "one-track-mind group." The latter, reported to account for three-fifths of all the non-listeners, are described as those psychologically incapable of listening and working at the same time.

If such a typology is to be adapted to television, the number of categories must be even greater, and their arrangement even more complex. There would have to be not only "radio-resisters" but "radio and television resisters" and just plain "television resisters" who are not averse to radio. Then too, the proportion of "television-restricted" whose work takes them away from the living room must be greater than for those who remain beyond earshot of radio. And the number who find it psychologically impossible to view and work simultaneously must be considerably greater for television than for radio. All this would lead to the conclusion that television will find it difficult ever to capture as large a share of the potential daytime audience of women at home as radio did at its peak.

Programs and Audiences

Unlike a magazine article or a newspaper report, a television or radio program normally continues in time. It is repeated day after day or week after week. Thus these programs tend to build up a steady and loyal audience. The typical weekly half-hour evening dramatic show on television is viewed about every other week by the average member of its audience.

Like most figures of this kind, this one can be regarded from two points of view. It can be considered evidence of a high degree of audience loyalty that most viewers are sufficiently aware of, and familiar with a program so that they keep coming back to it at least every other week, in spite of interruptions caused by other activities, and in the face of competing broadcasts.   (G)

On the other hand, the continual turnover of viewers may be seen as an indication that a program must fight for its life, broadcast after broadcast. This makes it difficult (in TV as in radio) to maintain any true dramatic continuity from one program to the next in a series. Where this is attempted each episode must be sufficiently autonomous in character to be able to stand by itself. Daytime serials must move at a snail's pace, and with constant reiteration of what has transpired, before, during and after the program itself.

The television audience is a constantly changing thing, as viewers consult program listings in their newspapers or television guides and sample the offerings on various channels, or as their other home activities are switched or interrupted.

The shifting pattern of the audience can best be traced through the measurements made by the A. C. Nielsen Company, which uses a device that actually records all tuning activity on a set. One recent analysis made by this method sought to determine where the audience of one evening television program came from. In this instance, the following happened:

> 49% came directly from the preceding show on the same network.
> 6% sampled both the preceding show on the same network and the one on the rival network.
> 20% came directly from the preceding show on the rival network.
> 8% tuned over to the competing show on the rival network, after first sampling our program.

3% came over after first sampling the competing show on the rival network.

3% tuned in after the show started, and had not been watching television before that.

11% came from other stations and networks.

The greatest amount of tuning in or out naturally takes place at the half-hour mark when programs change. But a substantial part of the TV audience stays with the same station, partly out of deliberate choice (because they want to see the next program), partly because it may be the clearest image that they are watching, but also partly because this represents the path of least resistance and effort. Because the networks recognize this tendency for many viewers to be governed by inertia, they are strongly aware of the value which any outstandingly popular show has for the following programs on the network schedule for any given evening. Conversely they recognize that a weak program can jeopardize the ratings of the programs which follow it.

The fact that timing may be far more important than the quality of programming is well understood in broadcasting circles. *Advertising Age* (June 27, 1955) states the point succinctly:

> "The time franchise is the only stable commodity in this wild game of programming. Time franchises reflect people's living habits. Programs come and programs go—even the best—but 9 or 9:30 PM, E.T., over the years still is the best place for your changing program schedule. To latch on to one of these prime times and hold on like a leech is the principal rule of succeeding in television."

As the competition among the networks has grown keener, their programming decisions have shown increasing deference to the principle of the strong continuous evening line-up. In a few notable instances this has meant even a refusal on the network's part to permit a long-established sponsored program to return to the air at its accustomed time, because of the feeling that other programs were threatened by its low rating.

As we have already seen, at some times of the evening more members of the family are at home watching television than at other hours. As Table 25 demonstrates, some programs manage to attract more viewers from within the family than other programs can. As a result, the total audience reached by a program is not necessarily indicated exactly by its rating—if this measurement represents the proportion of homes viewing or of sets tuned in.

TABLE 25

Two Programs with the Same Number of Sets
Tuned In May Differ in Audience Size

	Program X	*Program Y*
Number of sets tuned to broadcast	6,500,000	6,700,000
Viewers per set	2.3	2.7
Total audience	15,000,000	18,100,000

The size of audience which a program attracts is a reflection of its own particular appeal, rather than of its general format. This may be seen most clearly (in Table 26) when programs are grouped by type into five major categories: general drama, mystery drama, situation comedy, general variety (which includes comedy shows with singing and dancing), and audience participation or quiz programs. Table 26 shows the audience ratings received by the most and least successful programs, and by the middle programs, in each category, during one week in the 1955-1956 season.

TABLE 26

How TV Programs of the Same Type Vary in Popularity, 1955

(One week's audience ratings)

	High	*Median*	*Low*
General Drama	39 (Producer's Showcase)	24 (Goodyear Playhouse)	10 (They Stand Accused)
Mystery Drama	41 (Dragnet)	22 (The Line-up)	10 (Rocky King)
Situation Comedy	52 (I Love Lucy)	23 (Mr. Peepers)	10 (Life With Father)
General Variety	51 (Bob Hope)	29 (Texaco Theater)	23 (You Asked For It)
Quiz, Audience Participation	41 (You Bet Your Life)	24 (People Are Funny)	9 (Twenty Questions)

The general variety programs (which usually are the most lavish and expensive productions) do a little better, on the average, than shows of the other types, and they never do as poorly as the least successful shows in other formats. But apart from this, it is evident that viewers like to diversify their program choices. As a result the typical program of any one type does about as well as the typical show of any other type. Success and failure depend on the ingredients, not on the formula.

The Effect of Greater Program Choice

(H)   Because of the increasing number of stations, television is today a more selective medium than it was a few years ago, though it still does not offer the viewer the same great choice of programs that radio does. In 1952 only 32% of TV sets were within reception range of four or more stations. Today 72% are. A mere 4% of the sets can now receive only one channel, compared with 35% in 1952.

The effect of increased opportunity for choice on the part of the viewers has been heightened by competition for the public's attention. Network program *audiences* have continued to increase in size as more and more people have acquired sets. But program *ratings* (which represent the percentage of television homes that watch a particular show) have declined as an inevitable result of the fact that the available audience must be divided among more stations. This can be seen in Table 27, which shows what happened after the "freeze" was lifted.

TABLE 27

Increased Choice of Programs, and Its Effect on Ratings

	September 1952	1956
Number of stations	108	487
Per cent of TV homes within range of four stations or more	32%	72%
Average Nielsen ratings for all evening programs	26	20

If there are only a few channels available to the television viewer, it might be assumed that he would be more likely to turn to the radio set for entertainment, if the available TV programs are not to his taste. On the other hand, if he can select among a variety of television stations, one might expect him to turn to his radio less often. Actually, this is not the case. Television viewing and radio listening are both about the same in areas where only two television stations can be seen as they are in areas with three, four or even seven television stations. (See Table 28.)

TABLE 28

TV Viewing and Radio Listening in Areas
with Varying Freedom of TV Program Choice

(Adapted from C. E. Hooper Data)

Number of TV Channels in Area	Evening, Sets in Use	
	Television	Radio
One	41%	16%
Two	39	16
Three	40	16
Four	39	17
Five or more	41	17

Apparently people listen to the radio or watch television as an activity that fits in with their moods or their other activities. If they want to watch television, they will first check the available offerings, but if they don't care too much for any of them they will still watch *something* rather than turn on the radio.

This is why television viewing stays at about the same level every weekday evening, even though the calibre and popularity of TV programs may be different on different nights. (Total viewing does increase somewhat, though, when an extraordinarily popular program like "Twenty One" is on the air, showing that such a program does have the ability to attract some people who would otherwise not be watching TV.) It is also why extremely well-known entertainment personalities like Bob Hope, Jack Benny and Edgar Bergen (all with large audiences in homes without TV) have in recent years been unable to attract much more than 1% of the television owners to their radio audience, although not one of them broadcast at the same time as a TV comedy or variety program.

A 1955 study by the American Research Bureau also shows that the strength of the viewing habit appears to have little to do with a person's control over what he can view. The heavy viewers (the one-fourth of all TV families who do two-fifths of the total viewing) could receive about the same number of stations (about four) on their sets as could the light viewers (the lowest fourth of the families, in total viewing hours). Even though they had no wider choice of programs, the heavy viewers found themselves more easily satisfied with what was available.

Repeat Broadcasts

In its ceaseless search after something new to look at, the television audience will often turn to something it originally missed —or had rejected as its original first choice.

TABLE 29

Film Re-Runs Continue to Draw Large Audiences

(Source: A. C. Nielsen Co.)*

	Total	Winter	Summer
Nielsen Rating			
Original	31%	28%	28%
Re-run	22	23	19
Share of Audience			
Original	47%	43%	43%
Re-run	43	39	39
Total Shows	254	53	201

*254 repeat film telecasts analyzed

One solution to the television screen's insatiable appetite for fresh material has been the practice of running a kinescope or film of an original broadcast after an interval of time has elapsed. These repeat showings have demonstrated their capacity to win large audiences. Since repeat runs of film shows are most common in the summer months, when TV audiences are generally smaller, they only attract about two-thirds as large an audience as they did originally. But an analysis by Nielsen (Table 29) of 254 repeat film broadcasts, finds that the re-runs get almost as large a share (43%) of the available audience as did the original shows (47%).

In a questionnaire survey among 1381 insurance company employees in Los Angeles (1956), Jesse Bond found an even split of opinion for and against program reruns. A majority of the respondents reported that they cared "little" whether a program is live or on film.

In a telephone survey conducted during 1956, the Trendex organization found that 72% of the viewers of a filmed program which had been previously broadcast were unaware that it was part of a series of reruns. Those who knew the program was a rerun did not differ from the others in the extent to which they had watched the previous week's program in the same series or planned to watch the following week's show.

It is actually better to re-run films of previous broadcasts of a well-established program, during the summer months, than to introduce a summer replacement in the form of a completely new live show. An analysis by the A. C. Nielsen Company shows that filmed re-runs in the summer of 1955 were 38% below the February rating level for the same programs, while completely new summer replacement shows were 50% below the level of their winter predecessors in the same time period. Over-all audiences (including those of shows which remained on the air through the summer months) were 33% less in July and August than in February.   (I)

One tentative conclusion may be drawn from the relatively poorer showing made by replacement programs, compared with those which were continued either live or through filmed rebroadcasts. It appears that the summertime decline in ratings is at least partly due to the lower calibre of replacement shows (often the trying ground for new talent and ideas) or to the public's unfamiliarity with them and consequent lack of interest.

Different Programs Appeal to Different Audiences

While the time of day and day of week influence the composi-   (J)
tion of the audience by determining the availability of various members of the family, programs of different character necessarily appeal to different kinds of people. Differences in tastes and preferences may

be seen, for example, in some findings of the 1951 NBC-Hofstra survey of television in the New York Metropolitan area, shown in Table 30. In this study, TV owners were asked for a number of kinds of shows, whether or not they liked "most programs" of each type.

The extent to which people say they like most programs of a type bears no particular relation to their actual viewing habits, as measured by the program rating services. In general, persons with higher education are more critical of television fare than are the less well-educated. At least, they are considerably less likely to say they like "most programs" of any particular type.

News programs are preferred by men somewhat more than by women, and by young people more than by older ones. Although they are favorably mentioned to about the same extent by people at all educational levels, news looms larger (relative to other program types) in the preferences of the college educated. Forums, equally

TABLE 30

Program Preferences of TV Owners by Personal Background Characteristics

(Source: 1951 NBC-Hofstra Survey)

Per Cent of Each Group Who "Like Most Programs" of this Type

	News	Musical	Comedy-Variety	Dramatic	Sports	Mystery	Films	Quiz & Audience Partici- pation	Forums
Total	65%	63%	62%	51%	50%	49%	40%	31%	28%
Sex									
Men	70	58	65	43	72	48	36	27	28
Women	60	67	60	60	29	50	45	35	29
Age									
18-29	59	60	65	48	49	53	43	25	17
30-39	63	62	61	56	49	52	39	26	24
40-49	70	63	62	51	53	48	40	33	29
50 +	71	67	64	46	52	42	43	42	40
Education									
Completed Grammar School	67	70	69	47	53	51	55	38	26
Some High School	63	68	69	47	51	57	45	34	23
Completed High School	64	60	63	54	51	46	38	30	24
College	69	50	46	57	48	41	24	22	37

preferred by men and women, are most strongly favored by the better educated, and by younger persons.

Dramatic programs are better liked by women than by men and are best liked by the better educated. Perhaps because a high proportion of television drama deals with problems of domestic life, it has a greater attraction to persons in their thirties and forties than to younger or older people.

Mystery programs, on the other hand, are most favorably mentioned by younger viewers, least by older ones. Mysteries are equally popular among men and women, and they are better liked by people who have not finished high school than by those with more education.

Musical programs are favored by women and by the older and less educated. Quiz and audience participation shows follow the same pattern.

Comedy-variety shows are almost as well liked by women as by men. They are a favorite with people of all ages and all levels of education—except for the college educated. Sports programs are overwhelmingly an attraction for men rather than women, and preference for them appears to be slightly greater among older and less educated persons.

Feature films on television are more highly favored by women than by men. They are equally well regarded at all age levels, but approval of them is highest among the least educated. (This survey was made before the release for television of a considerable number of relatively recent films of a higher calibre than those originally available.)

Research conducted by Whan in Kansas two years after the NBC study shows a similar pattern of program preferences. In this research, summarized in Table 31, differences in tastes may be discerned between men and women, and among people of varying educational background.

As in the NBC New York study, Kansas men prove to be more partial to news and sports broadcasts, while women lean toward dramatic programs, audience participation shows, and musical programs of both the classical and popular variety. In Kansas as in New York, men and women are alike in their attitude toward comedy and variety shows. The Kansas study also notes the predilection of women for serial dramas and homemaking programs.

Because Whan makes a distinction between various types of musical programs, his findings indicate the usual differences: classical music is more favored by the better educated, "oldtime music" by those with only a grade school education. Popular music or jazz is better liked by the high-school educated group than by either the grade-school or college-educated.

While the New York study found sports telecasts about equally well favored at all educational levels, the Kansas survey finds the preference for them greatest among the college educated. (In part this may reflect the narrower range of sports events telecast over Kansas TV stations compared with those in New York.)

Preference for comedy and dramatic programs is heaviest among the college educated. On the other hand, variety shows are less popular with people who have not gone beyond grade school than with the other groups. News and audience participation shows appear to maintain their general level of popularity across the board. Farming programs, market reports, and religious programs are stronger among the less-well educated rural element.

In their study of television in New Haven, Everett Parker and his associates compared the viewing of different types of programs at different social levels. As in other studies, viewing of most types of shows was higher at the middle social levels than at the two extremes. Programs dealing with public issues were reportedly watched by 12% of the TV-owners in the highest social category, but by only 2% of those at the bottom of the pyramid. News, however, maintained the usual pattern, viewed by 80% at the top level, by 90% in the middle group, and by 82% in the bottom category. Such program types as general and comedy dramas, musical programs, quiz shows and religious programs were viewed by similar proportions at every social level. At the upper social level, there was relatively light viewing of crime and domestic dramas (soap operas) and somewhat lighter than average viewing of sports and variety programs.

In 1955, Raymond Stanley, Malcolm MacLean and their associates at the University of Wisconsin's Television Laboratory interviewed 225 residents of Stoughton, Wisconsin, on their preferences for various types of television programming content. The findings of this study closely parallel those already reported.

TABLE 31

How TV Program Preferences Differ by Education

(Source: 1953 Whan Kansas radio-television survey)

	Men			Women		
	College	High School	Grade School	College	High School	Grade School
News broadcasts	69%	66%	70%	58%	65%	57%
Comedians	70	63	61	67	62	62
Sports	70	62	55	47	37	33
Complete drama	60	55	42	67	59	47
Variety	49	50	34	52	56	47
Audience participation	37	42	38	48	53	54
Popular music	24	34	19	35	41	31
Talks, comment	28	18	23	21	14	15
Oldtime music	7	21	26	5	14	20
Market reports	3	17	21	2	4	6
Religious	9	15	18	12	18	27
Classical music	20	14	7	25	18	10
Talks on farming	8	9	24	2	2	8
Serial drama	4	9	12	14	21	36
Brass bands	6	8	7	6	10	11
Homemaking	3	1	3	10	12	15

While opinion surveys like those just cited show considerable differences in the program *preferences* of various population groups, actual audience measurements indicate fewer differences than might be expected in the extent to which various segments of the audience actually view programs of different types. It is not in the least surprising to find that seven out of ten viewers of a daytime serial like "Road of Life" are women, or that nine out of ten who watch "Howdy Doody" are children. But on the whole, as Table 32 shows, evening programs do not show so overwhelming an appeal for only one segment of the public (even though boxing matches appear to have nearly two male viewers for every woman).

An analysis (by the Pulse, Inc.) of audience composition for programs on film also fails to show great differences between programs of various types. This can be seen in Table 33. Understandably, the proportion of children is high in the case of children's and western-type programs. Children are also a strong audience component in variety and comedy programs, which appear to attract the entire family as a viewing group. But for most types of programs

---

TABLE 32

How the Composition of the Television Audience Differs by Program Type

(Source: C. E. Hooper, Inc., Winter, 1954)

	Men	Women	Children
Evening Shows			
General Drama (Armstrong Theater)	38%	48%	14%
Variety (Toast of the Town)	38	45	17
Sports (Pabst Fights)	59	33	8
Daytime Shows			
Children's (Howdy Doody)	4%	7%	89%
Daytime Serial (Road of Life)	10	70	20

---

the proportion of adult men to women in the audience remains roughly the same, with women somewhat preponderant except in the case of mystery dramas.

TABLE 33

How Audience Composition Differs, By Program Type (for film shows)

(Adapted from U. S. Pulse TV)

Program Type	Per Cent				*Total Viewers Per Set (100%)*
	Men	*Women*	*Teen-Agers*	*Children*	
General Variety	26%	32%	10%	32%	2.0
General Drama	34	42	9	15	1.9
Situation Comedy	32	35	11	22	2.0
Western	24	21	11	44	2.1
Mystery Drama	39	39	9	13	2.0
Children's Programs	22	25	11	42	1.9
Popular Music	32	49	11	8	1.8

What is the explanation for this absence of strong differences in the audiences of such distinct kinds of entertainment? Viewing takes place throughout the evening as a continuous activity in which all adult members of the family who are home usually participate. The selection of programs may now be resolved in favor of one family member's preference, now in favor of another. But it is rare to find anyone leaving the living room for a half hour because the program playing is not his first choice. Television viewing is the evening's pastime, and it continues regardless of content.

5. TV VIEWING IN ITS SOCIAL SETTING

Studies of television and other mass media generally present reports expressed in terms of aggregate activity. As demonstrated by the preceding chapter, emphasis is usually on the total numbers of people in the audience or on the differences in the viewing patterns of various sections of the population. Often such studies seem reminiscent of a mechanistic school of psychological theory, in which a stimulus (the communications medium) acts on an inert subject (the audience) and elicits an appropriate response. Actually, this is far from being an accurate description of what takes place.

The mass media audience is never exposed to any communication in a vacuum. The audience invariably receives the message in a social setting which profoundly influences the way in which the message is perceived, interpreted and absorbed. Communication via the mass media is more than an individual communication multiplied a thousand or a million times.

The child sitting on his mother's lap and hearing a story read aloud is responding not merely to the abstract symbols on the printed page but to the many sensations of love, security and mystery evoked by this shared experience. In later life, the solitary reader finds pleasure in reading not only because he has absorbed the author's wisdom or art but because he in turn can pass something of this on to others.

The importance of the social setting is even more readily apparent for viewing television than for reading. Since the days of TV's first appearance, the social character of viewing has gone through at least three major stages.

(A)   1. *The tavern phase.* In the earlier days, television sets were most often found in public places, notably in the taverns of large cities. The tavern audience was predominantly a male fellowship, particularly in workingclass neighborhoods, where the local bar is a kind of club in which men are accustomed to spend their evenings. The "crowd" at the tavern might include a core of intimates, a wider circle of nodding acquaintances, and a relatively small number of itinerant strangers.

The advent of television gave a focus to tavern life. The noise of the loudspeaker probably reduced the flow of casual small talk. However, TV provided a common denominator of experience which may actually have stimulated some conversation among people with little in common to talk about. On the evenings when television presented some outstanding attraction—especially an athletic contest —the tavern acquired even more importance than usual as a center of neighborhood life.

2. *The pioneer phase.* The first families to acquire TV sets were drawn from a higher income level than those who made up the tavern audience. Their viewing was no longer a public act. It took place in the familiar setting of the home, and the entire family participated. The pioneer set owners found their lives profoundly affected by the new medium. It kept them at home more, and cut down on outside activities like visiting or attendance at public events and meetings.

The singular aspect of TV viewing at this stage was that it was *more* than a family activity. The set-owning families were more frequently visited by friends and neighbors who had not yet acquired sets themselves. Their homes became social centers of a kind, though the sociability was sometimes superficial. This was the epoch of the "TV party," in which visitors gathered to see the programs, were fed beer and pretzels and left after only a minor exchange of amenities with the hosts.

3. *The mature phase.* In areas where television ownership has spread to the point of virtual universality, viewing reverts to a pattern which resembles that of radio listening in its prime. Viewing is now almost wholly within the family group, with outsiders not normally present. The television set remains the focal point of the family's typical evening activities. However, it probably no longer occupies the dominant position which it enjoyed in TV's earlier days, when other social activities slackened and even casual conversation was hushed in obedience to the set's demands. Television programs represent one of the family's principal shared experiences, and as such are a subject for small talk and occasionally for real discussion.

With a well-established habit of steady viewing night after night, it is not strange that the family which is suddenly deprived of television, through set breakdown or other circumstances, feels itself at a great loss.

The television set is typically located in the living room, at the heart of the family's life. A survey conducted by Alfred Politz for the Advertising Research Foundation in 1954 found 85% of the sets in the living room (Table 34).

(B)

TABLE 34

Distribution of Radio and TV Sets—By Location

(Source: 1954 ARF-Politz Survey)

	Location of All Television Sets	Location of All Radios
Living Room	85%	34%
Bedroom	3	29
Kitchen	—	22
All Other	12	15
	100%	100%

There is no reason to believe that the nature of television viewing has now entered its final phase. As more families acquire several sets, and as the sets themselves become lighter and less cumbersome, TV will spread through the various rooms of the house, much as radio has done, and viewing may become more of an individual activity and less of a family affair.

What TV Does for People

(C)   How did television enter the home in the first place? The obvious answer that it was acquired for purposes of family entertainment is not necessarily the whole story. Melvin Goldberg, asking 102 pioneer TV owners in New York what had led them to buy a television set, found a third referring to sports events, and a fourth to home entertainment. 18% said their children had wanted a set. 15% commented that they had been viewing TV at friends' homes and now felt they wanted a set of their own.

In a study of 740 persons in a Boston neighborhood (1951), Bernard Fine and Nathan Maccoby asked TV owners, "What were your main reasons for buying the set?" 45% gave entertainment as the reason, 13% said it was for the children, and 8% mentioned companionship as the reason. People of below-average education were most apt to mention TV's value for the children, as though protesting (too much) their own lack of interest.

94% of the TV owners interviewed in this survey said they would buy a set if they "had to do it over again"—but, on this question, two-thirds gave entertainment as a reason, and none mentioned the children. This suggests that while the children may have been the chief source of pressure to acquire TV in many households, once the set was installed it became an independent source of pleasure for the adult family members.

Of the non-television owners in this study who intended to buy a set, 71% said they wanted it for entertainment purposes. Of the non-owners who did not intend to buy a set, 42% said they had no interest, 18% said the programs were too poor, and 40% said a set would be too expensive.

On the other hand, the television owners viewed the main disadvantages of TV somewhat differently: 22% said it was distracting to the family or to work; 13% complained that "they never get to bed;" 10% mentioned specific programs as being harmful to children. (Middle-income persons mentioned disadvantages more frequently than did upper or lower-income people.) It is interesting that the bulk of the disadvantages listed by the TV owners reflect their inability to control themselves once the set had been installed in the house. This lack of confidence in one's own ability to control TV once it has entered the home is also mirrored in the apprehensions of non-owners.

The TV owners tended to state the main advantages of television in the form of generalities. 33% gave entertainment as the reason, 25% cited education, 16% said TV keeps the family at home together, and 4% said it keeps the children off the street.

A similar pattern of findings was reported in a study in Lexington, Kentucky, made by John McGeehan and Robert Maranville. When housewives in 400 TV homes were asked what were the good results of television ownership, 89% mentioned entertainment. 42% specifically mentioned that it cut the expense of entertainment. 16% reported that the family circle was more closely knit. 15% said it kept the children off the street, and 4% each mentioned TV's educational value or said it increased neighborliness. 2% felt that television had no advantages or good results. Half the women interviewed said their sets had been bought because of the interest of adults in the family.

It is evident that "entertainment" means different things to different people. Once television entered a community, many people felt that they had to acquire a set in order to keep up with the Joneses. In a study of 784 set owners in Atlanta in 1951, Raymond Stewart quotes the following remarks:

"Everyone expected us to have a set. I guess we wanted it because it was embarrassing not to have one."

"I didn't want it but my husband did. He saw them in so many homes and thought we ought to have one."

On the other hand, the first persons to acquire a set enjoyed the prestige of their pioneer status, and the special privileges of sociability and social leadership:

"It hasn't meant so much. I enjoyed it so much more when mine was new. I had one of the first anywhere around. Then so many friends came in to see it with me."

Television, Stewart found, also has a very special meaning for invalids, or for Southern Negroes who are similarly barred from public entertainments:

"It provides pleasure for us, especially since my husband has arthritis. It's a medium for him to feel like he's keeping up with things and it passes the time."

"It permits us to see things in an uncompromising manner. Ordinarily to see these things would require that we be segregated and occupy the least desirable seats or vantage point. With television we're on the level with everyone else. Before television, radio provided the little bit of equality we were able to get. We never wanted to see any show or athletic event bad enough to be segregated in attending it."

Television's Place in Family Life

Television viewing is characteristically a family activity, and as such it represents a kind of experience which is distinct from that of other media. Radio at one time had the same character, but radio listening appears increasingly to be something which people do by themselves, like reading. On the other hand, "going out" to the movies or to other forms of commercial entertainment is less likely to involve the whole family, and correspondingly more often occurs among persons of the same age group, whether this takes the form of teen-age dating or of adult socializing.

Elliott Freidson, examining the leisure-time patterns of Illinois grade-school boys of working-class background, found that "there is a strong tendency for particular situations to be characteristic of particular media: 52 per cent of the usual family situations were encountered with television; 75 per cent of the peer situations with movies; and 74 per cent of the alone situations with comics."

In the study made in Atlanta by Stewart, 57% of the television owners interviewed reported they prefer to watch television with someone. Only 9% prefer to watch it by themselves, and the remainder had no preference. (In practice, four out of five acknowledged that they had watched a complete show alone.)

The family character of TV viewing has from the start aroused a good deal of social commentary and speculation. Television's appearance was heralded as the beginning of a resurgence of American family life. The forecast was made that it would bring children in from outdoors to join with their elders around the hearth. Clerics, concerned about the decline of the family in an age of innumerable distractions and temptations, expressed the hope that television would enhance the attractions of the home for those who were inclined to stray outside its shelter. Accompanying this pious optimism there were also some skeptical voices. The rise of television, it was pointed out, represented an even further intrusion of the impersonal influences of the mass media into the intimate circle of family life.   (D)

Which of these contradictory predictions has been shown to be correct? Certainly television has proved to be a strong attractive force for all members of the family. It has brought more family groups together in the living room, of an average evening, than radio was able to do a few years earlier—as appears evident from TV's larger audiences.

Television provides the unifying effect of a common activity or interest on lives in which there is a scarcity of meaningful shared experience. In quotations like the following (from Stewart's study) it is also apparent that TV fills a void of boredom.

> "It keeps us together more. Friends drop in when they probably wouldn't otherwise. It's an entertainment that we take part in that isn't affected by the weather."
>
> "It makes a closer family circle. It draws our interests together. Instead of all doing different things, we are enjoying something together now. Before my husband was out a lot at night or was reading. My aunt would read and the boy would be playing. My brother-in-law usually slept."
>
> "We are closer together. We find our entertainment at home. Don and her boy friend sit here instead of going out, now. We sit and eat popcorn. Before television, I sat around and went nuts at home while my husband worked. He is tired when he gets home and would go to sleep just sitting around."
>
> "It keeps us closer together. It keeps down that wonder of where we can go and what we can do. My husband is very restless; now he relaxes at home."

In relieving boredom, television may also alleviate family tension:

> "It seems that family life is not as monotonous as before TV. We disagreed a little more before. Then one of us would go out of the house for a while; now we turn on television."
>
> "It keeps us happier. My husband and I get along a lot better. We don't argue so much. It's wonderful for couples who have been married ten years or more. It has been very entertaining for the boy. Before television, my husband would come in and go to bed. Now we spend some time together."

In fact, in some cases, the purchase of a set may actually have been motivated by the desire to eliminate family conflicts over the use of leisure time:

> "My husband did not like to go to shows. I did. He liked to go to ball games. I didn't. We decided this would be the answer for us."

In the judgment of one psychiatrist, Eugene David Glynn, "marriage after marriage is preserved by keeping it drugged on television; television is used quite constantly to prevent quarreling from breaking out by keeping people apart."

It might be expected that television tends to be a unifying influence in those families which, to begin with, showed the highest cohesiveness, and a divisive influence in homes where individual interests were already most dispersed. In a home characterized by tension or where family members pursue their own bents, television might simply represent one additional distraction to keep people separate, and disagreement about programs might mean only one more bone of contention in a struggle for power.

An interesting footnote to this subject is found in a survey of the relationship between leisure patterns and social status, made by Alfred C. Clarke among 574 residents of Columbus, Ohio. When asked, "What would you do with an extra two hours in your day?" none of those at the highest social level said they would watch television, and this response was mentioned by only 7% at the lowest level. By contrast, 40% of the latter and 25% of the upper-class group said they would relax, rest, loaf or sleep. Few said they would spend the time with their families. (E)

TV's Effects on Visiting and "Going Out"

A number of surveys, most of them made under university (F) auspices, have considered television's effects on family life. As in studies of TV's impact on other communications media, these researches have compared television families with families that had not yet acquired sets. In a number of cases the set owners have been asked their opinion of television's influence, comparing the present situation with the period before the set was obtained.

These studies agree completely that television has had the effect of keeping the family at home more than formerly, and has cut down a good many of its outside activities.

Of the pioneer New York set owners interviewed by Goldberg in 1948, 65% reported that, since television, they were spending more time at home, and 61% said they had more visitors than formerly. By contrast, 41% said they themselves were visiting less than they did before TV, and only 3% reported more visiting than formerly. Goldberg reports only slight evidence of any change in club membership or participation as a result of television.

Comparing the old and new set owners in his sample, Goldberg found that 70% of the old, but only 44% of the new, had at least some friends owning TV sets. This is easily explained if we assume that television ownership spread most rapidly among families who were tied together by some social bond. People whose friends had TV were the first to be exposed to the pleasures of home viewing, and also most strongly motivated to keep up with the Joneses. Those men who had few friends owning sets reported more visitors than did the men whose friends were set-owners.

The typical family decision to buy a television set seems to have come about after repeated exposure to programs at the homes of people who had already acquired sets. A survey among pioneer television owners was conducted in New Hyde Park, Long Island, in the fall of 1948 by House Organs Associates. Two-thirds of those interviewed said they had been influenced to buy their sets after watching TV at the homes of friends. (One in five cited the influence of sets in bars, hotels, restaurants and other public places. 15% mentioned advertising, news stories, and sets in store windows.)

In television's early days, "guest viewing" was a common practice, and the audience before the average set was proportionately larger than it has since become. In 1949, a New York Hooperating showed 3.9 viewers per set for the average show, with the number going as high as 4.9 for such extraordinarily popular programs as "Toast of the Town" and "We the People." Six years later, the average number of viewers per set was 2.4 in the evening and 1.6 in the daytime. Similarly, figures from the American Research Bureau show that in March, 1951, the average number of viewers per set was 2.6 in the daytime and 3.2 in the evening. In March, 1955, this had diminished to 1.9 viewers per set in the daytime and 2.7 in the evening.

In 1951, a Videodex study in New York found that 25% of the Sunday evening TV audience was composed of guests. On weekday evenings, about 15% of the viewers were guests.

In Thomas Coffin's (1948) study of "Television's Effects on the Family's Activities" in Long Island, commercial entertainment seemed to be feeling the impact of the medium more than non-commercial forms of sociability. Compared with the 498 non-owners interviewed, the 518 TV owners went to fewer public entertainments other than motion pictures. (Their weekly attendance rate was 45%, compared with 63% for the non-owners.) The greatest difference

(15% for the owners, 27% for the others) was in outside dining, dancing and night-clubbing. However, the television owners appeared to have just as active an informal social life as the non-owners—as represented by attendance at parties and other home entertainments.

Elmo Roper reported in a December 4, 1949, broadcast on the results of a national survey by his organization on the effects of television. He too observed that "the new world of video is primarily a home-loving life. Television owners go out in the evenings less than non-owners do." Roper found that 10% of the television owners usually entertained guests or went visiting in the evening, compared with 16% of the non-owners. Only 6% of the television-owning group said they "sit around and talk to other members of the family" but 15% of the non-owners said they did this. Roper also comments: "Fewer of the TV owners work around their house or in the garden. Fewer go to the movies, or go dancing, play bingo, or drink beer at the corner bar. And fewer told us they just rest and go to bed in the evening."

A mail survey made in the spring of 1950 by Fact Finders Associates, among 1800 readers of *TV Guide,* found two-thirds of those responding saying they went out less often than they had before television, but two in five said that they were doing more home entertaining. Similarly, a 1949 survey made for Duane Jones by Lawrence J. Hubbard found that of nearly 1600 television owners who returned questionnaires, three-fourths had more visitors than formerly—both children and adults.

Edward McDonagh, in a 1950 study of "Television and the Family" (among 160 TV owners and the same number of non-owners) in a southern California community, found the television-owning families reporting that they stayed home more than formerly, and also that they had more visitors. (The non-television families actually said they had *fewer* visitors than formerly.)

In the same year a study made in two towns in the Boston area by Franklin Sweetser (1950) found that 45% of the TV owners said they were spending more time at home since they installed TV. 32% said they were doing less visiting, but a relatively small proportion (16%) said they were going to dances or parties less than they had done formerly. Charles Alldredge, in a survey of 400 Washington, D.C., TV families, reported two out of five were spending more time at home.

In the "Videotown" studies of New Brunswick, N. J., entertaining friends and visiting was reported for the average week by 25% of the adults in TV families in 1950. By 1955 the proportion had declined to 10%.

In Lexington, Kentucky, McGeehan and Maranville found that family visits to TV homes (in a period of relatively low TV penetration) increased from a weekly average of 3.8 before TV to 4.8 afterwards. At the same time attendance at such public entertainment functions as athletic events, theatrical and concert programs fell from .7 per person weekly before TV to .4 afterwards.

Sherman Lawton, in a survey of 2864 families in Oklahoma City and Norman, Oklahoma, found that TV brought more guests into the house, at least in the first six months. However he found no indication that television kept people away from parties. The heavy television and radio fans seemed to go to fewer parties even before television appeared on the scene, and also attended church and organization meetings less frequently.

Stewart found that television owners in Atlanta reported decreased activity in clubs and organizations, though this was not as great as the over-all decline in their evening excursions. As in the other studies, he found that the TV owners reported staying home more, and entertaining more guests than they had done four years previously. Stewart's findings are summarized in Table 35.

TABLE 35

How TV Owners Compare Present Activity With That of Four Years Earlier

(Source: 1951 Stewart Atlanta Survey)

	More	Same	Less
Active in clubs, organizations	14%	53%	34%
Go out in evening	10	27	63
Stay home from things	58	31	12
Friends visit in evenings*	34	45	21

*1% report no visitors.

In comparing present activity with that of four years earlier, Stewart found that, in explaining their changed habits, people were more inclined to bring up the demands of parenthood, or considerations of health, than to cite television.

Two-thirds of the television owners had spent a recent evening outside their home. About 40% had stayed home recently from an event they felt they should have attended, but this was less true of the older set owners (who had higher incomes and presumably could better afford babysitters.)

Television's tendency to keep the family at home has frequently been advanced to explain a decline in outside entertainment. In June, 1951 Jack Gould, writing in the New York *Times,* reported opinion that television had hurt night club business: He quotes Monte Proser, a leader in the field, who believes that the larger night clubs have had their day and that smaller, more intimate, cabarets will gain in popularity instead, since they are better able to cope with the more lavish, but also more impersonal entertainment of TV. According to Gould, package store sales of beer and liquor remained steady or rose during TV's early years of growth, while bar custom fell off. Apparently other causes than TV's influence were at work in this case, however, for at the time of Gould's survey cities which did not yet have television also reported a slackening in the tavern trade.

Gould mentions another interesting observation on the part of the cabaret proprietors: "Television viewers are now seeing so many stars and variety acts that they've become more demanding. Where once only the professional critic saw everything in town, now virtually everybody does." Talent is also in shorter supply: "On television a chorus girl can get $112.50 for a half-hour show once a week, the fee including rehearsals. Leading night clubs pay $100 to a chorus girl and she must do eighteen shows a week."

A survey made in 1955 for the American Federation of Musicians by the Research Company of America provides further documentation of the decline of the cabaret. In this study, however, emphasis is put on the damaging effects of the federal tax, rather than on television, in explaining the decline in business.

TV and Conversation

(G)   Not every observer of television's effects agree that it has en-
hanced the intimacy of family life, even though it has kept the family
at home. Early comments often called attention to the inhibiting
influence of television on conversation. In the New York *Herald
Tribune* of June 9, 1948, John Crosby made this grim prediction:

> "The impact of television on our culture is one of the liveliest little
> topics of discussion to come along in some time, much of it conducted
> between clenched teeth. The most obvious and dire effect, one that
> strikes everyone who has seen more than two television broadcasts, is
> on conversation. There isn't any. The moment the set goes on, conver-
> sation dies. I don't mean it languishes. It dies. Messages are transmitted
> back and forth by means of eye-rolling, eyebrow lifting and frantic wig-
> wagging of the hands. (Only high priority messages are permitted: You're
> wanted on the telephone. Could I have another drink? That sort of thing.)
> People who will venture an occasional whisper in church remain awed
> and silent in front of a television set."

Of the television owners interviewed in Stewart's Atlanta survey, 85% said visitors came to their homes "just to talk to them." In
35% of these instances, the television owner and his visitor just
talked. In 35% of the cases, the television set was usually turned on.
27% reported varied activity, which sometimes included card playing
or television viewing. Stewart concludes that television causes no
more interference with conversation than "any other activity," but
occasionally his respondents were inclined to agree with Crosby. One
woman remarked:

> "It cuts down on the amount of family conversation. My husband
> requires that everybody be quiet when TV is on and it makes watching
> it disagreeable. Before we had television he just sat up and slept. Even
> then he talked very little."

Actually, two-thirds of Stewart's respondents said there was
not as much family conversation during television programs as there
had been in the evenings before they got their sets. Half said there
was less family conversation during television programs than on evenings "when each of you is busy with his or her own thoughts."

(Most of the remainder said it was about the same.) In the case of conversation, as for other activities, the greatest amount of interference was reported by the persons with least education.

Evidence that home conversation decreases when television appears on the scene is also provided by McDonagh's southern California study. Three-fifths of his television owners reported that they were now talking less to each other than formerly, while the non-owners noted no decline in this activity. He concludes on a pessimistic note: "In the evening in many homes the television set is making the family an audience rather than an intimate group characterized by much spontaneous talking and confiding. Table talk in the evening is greatly reduced so that family members may rush to their respective chairs to view their favorite program."

In their Boston TV survey, Fine and Maccoby asked respondents, "When members of the family are looking at a program together, how much talking is there during the program?" 29% said there was no talking, and 57% indicated that there was very little. 9% said there was quite a bit of talk and 5% said that the amount of talk varied with the program or the occasion. No one said there was talk "practically all the time."

TV and the Daily Routine

There is some evidence that television is changing the sleeping habits of the American people and possibly their meal schedules as well. 27% of the early TV owners questioned by Goldberg said that television was keeping the family at home and together. 17% mentioned that the children were staying up later and that it was harder to get them to sleep. 8% said that the dinner hour had been changed.

When questioned specifically on this last point, a fifth of the men reported some change in their eating habits; 11% were eating in front of the set rather than at the dinner table. Two out of five reported changes in the eating habits of their children. Sweetser in his 1950 study in the Boston area found that 47% of his respondents were sleeping less than formerly.

An Advertest study in early 1951 reported that before television 63% of the people interviewed were usually asleep between 11 PM and midnight, with the remainder awake. After television, 75% were viewing, 15% sleeping, and 10% were awake but not viewing.

McGeehan and Maranville (in Lexington, Kentucky) found two families in three retiring later, and 10% changing their supper hour. Stewart reports that in Atlanta 97% were eating at the same time as before television, but 44% were eating within viewing distance of the set. In this survey, 54% of the respondents said TV had changed their sleeping hours.

(H)

The Economic Differential

From a number of the studies already cited, it appears that persons of above-average income and education seemed to have felt the fewest effects from television. They were best able to fit it into their lives without drastically reshaping other activities.

While better educated and wealthier persons, with their greater resources, are best able to take television in their stride, they are also the very ones who are most sensitive to any possible harm done by the medium. This reflects their generally greater readiness, as determined by numerous surveys, to criticize the mass media or other social institutions. A 1950 survey for John Meck Industries found that 25% of the upper-income respondents, but only 4% of those with lower income, said television had made for objectionable changes in family life. Favorable changes were reported to the same degree by both groups.

High income people are more apt to be doing something else while they watch TV. In Fine and Maccoby's Boston study, 35% of the well-to-do reported some concurrent activity, compared with 17% of the poorer respondents. In this study too, the higher income people tended to be more critical of programs than were those of lower income. (16% of the upper income group rated programs excellent, 20% poor; 33% of the low income respondents rated them excellent, none rated them poor.)

Viewing by Inertia

At any particular time, a part of the television audience is not (I)
especially interested in what is on the screen. In part this represents
viewing as part of the family group; in part it represents simple
inertia: leaving the set turned on despite the lack of any interest in
the available programming.

To be sure, there may be intense interest — and conflict of
interest — with respect to programming choices. In "Videotown,"
about 30% of the television families acknowledged that there was
some dissension over the choice of programs. In half these cases, the
father was reported to get his way, and in the remainder the mother
and children made the decision about equally often.

Goldberg reports that in 1948 family disputes over the choice
of TV programs divided about evenly between adult-child conflicts
and husband-wife disagreements. But on the whole, peaceful accommo-
dation appeared to be the rule.   (J)

A study made among television families in Detroit in 1955
provides additional evidence on this point, as described in a speech
by Robert Kintner, President of the American Broadcasting Company:

"There is frequently more unanimity of appeal within the household
of lower-rated programs than for most programs appearing in the top 10
in terms of total homes delivered. I suppose that this may be traced to the
fact that the leading programs become more controversial, presumably
developing strong dislikes as well as likes which tend to fragmentize the
audience within the household.

"It appears that the housewife asserts herself to a greater extent in
the selection of a TV program when there is general drama or a situation
comedy available. As for mysteries, the housewife appears to have about
the same interest level as her husband. Naturally, as you would expect,
when sports events are on, the husband asserts his dominance, but what
surprised me is that he exercises it also for certain types of motion pictures. I can only guess that the same factors which keep men away from
home in Detroit must affect their choice of feature films on TV. Incidentally, the husband frequently reports, especially on weeknights, that
he would like to watch programs other than those chosen by his family,
so presumably the presence of a second TV set in the home will increase the male viewing activity."

65% of Stewart's Atlanta TV owners said they sometimes watch TV shows in which other members of the family are not interested. In these cases, other persons were present two-thirds of the time, and the respondents were watching the show (despite their lack of interest!) two times in five.

Of the Los Angeles insurance company employees questioned by Bond, about seven in ten report that they select half or more of their television programs in advance. 18% say they select all programs they watch, 46% select 3 out of 4, 22% select half the shows, 12% select one in four; only 2% say they select *none* in advance. Newspaper listings were the most important source of information about new programs, followed by weekly television magazine logs.

Bond also asked the (leading) question: "Do you sometimes try to follow more than one program at the same time, by shifting the dial back and forth during the same half hour or hour?" The answer was "no" by a margin of over 3 to 1.

In Boston, Fine and Maccoby asked, "Do you usually turn your set on for certain programs that you want to see, or do you more or less just leave it on?" 67% said they usually tuned to desired programs; 29% said they "just leave it on."

Using the statistical technique of latent structure analysis, Hanan Selvin examined further the program viewing patterns discovered by Everett Parker and his associates in their study of New Haven television. In this investigation, the extent of viewing for each type of program was related, for each household, to its viewing of every other type of program. It was found that no meaningful set of patterns or relationships emerged. Selvin concludes,

"The lack of relationship between the various program types revealed in the present data is not inconsistent with individual program preferment. It reveals primarily the heterogeneous character of television viewing. People are more likely to look at any program that comes along, just for the sake of viewing television, than they are to listen to whatever happens to be available on radio. More important, since most television viewing is done in the evening, the lack of pattern among program types probably reveals a willingness within the family to compromise individual preferences in favor of a family consensus . . . It appears that—again within the limits of current availability in relation to audience—a particular program type will be viewed in New Haven about in proportion to its relative importance in the schedules of the television stations."

This phenomenon of the viewer by default or by inertia raises a question that has perplexed many students of television's audience: what percentage of those in the audience are truly attentive to the program on the screen. In Stewart's study, 57% of the respondents said they sometimes listen to television but do not pay particular attention to the picture. This is particularly true of musical and news or weather programs. In nine cases out of ten, these inattentive viewers were doing something else at the same time—usually household chores. Pilot studies conducted at the University of Oklahoma on the "Distraction Possibilities of Television" indicate that this kind of dual activity reduces awareness of what the program conveys, without disturbing the speed and general efficiency of such an activity as washing dishes.

It is no wonder that the housewife audience during daylight hours has been regarded by many advertisers and broadcasting executives with some suspicion. There has been a disposition to question even the healthy audience rating figures which many daytime programs are able to show. These ratings, the critics have pointed out, measure either set tuning (in the case of the A. C. Nielsen service) or over-all recall of the program as determined from interview or diary studies. There has remained a good deal of skepticism as to whether the housewife actually watches her set—even though it is operating—what with all the other demands on her attention during daylight hours.

An interesting attempt to answer this question was made in Columbus, Ohio, in February 1955 by Joseph M. Ripley, Jr. Ripley conducted a telephone survey of nearly 8,000 Columbus homes between 8:00 AM and 10:00 PM on two typical weekdays. 4,779 calls were completed, 4,064 of them with housewives.

During every time period of the day, Ripley found that a substantial proportion of the women interviewed were not in the same room with the television set, even where the set was on. (See Table 36). The proportion of absentees, understandably, was greatest in the late afternoon when the children's programs were on the air. It was lowest during the peak viewing hours of mid-evening, when few family chores remained to be done. But at other times, about a third of the housewives were in a different room. Another third, though in the same room, were dividing their attention to the program by simultaneously doing other things: working at household chores, eating, or even reading.

TABLE 36

Attention of Women to Tuned TV Programs
at Different Times of Day

(Source: Ripley Columbus Telephone Survey)

| | In Same Room with TV Set | | |
	"Just Watching"	Other Activities	In Other Room
8:00-10:00 AM	31%	31%	38%
10:00-12:00 AM	33	26	41
12:00- 2:00 PM	32	27	40
2:00- 4:00 PM	38	34	29
4:00- 6:00 PM	23	20	57
6:00- 8:00 PM	38	31	31
8:00-10:00 PM	64	21	15

The types of programs during which the housewife was most apt to absent herself from the room were (as expected) children's programs and Westerns and (less to be expected) daytime news programs (the sound portion of which is relatively easy to follow without the visual element).

Some qualifications must be placed on Ripley's findings. They are not directly comparable to the familiar ratings produced by the broadcast measurement services, because Ripley questioned women who would not have claimed that they were watching TV at the time of interview. He also failed to interview other members of the family, who may have been watching avidly while the housewife busied herself elsewhere.

However, it is evident from his study that the television audience is by no means rooted to the set, and that television necessarily takes its place in an ongoing pattern of household activity. It comes as no surprise to discover that a good many housewives leave their sets turned on while they go about their daytime duties. Some wander in and out of the television room from time to time to refresh their familiarity with the figures on the screen, whose voices follow them around the house. Others remain in the living room, but continue with sewing or child care as they watch. What may seem more surprising is the discovery that during most of the day, a third or more of the housewives whose sets are on are seated in front of them with undivided attention.

Similarly, in a daytime telephone survey of six cities made in February and March of 1956 by the C. E. Hooper company (on behalf of the newspaper publishers' Bureau of Advertising), it was found that the television sets in use received undivided attention from only a minority of the housewives. In New York City, 11% of the homes had sets in use at the time of the interview. In 46% of these viewing homes, the housewife was not in the same room as the set (either because she had left the room or because someone else had turned the set on and was watching it); in 15% of the homes, the housewife was not in. In 13% of the viewing homes the housewife was in the same room with the set, but was doing something else besides viewing. In 26% of the viewing homes, the housewife was devoting herself to TV.

As a further check, each housewife was asked, "Did you tune in this program for yourself or for another member of the family?" In every city surveyed, more than one-fourth of those housewives tuned in to a program of their own choice were not in the same room as the set.

About a month after the Columbus study, the Chicago *Tribune* conducted a similar telephone survey in Chicago, on two weekday evenings. The *Tribune* found that 63% of the women who were watching television when the phone rang, and 73% of the men, said they had been giving TV their undivided attention. 5% of the women were reading, 5% eating, 3% sewing. Among the men 8% were reading and 6% were eating.

The inescapable conclusion is that while television competes with other activities during the daytime, evening television does manage to mobilize a very high degree of attention on the part of most of its audience. Evening viewing is, for most people, a full-time and absorbing occupation.

6. RADIO LISTENING IN THE TELEVISION AGE

Almost everyone who reads this has grown up with radio as a companion and as a source of certain memorable experiences—Roosevelt's fireside chats, the abdication of King Edward, Churchill's war speeches, the Louis-Schmeling fight. But this *kind* of radio, which flourished in the thirties and forties, is already history.

TV's growth, both as a leisure-time activity and as an advertising vehicle, has been largely at the expense of radio. Only a few years ago, radio stood undisputed as the main form of diversion in the American home. Enshrined in the living room, it was a major focus for family activity in the evening hours and a preferred source of news and entertainment. Today TV absorbs considerably more time and attention than radio did in its heyday.

TABLE 37	
	TV's Effects on Radio Listening
(Source: A. C. Nielsen Co.) March, 1956	
	Daily Hours Per Home
All Radio Homes	2.2
Radio-only Homes	3.3
Radios in TV Homes	1.8
TV-viewing in TV Homes	5.0

(A)

Surveys show that the public is highly aware that its interest in radio has slackened. In 1952, Harvey Zorbaugh and C. Wright Mills interviewed television owners in Metropolitan New York. Over half reported that they had stopped listening to the radio altogether —an exaggeration which is more interesting as a report on subjective sensation rather than on actual practice.

In 1948 the average family listened to the radio nearly 4.4 hours a day. (Part of this time represents individual listening, part of it group listening.) Now, the same average family listens 2.2

hours a day. In television homes, daily radio listening has dropped
to less than two hours. (See Tables 37, 38 and 39.)

TABLE 38

Average Hours of Daily Radio Listening, Per Radio Home

(Source: A. C. Nielsen Co.)

1943	3.6
1944	3.7
1945	4.1
1946	4.0
1947	4.3
1948	4.4
1949	4.2
1950	3.9
1951	3.4
1952	3.0
1953	2.7
1954	2.5
1955	2.3
1956	2.2

(B)

Even in homes which have no television set, radio listening
is down below its former levels. The families which still lack TV
today are below average in their general entertainment or media
interests.

TABLE 39

Radio Listening in Radio-Only and Television Homes

(Source: A. C. Nielsen Co.)

	Daily Listening Hours per Home	
	Radio-Only Homes	*TV Homes*
1951	4.0	2.0
1952	3.9	1.7
1953	3.9	1.7
1954	3.6	1.8
1955	3.4	1.8
1956	3.3	1.8

In the coming years, TV sets will enter more millions of American homes, and more and more television stations will come on the air. While no one is suggesting that this spells the end for *radio,* there have been dire predictions about the future of *network* radio.

In the New York Daily *News* of November 22, 1954, Ben Gross asks,

"Is network radio doomed? . . . Although no one wishes to be quoted, many leaders in the broadcasting field believe it is. One finds this sentiment echoed among executives, performers, sponsors and in the trade press, too. Some give network radio no more than a year or two. Naturally, for the sake of maintaining face, indignant denials are made in some quarters. Nevertheless, this is the picture as seen today by many observers."

The leading networks publicly admit that their radio operations are conducted at a loss, which must be offset by the profits earned from their ownership of major radio stations in the biggest cities, or from their television activities. To the pessimists who have suggested that the situation is irretrievable both Dr. Frank Stanton, President of CBS, and General David Sarnoff, Board Chairman of RCA, have issued strong denials.

General Sarnoff observed in a recent speech:

"I think I need not dwell upon the fact that if you were now making your will, and you had to decide on securities that you would select for your wife and children, for their sustenance and future after you are gone, that you are not likely to make that investment today in a radio network." But he later commented as follows: "We have no jitters about the radio network situation. Only last week, we met with a special committee of our affiliated radio stations and outlined NBC's intentions to proceed with practical evolutionary adaptations to meet radio's new requirements within the framework of the radio network business. This is the course on which we are set and we believe it holds out the best promise for an effective continuation of our radio network."

To buttress this position, the radio networks have been vigorously engaged in promotion and research designed to document and dramatize the assets of their medium.

One spokesman for radio has chided the industry for its defeatist mood in the face of television's advances. Says Gerhart Wiebe (formerly of CBS):

> "Radio has not yet recovered from the left to the chin it got from television. We in network radio are still fussing and complaining because a particular program commands an audience of *only* two or three or six or seven million people. Think of it! And this is not daily or weekly or bi-weekly or monthly circulation for the network. I am talking about the audience for a single fifteen or thirty minute show."

Is Anybody Listening?

In the average week 89% of America's 48,500,000 radio homes (C) listen to radio. During the average daytime minute, according to A. C. Nielsen data, there are 12,000,000 people listening at home; this decreases to 9,000,000 listeners during the average evening minute. Actually there are 6,500,000 home sets in use in the average daytime minute, with 1.8 listeners per set. In the evening average home set usage is 4,000,000 but there are more—2.2—listeners per set.

TV's inroads have been greatest in evening hours. Radio has shown its greatest strength in holding audiences at times when people are either least at leisure or most apt to be away from the living room, waking up, dressing, eating, driving, working, going to sleep.

Morning radio listening is at as high a level as it ever was. During almost all of the forenoon, more people listen to the radio than watch television. As a matter of fact, over half the listeners to daytime network radio shows are in TV homes; half of Arthur Godfrey's morning radio audience is in TV homes, even though his show is also on TV.

By contrast, with the decline in evening radio listening, the audiences of individual programs have steadily diminished. In 1948 the most popular evening program, "Lux Radio Theater," reached nearly 10,000,000 homes a week. In 1955 "Amos 'n Andy," the most successful evening radio show, reached only 3,400,000 homes. In 1948 the average evening radio program reached 4,800,000 homes. In 1955 it reached slightly more than 2,000,000 homes.

While almost all TV stations have network ties, about half of America's radio stations are affiliated with one of the four major networks. The radio networks have an overwhelmingly dominant position in the over-all listening pattern. In a recent analysis of listening preferences in 24 leading cities, CBS Radio found that, taking the 20 most popular programs in each city, 234 of the total 240 evening programs were network shows; 199 of the total 240 daytime shows.

However, since 1948 there has been a noticeable decrease in the networks' share of total radio listening, from 83% to 66% for evening radio, from 75% to 58% for daytime radio. Correspondingly, an increased proportion of all listening is now done to independent stations which tend to feature disc-jockeys, music and news, rather than the network type of radio programs which bear a closer resemblance to TV fare. (Table 40 traces the trend.)

TABLE 40

Networks' Share of All Radio Listening, 1948-56

(Adapted from A. C. Nielsen data)

| | Per Cent Listening to Network Programs, January | | |
	Morning	*Afternoon*	*Evening*
1948	78%	74%	83%
1949	78	73	85
1950	76	72	82
1951	75	71	82
1952	75	71	81
1953	74	70	79
1954	72	69	74
1955	67	63	71
1956	62	54	66

Of all local radio programming hours, 45% are in popular music, 12% in concert music, and 15% in "folk music," according to a survey of stations conducted by *Sponsor* magazine, 1955. 11% of program hours are in newscasts, and 17% in other types of programs.

Changes in Content of Network Programming

(D)   As the character of radio listening has altered, the content of network programs has also changed. It has become easier to listen to, and more distinctly different from TV programming. The content of sponsored network radio programs can be traced by the same method we employed for TV in Chapter 3, again looking at the classifications used by the A. C. Nielsen Company and making the necessary computations. Since radio has maintained its daytime audience, we have compared (in Table 41) the content of daytime as well as evening programs over a period of time going back to 1948.

TABLE 41

Changes in Sponsored Radio Network Program Content
(March)

(Based on A. C. Nielsen Program Categories)

	Daytime			
	1948	1950	1953	1955
News	1%	12%	11%	6%
Quiz, Audience Participation	25	15	20	22
Adult Serials	45	39	31	45
Concert Music	4	6	6	1
Variety Music	10	15	17	22
Popular Music	5	3	8	1
Children's Programs	10	10	7	3
Total*	100%	100%	100%	100%
	Evening			
News	14%	28%	40%	34%
Quiz, Audience Participation	7	6	8	4
Mystery Drama	15	18	11	11
General Drama	12	13	9	8
Concert Music	5	3	4	7
Variety Music	9	5	5	11
Popular Music	12	8	7	6
Variety Comedy	15	4	4	2
Situation Comedy	11	15	12	17
Total*	100%	100%	100%	100%

*Does not include sports, religious and other miscellaneous categories.

The emergence of television between 1948 and 1950 raised the percentage of sponsored radio and news programs on the networks from 1% to 12% in the daytime and from 14% to 28% at night. The proportion of evening news shows continued to rise until 1953, when they accounted for two of every five sponsored hours on the networks. In the last few years, news has lost position both in the evening and in the daytime.

Evening musical programs declined for several years, and then began to come back in their share of network time. News and music, understandably, gain relatively little by the addition of the visual element, and therefore may find it easier to compete with television

Daytime soap operas slipped after television entered the picture. They have regained their position in the last few years as advertisers have come to realize that they are continuing to hold their audience.

In general, quiz and audience participation shows have held their own both in the daytime and in the evening. Children's programs have declined since 1950.

Among the types of shows whose content is most closely duplicated by TV, evening radio dramatic programs have shown a sharp drop, particularly since 1950 when they hit their peak of sponsored network radio time. Variety-comedy shows have declined from 15% to 2% of evening network radio time. Situation comedies, which have risen on TV, also represent a greater proportion of the radio total than they did in 1948. In contrast with the relative stability of TV content in recent years, radio programming has undergone some major alterations.

In an attempt to revitalize network radio by providing a more flexible format for advertisers and listeners alike, the National Broadcasting Company launched "Monitor"—a continuous weekend programming arrangement—in the summer of 1955. Featuring frequent news, music, and special events and including a good many popular program of the traditional type, "Monitor" sought to break away from the conventional segmentalized schedule of earlier days while maintaining the network's preeminent position in the local affiliate station's broadcast time. This system has proved attractive to advertisers who wish to diffuse their messages at different times and to different segments of the radio audience at moderate cost. However, there is no evidence that "Monitor" has succeeded in increasing the amount of radio listening over the weekend. Nonetheless, NBC was sufficiently pleased with the success of its first venture with this "magazine" format so that it moved to extend it to the daytime scheduling during the week. The other networks have hewn more closely to the traditional programming pattern.

Radio's Two Audiences

The great dilemma faced by the radio industry today is that in effect it must simultaneously fulfill the functions of two different media. It is the primary medium of home entertainment for the one-fifth of all American families who do not have television. But it occupies a secondary place for the four-fifths who do own TV sets. The program requirements and needs of these two audiences are quite dissimilar.

If we look into the future we can only assume that, as television becomes as universal as radio (perhaps by 1960), the pattern of radio listening in America as a whole will be much like what it is now in the 41,000,000 television homes. But the broadcasting industry cannot guide its present policy by its expectations for the future. It must think of the vast audience of 25,000,000 people who do not now have television and who rely on radio for entertainment. Their needs have thus far kept evening network radio programming fairly close to its traditional pattern of dramatic, mystery, variety and audience participation shows, though the audience potential is much smaller.

In general, the radio-only listeners, as a group, spend less time with the mass media. The cream of radio's audience was skimmed away by TV at a relatively early stage. The first people to acquire television were those who had previously been the heaviest radio listeners.

In his report on what happens "When TV Moves In" (based

on surveys in Oklahoma), Lawton notes that purchasers of television, during its first year, were for the most part families with more radios at home than the average.

These findings find further corroboration in a survey made by Daniel Starch and Staff early in 1954, the results of which are shown in Table 42.

TABLE 42

Listening to Evening Radio in Television Homes

(Source: 1954 Starch Survey)

Length of TV Ownership	Per Cent Listening to Radio on Average Evening
Less than one year	16%
1-2 years	18
2-3 years	19
3-4 years	22
Five years or more	27

Here the results can be read two ways (either or both of which may be right): (1) the first to get television were the biggest radio fans—and are still relatively heavy listeners; (2) the longer people own television the more radio listening they are apt to do.

As a matter of fact, radio listening increases slightly as people get used to television, and as different members of the family watch TV and listen to radio separately, at the same time. The "Videotown" studies show that listening to the radio has increased every year since 1948 within television households, at the same time that television viewing has also increased. In ten percent of the television homes, both radio and TV sets were found to be tuned on simultaneously at some time in the day. A. C. Nielsen has found the same thing happening on a national scale, in the last two years.

Non-television homes (being smaller and not as well-to-do) actually have *fewer* radios than do the TV homes, though they listen to the radio more. However, 64% of the non-TV owners have their radios in the living room, compared with only 51% of the TV owners (according to Table 43, based on Politz's 1954 survey for the Advertising Research Foundation).

TABLE 43

Where Radio Sets Are Located in TV and Non-TV Homes

(Adapted from ARF-Politz Survey)

Per Cent Who Have a Radio in the	TV Homes	*Non-TV Homes*
Living Room	51%	64%
Bedroom	57	35
Kitchen	44	24
Dining Room	10	9
Den, Study, Library	4	2
Other Location	17	7
Automobile	71	40
Total Home Radios	1.8	1.5

A survey made in 1953 in Metropolitan New York by the Pulse, Inc., finds that the families with the greatest number of radios at home do the most listening (Table 44.) This is so in spite of the fact that these multi-radio families are more apt than the one or two-set families to own a television set as well. The explanation, very likely, is that these are larger families with a more than average interest in all the media.

TABLE 44

The More Radios at Home, the Most Listening

(Source: Pulse 1953 Metropolitan New York Survey)

Number of Radios	*Per Cent of All Radio Homes*	*Share of Radio Audience*	*6 AM to Midnight Homes Using Radio Average ¼ Hour*
One	33%	21%	13%
Two	28	27	19
Three or more	39	57	27
	100%	100%	

Some indication of how the television owner uses the two broadcast media for different purposes is seen in the findings of Whan's 1953 television survey in Kansas. The radio and television program preferences of TV owners are compared in Table 45.

Television receives more frequent mentions for the following types of programs: sports, comedians, drama, audience participation and variety shows (where the preference for it is most clearly marked).

Radio is favored for music of all kinds, market reports, farming talks and serial dramas, and it outdistances television by a narrow margin in the case of news programs.

Curiously enough, "talks and comment" appear to be more heavily preferred on television than on radio. Apparently the sight of the speaker's face does provide a desired extra dimension of personality which was lacking in radio commentary.

TABLE 45
A Comparison of the Radio and TV Program Preferences of TV Owners

(Source: Whan 1953 Kansas Survey)

	Men		Women	
	Radio	Television	Radio	Television
News broadcasts	80%	73%	75%	70
Sports broadcasts	52	70	24	41
Featured comedians	48	72	52	69
Popular music	47	23	59	32
Complete drama	38	67	39	68
Audience participation	32	47	44	57
Variety programs	28	60	38	60
Market reports	22	5	10	2
Serial drama	17	12	37	23
Oldtime music	16	10	15	9
Talks and comment	14	20	9	14
Talks on farming	14	10	6	3
Classical and semi-classical music	12	8	17	16
Religious music and devotionals	11	10	16	13
Brass band music	9	4	8	5
Homemaking programs	4	3	12	10

The music and news format into which radio has increasingly tended in its programming structure thus appears to have a foundation in listener tastes and expectations—or at least in the tastes and expectations of those listeners who have come to rely on television as the major source of their broadcast entertainment.

Radio's Continuing Vitality

For all its current woes, radio remains an extraordinary vital medium of communication. Four out of five people have TV at home. Four out of five read magazines and newspapers; but nearly every one has a radio. There are more and more radios all the time, an estimated total of 113,000,000. And there are more radio broadcasting stations now than ever before—3079 AM and 530 FM outlets in January 1957 (compared with 1522 AM and 158 FM stations operating in 1948, radio's peak year).

In 1956 alone (according to the Radio-Television Manufacturers' Association), 8,925,000 home radio sets were made, three-fifths of them portable and clock radios. In addition, 5,057,000 new radio-equipped cars set forth on the highways. That makes a total of 14,000,000 new radios—compared with 7,400,000 television sets made that year.

In May, 1955, interviews conducted by the Pulse, Inc., with 39,000 families in sixteen major cities, indicated that 8% had acquired at least one new home radio set in the preceding year and a half. Less than a third of these were replacements for existing sets. One of every four radios sold was for use as a gift. 63% of the sets purchased were table models, 29% were portables (though most of the latter are not used as portables).

Two-thirds of all U. S. households have two or more radios, including auto radios. (In Iowa, Whan found that the proportion of multi-set homes tripled between 1940 and 1954.) Two-thirds of the 54,000,000 passenger cars in America have radios, and these radios are *used*. They add over a third to the in-home radio audience at around five o'clock on weekday afternoons in winter months, as much as two-fifths on Saturday and Sunday afternoons (and this goes substantially higher in the summer). A survey made in 1954 by CBS-Radio (among motorists on the New Jersey Turnpike) indicates that people listen to much the same programs in their cars as at home.   (E)

Radio is everywhere (there are 10,000,000 sets in public places), or at least it can be taken anywhere. There are now about 12,000,000 portable radios, and these have steadily become smaller and more efficient, as a result of new developments in electronics—printed circuits, tiny tube-replacing transistors and miniature batteries with miraculously long lives. Radio has become a mobile, intimate and *personal* companion, while television replaces it as the center of *family* entertainment. For the TV set owner, listening to the radio today fills a different purpose and takes place under different circumstances than before television.

During the morning hours and at all mealtimes much listening takes place in the kitchen. In the afternoon, more of it takes place in the living room; by evening, the bulk of it. Two independent surveys conducted at about the same time produce similar findings:

A study made in 1953 for the Mutual Broadcasting System by J. A. Ward found that 37% of the morning listening took place in the living room and 40% in the kitchen. In the afternoon, 42% of the listening was in the living room, 31% in the kitchen. By evening, 53% of the radio listening was in the living room, 23% in the kitchen. (By 8 in the evening, Ward found, three-fourths of the home audience was at leisure, compared with only one in five between 11 AM and noon.)

In the winter of 1952-3, the research firm of Alfred Politz, Inc., in a study sponsored by the Henry I. Christal Company and a number of radio stations, interviewed nearly 5,000 persons aged fifteen and over in the areas covered by television (at that time inhabited by 61.6 million people in 26.7 million households). In the published findings of this survey no breakdown is made to distinguish television owners from non-owners. The results, therefore, are a composite of two different sets of activities and opinions, combined in a ratio characteristic only of that moment of time, — a ratio which would change as more homes acquired TV. Allowing for this limitation, the study sheds light on radio's new position.

Two years after his first survey, Politz conducted similar research in three areas in Michigan, Kentucky and upstate New York. His findings were much the same as in the first study.

Politz reports that in daylight hours, most listeners are engaged in other simultaneous activities (home chores, preparing food, eating or driving).In the evening, only 37% of the radio listeners are doing something else. The remainder are concentrating on their listening. Of the evening listeners, only 9% are reading at the same time;

6% are writing, sewing or studying; 4% are entertaining guests. Most of the other things which people do while they listen to the radio require very little mental effort. Only 16% of radio listening takes place at a time when attention is seriously diverted by another activity.

TABLE 46

Where Radio Is Heard at Different Times of the Day

(Source: 1953 Politz-Christal Study of Radio in TV Areas)

Men Who Listen to the Radio on an Average Day During the Period

	Between Waking and Breakfast	During Breakfast	Between Breakfast and Lunch	During Lunch	Between Lunch and Supper	During Supper	Between Supper and Going to Bed
Kitchen	45%	81%	12%	50%	15%	67%	14%
Living room	18	6	30	8	29	9	56
Bedroom	40	1	6	1	9	2	23
Dining room	5	8	4	7	5	23	4
Other place at home	7	—	3	4	5	1	4
In car, while driving	4	1	37	2	31	*	5
At work	2	*	14	13	13	1	1
Other places outside home	1	1	4	7	5	*	1
Don't remember where, no answer	2	4	4	10	3	2	2

Women Who Listen to the Radio on an Average Day During the Period

	Between Waking and Breakfast	During Breakfast	Between Breakfast and Lunch	During Lunch	Between Lunch and Supper	During Supper	Between Supper and Going to Bed
Kitchen	66%	80%	58%	68%	43%	64%	21%
Living room	14	6	38	10	46	13	55
Bedroom	32	3	24	4	19	3	22
Dining room	4	6	14	9	12	15	5
Other place at home	5	2	10	3	7	2	4
In car, while driving	*	—	2	*	4	—	1
At work	1	*	3	2	3	*	1
Other places outside home	1	1	2	4	3	2	3
Don't remember where, no answer	4	5	4	6	3	6	4

*Less than 1%

　　Listeners (especially younger and middle-aged persons) often cite as radio's chief advantage the fact that it does not require complete concentration, that it permits them to do other things at the same time. (In this connection, it should be noted that radio is hardly the only medium which must compete for attention with other activities. Its spokesmen point out that there may be an advantage for the advertiser to talk about soap powder or cake mix to a woman while she is in the act of doing her laundry or baking a cake, rather than while she is in the living room resting from her labors and trying to forget household drudgery.)

People look to radio primarily for entertainment and for information, according to the Politz findings. When asked, "Why do you have a radio?", 45% of the respondents say that radio's main function is to provide entertainment, relaxation or enjoyment, and an equal number say its main function is to give the news. In total, 70% give reasons which refer to radio's entertainment features and an almost equal number (66%) give reasons referring to its information features. Younger and older people are most apt to say that entertainment and relaxation are the most important reasons why they have a radio, while middle-aged people stress news. Not surprisingly, persons of better-than-average education and income are most apt to stress the educational or informational advantages.

When people are asked what they like most about listening to the radio, 42% (and an even higher proportion of the younger people) say they like music best. 32% mention news, 13% mention stories or plays, 11% give general entertainment reasons.

"Too much advertising" is radio's most frequently mentioned unfavorable feature, volunteered especially by those of above-average education and income.

Respondents were asked which medium they consider best for keeping up with the news and for sports coverage. Politz does not report the answers to these questions, but he indicates that those people who like radio news best primarily cite its speed and its convenient availability.

People who prefer radio for sports coverage cite its play-by-play accurate reporting, or note that it covers more sports than television does.

Radio's chief disadvantage, as reported by Politz's respondents, is that it is less entertaining than television, because it can only be heard. This reason is most often voiced by younger people who are less familiar with radio as it existed in the pre-television era.

Radio is now considered a necessity more than a luxury, while television is overwhelmingly considered a luxury item. (Respondents were presented with a list of household items and asked (1) "Which of these things does your family happen to have now?" (2) "Which of these things do you consider a necessity?" (3) "Which of these things do you consider a luxury?") The results are shown in Table 47.

TABLE 47

How Household Items Are Classified as "Necessities" or "Luxuries"

(Source: 1953 Politz-Christal Study of Radio in TV Areas)

	Have Item in Home	Consider Item a "Necessity"	Consider Item a "Luxury"
Radio	95%	49%	31%
Refrigerator (not ice box)	93	85	5
Bathtub	85	82	6
Telephone	79	71	14
Washing Machine	76	73	12
Television	72	23	66
Automobile	71	58	27
Sewing Machine	60	51	19
Home Freezer	9	10	62
Air Conditioner	3	6	69
Electric Dishwasher	3	4	74

The indispensability of radio in an era dominated by television is well described by William McPhee and Rolf Meyersohn who in 1955 directed a study on "The Future of Radio" for the National Broadcasting Company. McPhee and Meyersohn note that radio's present uses cannot be separated from its past history:

"A radio was once only a radio, but after people have spent a generation weaving it into their lives, it is many things—an alarm clock to wake people up pleasantly, a kind of morning newspaper to bury one's thoughts in at breakfast, a travelling companion in the car, a day-long visitor to help pass the drearier hours of the day for a housewife, an education for the woman who learns about life from soap operas, a game of suspense for the up-to-the-minute news follower or sports fan, a record player for teenagers, a partisan ritual for the avid follower of Fulton Lewis, Jr., a Muzak sound system for people whose moods respond to music, a prized personal possession for a child, and so on through many more. The uses to which people put a device even include contradictory ones, as for example, when insomniacs use the same radio program to go to sleep to as drowsy drivers use to help keep awake!"

In McPhee's survey (conducted by the Columbia University Bureau of Applied Social Research), intensive interviews were made with over two hundred television-owning families in half-a-dozen cities. Radio listening in TV homes, the findings suggest, takes either a "random" or "reference" form.

By "random" listening, McPhee refers to the constant flux of the radio audience which listen in odd bits of free time scattered throughout the week, and which contrasts with the "loyal, regular" audience that major evening radio programs received in their heyday. One housewife's remarks illustrate this type of listening pattern:

"It's only occasionally that I can have it on (kid's programs on TV interfere), but I do like to have a music program then. Just soft music, low volume. I don't know what station, perhaps WLW but I can't say for sure . . . No special program, just music and news. They come on and I don't know what station or what recording it is most of the time (but) I always enjoy music when I work or rest."

"Reference" listening, by contrast, describes the use of radio for a specific purpose, as in the case of the individual who has a clock radio bring on classical music to wake him up, or the one who knows he can always get the news on the hour on a certain station.

The great advantage of radio, in the opinion of the persons interviewed in this study, is that it permits the listener to do other things while he listens. As one woman puts it, radio is something that "you let run continuously" all day. Another housewife says:

"I don't like housework. It's revolting. Radio makes my work go faster and makes it less revolting. I don't think about it so much. I like the disc jockey programs with popular recordings."

McPhee goes on to suggest that the possibilities for expanding radio listening involve the possibility of developing programs other than those of the disc-jockey type which are still suitable to multiple-activity listening.

McPhee compares the survival of radio alongside television to the parallel existence of silent films and the talkies. He points out that television often "takes away something" when it adds sight to sound. At breakfast, supper, on rising or retiring, most people he interviewed prefer nothing more than a radio:

"There is no question that the picture and voice of Dave Garroway is more entrancing at breakfast than that of the harassed family bread-winner stumbling off to work, nor is there any serious doubt that Dinah Shore is more eye-filling than the family housewife serving the potatoes at suppertime. Nevertheless, among many modern families, there is a profound — almost instinctive — resistance to television at such times . . . Who would really like to see a Max Liebman spectacular in full color — if he were just getting out of bed in the early dark of a winter workday, or greeting his children and wife after an absence, or turning a fine piece of machinery on a factory lathe, or washing the dishes and making beds on Tuesday morning? In every one of these instances, an unobtrusive radio would not be out of place, but the full impact of the 'best' entertainment that television can offer—that would be self-defeating."

It is evident that radio continues to be used and to be useful in even the most avid television home. People will turn eagerly to radio when TV fails to cover some event of extraordinary interest. The Marciano-Moore heavyweight championship fight, in 1955, was heard by 12,225,000 families (27% of the total.)

Because of its greater flexibility, radio is less seasonal a medium than television. (Viewing of evening television programs dips in the summertime when people spend more time outdoors. But radio's summer audiences are almost the same size as in winter. This was seen in Table 24, Chapter 4.)

Because of its greater economy of operation, radio can offer programming directed to audiences too small for TV to touch — foreign language groups and other minorities, specialized professional, occupational, hobby and other groups. More than ever before, radio stations are now broadcasting at odd hours (for example, all through the night) to catch segments of the audience which were formerly not considered important. Just as television is especially useful in demonstrating and depicting the concrete, so radio has a peculiar capacity to set a mood and to convey abstract messages persuasively.

7. TELEVISION AND READING

Television's effects on books, magazines and newspapers, are harder to trace than its effects on radio. Radio and television audiences are measured by the same or similar methods, and exact comparisons can be made of the amount of listening and viewing. But no such common denominator exists between TV viewing and reading. During the post-war years of television's great growth, the total circulation of magazines and newspapers has also continued to grow, and more books have been sold than ever before. But there is no way of knowing whether or not the growth of the print media might have been even greater had television not appeared on the scene.

In measuring the effects of television we are faced with a limitation in the available evidence. Only two major studies have traced the influence of TV by questioning the same people at different points in time, before and after some of them acquired television sets. (This procedure, in research terms, is known as the "panel" technique of observing change in attitude or behavior.) The great bulk of the numerous studies of this general subject entail a comparison of TV set-owners and non-owners, interviewed only once, and at the same time. If the owners and non-owners were exactly alike in every respect except that of television ownership, conclusions could be drawn readily from this sort of evidence. But the fact of the matter is that they are not exactly alike, and one of the ways in which they differ is in their interest in all the mass media—TV apart.

When we try to determine the impact of television upon print, we face a familiar problem in tracing cause and effect. The first people to acquire television sets were drawn from the ranks of those who read the most to begin with. The pioneer TV owners were above average in education and income. This means that they were more apt than the average person to have acquired the habit of reading, and also that they were better able to afford the expense of buying periodicals and books.

Direct comparisons of the reading habits of TV and non-TV owners often yielded results which were difficult to interpret, since the TV owners read more before television, but were also more likely to have their reading interfered with.

From the very beginning of TV, studies of its impact have indicated strongly that reading as an activity had suffered even among the formerly heavy readers who made up the early television public:

1. Coffin, in his pioneer study (1948) of TV's effects in Long Island, found set owners reading eighteen hours a week, compared with twenty-one hours for the non-owners.

2. In McDonagh's 1950 study of a Southern California town, over two-thirds of the television owners said they were reading less than they did formerly, compared with less than a fourth of those without television sets.

3. A study made the same year in the Detroit area by Walter Kaiser found that two-fifths of the television owners said they were reading less than formerly.

4. In the study of Metropolitan New York made in 1951 by Zorbaugh and Mills, 49% of the television owners reported that they had stopped reading books, 24% magazines, 3% Sunday newspapers, and 2% daily newspapers. (Although limited in geographic scope, this was the first study of the subject which employed both a large and well-designed sample and also sophisticated techniques of analyzing the data.)

5. Nancy Faulkner, interviewing Bloomington, Indiana, housewives in 1954, found that those who owned television said their book and magazine reading had been cut in half.

This is slender evidence both because these studies (except for the one by Zorbaugh and Mills) are modest in scale, and because retrospective judgments are apt to be far from accurate. However, all the signs point the same way, and studies of individual print media also tell a consistent story.

Television and Book Reading

An important distinction must be drawn between books and other forms of reading matter, to which our previous discussion of "media-mindedness" applies more directly.

In their 1945 and 1947 researches on "Radio Listening in

America," Lazarsfeld and Kendall found that among those who read at least one magazine regularly, only 22% listened to the radio for less than one hour in the evening, compared with 30% of those who did not read magazines. However, such differences did not appear when listening habits were compared for those people who read books and those who did not.

This finding can be explained in the light of a study of Book of the Month Club members which Lazarsfeld had made some years before. At that time he reported that people who read many books also read a high proportion of serious books, whereas in the case of radio the heaviest listeners listened to the lowest proportion of serious programs.

This suggests two contradictory tendencies at work when we analyze the relation between book reading and radio listening or television viewing. On the one hand are the better educated, more serious book readers, whose tastes are sufficiently cultivated or specialized so that the bulk of broadcast fare is uninteresting to them; they were light radio listeners and are now light television viewers. On the other hand are those persons who read books largely for light entertainment and who are, like the heavy magazine readers, among the more avid listeners and watchers.

While these two contrasting groups represent extremes which shade into each other, they apparently exist in sufficiently similar numbers so that they cancel each other out when they are averaged together. This might explain why the listening (and now perhaps the viewing) of all book readers resembles that of the remaining three-fourths of the population who do not read at least one book a month.

In Boston (1951) Fine and Maccoby found that television owners reported spending about two hours reading on the average weekday, while the non-owners claimed to spend only 1.2 hours reading. Nonetheless, only 22% of the television owners were in the middle of reading a book at the time of the survey, compared with 31% of the non-owners.

The television owners spent less time on books, but apparently more with newspapers and magazines. The explanation may run like this: At this phase of television's growth, TV was owned predominantly by people who were strongly attached to all of the *popular* media but who were not necessarily serious book readers. The non-television owners included many "high-brow" heavy book readers who eschewed both TV and the popular magazines; they also included many people of below-average education who did very little reading of any kind.

Some corroboration for this theory may be found in Zorbaugh and Mills' study of television's impact on Metropolitan New York. Television owners who had had their sets for some time did more magazine reading than either the more recent owners or the people who lacked TV. They also read more books than did the newer set owners, but no more than the non-owners. (See Table 48.)

TABLE 48

Length of TV Set Ownership and Reading Habits

(Source: Puck Survey, New York Metropolitan Area, 1951)

| | *TV Owners* | | |
	For 2 Years or More	*For Less Than 2 Years*	*Non-Owners*
Read one or more magazines regularly	60%	51%	52%
Read one or more books in last month	34%	27%	35%

An interpretation can be given along these lines: The pioneer television owners were those who had listened to the radio most and who also read the most magazines. They were above average in income, but were concentrated in the middle educational brackets. As time went on, television became accessible to more and more people of lower income and education, who read fewer books and magazines. But a substantial number of better-educated persons, including the heaviest book readers, continued as hold-outs, at least up to 1951, when the study was made.

It should be noted that Zorbaugh and Mills report the better-educated no exception to their general conclusion that television has cut into book-reading. They found that 35% of the non-TV owners had read a book or more during the preceding month, while only

29% of the television owners had done so. However the median individual in both groups read the same number of books in a month: 2.2. While college educated persons read more books than the average, 47% of the set owners among them had not read a book in the preceding month, compared with 30% of the non-owners.

Lawton's study of the effects of television in Norman and Oklahoma City shows a somewhat different pattern, perhaps reflecting a difference in the kind of books read in these smaller cities, compared with Boston and New York. The people who acquired television in its first year in those communities were the very ones who had done the most reading in the first place. Before television they bought more newspapers and magazines, but they also read an average of .57 books each month, compared with .28 for the people who did not subsequently get television (see Table 49).

In spite of this initial lead, Lawton found television cutting into book reading as an activity, when he repeated his interviews six months and a year after the inauguration of TV service. The pattern of results in Norman, Lawton's other test city, was highly similar.

TABLE 49

Television Ownership and Book Reading in Oklahoma City, 1949-50

(Source: Lawton Oklahoma Survey)

| | Books Read per Month | |
	Television Owners	Non-Owners
Before TV	0.57	0.28
Six Months After TV	0.33	0.20
One Year After TV	0.15	0.29

Other studies of varying professional calibre have documented the inroads of television on book reading:

1. In his study in New York (1948), Goldberg found less book-reading was reported after television than before.

2. In a survey of 1580 persons who had responded to television offers by the Duane Jones Company (1949), three out of five reported that they were reading fewer books than formerly.

3. Half of 133 television families interviewed the same year by James Jump said they were reading fewer books.

4. In Washington (1950), Alldredge found three out of ten reporting less book reading than before.

5. McGraw-Hill, surveying 940 subscribers to business publications (1951), found that 36% of the television owners said they had read a book the previous day, compared with 46% of the non-owners.

6. In 1951, a mail questionnaire sent out by the advertising firm of Batten, Barton, Durstine and Osborn to 5,657 persons in cities and towns, inquired "What's Happening to Leisure Time in Television Homes?" In this case, the percentage who had done any book reading in the previous month was higher (32%) among non-television owners than among those who owned television (23%). The non-owners who read books also claimed to spend more time with them—an hour and thirty-four minutes daily, compared with an hour and seventeen minutes for the TV owners.

7. In Atlanta, Stewart (1951) found only 8% of the television owners, compared with 13% of the non-owners, stating that their book reading had increased in the preceding year. However slightly more television owners (34%) than non-owners (28%) said they had read a book in the two month period before they were interviewed. (The difference is barely significant in the statistical sense.) Nine per cent of the women interviewed said they had "dispensed with all types of book reading because they claim that television viewing is now taking all the time that was once spent in this manner." The author notes that of the great majority who reported "no effect" on their book reading, a good many were not book readers to begin with.

8. Donald Johnson (1954) studied the book-borrowing habits of 123 TV owners and 208 non-owners in the Free Public Library of Montclair, New Jersey. He found that set owners used the library 22% less after they acquired sets, and they also used the library less than did people who had not acquired sets by the middle of 1951. The loss was not in the percentage who used the library, but in the number of books the borrowers withdrew. The decline was just as pronounced among college graduates as among other persons, though

it seemed to affect older people more than younger ones. Johnson also reports indications that television's adverse effect on reading diminishes about a year after the set is acquired.

9. Mary Peerless (1954) submitted a questionnaire to 500 borrowers in the public library branch at Elmhurst, Queens, a middle-class New York City neighborhood. Three out of five who owned television reported their reading habits had changed "to some degree" since they had acquired a set, and 6% said they had changed greatly. Older people, and persons holding clerical and sales jobs were most apt to say their reading habits had not changed at all. About three borrowers in ten said they were reading fewer books than previously, but one in eight claimed to be reading more.

(A)

The story revealed by these surveys is parallelled by developments in the publishing business.

Groff Conklin, writing on "Rental Libraries: Problems and Prospects" for the *Publishers' Weekly* of April 24, 1954, reported that the average rental library's gross income had dropped by 50% since 1948. A mail survey of over 100 bookstores found 41% blaming television for the decrease in business, while 30% mentioned pocket books.

In spite of this grim conclusion, publishers continue to put out more titles each year and to sell more copies of their hard-bound books. The American Book Publishers Council, Inc., reports an increase in dollar sales from $421,900,000 in 1947 to $663,500,000 in 1953.

(B)

It is interesting to note that publishers report both a lessening public demand for fiction, and also a decline in the proportion of novels submitted to them by authors. While the underlying reasons for this trend must be sought in the temper of the times, television may well have something to do with it. TV competes with books in the area of fiction and fantasy entertainment, but hardly at all in the sphere of information. Between 1946 and 1955 the number of new fiction titles published grew at only half the rate of non-fiction.

(C)

The book industry has been revolutionized, during the very period of television's growing influence, by the increasing popularity of paper-bound pocket books. (In 1947, 95.5 million paper-bounds were sold; by 1953 the number was 292 million.)

Television—like motion pictures and radio before it—stimulates curiosity in a diverse range of subjects among people who do only a limited amount of reading. Librarians report that children frequently ask for books on subjects in which their interest has been aroused through watching a television program. Television's unique capacity to make complex information understandable and exciting may lead people to look further into subjects which had not previously seemed interesting or important to them.

Of the borrowers in a New York City branch library, 11% said, in answer to a direct question raised by Peerless, that they had at one time or another reserved a book at the library because they had heard it discussed on television. This might well be an exaggerated claim. We must take with similar caution the report, by 15% of the borrowers, that they had sought out books by authors they had seen on television. 17% checked "yes" in answering the question, "Have you ever seen a TV drama adapted from a famous book or short story and later obtained the title for reading?" High school and college students most often answered this question affirmatively. 44% of the borrowers said they had at some time "wished to know more about a subject you heard discussed on television." The subjects most often mentioned were science, social studies and sports.

Recently, Quincy Mumford (who is Librarian of Congress and President of the American Library Association) sent questionnaires to 38 leading libraries; "there was general consensus that an active policy regarding television has visible results. Calls for books mentioned in telecasts; general communications about programs; greater attendance at library activities could be attributed to the television programs."

Library book circulation has continued to rise in the post-war years, primarily in non-fiction. If the libraries are flourishing, it may (D) very well be that this is neither in spite of television, nor because of it, but because of the great distinctness of function between the oldest mass medium and the newest.

Television and Magazine Reading

Of all the print media, magazines most clearly reflect the influence of television's presence. While magazines are read by about four Americans in five, the better educated and better-off do the most magazine reading, and they, of course, were the first to get TV.

Magazines feel the competition of television more seriously than newspapers do. Newspaper reading is a daily ritual, typically associated with certain transition periods in the day. Magazines are read less frequently and with less regularity. They have less immediacy and urgency than newspapers do, and therefore are in more direct conflict with television as a medium of entertainment.

As in the case of book reading, a number of miscellaneous studies show a similar pattern of declining readership as television enters the picture. However, where TV owners and non-owners are compared in these surveys, it is apparent in many cases that the "media-minded" people who first acquired television were a heavy magazine-reading group.

1. A decline in magazine reading was reported by half the television owners interviewed by Duane Jones (1949), by two-fifths of those surveyed by Jump (1949) and by one-fourth in Alldredge's study (1950).

2. In 1950 a mail survey of Omnibook subscribers revealed that 69% of the television owners were subscribing to four magazines or more, compared with 52% of the non-owners.

3. In the same year a survey made by Macfadden Publications in two midwestern cities found that television owners read slightly more magazines than non-owners, averaging 2.0 per family, compared with 1.8 for the non-owners. However, 22% of the television owners reported that they were reading less magazines than they did the year previously.

4. The B.B.D.O. mail survey came up with a different set of findings: 69% of those in homes without television reported reading weekly magazines, compared with 60% of the set owners. Moreover, among the magazine readers, more time was spent reading in the non-television households (an hour and 12 minutes) than in the television households (59 minutes).

5. A survey of 1200 New York television owners made by Young & Rubicam (1951) reported that magazine reading fell off 20%, on the average, after the TV set was bought.

6. The study made in Atlanta by Stewart (1951) showed the

TV owners to be heavy readers. About half read three magazines or more; only a third of the non-television group read as many. Yet 38% of the television owners and only 30% of the non-owners reported they were reading magazines less than they had the year previously.

7. Zorbaugh and Mills' New York survey found virtually no differences between the two groups. 54% of the television owners read magazines regularly, and the median time spent on them was 59 minutes a week. Among non-owners, 52% read magazines, and the median time spent on them was an hour and four minutes weekly.

8. A nationwide mail survey conducted in 1952 by the National Family Opinion Poll found that 36% of the housewives in television homes had not read a magazine in the past 24 hours. Only 43% had spent an hour or more reading a magazine. By contrast, in non-TV homes, only 24% had not read a magazine, and 61% had spent an hour or more reading.

9. In Lexington, Kentucky, (1953) McGeehan and Maranville found that the average number of weekly hours spent with magazines was 4.2 per person weekly; the same women reported an average of 4.8 hours per week had been spent reading magazines before television. The number of magazine subscriptions reportedly had declined from an average of 3.4 before TV to an average of 3.2 afterwards.

By contrast with most of the studies thus far reported, many of which were made on limited budgets and used samples of only limited scope, a highly accurate and large national sample was employed in the survey made by Willard Simmons in 1953 for the Crowell-Collier Publishing Company. In this survey the average reading time was noted in both television and non-television households for a number of leading magazines. This study, made at a time when television had passed beyond the pioneer phase and had already clearly become a national mass medium, showed very small but persistent and reliable differences which indicated that readership had been affected. The findings are summarized in Table 50.

Two surveys made under Coffin's direction for the National Broadcasting Company showed the same story with even more dramatic effect. The first was a study which compared the leisure-time (and buying) habits of a probability sample of 5,067 television owners and non-owners in Metropolitan New York in 1952. (Both male and female heads of households were interviewed.) This study includes a careful and comprehensive analysis of television's effects on magazines and newspapers.

TABLE 50

Magazine Reading Time (Per Issue) in TV and Non-TV Homes

(Source: W. R. Simmons National Survey, 1952)

Magazine	TV Owners	Non-Owners
Collier's	1 hr. 24 min.	1 hr. 34 min.
Life	1 hr. 8 min.	1 hr. 24 min.
Post	1 hr. 25 min.	1 hr. 58 min.
Look	1 hr. 4 min.	1 hr. 13 min.
Average	1 hr. 12 min.	1 hr. 29 min.

Again the familiar pattern emerged. The total amount of time spent reading magazines on the day before the interview was found to be nearly eleven minutes among individuals who had television at home. It was fifteen minutes for non-owners. Of those who actually had spent some time "yesterday" reading magazines, television owners had spent an average of 47 minutes; the non-owners had spent 54 minutes.

Going further, Coffin compared completely "unexposed" individuals in non-TV homes who were matched with the television sample with respect to sex, age, family size, education, income and area of residence. With this careful control, almost identical results were obtained: eleven minutes daily for the TV owners, sixteen for the non-owners. On the average day, 23% of the television owners had spent some time reading magazines; among the matched non-owners the proportion was 27%.

The differences between television owners and the entire (unmatched) group of non-owners persisted at every level of age, income and education, even though these factors are independently related to the amount of magazine reading. This can be seen in Table 51.

TABLE 51

Time Spent Reading Magazines by Owners and Non-Owners

(Source: NBC Metropolitan New York Survey, 1952)

	Minutes per Person per Day	
Age	*TV Owners*	*Non-Owners*
18-29	12	17
30-39	12	15
40-49	10	15
50 +	8	13
Income		
$100-3,000	7	12
$3,001-4,000	10	12
$4,001-5,000	11	17
$5,001 +	15	22
Education		
Grammar School	5	8
Some High School	8	13
Completed High School	12	17
College	18	24

To see whether reading habits changed as television became an established feature in the home, Coffin compared the time spent with magazines each day by new and old TV owners (Table 52). Since he knew that people of above-average income were the first to acquire sets, and were also more apt to be heavy readers, Coffin broke his results down by low and high income groups. As Table 52 reveals, he found practically no differences in reading time between old and new set owners in the low income bracket, but among those of above-average income he found that the pioneer TV fans were doing more reading than those who had acquired sets within the past year.

These figures could suggest two possible explanations, both of which may be correct: (1) that the first to acquire TV were most strongly interested in *all* the popular media, and (2) that as time went on, television owners were finding time for more additional activities.

Why was the same pattern not found for the persons of below-average income? The novelty effect of television on reading may have been less for this group since they did less reading in the first place. Moreover, it is possible that at the lower-income level, pioneer television ownership was more a matter of ability to afford a set, or of family size, than it was of "media-mindedness."

TABLE 52

Time Spent Reading Magazines by Length of TV Ownership

(Source: NBC Metropolitan New York Survey, 1952)

	Minutes per Person per Day		
	TV Owners With Incomes Under $4000	*TV Owners With Incomes Over $4000*	*All TV Owners*
Less than 1 year	8	11	10
1-2 years	8	14	11
More than 2 years	9	15	13

In another study directed by Coffin for the National Broadcasting Company (1953-4), interviews were conducted in 6554 homes in Fort Wayne, Indiana, just before, and again six months after, that town acquired its own television station.

Thus a comparison could be made of the time spent on magazines (1) by people who already had sets which were tuned to distant stations before the local one came on the air, (2) people who acquired sets after the local station opened, (3) people who occasionally watched television over friends' sets, and (4) people who were for practical purposes unexposed to television altogether.

Before television appeared on the local scene, the new set owners spent about the same amount of time reading magazines as those who later remained unexposed to TV (17 minutes daily for the new TV owners, 16 for the unexposed). After television, the set owners reported only 10 minutes of daily magazine reading, while the unexposed showed virtually no change (17 minutes). Again, television appeared to have reduced the amount of magazine reading time, though perhaps not as dramatically as is indicated by the rough answers which respondents are apt to give to this sort of question.

In their continuing studies of "Videotown", Cunningham and

Walsh's researchers reported a 53% drop in the number of adults reading a magazine during their first year with television. However, in 1953 magazine reading was 5% higher than in television's first year, and it jumped by another 70% in 1954. This revival of interest in reading parallels a revival of other activities as television approaches complete saturation of the community and loses its overwhelming novelty.

Trends in Magazine Circulation and Content

The "Videotown" findings suggest that magazines may recover the losses in reader interest which have been inflicted by television. But reader interest is not immediately reflected by the trend in circulation figures. An individual's changing habits of readership may be reflected more in the amount of time he spends with magazines rather than in the number he buys.

Since television appeared on the scene, circulation has continued to grow, but the rate of its growth has slowed up in recent years; in the last few years it has failed to keep pace with the increase in population.

A smaller proportion of magazine circulation today represents independent purchase decisions by the ultimate readers, and more of it represents habitual exposure. At the war's end about half of all magazine copies were sold on the newsstand. In 1954, the percentage had declined to 38. Part of this transformation may have been due to the trend toward suburban living (with less frequent access to newsstands) or the increased level of income (which made the price of a subscription a smaller investment). But it seems likely that television too had something to do with the change. (E)

A more striking indication of television's effects may be seen by comparing the pattern of circulation growth in metropolitan areas and in the remainder of the country. The original heavy growth of television was in the metropolitan areas, and TV growth in the smaller cities and towns developed momentum only after the lifting of the F.C.C. "freeze" on new stations in 1952.

As Table 53 suggests, between 1946 and 1952 magazine circulation grew only slightly, (and actually declined relative to population growth) in cities over 100,000, while it soared in the rest of the country. In the last few years, however, the non-metropolitan areas have come within reach of television, and magazine circulations have fallen there, while they have begun to recover in the bigger cities.

TABLE 53

Changes in the Circulation of Top 30 General Magazines*
1946-1954

Magazine Circulation	Single Issue Circulation (in millions)			Per Cent Increase		
	1946	1952	1954	1946-52	1952-54	1946-54
Cities over 100,000	17.75	19.16	20.48	8%	7%	18%
Other places	30.67	37.75	40.96	23	9	33
Total	48.42	59.91	61.44	18	9	28
U.S. Civilian Population**	138.34	153.32	160.44	11%	4%	19%

*This table is partly based on data supplied by the Magazine Advertising Bureau, and covers the following major magazines:

**The rate of population growth has been approximately the same in metropolitan and non-metropolitan areas.

American Home	Living for Young Homemakers
American Magazine	Look
Better Homes & Gardens	Mademoiselle
Collier's	McCall's Magazine
Cosmopolitan	Newsweek
Esquire	New Yorker
Fortune	Outdoor Life
Glamour	Popular Science Monthly
Good Housekeeping	Redbook Magazine
Harper's Bazaar	Saturday Evening Post
House Beautiful	Time
House & Garden	Town & Country
Household	Town Journal
Ladies' Home Journal	Vogue
Life	Woman's Home Companion

(F)

Since television is primarily an entertainment medium, with most of its programming time devoted to drama of one sort or another, it might be expected that those magazines which would suffer most from its inroads would be those which are primarily entertaining rather than informational in character. A breakdown of circulation figures for magazines of various types indicates that this is indeed so. The smallest gains were recorded by the great general weeklies and bi-weeklies and the general monthlies, whose fiction picture stories, human interest articles and other features of broad appeal bear a generic resemblance to much television programming. Subsequent to this analysis, the demise of *Colliers'* and *American* further reduced the strength of the general magazines.

The greatest gains in circulation were made by magazines which offer information more than entertainment, and particularly those with a definitely specialized character, which cater to tastes, interests and needs which television, because of its very massive character, cannot possibly provide. (See Table 54.)

TABLE 54

Changes in Circulation of Different Magazine Categories

(Based on A.B.C. circulation data)

	% Increase 1940-1946	% Increase 1940-1954	% Increase 1946-1954
General Weeklies (and Bi-Weeklies)	+ 26%	+ 67%	+ 33%
News Weeklies	+ 99	+176	+ 39
Other Weeklies—Small Town	− 23	+ 37	+ 77
Other Weeklies—Big Town	+ 64	+132	+ 41
Women's Service	+ 19	+ 39	+ 17
Grocery Store Women's	+ 61	+278	+135
General Women's Monthlies	+ 46	+ 69	+ 16
Men's Monthlies	+136	+324	+ 80
General Monthlies	+ 18	+ 61	+ 36
Fraternal Monthlies	+ 60	+138	+ 49
Class Monthlies	+ 32	+153	+ 91
Literary-Political Reviews	+ 97	+392	+150
Home	+ 37	+116	+ 58
Fashion	+194	+320	+ 43
Business	+ 37	+106	+ 51
Youth	+ 82	+186	+ 57
Outdoor and Sports	+ 32	+133	+ 76
Mechanics and Science	+ 62	+141	+ 49
Farm	+ 1	+ 31	+ 29
Negro Magazines	—	—	+281
Romance	+ 66	+ 48	− 11
Screen-Radio-TV	+146	+249	+ 42
Picture Magazines	+170	+ 65	− 39
Total	+ 40%	+101%	+ 44%

NOTE: Figures represent December 30th, ABC reports on all magazines published each year.

One interesting trend in circulation is apparent when magazines are grouped into several different cultural or intellectual levels. In this crude classification they can be called "high brow," "middle brow," and "not too-middle brow." This might put the *Atlantic* at one end of the continuum and *True Confessions* at the other.

High-brow magazines more than doubled circulation between 1946 and 1954. In fact, the higher the intellectual level, the greater the growth. The great mass of general circulation or middle-brow magazines grew by about half. Magazines appealing to the *least* educated element stayed at about the same circulation level. Non-ABC magazines, many of which are at the lower levels of taste, dropped a fourth of their circulation, and comic books are struggling to hold their own. At least a partial explanation for this development is that television presents a greater distraction for the person of average or below-average education than for the better-schooled, who are also less apt to be repelled by the printed word.

We can study circulation figures from another angle. Magazines appealing mainly to women did not grow as fast as those appealing mainly to men or to the whole family. Here television is probably at least partly to blame, since daytime TV programming, with its serial drama, variety and homemaking features, bears an unmistakable resemblance to a good deal of magazine fare.

The influence of television can be traced in magazine content as well as in circulation. Monthly reports prepared by the Lloyd Hall organization provide an analysis of editorial matter for leading general magazines. From these reports it is possible to discern the trends in magazine content during the years which coincide with television's great growth.

There are two noteworthy changes: (1) There is a striking decrease in the amount of fiction carried by all types of publications. This parallels the developments in the book field, already described. (2) Magazines with a special informational character or function, like farming publications, homemaking magazines, or *Popular Science* and its competitors, are becoming more specialized. They all appear to be devoting less space to extraneous matters and more to their
(G)   central editorial subjects.

Television, like radio or the movies, competes directly with magazines and books as a source of fantasy and of dramatic identification and excitement. It is no wonder that, since the war, magazines have steadily reduced the amount of fiction which they carry. This is only in part due to the strong diet of TV drama on which the magazine-reading public daily feeds. It also reflects the increased popularity of the inexpensive paper-bound book. To meet both these threats, magazines have become more and more specialized. Yet taken altogether the changes in content parallel the trends in circulation for magazines of different types and they are exactly the sort of changes which the competition of television might have influenced.

Television and Newspaper Reading

Television's effects on newspaper reading are, from all the evidence, less pronounced than its impact on magazine or book reading. A whole series of studies document this point, though they also suggest that newspapers are not completely immune to the new influence.

1. Studies which asked television owners whether they were reading newspapers less than formerly produced a response similar to that for book and magazine reading—though the reported decline in newspaper reading was of a much lesser order. Of the TV owners interviewed by Duane Jones (1949), one in four said he was reading newspapers less than formerly. Jump (1949) reported one in five slackening readership, Alldredge (1950) only one in twenty. Young and Rubicam (1951) report one in four dropping in readership of evening papers, but no change for the morning press.

2. In Oklahoma, Lawton found that television set owners read more newspapers than non-owners, but that the most avid viewers took fewer papers than the TV owners who spent less time with their sets.

This can be explained as follows: The TV owners, being a better educated group on the whole, read more papers to begin with. However, the most highly educated TV owners do more reading, but less viewing, than do those at the middle educational level. The latter group read less, but are more apt to be strong television fans.

The same study found no evidence that television owners were spending less time with their daily newspapers than they did before acquiring television. They spent about the same amount of time reading papers as did the people who had only radios at home. Moreover, the families who took only one or two papers a day spent almost as much time reading them as did the families who took three or four. In short, television appeared to have no direct effects on newspaper reading.

3. Similarly, in Atlanta, Stewart found that television owners and non-owners alike reported they were reading the newspaper "more thoroughly" than they had done three years previously. (This may well have been an accurate report, for the Korean War had started a year earlier.) Slightly more television owners than non-owners received a local newspaper, but considerably more read *both* the *Journal* and the *Constitution*. This fails to indicate that their reading was affected by TV, though it confirms our assumption that they were better-educated, and accordingly more serious newspaper readers.

4. Further confirmation comes from Zorbaugh and Mills' study in Metropolitan New York. They found reading slightly higher among TV owners (90%) than non-owners (86%) both for daily and for Sunday newspapers. The TV owners spent more time—an hour and eighteen minutes—with the daily paper, the non-owners an hour and eight minutes. The TV owners spent an hour and 38 minutes with the Sunday paper, the non-TV owners an hour and 23 minutes.

The time spent with the Sunday paper was distributed differently by the two groups. As an indication: the television owners, with their higher average education, spent only 27 minutes (30%) of their total Sunday newspaper reading time on the comics, compared with 40 minutes (44%) for the non-owners.

The difference is in part accounted for by the probability that proportionately fewer readers of the New York *Times* (which prints no comics) were included in the non-television group. However, a nationwide survey by the National Opinion Research Center produced similar findings: the television owners spent an average of 44 minutes reading the Sunday comics, the non-owners 53 minutes.

5. By contrast, the national survey by Batten, Barton, Durstine & Osborn found virtually no difference between TV and non-TV

families in the patterns of Sunday newspaper reading. (See Table 55.) Because of technical shortcomings of the sample and questionnaire, the findings of this study cannot be taken as seriously as the Zorbaugh-Mills research.

TABLE 55

Reading of Daily and Sunday Newspapers

Source: (B.B.D.O. Mail Survey, 1951)

	Per Cent Reading		Average Reading Time	
	TV Owners	*Non- Owners*	*TV Owners*	*Non- Owners*
Daily Paper	92%	93%		
Morning Paper			37 min.	40 min.
Evening Paper			43 min.	48 min.
Sunday Paper	93	94	1 hr. 46 min.	1 hr. 57 min.
Comics	70	71	32 min.	27 min.
Picture Section	58	57	30 min.	28 min.
Magazine Section	55	56	32 min.	37 min.
Other Sections	80	84	52 min.	1 hr. 4 min.

(H)

Further corroboration comes from a study of trends in readership of comic strips in Minneapolis. Jack Haskins and Robert Jones report that the pattern for strips in the morning newspaper remained fairly stable in the years since television entered the local scene, while readers of afternoon papers have been reading fewer strips than formerly, and are becoming more variable in their selections. The authors suggest that television may be one of several possible causes of change in the habits of reading the evening paper.

Unlike some of the other studies we have cited, the B.B.D.O. survey did not show television owners to be heavier newspaper readers than non-owners; if anything, it suggested the opposite. It also indicated that television's inroads were no more evident in the case of the morning newspaper (which has relatively little competition from TV) than in the case of the evening newspaper (whose reading period corresponds with television's main viewing hours).

6. In Lexington, Kentucky, McGeehan and Maranville found virtually no difference in the average number of hours reportedly spent with newspapers before television (10 per week) or after (9.4),

nor in the average number of newspaper subscriptions (1.3). However, 10% of the TV owners interviewed said they were now neglecting the main news section of the newspaper.

7. In the National Broadcasting Company's 1952 survey of
Metropolitan New York, virtually no differences in newspaper reading time were found between television owners and non-owners (even
when these were matched with the owners according to their characteristics). The results may be seen in Table 56.

TABLE 56

Newspaper Reading Among TV Owners and Non-Owners

(Source: NBC Metropolitan New York Survey, 1952)

	TV Owners	All Non-Owners	Matched Non-Owners
Minutes per person per day spent reading newspapers	47	50	50
Minutes spent per day by those who read newspapers	62	61	
Per cent exposed to newspapers on average day	78%		83%

A breakdown of the same information (in Table 57) by
separate age, income and educational groups shows that this lack of
significant difference persists at every level, except among those of
lowest income and schooling (where TV cuts in noticeably).

Among those with incomes over $4,000 (who were in a posi-
tion to afford TV relatively early in the game), the first to acquire
television were the ones who spent the greatest amount of time reading newspapers. (See Table 58.)

8. A survey of 700 families in the Chicago area, made by the
Television Bureau of Advertising in March, 1956, finds that time
spent reading newspapers is lowest in those families where television
viewing is heaviest—where the housewife is youngest. In these
families (where the housewife is under 35) the aggregate daily time
spent with newspapers (for all individuals combined) is 66 minutes,
on television 794 minutes. In the families whose housewife is 35-49,

124 minutes a day are spent with newspapers, 570 with TV. In the older families (housewife over 50), 103 minutes go to newspapers, 377 to television.

TABLE 57

Time Spent Reading Newspapers by TV Owners and Non-Owners

(Source: NBC Metropolitan New York Survey, 1952)

| | *Minutes per Person per Day* | |
	TV Owners	*Non-Owners*
Age		
18-29	41	43
30-39	47	48
40-49	48	53
50 +	50	55
Income		
$100-3,000	41	48
$3,001-4,000	48	50
$4,001-5,000	47	52
$5,001 +	50	53
Education		
Grammar School	40	48
Some High School	46	50
Completed High School	49	51
College	51	53

TABLE 58

Time Spent Reading Newspapers, By Length of TV Ownership

(Source: NBC Metropolitan New York Survey, 1952)

| | *Minutes per Person per Day* | | |
	TV Owners with Incomes Under $4000	*TV Owners with Incomes Over $4000*	*All TV Owners*
Less than one year	47	46	47
1-2 years	43	49	45
More than 2 years	45	52	50

A Comparison of News Media

(I)   It is not surprising that newspapers should have been less directly affected by television than any other medium. Newspapers are often read under circumstances in which television cannot compete, — at meals, while travelling to and from work, or even at work itself. Unlike the magazine which appears once, twice, or four times a month, the newspaper is read daily; buying and perusing the newspaper is a much more deeply engrained habit than reading a magazine or book. And newspaper reading often fills moments of idleness during the day. When the daily paper is not available (Bernard Berelson found in studying the effects of a New York newspaper delivery strike), many people feel acutely uncomfortable because of the interruption in their customary pattern.

In his early study of New York TV owners, Goldberg asked two parallel questions: "Which do you think gives the most complete news coverage—radio, newspapers or television?" and "Which do you think gives the most interesting news coverage?" Newspapers were rated "most complete" by 75%, television "most interesting" by 68%.

In the scope of its content it is clear that the newspaper serves functions which television cannot completely fulfill. In reality the paper may serve primarily as a means of passing the time, but in the consciousness of the reader it is a source of (important) information, while television is a source of (unimportant) entertainment. The newspaper has enough space to cater to some of the private and special interests of all its readers: stock market reports, crop prices, baseball line-ups, stamp columns and so on. Television, because of its greater operating costs, must appeal to at least a sizable segment of the public with every program it puts on the air; it cannot be highly specialized. Television programming is for the most part national in scope, whereas most newspapers in the United States are predominantly oriented to the local scene and can adddress their readers in terms of their private concerns.

Newspapers are more directly competitive with radio, which has always been a more local medium than television. Samuel Stouffer, examining "the effects of radio upon newspaper circulation" between 1930 and 1940, noted that "the radio's advantage to rural listeners was greater relatively than its advantage to urban listeners," who had more ready access to the daily newspaper. He therefore predicted that newspaper circulation in rural areas was likely to be most directly affected by radio's growth.

An examination of newspaper circulation figures revealed that this was indeed the case. City-zone circulation held up better than in outlying areas for the same newspapers. Newspaper circulation in small cities was found to be holding up better than in larger ones, conforming to Stouffer's prediction that "since radio news tends to favor national news at the expense of local affairs, the local newspaper might hold up more successfully (than the great metropolitan newspaper) because it still perfoms a function which radio has not taken over." Similarly, he found that "the morning newspaper did somewhat better than the evening paper, and this might be due to the fact that the morning paper is frequently 'analytical' and therefore less subject to radio's competition."

It is worth noting in this connection that radio news provided a basic informational function for a different (lower) educational group than newspaper news. As a news medium, television appears to be functioning in a somewhat different manner.

Newspapers continue to be the main source of news information for the urban public, according to the 1956 study by McCann-Erickson, Inc., in New York, Philadelphia and Charlotte. In New York, they were named by 50% of those interviewed, while television was cited by 32%, radio by 15% and magazines by 2%. (The pattern of response was similar in the other two cities.) However, the proportions were reversed on the question, "Which makes the news most interesting to you?" In New York, 49% named television, 36% newspapers, 11% radio, and 4% magazines.

It appears from these findings that TV has replaced radio as the main news source for the sector of the public which is accustomed to assimilating information aurally rather than by reading. It has not displaced newspapers as the main news source for the people who are readers rather than listeners. However, a certain proportion of these readers find that television enlivens the presentation of the news more than newspapers do—even though they rely more heavily on newspapers. Apparently, television has become the primary news medium for some people, but for others it has become an important supplement to newspaper accounts, visualizing and dramatizing the events and personalities of the day.

The people who select television as their principal news source are essentially those who in earlier years chose radio over newspapers: those of lower income and lesser education. (43% of the grade-school educated say they rely on newspapers and 40% on television, whereas 64% of the college educated rely on newspapers, only 20% on TV.) Women depend more on the broadcast media than men do (45% mention newspapers, compared with 55% of the men). Young persons of 16-25 and older persons over 55 express greater dependence on TV news than do those in the years of peak activity. Radio is actually mentioned less often than television as the medium that brings the news most quickly. In New York, for example, 44% mention television, 37% radio, and 18% newspapers. These findings are rather startling in the light of the fact that the TV viewer can see only a limited number of news programs in the course of the day, whereas the radio listener can hear news almost every half-hour. The explanation lies in the average person's changed leisure time habits. The fact that far more time is now spent watching television than listening to the radio means that people are more apt to think of TV as the medium which is first to reach them with the latest news. At the same time, they may instinctively turn to the radio at a moment of crisis.

Evidence on this point comes from the survey of radio listening in television areas made in 1953 by Alfred Politz Research, Inc. Radio looms far ahead of newspapers and television as a source of fast news information. (Unfortunately separate breakdowns of television and non-television owners are not provided in the published releases on this survey. At the time it was made, 72% of the homes in the areas surveyed owned television sets.)

Politz asked, "Suppose you were at home and heard a sudden rumor that war had broken out. What would you do to see if the rumor were true?"

55% would turn on the radio.

15% would turn on the television set.

11% say they might turn on either the radio or television.

8% would call up a newspaper.

7% would call the police or other public authorities.

3% would call their neighbors.

3% would wait to read about it in the newspapers.

If radio may be said to provide fast reports of the news after it has happened, and if newspapers are looked to for full details and for interpretation of what the reader already knows in capsule form, as well as extensive coverage of minor items which other media cannot handle, then television may be said to fill two entirely different news functions:

1. The regular news programs provide a newsreel-type pictorial documentation of news which the viewer may already know about in a general way. Television news faces a special problem in that it is broadcast less frequently than radio news, so that its spoken content is more apt to be already familiar to the viewer. In its reporting of international and much national news it cannot provide filmed footage to match the spoken reportage, and the camera must therefore focus either on a still photograph which may already have appeared in the evening newspaper, on stale "background" films, or on the face of the announcer. When films of distant news events are available a day or two after the news has broken, they can be placed on the air only at the risk of changing the show's character from a news to a feature emphasis.

2. The chief and extraordinarily unique news function of television is that it permits the viewer to be an eyewitness of news in the making, whether this be a Congressional hearing, a presidential speech, a world series baseball game or an atomic explosion. In providing this service television by no means detracts from the appeal of the newspaper. Persons who have vicariously participated in an event via television (just like those present in the flesh), turn eagerly to the paper the following morning to refresh their memories of the experience, to check their observations against those of a specialist, and to get some analysis or reflections on what they have witnessed.

The television medium can actually create news, as in a speech, interview or panel discussion involving an important political figure whose pronouncements are inherently newsworthy, like Nikita Khrushchev.

The McCann-Erickson study found that persons at different social levels have different expectations and wants with respect to the content of the TV newscast. Of every ten news viewers, only one prefers to see television news programs consist largely of local news. Five prefer a concentration on national and world news and four volunteer that they want equal attention to both. The minority who prefer local news are most often found at the bottom of the social scale, and among the young. They are the very people who rely most strongly on television as their major source of information, whereas those who prefer national and world news are the better educated and older people who lean most toward newspapers.

A similar division is found when people are asked whether they prefer the latest news bulletins spoken by an announcer or films showing the actual events that might already be a day or two old. One person in four prefers the latest news bulletins even if no films accompany them. Two out of five prefer film. One in three volunteers that he wants both. At the upper income level the preference runs over two to one for bulletins as opposed to film, whereas at the other income levels it runs about four to three in favor of film. The people who prefer television to print are the very ones who favor films over the fast bulletins, since it is thus that TV uses its full capacity for humanizing the events which print makes relatively impersonal and abstract. These findings differ from those of a small experiment conducted by Erling S. Jorgensen at the University of Michigan in the fall of 1954. Jorgensen prepared kinescopes of three fifteen-minute television news programs, using the same twelve news stories arranged in three groups. The order of presenting the material was rotated, and the presentation of each set of stories was varied to permit the use of three techniques: the newscaster alone, the newscaster using still pictures, and the newscaster using motion pictures.

Jorgensen tested these three programs on nine audiences, comprising a total of 142 subjects: college students, young adult

Community Center members, and Air Force enlisted men. He failed to find any significant difference among the techniques in the amount of information gained by his subjects. The highest approval was, surprisingly, achieved by the technique which used the newscaster alone, with films lowest. The three test programs differed markedly in approval, indicating that certain techniques were most suitable for certain stories. Jorgensen remarks, "The subjects in this experiment tended to react more strongly in either direction (i.e. approval or disapproval) during film than during newscaster treatment. In other words here is evidence that the films used in a newscast had better be *good* pictorial treatment or they may detract from the story rather than add to it." This seems to leave open the possibility that the locally produced films used in the experiment may not have been up to the audience's expectations and may have produced a negative impression.

A content analysis made by the writer, of one week's local news broadcasts on stations in twenty cities (1956), shows that programming generally accords well with public preference. Content is slanted to national and world news more than to local news. There is virtually no difference in the distribution of air time between big and small city stations. The small-city stations, however, make relatively greater use of film. The big-city stations are more likely to give the latest bulletins even when no motion pictures are available. In general, filmed items are given more time than bulletins. World news, particularly, is apt to be shown on film. In their selection of the principal stories each day, the individual TV news editors show a remarkable similarity of judgment. However, there are tremendous variations in the choice of national and world news items and in the use of film. Local news items most often deal with disasters or natural catastrophes, next with the activities of local legislators or officials.

A comparison of public issues covered on television and in newspapers during one week in 1954 was made by Remmers and his associates in connection with their content analysis of New York television. Monitors of public affairs broadcasts found that 55% presented only one point of view, with the "selling" of that viewpoint. The subjects discussed in these broadcasts differed from those on the front pages of newspapers in the same period. The TV programs focussed on recession and the economy, whereas the headline news dealt with the Berlin Conference and the repatriation of U. S. soldiers in the Far East. However, as Remmers points out, the comparison is not strictly valid, since the public affairs broadcasts are more comparable to newspaper editorials or columns than to news items.

Television and Newspaper Circulation

(J)   The opinion surveys indicate that television has had only negligible effects on newspaper reading. Further light may be shed on the subject by an analysis of newspaper circulation trends in the post-war period.

In 1940, U. S. newspapers circulated 118 copies daily for every one hundred households in the country. News-hunger and rising incomes raised this figure during the war, so that by 1947 circulation stood at 132 copies per 100 households. From this point, which coincides with television's beginnings, growth in households was faster than the growth in circulation. By 1954 newspapers were again circulating 117 copies for every 100 households.

While these figures seem to point to the adverse effects of television, an analysis by Allan Donnahoe, research director of the Richmond Newspapers, leads to no such conclusion. Taking the 43 metropolitan areas whose central cities have a morning, evening and Sunday paper, Donnahoe finds that in 1953 circulation per 100 households was highest in the areas where the largest percentage of homes owned television. (These are, of course, the largest metropolitan areas, first to get TV.) Donnahoe finds that the differences in circulation per 100 households can be explained by differences in family income and newspaper subscription rates. The degree of television penetration is no longer related to circulation when these other factors are controlled. The general decline in circulation per 100 households Donnahoe ascribes to the problems of delivery to the growing suburbs.

Somewhat similar results emerge from an analysis made by the writer of newspaper circulation trends from 1946 to 1952, the year the television freeze was lifted. The results are summarized in Table 59. All cities with populations over 500,000 had television stations in them by 1952. Cities ranging in size between 95,000 and 500,000 have been grouped into three categories: (a) cities which had TV stations in them, (b) cities within reception range of stations located elsewhere, and (c) cities with no television coverage at all.

In the larger cities newspaper circulation dropped by 7% between 1946 and 1952, while the population grew by 19%. In all three categories of the smaller cities newspaper circulation increased by about the same margin. However, population increased much faster than newspaper circulation both in the cities *with* television stations and in those *without* television stations. In those covered by outside stations, population grew only a little faster than circulation.

Of course many other things beside television were responsible for changes in newspaper readership trends during this period. Papers merged and went out of business. The big cities gained less in population than did their suburban satellites. But the specific influence of television cannot be discerned in these data.

TABLE 59

Newspaper Circulation Trends, 1946-1952

City of Publication	Circulation (in millions) 1946	1952	Per Cent Change in Circulation	Per Cent Change in Population, 1946-1952
Population over 500,000 (with television station)	21.98	20.38	− 7%	+19%
Population 95,000-500,000 (with television station)	7.85	8.71	+11%	+27%
(covered by outside television station)	1.66	1.81	+ 9%	+12%
(no television coverage)	2.79	3.04	+ 9%	+33%

Summary of TV's Effects on Reading

The evidence we have reported in this chapter is far from being completely consistent. Studies made by varying methods and standards, in different places and at various times, could hardly be expected to produce identical results. Yet there is overwhelming agreement that television has reduced the amount of time which the American people spend in reading magazines and books, not newspapers. The effects appear to be substantial, even though they may be somewhat lessened as television becomes a long-established feature of family life.

To make such a generalization is to speak of a hypothetical average American family into whose life TV has come. Other forces besides television are also at work to influence reading habits. Better educated people do more reading. As the average American continues to become better off and more highly schooled it appears inevitable that over the long run he will do *more* rather than *less* reading in spite of the influence of television. For the moment, however, reading will be reduced. This has some implications which are worth noting:

1. It represents a transfer of time from an individual activity (reading) to a collective one (watching TV).

2. It is a shift from an active pursuit of positive interests to a passive acceptance of the proffered fare.

3. It is a gain for a medium (television) which provides literal depiction of life, in real or dramatized form, at the expense of a medium (reading) which makes great demands on the imagination and on the capacity for abstraction.

4. It is a change from a medium (reading) which provides an opportunity for infinite choice of subject matter to one (television) which is a tremendous force for social and cultural conformity.

8. TELEVISION AND THE MOVIES

Television has probably had a greater impact on the motion picture industry than on any other medium except radio. This effect has been explored in many surveys, but it has been most impressively recorded at the box office. Average weekly motion picture attendance dropped from 82,000,000 in 1946 to 34,000,000 in 1956.

The motion picture industry's first reaction to television took the form of reiterating pious assurances that there was nothing wrong with the movies that good pictures wouldn't cure. J. Myer Schine, operator of 150 theatres, announced in print that television might prove a boon to movie attendance by getting more Americans in the habit of looking at pictures. Another film mogul made this observation (as recently as 1951): "Video isn't able to hold on to the market it captures after the first six months. People soon get tired of staring at a plywood box every night." Nonetheless, motion picture houses kept closing throughout the country as television spread. Of the 19,000 houses in operation in 1946, a fourth had closed by 1953. (A)

The woes of the film industry could not all be laid at the door of television. The established distributors began to face the competition of drive-in theaters in the new suburbia. And over-all movie attendance dropped even in areas into which TV had not yet penetrated. At the start of 1949, long before television became a force to be reckoned with, a *Wall Street Journal* survey of twenty cities found that attendance was down in all parts of the country. In November 1950, *Business Week* observed that the box office slump was as bad in Honolulu, which had no television, as in New York, which abounded in television homes.

The decline of the movies has been measured not only at the box office but by every survey in which television owners have been asked about their film-going habits. In fact, once people acquire television, they tend to exaggerate the frequency of their film attendance before TV, and to minimize their present attendance.

Early studies of television's impact invariably found a sizable proportion of set owners reporting a decline in their movie attendance:

1. In a survey by Television Research, Inc., in Los Angeles (1947), 46% of the set owners said they were going to the movies less often. The following year, Advertest, interviewing 150 families in Northern New Jersey, found 63% agreeing that television had had "a great effect" on their movie-going.

2. At about the same time, the advertising firm of Foote, Cone and Belding conducted a telephone survey of 415 TV owners in New York City. 51% said their visits to the movies had decreased. 57% said they had gone to the movies "every few days" before television, but only 4% said they now went this frequently. Of those who had formerly gone several times a week, 68% now went once a week, and all but 5% of the remainder went even less often. Of those who had formerly gone once every week, 62% now went every two or three weeks, the others even less frequently.

3. Of the people interviewed in 1949 by Duane Jones, 81% said they were going to the movies less than they did formerly. A year later, in a study of subscribers to TV Guide, Fact Finders found that 63% reported a decline in movie attendance.

4. In two midwestern cities (also 1950) Macfadden Publications found that 64% of the television-owning families said they went to the movies less often than they did before TV. In Washington, D.C. that year, Alldredge reported 72% of the TV owners were going to the movies less frequently.

5. In 1951, 68% of the TV owners in two Boston suburbs were going to the movies less often, according to Sweetser. In the Southern California community surveyed by McDonagh, three television owners in four reported that their film-going had decreased.

6. More recently (1953), television owners in Lexington, Kentucky, told researchers McGeehan and Maranville that before TV they had gone to the movies 2.8 times a week, and that they were now going about three times a month (0.7 times a week, on the average). With due allowance for exaggeration and faulty memory, this is still quite a dip.

TV and the Movie Fans

In his early survey of the effects of television, made in Long Island in 1948, Coffin found that 59% of the respondents reported that they went to the movies less since they had television at home, and 13% said that they actually enjoyed movies less than they did formerly. The effects were present regardless of how long television had been owned, and it was true of people at all income levels. Comparing his television owners with other people who did not have TV, but who lived in the same neighborhoods and were otherwise similar to them, Coffin found that the TV owners were going to the movies less often—49 weekly attendances per hundred persons, compared with 62 for the non-TV group.

This finding has particular interest, because the people who acquired sets so early in television's history were among the most ardent movie fans. This means that the motion picture industry felt the effects of television rather quickly, as its best customers were attracted to its rival. A survey made by the National Opinion Research Center in the fall of 1947, before TV began to grow, showed that people went to the movies more often in the cities and towns than in rural areas—and the big cities were, of course, the first to feel television's impact. Moreover the heaviest movie-goers were also the heaviest radio listeners, and these in turn, as we already know, were the first persons to buy television sets.

A nationwide study made by Audience Research, Inc., in the spring of 1950 found close resemblances between the movie and TV audiences with respect to age, education and concentration in urban areas. Here note was made of a tendency "for persons in television set owning households to have those characteristics more likely to accompany high movie attendance frequency than the opposite." Even when the sample was broken down into separate age, educational and city-size groups, the TV owners within any given sub-group always were found to attend the movies less often than the non-owners.

This survey found movie attendance among TV set owners to average 4.4 visits in a hundred days. Non-owners attended more frequently: 6.2 visits in television areas, and 6.3 visits in areas to which television had not yet come. The non-TV areas contained fewer of the big cities in which movie attendance was higher at the outset. This explains why the non-TV owners in such areas, including people who would have bought TV if it had been within reach, did not attend the movies even more frequently than the non-TV owners in TV areas.

There is one study, however, which fails to show that the first people to acquire television were the heaviest movie-goers. Lawton's research in Norman and Oklahoma City suggested just the opposite, namely, that the first television owners attended the movies less often even before they acquired their sets. The first part of this survey took place just before television came to the area. The interviews were repeated six months later, and again after six more months. A decline in movie attendance was found among television owners, but a very similar decline occurred among people who only had radios at home. None of these findings jibe with any other evidence. The easiest explanation of the discrepancy might be a technical shortcoming in this study—for instance, if the people interviewed in the three "waves" of the survey were not exactly comparable. (It should be noted that Lawton's findings on book reading are also at variance with other research).

TABLE 60

Education and Movie Attendance

	Educational Level		
	College	High School	Grade School
Per cent of general public who saw four or more movies in previous month (1947 N.O.R.C. nationwide survey)	25%	28%	16%
Per cent of television owners who go to the movies at least once a month (1952 Metropolitan New York survey by Zorbaugh and Mills)	45%	50%	34%

Lawton's findings reporting a similar decline in motion picture attendance for both television owners and non-owners are contradicted by the nationwide mail survey made at approximately the same time by Batten, Barton, Durstine and Osborn. Of those respondents who had television sets at home, 12% reported they went to the movies on the average day, compared with 18% of those without TV.

Similar findings were produced in the New York study of Zorbaugh and Mills. 45% of the television owners interviewed said they went to the movies at least once a month, with a typical (median) frequency of 1.7 times a month. 16% said they had stopped going to the movies altogether since they had television. By contrast, 59% of the people in non-TV homes went to the movies at least once a month, with a typical frequency of 3.1 times.   (B)

Not unexpectedly, this study found that movie-going remained strongest, even after TV, among people at the middle educational level. This very group had originally been the biggest movie fans. They also had been the heaviest radio listeners. Now they became the greatest devotees of television, as Table 60 suggests.

The Movie Industry's Response

The motion picture industry responded to its falling revenues   (C) by cutting costs and raising rentals, while distributors upped attendance prices, or introduced bingo and free dishes to stimulate trade. Producers quickly recognized that in color and screen size motion pictures had an enormous advantage over television both in reproducing reality and in heightening dramatic effects. As a result more and more films were made in color, and the film makers brought forth a series of new inventions which either created a three-dimensional illusion or which gave greatly increased size and scope to the theater screen.

Hollywood also knew that its vast experience and the enormous resources it could invest in the production of a single 90-minute feature film could not be matched by the television producers who operated on much more slender budgets. One answer to television was therefore to make fewer films (about three-fourths as many as in the post-war period), but to make their production so spectacular and lavish that TV could not possibly rival their entertainment values. By contrast, another approach was to make more rather than fewer films. The *Wall Street Journal* of March 30, 1949, reported that "the grand strategy now is to throw a larger number of pictures at the public, and thus get more 'first week' box office results."

One leading film producer heralded the new era by saying that from now his studios would produce only quality motion pictures, and would no longer produce inferior films. (This statement was greeted with some derisive questions as to who had ever deliberately set out to make an inferior film).

But the movie industry did more than adapt its techniques to meet the television threat. If TV could not be licked it could be joined. From television's earliest days, a few farsighted producers recognized the money-making potentialities of adapting their production facilities to television. Television quickly proved to be a prodigious consumer of talent. Although the film studios refused to release their recent products for broadcasting they had no such reluctance about old pictures which had outlived their revenue-producing powers in American theaters. From TV's infancy, old films (but not the best ones which still merited an occasional theatrical revival) became a staple item of its programming and a source of income for Hollywood. But there was an even more rewarding opportunity for the movie-makers in the production of short low-budget films especially for television. And as television itself moved into the era of the "spectacular" shows of great length and budgets, many leading film producers themselves became directly identified with the new medium.

Motion picture stars had for a number of years been among the leading personalities of radio, and insofar as their studios permitted, they now became television performers as well— if only to make brief guest appearances heralding their latest film offerings. As a reservoir of entertainment skills and talents, Hollywood became the site of more and more live TV productions. Its television studios came to rival those of New York, which had long been the radio capital. Recently Hollywood has drawn on television drama as a source of film plots as well as talent, and successful TV plays (like "Marty" and "Patterns") have been turned into feature films.

The premiere of Sir Laurence Olivier's motion picture version of Shakespeare's "Richard III" coincided with its release over the television network of the National Broadcasting Company. The intimate interrelationship between television and the other dramatic arts was also apparent on the stage. The television networks have provided backing for a number of Broadway hits, including "My Fair Lady."

The marriage of Hollywood and television may be illustrated

by the findings of a Sindlinger survey. During a week in March, 1957, 27% of the adult and teen-aged public spent a grand total of 138,200,000 hours attending movies. But in the same period, a like proportion (24%, undoubtedly including many of the same individuals) spent a total of 276,500,000 hours watching movies on television.

The motion picture industry's most direct move into television came about in 1952, when United Paramount Theaters, Inc., acquired control of the American Broadcasting Company, and invested substantial capital to build the third network into a serious rival of the NBC and CBS television empires. The very opposite step occurred in the summer of 1955, when the General Tire and Rubber Company, owners of the Mutual Broadcasting System (radio) and of some leading television stations, bought RKO Pictures, Inc., from Howard Hughes and thereby acquired a valuable library of recent films. General Tire's WOR-TV in New York had fought its way to financial health as an independent station by taking recent films, new to television, and showing them repeatedly for a one-week period. Under the program title of "Million Dollar Movie" these films achieved a larger total audience than any other TV program in New York. The RKO film library of 740 features and 1000 shorts was bought by the C. and C. Television Corporation, which plans to sell exclusive rights to one station in each market.

Within the first half of 1956 nearly 2,000 feature films were made available for TV showing by the motion picture industry, and Metro-Goldwyn-Mayer announced the release of an additional 770 produced between 1929 and 1949. Columbia Pictures, through its subsidiary, Screen Gems, was an active package producer of TV film shows, and other companies were following suit.

While all these developments were taking place, movie theater attendance continued to decline, at a slower rate. But new threats loom on the horizon. Color television matches one of theater movies' great advantages. Less imminent is projection television which throws an image on a large-size screen instead of on the end of a picture-tube. "Pay-as-you-see" television poses a different kind of problem. For producers it may represent an enlarged audience and an opportunity for increased profits, but it is clearly a threat to movie theater owners. It is doubtful whether even "pay-as-you-see" TV will break people of the habit of going to the movies.

In Atlanta (in 1951) Stewart found 49% of the television owners reporting their movie attendance had dropped, but at the same time, virtually all the set owners (95%) said they were now watching feature films on television. Stewart went on to ask them what they liked about seeing a motion picture in a theater that they did not get from seeing one over TV. The advantages most often mentioned were (1) the pictures were newer and better, (2) the screen was larger, and (3) going out to the movies meant being away from home and getting among people.

The motion picture theater is bound to survive as long as the technique of film production continues to stress panorama and massive display to achieve dramatic impact. The heroic-sized figures on a theater screen create a mood and convey an effect which is very different from that of the intimate atmosphere of the living room. The movie-house will remain as a focus of interest for those who are bored with their familiar surroundings, as a refuge for lovers, and as an answer to the need for "going out" as a form of sociability. In this latter respect, the film itself is incidental and the theater is a point of reference rather than a point of pilgrimage.

Since 1948, the Cunningham and Walsh surveys of "Videotown" (New Brunswick) have traced the inroads of television upon movie attendance. Although the complete figures on this point have never been publicly released, it is reported that "the number of people attending a movie on a week-day evening dropped 77% when a TV set was purchased. It continued to decrease until 1953 when a 17% increase over 1952 was noted. 1954 shows a very substantial increase, with about twice as many people reporting movie attendance on a week-day evening as in 1953."

In 1955, two-thirds again as many adults as in 1954 reported going to a movie on the average weekday evening. By mid-1955, over three-fourths of the families in New Brunswick owned television sets, and they were watching them as much as ever. Yet somehow or other they were finding time to see more movies as well as to do other things which TV had curtailed. By 1956 the trend was reversed, and movie attendance had dropped to the level of the early TV years.

For a rising generation which hardly knows of a world without television, the findings of adult surveys do not apply. In 1954, T. C. Battin, questioning grade school children in Ann Arbor, Michigan, discovered that 75% of the boys and 79% of the girls reported no change in their movie-going habits as a result of television. Among the boys, 16% said they were actually going to the movies more often, 9% less often. Among the girls there was a balance: 10% more, 11% less. To children it appeared that television and movies alike had always been constant and predictable elements in life's choice of entertainment. It is in such findings that the pattern of the future must be discerned.

9. TELEVISION'S EFFECTS
ON SPECTATOR SPORTS

(A)

Television has brought outstanding athletic events within the reach of millions who would otherwise not see them. In 1956, one game of the World Series was viewed in 22,300,000 homes. The New Year's Day Rose Bowl game was seen in 20,200,000 homes.

Radio coverage of sports events has long been accepted and welcomed in college football and professional baseball both as an added form of income and as a stimulus to popular interest. By contrast, television was from the start regarded as a menace by organized athletics since it actually permitted the game to be watched and followed, play by play, much as it might be from the stadium. And these anxieties have been well justified.

While television has damaged attendance at baseball and football games, it has from time to time aroused interest in minor sports. The roller derby, a kind of roller-skating marathon, not only won a huge television audience for the few years of its popularity, but managed to attract a good many people to view the spectacle in the flesh. Wrestling, never one of the more popular spectator sports, developed, through television, a vast circle of devotees. In wrestling as in professional boxing, which for some time permitted heavyweight championship bouts to be televised only in theaters, the small size of the screen does not cramp the view of the spectacle in the same way as it does in a football or baseball match where the camera must follow the action over a wide field.

The single outstanding piece of research on the subject of television's influence upon organized sports has not received more publicity and comment than far less substantial studies. Indications of television's effects are easier to trace in terms of attendance figures or gate receipts than in terms of actual public interest in the sports.

A few scattered reports are indicative:

1. Ruth Taylor, in a 1949 survey among 549 subscribers to *Television Forecast* magazine, found that 85% of the respondents said

they had become interested in sports events which they had not been interested in before TV.

2. Stewart, in his 1951 survey of Atlanta, found that nine-tenths of the television owners said they had watched sports on TV. Two-thirds said their interest had increased as a result. About two-thirds said their attendance had not been affected. But one in three of the TV sports viewers said they had been going to fewer athletic events since they acquired television—and this was especially true of the better educated respondents who probably (since they also had the highest incomes) attended most frequently.

3. In McDonagh's Southern California survey, 39% of the television owners, and only 22% of the non-owners, reported that they were participating less in sports. This again suggested a decline.

4. In 1951, the New York *Times* interviewed principals of leading high schools in the suburbs of New York, and found a uniform picture of declining attendance. At White Plains, attendance at football games dropped from an average of 15,774 admissions in 1948 to 12,856 in 1950. In the same period basketball receipts dropped by $100 a game. The implications went beyond athletics, reported *Times* Radio-TV editor Jack Gould: "Football and basketball revenues formerly supported baseball, track and other sports, as well as activities such as the dramatic, riding and French clubs, and the school newspaper. With such revenues showing a $3,500 loss for the year, it was said, taxpayers ultimately would have to meet the deficit."

The story was exactly the same at New Rochelle High School, whose band was left with insufficient funds to buy new uniforms. The school's "big game" which produced gate receipts of three to seven thousand dollars before television, yielded only $700 in 1950. At Stamford, Connecticut, the high school stadium, with a seating capacity of 10,000, was only half-filled at many games. School sports, formerly self-sustaining, showed a deficit.

In contrast to these isolated case histories, Jerry Jordan, first in a college thesis and later in studies underwritten by the Radio-Television Manufacturers' Association, sought to assemble attendance histories for a number of organized sports, and supplemented this with several small-scale opinion surveys.

Rejecting the thesis that telecasting of sports events led automatically to a decline in attendance, Jordan drew attention to the variations and cycles in popularity which affected sports like baseball long before the advent of TV. He listed fifteen factors which could affect attendance: (1) economic conditions; (2) management; (3) performance (of both home and visiting teams); (4) publicity-promotion; (5) employment-working hours; (6) kind of games or schedules; (7) general population; (8) college population (at least insofar as college football is concerned); (9) weather; (10) accommodations; (11) ticket prices; (12) individual attractions; (13) competition; (14) radio sportscasting; (15) television sportscasting.

Seen in this light, television could be regarded as only a minor influence among many other influences. To illustrate that factors other than television might cause attendance to drop, Jordan cites a loss of 26,778 admissions per game in Los Angeles college football in 1948—at a time when only 2% of the homes in the area had TV. In 1949, when the number of sets had grown sixfold, the decline in admissions was less than half what it had been the previous year. (Jordan fails to underline a point, however, which is apparent from his accompanying data: that 1947 was an unusually good year.

In further support of his point Jordan quotes a newspaper column by Grantland Rice, who noted that in 1932 the Eastern Intercollegiate Association passed a resolution banning radio broadcasts of football games, and that much earlier there was talk of banning newspaper men from ball parks so that people would have to attend the game to find out the score.

The real secret of the attendance figures, Jordan believes, is in the quality of a team's performance record. He notes that baseball teams with good records increased attendance in 1949 over 1948, while attendance declined for teams with less satisfactory performance. On the other hand, he finds no relation between the attendance standing of the teams and the size of the television audience in their home towns. On days, nights and weekends, games which were good enough to attract large television audiences also drew crowds to the ball parks.

In football too, Jordan finds no evidence of TV's adverse influence on attendance. Of 106 colleges in TV areas, 56% showed an increase in attendance between 1948 and 1949, compared with 51% of the 88 colleges in non-TV areas. He reports the least improvement in the case of small colleges in non-TV areas.

Moreover, Jordan observes that (at this relatively early point in the history of television), the TV owners were especially apt to be represented among the crowd at the stadium. At a time when 17% of Philadelphians had television, ownership stood at 36% among season ticketholders of University of Pennsylvania football games. At a time when 19% of the city had television, Jordan interviewed 303 persons at two Philadelphia baseball games—one well- and one poorly-attended. In each case 27% said they had a TV set at home.

But in the light of his researches Jordan could not discount the effects of television altogether. He does find that it cuts into attendance, but he believes that this is the result of a novelty effect which wears off after a while. Interviewing 600 male heads of families in the Philadelphia area, in the fall of 1949, he finds that among the non-TV owners, 46% went to see a football game of some kind (high school, college, or professional). Only 24% of the new television owners (who had owned their sets for less than three months) had gone to a game, compared with 41% of those who had owned their sets between four months and a year, 45% of those who had owned their sets for one or two years, and 54% of those who had owned their sets for over two years.

Similar findings were produced in the case of baseball: 45% of the non-TV owners had seen a big-league game in Shibe Park in 1949, for an average of 4.4 games. 44% of the new TV owners (who had owned their sets for less than a year) saw at least one game, or 3.7 on the average. Of the old TV owners (who had owned their sets for a year or more), 58% saw an average of 5.9 games.

The new television owners were less apt to take other members of their families with them to the baseball games than were either the old owners or the non-owners. However, interviews at the ball park itself suggested that television was the most important factor stimulating other members of the family (mostly wives, no doubt) to attend a game.

Minor baseball league attendance reacts to performance more than to television competition from the big leagues, Jordan believes.

However, this conclusion is not necessarily buttressed by his report on 300 interviews with television set owners in Wilmington, Delaware. 40% said they would prefer to see the Wilmington Blue Rocks play locally than watch the Philadelphia teams on television, but 53% said they would prefer TV; 7% had no choice.

Summing up his findings, Jordan says, "There is a temporary decrease in football attendance during the first year of ownership. After the novelty wears off, attendance picks up again, and returns to normal in about one year. Owners of two or more years have higher attendance than non-owners. This temporary loss in attendance among new owners, indicated by the public opinion surveys, is not reflected in national attendance figures. There are three reasons for this: (a) the higher rate of long-term owners balances out part of the loss. (b) This temporary loss is not found among alumni, who represent a large proportion of the football crowd. (c) Television helps create new fans. The effect of these three factors just about neutralizes the loss among short-term owners."

The Jordan studies have been described here at some length not so much because of the inherent importance of the findings but because the surveys were widely publicized by the sponsoring Radio-Television Manufacturers' Association, which was understandably eager to discount the theory that TV posed a menace to any established American institutions. Accordingly these studies have had a disproportionate influence on discussion of the subject.

Actually Jordan's findings were largely based on small and unrepresentative samples, and most of the differences he reports (for example on the sports attendance of old and new set owners) are statistically not significant. As a devastating critique later pointed out in commenting on Jordan's prize theory of the novelty effect, "It is improper to conclude that the attendance of newer owners will ever reach the level of the older owners, since their prior or normal attendance was unquestionably lower. They are less well off economically and their average interest in college sports is less."

While Jordan in his reports discussed the whole broad area of TV's impact on athletics, without marshalling sufficient evidence to produce a completely convincing story, the most thorough investigation of the subject has confined itself to only one sport—intercollegiate football. Since 1950, the National Collegiate Athletic Association has sponsored a series of studies made by the National Opinion Research Center and directed by Paul B. Sheatsley and Paul N. Borsky. Year by year, as the television-viewing area has been extended, NORC has carefully examined attendance statistics and has interviewed thousands of men about their interests in college football. The general conclusion has been that television cuts into sports attendance as seriously as into other activities.

These studies represent a clear-cut example of research influencing policy and action, for as a result of the first reports, the NCAA at its annual meeting in January, 1951, voted to restrict direct telecasting of its members' games. An experimental plan was set up which permitted only seven live games to be televised in a season in any one TV reception area, with each area shown an approximately equal number of nearby and distant games. No single team could appear on television more than once or twice.

In the 1950 season, the greatest decline in attendance occurred where a college's games were telecast. The next greatest decline was shown by other colleges in the same areas. The least effects were felt by colleges whose only television competition came from games in other areas.

Unlike Jordan, Sheatsley and Borsky began their researches by asking who the sports fans were. In a national survey they found that over half the adult public had never attended an intercollegiate football match. About the same number reported no interest at all in the game. Only one person in seven attends a game in any given season, and fewer than one in five can be classified as a fan. College football is therefore a minority sport, of particular interest to younger men, and particularly to those who have gone to college.

Interest in football develops early, and only one fan in a hundred said that television was responsible for arousing his interest in the game. By contrast, in two cities, 10% of the people who had gone to a game some time between 1947 and 1950 said they did not plan to attend any in 1951, but would watch televised games instead.

Like Jordan, Sheatsley and Borsky point to the factors other than television which might affect attendance, including "the weather, the calibre of the opposition, and special promotional efforts

. . . the size of the stadium, the performance of the team . . . local interest in college football . . . the level of student enrollment, the pinch of inflation or the ready spending money of boom times."

Of these factors, the attractiveness of the game appeared to be most important, but competition from televised football made quite a difference regardless of how good the game was. To arrive at this conclusion, the 1947-8 attendance figures were taken as the "expected" norm, and comparisons were made in such a way as to carefully control for extraneous influences. The results of this analysis for the 1952 season are shown in Table 61. (Similar findings were obtained in 1951.)

TABLE 61

Game Attractiveness and TV Competition as Factors Affecting College Football Attendance

(Source: NORC-NCAA Report #3)

		Per Cent of "Expected" (1947-8) Attendance		
	All Colleges	No TV Competition	TV Competition	TV Differential
All games	93.1	110.5	83.8	26.7
More attractive	122.0	141.7	102.3	39.4
Less attractive	72.3	79.3	65.3	14.0
Attractiveness differential	49.7	62.4	37.0	

It is clear that the more attractive games, particularly, did much better when they did not face TV competition. The explanation given by the NORC researchers is that these are the games which normally draw the largest number of less interested or "marginal" fans, who are more apt to accept a substitute on TV. The most enthusiastic fans, who don't consider a televised game a proper substitute, are also the ones who show up at the less attractive games as well as the big ones.

For the same reason, television has had a more serious effect on the big and middle-sized colleges than on the smaller schools. It is the big games which draw the general public, and consequently more of the marginal fans. At small college games, attendance is more apt to be made up of loyal alumni and others with a very special interest.

Because the small college games have a relatively heavy day-of-game sale (while the big colleges rely more on advance bookings) and because the public had no advance knowledge of which games would be telecast, the NCAA restriction on football telecasts aided the small colleges more than the big ones. This made the first findings of the NCAA experiment somewhat inconclusive.

The very fact that few fans knew in advance what games would be on the air meant that the size of the TV football audience remained surprisingly stable, regardless of the intrinsic quality or interest of the games themselves. As the fourth NORC report points out, "If 23% watched the average game, one might have thought that the less attractive telecasts would be watched by only 5% to 10% of the fans, and the most attractive ones by 70% or 80%. This is not at all the case. No game was lower than 17% and no game was higher than 35%." (The implication of this might be that home viewing of football is for the most part a kind of second-choice activity. Few of the viewers are people who have actively planned in advance to stay home Saturday afternoon and watch the game, in the same way in which a fan might plan ahead of time to *go* to the game.)

Under the NCAA plan of restrictions, the televised game of the week was not necessarily the one a given football fan was most interested in. However, radio continued to offer him a choice of the best games in the country. An NORC survey found that, in television areas, more fans (34%) listened to college football on the radio than watched it on television (23%) on the average Saturday afternoon in the 1953 season. Yet these figures contrast with a mere 3% of the fans who actually attended a game on the average Saturday. Sheatsley and Borsky conclude that if no games were telecast, the result would not be more listening to radio broadcasts, but an upward surge in attendance at the games themselves.

Watching football on television, they observe, actually breaks the habit of attendance. In support of this they point out that attendance is lower among those who have owned TV longest. In 1953, 84% of those fans who had owned their sets for four years or more did not attend a single game; this compares with 73% of those who had owned a set for two or three years, and with 69% of those who had owned their set for a year or less.

With these findings, the NORC researchers effectively dispose of Jordan's theory of TV's "novelty effect." In fact, their analysis leads them even further in the opposite direction. They note that strong interest in college football is heavily concentrated among the minority of college-educated. "The best seats are reserved for alumni and students, and a large part of the game's appeal lies in the songs and cheers, the campus associations and the pleasures of meeting old friends and classmates, which the non-college attender cannot fully appreciate."

But the select group who constitute college football's chief supporters were also among the first persons to acquire television. By contrast, those who bought sets later on were more apt to be "marginal" fans, if they were interested in the game at all. The last persons to acquire television had even lower incomes, and were less apt to have college ties. Such persons were far more ready than the TV pioneers to be wooed away from actual attendance, and less apt to have a strong attachment to a particular team. The result is that televised football would have a greater, rather than a smaller, effect as time goes on—if not for the NCAA restrictions on telecasting.

TABLE 62

Football Attendance in Areas With and Without TV Competition

Year	Per Cent of Expected (1947-8) Attendance		
	Colleges With TV Competition	Colleges Without TV Competition	TV Differential
1950	88.6	115.1	26.5
1951	85.1	103.7	18.6
1952	83.8	110.5	26.7
1953	81.6	109.3	27.7

Actually the Sheatsley-Borsky analysis shows a fairly stable attendance pattern over recent years, at a level well below the pre-television norms of 1947-8, and with a clear-cut differential between TV and non-TV areas. Table 62 shows the results of this comparison for the years 1950-3. By 1954 there were practically no non-television areas left to measure.

The NORC studies not only reveal an unbroken array of evidence that TV cuts into attendance; they also fail to support the theory that telecasts stimulate interest in football among those who previously lacked it. "While televised games, just like radio and the sports pages, undoubtedly provide satisfaction to fans who are already interested, they clearly have not made many new fans for the game." Four fans of every five were found to have at least one strong favorite team whose fortunes they follow, and these attachments are based overwhelmingly on personal or geographic ties rather than on performance or quality.

To what extent are the conclusions of the NORC-NCAA studies applicable to other sports? The finding that television does not create interest probably cannot be made into a general statement. It seems likely that in the case of baseball, boxing and a number of other sports (and perhaps to a lesser degree even in the case of football), television combines with other media and channels of publicity to generate an atmosphere of interest and discussion which lifts the general level of awareness to the point where some people move from a position of apathy to one of marginal interest, or from the latter category to become true fans.

The major reason for hesitation in generalizing to all sports from the NORC findings is that college football and basketball are different from professional baseball and boxing in the degree to which their principal fans are drawn from a distinct social stratum. Because the professional sports have a broader mass following, it would probably be wrong to assume that the first owners of TV were also the most enthusiastic fans. Moreover, since baseball telecasts have not been restricted like college football games, it is impossible to trace the pattern of cause and effect in the exacting manner of the NORC analysis.

The period of television's growth has been a period of decline for professional baseball. Big league attendance fell from a high of nearly 21 million in 1948 to a low of 14 million in 1953. In 1954 it climbed back to 16 million.   (B)

A survey made in 1955 for the office of the Baseball Commissioner by the public relations firm of Stephen Fitzgerald and Company came up with an optimistic view of the subject. Since the sampling and interviewing were not carried out by professionals, the findings cannot be taken literally in spite of the 20,000 persons reportedly interviewed. Seven out of ten reported that radio broadcasting and telecasting of baseball games had increased their interest in the sport. Of those who felt that broadcasts had increased the public interest in baseball, 39% believed that they had decreased actual attendance, but 27% thought that attendance had increased.

Half of those interviewed said they would favor a blackout of home games if baseball were threatened by the telecasts. About one in three indicated a willingness to pay 25-50 cents to see games on "pay-as-you-see" TV.

Two major-league teams have taken the step of banning television. The Braves, after moving from Boston to Milwaukee in 1953, showed the biggest attendance increase of any team in either league. The Athletics, when they moved from Philadelphia to Kansas City, raised their attendance by over a million. In both cases it is hard to say how much of the improvement was wrought by the move, how much by the exclusion of TV.

TABLE 63

The Rise and Fall in Minor Leagues

(Source: Sports Illustrated)

Year	Number of Leagues	Number of Teams
1935	21	150
1937	37	249
1940	43	296
1943*	9	62
1946	42	310
1949	59	448
1952	43	324
1955	33	241

(C)

*Most minor leagues suspended play during World War II. 1943 marked the lowest point.

However, television has provided the big leagues with some fresh source of revenue. Television fees do not have to be split with the visiting club, which gets 25¢ for every customer at the gate.

In 1947, radio rights for the world series games were $175,000,

TV rights $65,000. In 1949 radio cost $154,000, TV $200,000. By 1950 radio cost $175,000, TV $800,000. In 1953 radio cost $200,000, television $925,000. The National Broadcasting Company and a sponsor, Gillette, will pay $16,250,000 for TV rights to the World Series and All Star games for five years starting 1957.   (D)

By contrast, television has meant nothing but continued losses for minor leagues, which must compete with the majors on TV. *Sports Illustrated* mentions a number of other factors contributing to their decline, including the growth of other sports, outdoor movies, and miscellaneous summertime diversions. The story is told in Table 63.

In summary, the evidence suggests that unrestricted televising of sports events can cause attendance to drop *but* at the same time heighten popular interest in the sports themselves.

10. TV AND THE ADVERTISERS

From the very beginnings of wireless telephony, broadcasting in the United States has developed under a system of commercial sponsorship by which air time is sold by the broadcasting station or network to companies with goods and services to advertise. This system is subject to the regulations of the Federal Communication Commission, which requires that a certain amount of broadcast time be devoted to public service features.

For the advertiser, the radio or television audience is part of a market. He sees the listeners or viewers as potential customers whose attention he buys in order to persuade them to buy his product.

Television's emergence as a popular medium of entertainment and information coincided with the post-war economic boom. The boom accelerated television's growth, and in fact the growth of all the media.

1. Consumers with more money to spend have been able to buy expensive television sets, as well as more newspapers, magazines and radios.

2. The increased prosperity of industry has made more money available for the advertising which provides the main direct support of television and the other mass media.

If the rise of television was made possible by a high order of economic prosperity, it has also played a part in sustaining that prosperity. The television industry — broadcasting, manufacturing and servicing—has grown to proportions which give it an important place in the economy. Apart from this, television has provided American business with a powerful new advertising vehicle by which to rouse the buying instincts of the public and keep its spending up and up. But the mass media have always whetted the appetites of the American consumer to a far greater degree than advertising alone would indicate. More than radio (because it adds sight to sound), more than newspapers and magazines (because it has sound and motion), more than motion pictures (because it is a much more constant companion), television is helping to shape values and set standards simply by depicting a world somewhat more glamorous than present reality. And the perquisites and comforts of this fantasy world become the very objects to which the audience aspires, and which it ultimately acquires.

A few years ago, there was virtually no investment in television by advertisers. In 1955 their investment passed the billion dollar mark. Yet this fabulous growth is only part of the fantastic history of advertising in the past two decades, from $1.7 billion in 1935 to $3 billion at the war's end, and to $10 billion in 1956.

TABLE 64

Advertising Expenditures in Five Major Media
(in millions of dollars)

(Source: McCann-Erickson, Inc.)

	1935	1940	1948	1952	1956
Television	$ —	$ —	$ —	$ 453.9	$1,209.9
Radio	112.6	215.6	561.6	624.1	570.7
Magazines	136.3	197.7	512.7	615.8	794.7
Newspapers	762.1	815.4	1,749.6	2,472.8	3,235.6
Outdoor	31.1	44.7	132.1	162.1	199.6
Total for Five Media	$1,042.1	$1,273.4	$2,956.0	$4,328.7	$6,010.5
Total for All Media*	$1,690.0	$2,087.6	$4,863.6	$7,809.2	$9,904.7

*Including direct mail, matchbooks, etc.

(A)

This enormous expansion (shown in Table 64) has directly reflected the rise of the economy, rather than an increase in the proportion which advertising represents of the cost of products to the consumer. (This proportion stands at around 3½% over-all, though lower or much higher in individual product fields.)

The increased prosperity of the mass media is more than a reflection of the increased volume of advertising which they carry. Actually the increase in advertising support only reflects steadily increasing support on the part of the audience. This support has grown not only as people can afford to spend more money and more time on their own entertainment, but as their better education and their changed mode of living broadens the scope of their interests.

Though vast sums are spent by advertisers on the mass media

these sums are actually dwarfed by what the public pays voluntarily. (The figures are shown in Table 65.)

TABLE 65
The Advertiser's Share of Media Costs—And the Consumer's (1954)

(Source: McCann-Erickson, Inc.)

	Advertiser's Share	Consumer's Share	Estimated Total (100%) (in billions of dollars)
Television	20%	80%	$4.0
Radio	40	60	1.5
Magazines	52	48	1.3
Newspapers	66	34	4.0
Outdoor	100	—	0.185
Five Media Total	31%	69%	$11.0

(B)

In 1954, for every dollar spent by advertisers to buy magazine space, consumers spent another dollar to buy copies of the same magazines. For every dollar advertisers spent in newspapers, the public spent 50 cents. For every dollar advertisers invested in radio, consumers spent one and a half to buy, run and service radio sets. For every dollar spent by the advertiser on television, the viewers spent four. (In preparing this estimate allowance was made for electric consumption, servicing and installation charges, and the cost of sets and replacement parts.) An estimate by *U. S. News and World Report* is that radio accounted for 0.5% of the family budget in 1935-9. Radio and television accounted for 0.8% in the 1945-9 period, 1% for 1950-54.

All media have profited by the rise in advertising revenue. The steady growth of advertising budgets has meant that new sums have been available in each successive year to finance the progress of television, without actual loss in dollar volume to any other medium except radio. But even radio's losses in the last few years represent only a small fraction of the television advertising investment.

When the dollar expenditures in the five principal advertising media are expressed in percentage form, it is evident that television has spurred a tendency, already apparent before it arrived, for advertisers to reduce the share of print media in their total spending. Newspapers in particular represent a declining share of the advertising dollar, although they are still by far the major medium, and although their actual income has continued to grow.

Before too many tears are shed over newspaper's diminishing share of advertising, it must be remembered that the publishers themselves have shared heavily in the profits of the new medium. At latest count, 164 of the country's 502 TV stations, or 33%, were owned by newspapers, or associated with them, compared with only 14% of the AM radio outlets. The newspaper-affiliated TV stations have over 90% of the nation's receivers within their coverage areas.

Television may actually have spurred the growth of advertising in the other media, both directly, in the sale of sets and promotion of programs, and indirectly, by sharpening competition and increasing awareness of advertising in general. In an analysis of the effects of radio, Harvey Levin makes a number of points which apply very well to television:

"Radio advertising, according to some authorities, stimulated newspaper advertising directly on a number of counts. First, there was simply the effect of introducing newcomers to the role of advertising, after which they simply 'got the bug' and turned to other media too. Then, there was the phenomenon of 'competitive advertising' where outlays by one firm in a new medium forced its rivals to follow suit while maintaining their older appropriations, or to counter with increased outlays in established media. Radio set manufacturers, moreover, poured millions into newspaper advertisements. Furthermore, though there is no evidence that radio seriously deterred movie receipts, what inroads there were would seem to have brought new money into advertising. Lastly, newspapers turned to radio for promotion, which is not at all the same as saying that radio took revenues that would otherwise have gone into newspapers. But newspapers plugging their circulation over the radio may not have advertised at all in other newspapers or magazines."

Regardless of television's effects on advertising appropriations for rival media, or on audiences for those media, there is no evidence that it has reduced the attention paid to other forms of advertising. An analysis of magazine ad observation figures, prepared by the Magazine Advertising Bureau, shows no perceptible trend during a five-

year period of great TV growth. Both in 1947 and in 1951 full page
ads in nine magazines measured by Daniel Starch and Staff were noted
by 28% of the men readers and by 33% of the women.

TV's Effects on Radio Advertising

The two broadcast media together today represent a much
larger share of all advertising than radio did at its peak. (See Table
66.)

TABLE 66

How Advertising Expenditures Are Divided
Among Five Major Media

(Source: McCann-Erickson, Inc.)

	1935	1940	1948	1952	1956
Television	—%	—%	—%	11%	20%
Radio	11	18	21	15	10
Newspapers	73	63	58	56	54
Magazines	13	15	17	14	13
Outdoor	3	4	4	4	3
Total for Five Media	100%	100%	100%	100%	100%

(C)

But it is not altogether accurate to assess television's impact
on radio's income on the basis of total expenditures. The most significant effect has been on the patterning of media usage by different types
of advertisers. The great network programs sponsored by national
advertisers have undergone a steady decline on radio, at the same
time that they have become an increasingly dominant feature of television advertising. National advertisers on radio have tended to switch
from direct sponsorship of network programs to "spot" commercial
announcements and programs which permit far more flexible scheduling. On television, network programs continue to represent the
bulk of their spending.

But a still more important development has taken place, as
radio has sought and won increasing support from local and regional
advertisers to offset its decline on the national level. Between 1950
and 1956, radio's revenue from this source increased from 45% to

60% of its total. At the same time television's dependence on these small advertisers declined, from 32% of its revenues in 1950 to 21% in 1956. The details are given in Table 67.

TABLE 67

Trends in Broadcast Advertising Expenditures, by Medium and Type

(Source: McCann-Erickson, Inc.)

	Radio					Television				
	National		Local	Total	Local as % of Total	National		Local	Total	Local as % of Total
	Network	Spot	Local	Total	of Total	Network	Spot	Local	Total	of Total
1935	62.6	14.9	35.1	112.6	31%					
1940	113.3	42.1	60.2	215.6	28					
1946	199.6	98.2	156.6	454.4	34					
1948	210.6	121.1	229.9	561.6	40					
1950	196.3	135.8	273.3	605.4	45	85.0	30.8	55.0	170.8	32%
1952	161.5	141.5	321.1	624.1	51	256.4	93.8	103.7	453.9	23
1954	114.5	135.4	315.0	564.9	56	417.9	205.2	180.5	803.6	22
1955	84.4	134.1	326.4	544.9	60	540.2	260.4	224.7	1,025.3	22
1956	71.0	158.9	340.8	570.7	60	629.7	325.0	225.2	1,209.9	21

(D)

Between 1948 and 1954 the number of national advertisers sponsoring or participating in network radio programs fell from 143 to 116, though the total number of national advertisers in the U. S. grew by more than a third. Sponsored network programming fell from 202 hours a week to 187. In 1948, 37% of all sponsored time periods were segments of 30 minutes or more; in 1954 these were only 15% of the total. Between 1955 and 1957 radio began a revival. The number of network sponsors rose to 130. (E)

In spite of a general rise in advertising costs, sponsors are investing less money today for the talent and production needed to attract radio audiences. As recently as 1950, the average half-hour evening broadcast cost $8,283 for production and talent. In 1954 only about half as much was spent—$4,223 (according to published estimates in sources like *Sponsor* or *Variety;* it may actually be lower). In part, this reflects the introduction of a number of low-budget shows. But established programs have also cut their production costs. (Evening radio shows which were on the air both in 1950 and in 1954 cut their production budgets by at least two-fifths in this period.)

National advertisers spent $230,000,000 in radio in 1956, only

24% as much as they spent in television. Yet radio as a whole has held its own as an advertising medium (with estimated revenue of $570,700,000 in 1956), despite increasing expenditures on television by many national advertisers. Partly this reflects the fact that more and more money has been spent on advertising.

Between 1948 and 1956 advertising expenditures in the two broadcast media tripled. The revenues of the radio industry, over-all, continued to grow until 1952, dropped until 1955 and then gained slightly.

While spending on network programs has fallen drastically (67% since 1948), national advertising expenditures in radio only declined by 2% in the same period, because of increased use of spot. Moreover, there has been increased support from local advertisers like supermarkets and department stores who had traditionally used newspaper advertising almost exclusively. In 1956, such locally supported advertising was at a high level—341 million dollars—48% greater than in 1948.

To attract advertisers in the face of declining audiences, the radio networks have lowered their time charges substantially for evening shows, have provided special discount incentives for sponsors of both daytime and evening programs, and have offered a variety of new sponsorship plans to permit far more flexible placement of advertising messages. Under these plans an advertiser can have his message appear on a number of different programs, attracting differ-

(F)   ent audiences, instead of confining himself to a single program. This enables him to reach far more prospective customers, although he loses at the same time the advantage of exclusive association with the program or its star.

A radio network program is usually broadcast on a chain of stations whose combined signal can be heard by virtually every radio set in the country. By contrast the limited number of television stations (some of which, in smaller cities, service several networks) is unable to achieve this kind of universal coverage, even of television homes. The coverage picture has been improving, however. By one recent estimate, the average evening TV program could reach 70%

(G)   of all U. S. TV homes three years ago, but now reaches 90%. Nonetheless, television scheduling on the major networks represents a problem during peak viewing hours.

Radio offers a way for the advertiser to reach large numbers of people more cheaply than with television. There are limits to available TV facilities and air time. TV ratings have declined and will continue to do so as competition increases. At the same time, television costs have risen and will continue to rise. (They may jump as much as 10% in 1958.) Daytime radio's cost/1000/commercial minute is much lower than that of daytime TV ($1.35, compared with $1.75), but evening radio is comparable ($3.25, compared with $3.28 for half-hour programs on television). The cost/1000/commercial minute is the cost of reaching 1000 homes with one minute of a sponsor's commercial message.)

To illustrate daytime radio's economy: "Road of Life," a daytime serial which was both broadcast and telecast in 1955, reached a larger audience on radio than on television, and at one-third the cost/1000/commercial minute. (H)

Network radio has shown its capacity to compete successfully with television during daylight hours, even in TV homes. For the time being, and for a few years to come, evening network radio provides an extremely efficient way of supplementing television. (About 85% of the listeners to an evening radio program like Amos 'n' Andy were in radio-only homes in 1955.)

TABLE 68

National Advertisers' Expenditures as a Proportion of Total Advertising
(1956)

(Source: McCann-Erickson, Inc.)

	National Advertising As a Per Cent of Total
Television	79%
Radio	40
Newspapers	24
Magazines	100
Outdoor	67
Five-Media Total	48%
All Advertising*	60%

*Including Direct Mail, Transportation, etc.

(I)

When TV has achieved universal penetration, evening radio may no longer be able to meet its competition; at least this may not be possible for four networks operating on their present scale. But network radio should continue to flourish on the basis of its daytime schedule, though its internal budgeting and management will require some adjustments.

Radio today is a predominantly local advertising medium, increasingly competitive with newspapers, which depend overwhelmingly on local advertisers. By contrast television gets four dollars of every five from national companies, and accordingly finds itself in direct competition with magazines. (See Table 68.)

But the number of national advertisers has continued to grow steadily, as Table 69 demonstrates. The number of nationally advertised brands produced by these companies has grown at an even faster pace. This reflects more and more competition for the market, and for a share of the consumer's attention. Thus the pressure for larger advertising budgets is accelerated.

TABLE 69

Growth in the Number of Major National Advertisers
(Spending over $25,000 a year in magazines, network radio
and network television)

(Source: Magazine Advertising Bureau)

1940	1,129
1945	1,884
1950	1,964
1954	2,379
1956	2,600

(J)

Television, at the very start, attracted the big national advertisers as sponsors of its network programs. Smaller national and regional advertisers, who could not afford the cost of sponsoring shows, have used spot announcements at an ever-increasing rate, as Table 70 shows. Between 1951 and 1955 their number grew by 120%; in the same period the number of network advertisers rose 36%.

The relatively slow growth in the number of network advertisers is caused by the limited time availabilities on the major networks and by the high costs of network program production, which only the very biggest advertisers can afford to bear. The result of this is that ten companies spend one third of all the money that goes into television network advertising, as Table 71 indicates. Similarly,

TABLE 70

The Growing Number of TV Advertisers

(Source: Television Bureau of Advertising)

	National and Regional Spot Advertisers	Network Advertisers
1949	530	71
1950	970	107
1951	1,540	187
1952	1,632	197
1953	2,009	196
1954	2,789	243
1955	3,355	255
1956	4,399	321

(K)

the television billings of ten advertising agencies account for half the money spent on national television advertising—network and spot. These big advertisers and agencies understandably wield greater power in television than in other advertising media whose sources of income are more widely distributed.

TABLE 71

Network Time Expenditures of Top Ten TV Network Clients, 1956

(Source: Publishers' Information Bureau)

Procter & Gamble Company	$43,449,027
Colgate-Palmolive Company	19,880,282
General Motors Corporation	19,086,646
Chrysler Corporation	18,198,264
American Home Products Corporation	15,758,019
General Foods Corporation	15,688,789
Gillette Company	15,257,871
R. J. Reynolds Tobacco Company	11,424,421
Lever Brothers	11,322,643
Ford Motor Company	10,316,421
Total Top 10	$180,382,383
Total TV Network Time Billings	$488,167,634
% Top Ten of Total	37%

(L)

Advertising Practices and Costs

While the preceding discussion refers to all national advertising, it must be kept in mind that practices vary widely among different industries, and even among individual companies in the same industry. Partly this reflects traditional practice and a tendency to follow the leader or leaders in each field. Partly the differences among industries arise from the inherent advantages of a given medium in calling attention to the merits of the particular product (for example, the unique advantage of television in permitting appliances to be demonstrated). They may be related to the marketing structure of the industry (for example, the concentration of many oil companies in restricted marketing territories). Table 72 compares the media scheduling practices of four principal industries, to illustrate this point.

TABLE 72
How Different Kinds of Advertisers Spend Their Money (1956)

(Source: McCann-Erickson, Inc.)

	Food	*Appliances*	*Industry* *Gasoline and Oil*	*Automotive*	*All National Advertisers*	*All Advertisers*
Television	39%	34%	25%	23%	34%	21%
Radio	17	3	5	2	7	9
Newspapers	26	26	35	50	28	54
Magazines	15	35	13	18	27	13
Outdoor	3	2	22	7	4	3
Total for Five Media	100%	100%	100%	100%	100%	100%

(M)

Television network advertisers are drawn from every industry, but their expenditures come much more heavily from certain product fields than from others. Of every ten dollars spent in network television, seven come from manufacturers of food products, toiletries, automobiles, soap, cigarettes and related commodities. (See Table 73.)

The great boom in advertising expenditures has paralleled the great growth of media audiences, which has already been described. With rising audiences, the media have raised their rates, at a faster

TABLE 73

Sources of Network Television Revenues
by Major Industry Classifications

(Based on Publishers' Information Bureau Data, 1956)

	% Share of Total
Food and food products	18%
Toiletries & toilet goods	18
Automotive, automotive accessories & equipment	12
Soaps, cleansers & polishes	12
Smoking materials	8
Drugs & remedies	8
Household equipment & supplies	7
Industrial materials	2
Beer, wine & liquor	2
Confectionery & soft drinks	2
Radios, television sets, phonographs, musical instruments & accessories	2
Apparel, footwear & accessories	1
Office equipment, stationery & writing supplies	1
Jewelry, optical goods & cameras	1
Household furnishings	1
Gasoline, lubricants & other fuels	1
Miscellaneous	4
	100%
Total	$488,167,634

(N)

pace than the growth in the cost of living since the war. During the past ten years, the cost of advertising has doubled for companies which have sought only to sustain constant pressure. This is shown in Table 74.

Among the major media, only radio, with falling audiences, has lowered its rates, but even radio cannot deliver as many advertising impressions for a dollar as it could at the end of the war. Rising costs of paper and production have also hit print advertising. When both cost and audience changes are considered, this too is more expensive than it was ten years ago.

But television is the biggest single reason why advertising

expenses have grown. With more stations and more sets, TV rates have tripled in five years. But the expansion of the television audience has taken place even more rapidly, so that this medium, a far from economical buy in 1950, can now compete with other media on a "cost-per-impression" basis. The cost to the TV advertiser, to deliver his message to 1000 homes, is a third less than it was five years ago.

TABLE 74		Changes in Advertising Costs, 1950-1957
(Source: McCann-Erickson, Inc.)		
	Rate Changes	*Cost of Reaching 1000 Households*
Network Television	+210%	−71%
Spot Television	+399	−53
Network Radio	−43	+ 8
Spot Radio (Day)	− 6	+40
Newspapers	+34	+26
Magazines	+47	+28

(O)

Increased network and station time charges represent a substantial part of the growing television budget. A half-hour of evening time on the "basic" 54 stations of a major network costs about $42,000, though discounts bring this figure down considerably for a regular advertiser.

Time costs depend upon (a) the time of the program (evening hours on television are twice as expensive as daylight hours, and the period from 5-6 is half again as expensive as daytime); (b) the length of the program; and (c) the size of the network, the number of stations carrying the program. But heightened competition for the viewers' interest has raised production costs even more rapidly than time charges, as more expensive talent and more lavish staging has become the general rule. Television has made ever greater use of Hollywood and Broadway stars, and the shortage of skilled performers, producers, writers and other program personnel has also meant mounting fees. A contract recently announced for one entertainer provides a salary of $25,000 a week. Perhaps the highest talent

TABLE 75

Average Production Costs of TV Programs

(Source: McCann-Erickson, Inc.)

90 Minute "Spectaculars"	$200,000
One Hour Variety Shows	88,000
One Hour Dramas	62,000
Half-hour Dramas	34,000
Situation Comedies (Per ½ hour)	40,000
Quiz, Audience Participation (Per ½ hour)	28,000
Daytime Quarter-hour	2,000

and production cost for a single broadcast has been paid for "Mayerling"—estimated to have cost $450,000.

The typical evening program costs far less, of course, but (as Table 75 indicates) there is a substantial range in the average figure for different types of shows. In general, variety shows, with their high-salaried stars, large casts, and frequent changes of scenery and costume, are the most expensive. Audience participation shows, despite what often appear to be fabulous prizes (as in the case of the "$64,000 Question"), are the least complicated and costly. Sports events, children's programs, and daytime serial dramas cost far less than most evening productions. (P)

TABLE 76

A Program's Cost Is No Clue to its Efficiency

(A Comparison of Three ½-Hour Dramatic Shows)

	Program A	*Program B*	*Program C*
Total Cost, time and talent	$87,285	$70,894	$48,835
Cost of reaching 1000 homes with one minute of commercial time	$2.85	$3.76	$2.08

It must not be assumed, however, that the cost of a program provides any clue to its efficiency as an advertising medium for the sponsor. The most expensive show does not always draw the largest audience, and the show with the biggest rating is not always the most economical, when its costs are considered. Table 76 illustrates this by comparing three half-hour evening dramatic programs of essentially the same format but differing costs. In this particular comparison, the least expensive show also happens to be most economical, in terms of its audience size. But the most expensive of the three is *not* the least economical. (In other cases, the pattern may of course be different.)

Although network television programs vary tremendously both in cost and audience size, there is no way for a sponsor to assure himself of getting the most for his money simply by putting on a certain type of program. All types of evening programs (except quiz and audience participation shows, some of which are scheduled in afternoon and morning hours) have very similar efficiency ratings, on the average. (Table 77 gives the details.) Half-hour programs are generally more than half as expensive to produce as hour-long programs, and the cost of delivering 1000 commercial minute messages is accordingly greater.

TABLE 77

Comparative Efficiency of Different Types of TV Programs

(Source: McCann-Erickson, Inc.)

Average Programs	*Cost of Reaching 1000 Homes with One Minute of Sponsored Commercial Time, January, 1955*
General Drama (½ hour)	$3.56
Mystery Drama (½ hour)	3.33
Situation Comedy (½ hour)	3.40
General Variety (½ hour)	3.31
Quiz, Audience Participation	3.12
News Commentary	2.93
Sports Events	2.77
Children's Programs	2.27
Daytime Serials	1.46
77 evening ½ hour shows	$3.80
28 evening one hour shows	3.57
6 daytime ¼ hour shows	1.59

(Q)

While daytime programming is more economical, on a relative basis, it reaches smaller audiences, and is therefore less attractive to the advertiser who wants to reach as many people as he can.

TV's Values for the Sponsor

Dollar and cents figures in themselves provide no indication   (R)
of a program's value for the advertiser. He may be willing to sacrifice something in per-unit cost efficiency if a larger investment will
raise his total audience. This choice may occur either in fixing production costs, or in program scheduling.

An advertiser invariably faces problems in determining how
many of a network's affiliates should be asked to carry a program
beyond those stations which constitute the basic list. Up to a point
his efficiency increases as he adds additional stations, because he has
a heavy investment in production which can be spread more widely
to a larger audience. But a point of diminishing returns is reached
as he adds new stations in smaller markets where there are few television sets and viewers are harder and more costly to come by.

The advertiser cannot make his decision to add a station on
the basis of efficiency alone. He may want to buy time on a station
in a market which formerly had not had local TV service, on the
assumption that the viewing public will grow in size, and in order
to secure his right to a prime time period which might not be available later. Or he might have to add a market to his list in order to
provide support for important distributors or dealers who like the
idea of being associated with a big network television program, even
though some other form of advertising might work more efficiently
for them.

A program should be scheduled in such a way that it covers
the geographic territory in which the sponsor sells his product, and
wastes no effort elsewhere. In one notable violation of this rule, a
brewing concern spent two million dollars on a network television
show which reached an audience throughout the country—while 90%
of the sponsor's beer was sold in twelve states.

In selecting a program, an advertiser considers not only the
size of his audience, but also the kinds of people who watch it. Since
he generally knows who the best prospects are for the commodity he
is selling, he tries to find a show that will reach these very people.
This is why it makes sense to advertise razor blades via boxing
matches, dry cereals and candy bars with a children's program, and
laundry soap with a daytime soap opera.

Only in rare cases does a prospective sponsor actually begin by specifying the kind of audience he wants to reach and by actually building a program to those audience and marketing specifications. Normally a program is bought by an advertiser only after it has already been developed by a broadcasting network, an advertising agency, or a "package producer" who undertakes on a speculative basis the development of a format and then the actual production.

Before a program goes on the air there can be conjectures about its probable future audience, based on its type, timing and competition. But most new programs are judged for their attractiveness as entertainment by the sponsor or his advertising agency. Sometimes their judgment is excellent. Sometimes they mistakenly identify their own likes and dislikes with the likes and dislikes of their customers, even though these may be drawn from a very different level of taste. (An extreme example of this is the case of a company president who opposed advertising on television because he thought that the only people who owned television sets kept them in their servants' quarters—as he did—and never watched them.)

The procedure of matching the market and audience may seem most elementary. Yet some advertisers—particularly those who buy a new program on the strength of its own inherent merits or promise, or those who never look beyond the over-all rating figures—disregard the principle and thereby short-change themselves.

This is one reason why a show which is successful in attracting large numbers of viewers is not always successful in moving goods. It may be more than the obvious factors of sex, age and income which are crucial in determining whether a program is an appropriate selling vehicle. The personality of the program must not be too sharply inconsistent with that of the advertised brand.

A comedian like Milton Berle unquestionably has his strongest appeal to a different type of viewer than someone like George Gobel. Similarly, personality differences are reflected in the choice between competing brands of cigarettes, soft drinks or gasoline—since different companies create different public images of themselves and their products. If the program does not reinforce the tendency to use a particular brand, it serves no purpose for the advertiser, regardless of its qualities as entertainment. As a simple illustration of this thesis

—a manufacturer introducing a radical innovation, whether it be an aerosol-bomb shaving cream or an atomically fueled automobile, would probably do much better to sponsor a liberal news commentator than a conservative one, if he wanted to attract the venturesome type of consumer.

Of course there are other ways in which the program should suit the product. An institutional, public relations type of advertising message would be out of place in a variety show and be perfectly at home in the setting of a serious dramatic program—even though both shows attracted the same group of viewers in different moods.

The subject of mood is sometimes brought up in criticisms made by rival advertising media. A promotion brochure issued by the Magazine Advertising Bureau puts the argument succinctly:

> "It's Saturday evening; the week's work is done and the children are in bed. The little woman settles down with a sigh of relief to watch 'Your Show of Shows.' But two of the sponsors of that most entertaining variety show are a pot and pan cleaner, and a household disinfectant. Their commercials abruptly jerk the little woman from the theatre, send her back to the kitchen she's just left with a sigh of relief."

Despite the strong note of special pleading in this description, it contains a grain of truth which the television industry itself has been ready to recognize. With even the best of opportunities to reach large numbers of the right people, a sponsor can fail to get his message across effectively if it is unsuited to its setting in the program itself—or if it is inherently incapable of gaining attention, interest and conviction.

A manufacturer whose competitors are advertising on the new medium often feels that he cannot afford to stay out of it either. Yet there are a number of reasons why a sizable advertiser might want to stay out of television: because of the substantial expenditure it requires, because his market is limited geographically, or because his customers are concentrated in a particular social or occupational group. In the latter case it may be much more efficient to use magazines, or some other medium which focusses directly on a functional interest of that group, rather than to spread his effort via a mass medium like television.

It is not too common to find a direct relationship between the type of program and the type of sponsor. Soap manufacturers have traditionally sponsored daytime serials, but they are by no means the only sponsors who have used this type of program to reach housewives. Conversely, these same sponsors have used evening programs which reach the housewife in the context of her family. This permits messages directed to other members of the family to reinforce the appeals to the housewife herself.

Large industrial corporations like the Aluminum Company of America, Standard Oil Company (New Jersey), U. S. Steel, General Electric and DuPont, sometimes advertise to build regard for themselves as institutions, both for public relations reasons and because they wish to acquire prestige for their products. Since the days of radio, they have required that their programs be suitably dignified and serious. In practice this means that they have often tried to reach a selective audience with which a manufacturer directly selling consumer goods would not necessarily be satisfied.

The increasing cost of television programming has brought about two developments: (1) cooperative sponsorship of the longer and more expensive shows (including the extra-length "spectaculars"), and (2) sponsorship of the same show by different sponsors in alternate weeks.

Three-fourths of network television advertisers are today involved in some multiple-sponsorship arrangement. Robert Kintner, ex-President of the American Broadcasting Company, describes the advantages of multiple sponsorship as follows:

"This has come about for budgetary reasons; from a desire to spread the risk of a flop over several shows; and from a desire on the part of the larger advertisers to distribute their commercial minutes over different time periods and days of the week for different products."

To this list one disadvantage must be appended. The joint sponsor of a program may lose something of the favorable association he wants to build with the show and its stars. There appears to be less ability on the part of the public to correctly remember that he is the sponsor. Where commercials for several products are advertised on the same program, recall of what they have said appears to weaken, though the unconscious impact may be just as great.

Spot placement of filmed programs and the use of spot announcements have also grown. Spot programs on film may be sponsored by different companies in different cities, thus giving the small local advertiser the opportunity to use talent of national calibre. Spot announcements sandwiched in the breaks between programs come within reach of the great audiences already assembled for entertainment, but the advertiser does not underwrite the cost of the entertainment, though he pays disproportionately heavily for air time.

How much extra value, in the way of gratitude, prestige, or pleasant associations, an advertiser gets from sponsoring a program is not known from research.

Television, like every other medium, can best be judged as a vehicle for advertising, not in the abstract, but in relation to specific products or services. In selecting or evaluating advertising media, many different points must be considered, some of intrinsically greater importance than others, but all of them relevant in certain cases. Here are a number of questions that might be raised about every medium, — and the answers which might be given for television in each instance:

Coverage

1. How well does it concentrate on the best customers or prospects for the product? The answer would depend on the particular TV program used, and the congruence between its audience composition and the character of the market.

2. Does it get into the major markets for the product? The answer here depends on whether the advertiser uses a network program, which allows only a limited choice of stations (beyond the "basic" network), or whether he uses spot programming or announcements (which can be scheduled on any station desired—provided that time is available). Since all principal American cities have television, even a regional advertiser can use the medium to good advantage.

3. Does it penetrate into the areas of low advertising pressure?

No, TV cannot reach into a fifth of the homes in the country, and these are the very homes which are hardest to reach with all other media—except radio.

4. Does it provide national coverage? Still not quite as completely as other media.

5. Does it permit flexible geographical coverage? Bought on a spot basis, yes.

Economy

6. What is the cost/1000 people reached? Television looks expensive, compared with Sunday supplements, radio, or the largest magazines, but less expensive compared with newspapers bought individually.

7. What is the cost/1000 messages delivered? The sponsor of an hour-long television program has six minutes of commercial time, which he might split into six one-minute messages. On this basis, television compares favorably with other media in economy.

8. How big a basic investment is required? For network programming, a sizable one. While many small local advertisers use television on a spot basis, this is still an expensive medium to break into, and it offers nothing for the low-budget national advertiser that can compare with small-space ads in newspapers or national magazines.

9. Can the campaign be contracted or expanded within the limits of the medium? With spot television it can be, with network programming it can't.

Perception

10. Does it permit vivid visual impact? It certainly does, and color will heighten this advantage.

11. Does it allow the product to be demonstrated? This is a unique advantage. No other medium can make this claim.

12. How well does it convey abstract ideas? Not as well as the printed word, or even as well as radio's spoken word. At its best, television can be used to dramatize abstractions and to make them vivid in concrete examples, but this requires effort and ingenuity.

13. Does it have a news value, or convey a sense of urgency? It can be used in this way, though the effect is different from that of a department store sale announced in a newspaper spread.

14. Can the advertising message be integrated with media content? It can be, and it's done all the time, for instance when Arthur Godfrey talks about tea.

15. How well does the medium go with simultaneous activities? Not too well. It's known that people sew, talk, and even read while they watch television, but the results are not as successful as when they listen to the radio. On the other hand, the print media require complete concentration.

16. Does the audience get the message with a minimum of distraction? To a greater degree than with radio, but certainly less than with magazines.

17. What is the life of the advertising message? Like all broadcast words, it is evanescent, while printed words last. On the other hand, a really catchy commercial slogan or jingle develops a life of its own and is embodied, through repetition, in the public lore.

18. What is the potential for repeated impact? Since television viewing is a sustained activity in which people return to their favorite programs, there is a good opportunity to reach the same people again and again. (TV comes out better than radio in this respect, though not nearly as well as the Sunday supplements.)

19. To what extent are prospects reached who are not touched by other media? Hardly at all.

Associations

20. How believable or authoritative is the medium? Perhaps not as much as the New York *Times* or *Life,* but it carries considerable weight.

21. What good will or prestige comes from sponsoring entertainment? The assumption has always been that this factor adds considerably to the value of broadcast advertising compared with print, but there is no evidence really to prove the point.

22. Is there a favorable association with a well-known personality? Television and radio have an advantage over the print media in this respect, for advertisers.

Merchandising

23. Does the medium provide promotional support for its advertisers? Individual television stations may place audience-building

ads for a program on the TV-radio program pages of the newspapers, but television as a medium does not have the same aggressive practice as leading magazines and newspapers, who actually employ crews of representatives who work directly with placards, stickers and other devices that the retailer can use at the point of sales or in his windows. In many cities local television personalities cooperate actively in store appearances, dealer meetings, and the like.

24. How does the medium rate with the retail dealer? Very highly. As part of a study made in Fort Wayne, Indiana, the National Broadcasting Company found that television was particularly effective with the local merchants whom any national advertiser must court to get his product properly stocked, displayed and promoted. Half the managers of food and drug stores in Fort Wayne had owned television sets before the local station came on the air, compared with only a fifth of the population at large. Three out of four had sets by the time the survey entered its second phase—compared with only two out of five in the general public. Half of them named television as the national advertising medium that did "the best job of moving goods in your store," while newspapers, the runner-up, were named by 17%. Commenting on this, the NBC report observes that "for reasons of sound merchandising they began to favor the TV-advertised brands: stocked items they hadn't carried before . . . gave TV brands better shelf space . . . put up special displays featuring the TV brands. Activities like these naturally leave their mark on customers—whether they own TV sets or not."

CBS-Television also sponsored a survey in February and March, 1954, among 3100 grocers, druggists, gasoline, new car and appliance dealers in 17 cities. The dealers were asked, "Which one of these types of advertising placed by the manufacturer helps you the most in selling advertised brands to your customers?" 63% named television as their top choice, 23% named newspapers, 5% radio and 4% magazines. The outstanding preference for television was true in every product field. Grocers and druggists gave television a particularly high vote of preference, compared with automotive and appliance dealers. Independent retailers named television as their favorite even more frequently than did managers of chain stores. The preference for television was almost as high among dealers who watched the medium least as among those who were heavy viewers.

Despite their enthusiasm for TV, small merchants frequently find the medium out of their reach. This is indicated by a survey of television's use by department store advertisers, reported in the Department of Commerce's Business Service Bulletin (Number 53, July, 1954). At this time, 9% of the "typical" retail advertising budget went into television, compared with 80% in newspapers, 4% in radio, 3% in direct mail, and the remainder in all other media. In most cases, the television budget came out of increased advertising expenditures, in other cases from newspaper budgets.

The merchants questioned found the chief advantages of television advertising to be the opportunity for visual demonstration, and the personal touch in the sales message. They also pointed to television's prestige value. Some felt the medium could reach a different audience than other forms of advertising. High costs were the major source of dissatisfaction. Objections were also raised to the lack of available broadcast time at good hours, and the shortage of experienced or talented personnel to prepare the ads.

A supplementary survey was made among department stores who had discontinued television after using it for a while. The most common explanation was that the medium was too costly for the results it produced. Blame was not placed on television, but on the lack of talent available to make it work at its best for the advertiser with a small budget.

The Television Commercial

From the advertiser's standpoint, the best commercial is the   (S)
one that works most effectively to persuade the viewers to buy his product.

Commercials on television, as on radio, are accepted by the audience as part of the nature of things. The public's attitude toward them, from the available evidence, seems to lie somewhere between uncritical apathy and positive interest.

In Lexington, Kentucky, McGeehan and Maranville found the public generally willing to approve television advertising. 74% said there was about the right amount of it. 81% called it "clever," 74% "powerful," and 69% "helpful," in a series of multiple choice questions.

In Whan's 1952 Iowa survey, only 26% of those interviewed answered "yes" to the leading question, "Does any of the advertising on television annoy or irritate you?"

More recently a Trendex survey of 1000 television homes found that 90% of those interviewed said they "liked" the last commercial they heard.

Paul Lazarsfeld, in his analysis of two major studies of public attitudes toward radio, observes that favorable comments are made about commercials which are integrated into the body of the show and which sustain the prevailing mood. (Similarly, in a survey of 200 Chicagoans in 1951, the Gourfain-Cobb agency found 57% preferring integrated commercials on television.) By contrast, he notes that great annoyance is expressed toward commercials which interrupt the listening mood (for instance, the middle commercial in a program). He quotes a school teacher's remark about a commentator:

> "He makes me so mad. He gets me so interested and then switches to the product. He's a good guy but when he interrupts with the commercial he is terrible."

Lazarsfeld and Kendall found preferences almost evenly divided between singing and straight commercials. The chief criticism of radio commercials (in 1947) was that they were boring and repetitious. Fewer people called them noisy and distracting. Lazarsfeld and Kendall note that "people dislike what is known to the trade as 'hard selling'. It may be that such techniques lead to increased sales, but there can be little doubt that they also create hostility in the audience. Listeners feel disturbed, and also irked, when claims which they consider extravagant are made for many products."

Because television viewing makes greater demands than radio listening on the full attention of the audience, the shift in mood and the relaxation of tension may be all the greater when the commercial comes on the air, particularly if it differs substantially in format from the rest of the program.

A commercial may be irritating, and yet be effective for certain kinds of products (particularly those which are apt to be bought on impulse) if it brings the name of the brand to the forefront of the consumer's consciousness at the moment he finds himself in the store and must make a purchase decision. Of course, no advertiser sets out deliberately to irritate his audience. His commercial must capture attention and interest, and should impress the viewers with the name of the product and the special merits it offers.

According to Daniel Starch, no correlation can be found between the sales effectiveness of a commercial and the extent to which it is liked. Research conducted at McCann-Erickson, Inc., indicates that test audiences do not always select the same commercial as most interesting and most convincing when several are presented for comparison. Horace Schwerin observes that the best remembered commercials are not necessarily the ones which are either best liked or most effective in influencing brand choice.

In 1953, the city engineers of Toledo, Ohio, raised a mild furor in advertising circles by releasing a chart of water consumption during evening hours, which showed great spurts of activity every half-hour. This suggested that during the station break, when many commercials typically appear, a substantial part of the living room audience left for the kitchen or bathroom, resuming their viewing when the entertainment returned to the air. At the same time it is evident from minute-by-minute measurements of set usage (made by the A. C. Nielsen Company) that receivers remain on at this time, though there is considerable shifting and searching among the channels. It may well be that whatever loss in audience takes place during the station breaks is felt chiefly by the sponsors of spot messages which are sandwiched between programs. The advertiser with a program of his own typically tries to place his commercials within the body of the show itself rather than at the very beginning or conclusion.

That the television audience does see and remember commercials is attested to by the findings of numerous surveys, notably those conducted on a continuing basis by the firm of Gallup and Robinson. Their "commercial impact" measurements (on the day after a broadcast) reveal a high (though varying) degree of recall by a program's viewers of the points made in the commercials.

The most effective commercials, according to Gallup and Robinson, are those which use animation to demonstrate the superiority of the product. The least effective ones attempt a "straight sell" while merely displaying the product.

Continuing studies made by different audience research organizations provide similar conclusions about the ingredients of a successful television commercial:

1. It should be simple in concept and technique, with a few scenes or elements. The sound track should deal with the same subject as the visual part, and the video, in turn, should be self-sufficient. There should be a minimum number of different ideas, but each idea should be repeated, if possible in several different ways. In short, the viewer should be able to absorb the message with a minimum of effort.

Leyton Carter, a spokesman for Gallup and Robinson, offers the following advice:

"In the shortest ones, if you can't do anything else, at least have some memorable gimmick which sticks out from the rest of the format in which the commercial is put—like Flamingo's flapping bird. According to our research the really effective commercials set up a problem, settle it quickly via product use, close up and go home."

2. Emphasis should be directly on the product and its specific benefits for the consumer. The ideas and benefits should lie within the consumer's experience. According to George Gallup, people are interested in products, but a good many commercials begin by talking about something else, on the mistaken notion that this is of greater interest.

3. The product's values should be demonstrated in simple terms. Sensory impressions should be aroused, where possible (as in the appetizing sight of food in preparation). Charts, reports on laboratory experiments and other technical information should be kept out. There should be no implausible or unlikely claims. Camera tricks and special effects should be avoided unless they strengthen a sales point.

4. The product spokesman and the setting should be appropriate. The person who presents the product should appear on the screen (rather than as an off-stage voice), and he should be identified. He should be shown in a credible role, one which lends authority

to what he says. The commercial should show the advice of the authority or spokesman being followed by someone, with beneficial results. The spokesman should not distract attention from the product, as might happen if the presenter is a scantily dressed young woman. or if he is the star of the show. This star may be very good if he manages to play up to the product.

Integrated commercials delivered by the star of the show are particularly successful, but if he is too entertaining, the point he is trying to make for the sponsor may be overlooked while his antics are remembered. There is no value for the advertiser in having a star deliver a selling message if his stage role is that of a buffoon or zany whose earnest pleas on behalf of the product may carry no conviction at all for even his most faithful fans.

Schwerin warns that mention of the product during the entertainment portion of the show can adversely affect reactions both to the entertainment and to the commercials, when they occur. He concludes that it is impossible to generalize about the ingredients of a successful commercial, since a treatment which may work well for one product will not necessarily work for another. A logical, reasoning type of commercial, Schwerin believes, is best when it utilizes demonstration to the full, whereas an imaginative treatment is best when it makes extreme use of fantasy. (In both cases what he recommends is full use of the medium's technical potential.)

Schwerin also points out that care must be taken to avoid negative elements which offend a section of the audience. "An instance of negative involvement was a commercial that showed a wife nagging her husband about his failure to use the product. Men resented it because the husband was presented as not caring enough about his appearance to make the effort; women, because the wife was shown as an unreconstructed shrew."

TV's Sales Effectiveness

Television's power to produce sales for advertisers is demonstrated in hundreds of case histories. Perhaps the most dramatic (T) example is the case of Revlon, which began sponsorship of the popular "$64,000 Question" in the summer of 1955. Its total sales for the year were 54% over those of the preceding year, an achievement which the company readily ascribed to the success of its new program.

In Stewart's study in Atlanta, 27% of those interviewed said that someone in the family had telephoned an advertiser directly to buy a television-advertised product, and three-fourths of this group said that the television commercial created the need for the product. 39% of those interviewed said they had gone on to look at TV-advertised products in the store.

The comparative sales influence of television, radio, newspapers and magazines was examined in 1955 in a study conducted by Ernest Dichter for the Television Bureau of Advertising. Supermarket shoppers in two cities in California and three in New York, after completing their normal shopping, were asked to sort each nationally advertised brand they bought into one of four bins, each labelled with the name of a medium, according to which had had the greatest influence in making that particular purchase. In terms of dollar values, half of the merchandise bought was assigned to television as the medium which had carried the greatest influence. 27% went into the magazine bin, 14% to newspapers, 10% to radio.

Surveys attempting to measure sales effectiveness systematically run into a number of difficulties. To begin with, it is hard to track down the specific influence of one particular advertising message among the vast number to which consumers are continually exposed. Moreover, a rise or fall in sales may be due not to anything the advertiser does, but to the activities of his competitors or to the general conditions of the market. Changes in pricing and at the retail merchandising level are often hard to avoid. Yet stability and control of other factors is essential for a proper test.

There appears to be a tendency for users of a particular brand or product to be drawn to its television programs, and to its other advertising, as though they wanted reassurance in their buying decision. (Of course, this very function of maintaining the loyalty of existing customers is an important purpose of advertising.)

Another problem is that television owners as a group have more money and larger families—and therefore buy more of most things—than do non-owners. Elaborate comparisons and controls are required to determine whether possession of a television set and exposure to television programs advertising a product results in greater sales among the exposed group than among the unexposed. Such other variables as income, family size, and education must be taken into account.

The National Broadcasting Company, in three major surveys directed by Thomas Coffin, has sought to document the effect of television upon consumer preferences and purchases of advertised products.

The first of these studies was made under the auspices of Hofstra College in a number of communities in the Metropolitan New York area. 1600 persons were interviewed in January, 1949, and again in May. The sample consisted both of TV owners and non-owners, matched on a number of socio-economic variables. On both waves of the survey it was found that television-advertised brands were bought more often by owners than by non-owners. The reverse was true for products not advertised on TV.

Those who saw and liked the commercials advertising a product were found to be more apt to buy the brand than those who saw the commercials but did not like them. And the more frequently a program was viewed, the more often the advertised product was bought by the viewers, as Table 78 indicates.

TABLE 78

Frequency of Viewing Program and Brand Purchase

(Source: 1949 NBC Hofstra Survey)

Per Cent Buying Average of 15 TV-Advertised Brands

Non-viewers	28%
Occasional Viewers	35
Regular Viewers	38

Persons who acquired television between the two waves of the study increased their purchase of 15 TV-advertised brands, while their consumption of 13 non-advertised brands declined. (See Table 79.)

The second Hofstra study, made in January, 1951, was conducted with 5,067 male and female household heads in the New York

Metropolitan area, using a probability sampling plan. By this time about half the homes in the area owned TV.

65% of the television owners said they considered television the most "convincing" medium, while other media were named by 28%. The heavy viewers (who watched television 25 hours a week or more) were more apt to name television as most "convincing" than were the medium or light viewers (who viewed less than fourteen hours a week).

Similarly the heavy viewers correctly recalled more TV-advertised brands than did the light viewers. Persons who had owned their sets longest were able to recall more different brands, but they did not buy them more than did the newer set owners. Viewers who reported that they enjoyed programs they had seen recently were also best able to recall the sponsor's advertising. General attitudes toward the television medium were also reflected in the opinions of advertising for specific brands. (Of those who rated television as "poor," only 19% said they liked at least one television-advertising campaign for a brand whose TV advertising they had noticed; for those who rated television "excellent" the corresponding figure was 54%.)

TABLE 79

Purchases Before and After Owning a TV Set

(Source: 1949 NBC Hofstra Survey)

Per Cent Who Buy Regularly	15 TV-Advertised Brands	13 Brands Not Advertised On TV
Before owning a set (January)	24%	14%
After acquiring a set (May)	33	10

The most important aspect of this study was its careful effort to compare the buying patterns of TV owners and non-owners, for both TV-advertised and non-advertised brands. Averaging the findings for 30 different product categories, it was found (as shown in Table 80) that purchase of television-advertised brands was highest among those whose exposure to television was most intense.

More detailed analysis revealed that the advertisers who made the greatest use of television got a greater sales effect from it—in proportion to the volume of their advertising—than did average or small-scale TV sponsors. Moreover, the heavily advertised brands were most apt to find a high level of approval and a high measure of recall for their advertising.

Competing brands whose television advertising is recalled equally well may be radically different in the extent to which they are bought. Noting this, Coffin points to the differences in the persuasiveness of their selling messages—"in the creative skill with which the medium is being used."

TABLE 80

Exposure to Television and Purchase of Television-Advertised Brands

(Source: NBC 1951 Hofstra Study)

Amount of TV Viewing	*Per Cent Buying a TV-Advertised Brand Recently (average for 30 products)*
Non-owners who watch no television	43%
Non-owners who watch some television	49
TV owners: light viewers	50
TV owners: medium viewers	52
TV owners: heavy viewers	55

About three years after its second New York study, NBC, again under Coffin's direction, launched a new piece of research on television's sales effectiveness, — this time interviewing a panel of 6,554 housewives in Fort Wayne, Indiana, before and after the local television station came on the air. This made it possible to compare buying patterns for old and new television owners and for non-owners. This study showed that people who acquired television after the Fort Wayne station came on the air bought more TV-advertised products than they did before, and actually less of the competing brands which were not advertised on TV. By contrast, their neighbors, who had no television sets, did not change substantially in their brand preferences. The new TV owners also became more aware of the slogans and trade marks of television advertisers. The results are summarized in Table 81.

Television appeared to produce an extraordinary degree of public awareness, as an advertising medium. In a supplementary survey in Fort Wayne 2500 men and women were asked whether they had noticed any recent advertising for automobiles, and they were separately queried about laundry soap and cigarettes. Those who said they had noticed such advertising were then asked, "Would you

TABLE 81

TV's Effects on Consumer Attitudes

(Source: NBC Fort Wayne Study)

Per Cent Who	New Set Owners		"Unexposed"	
	Before TV	After TV	Before TV	After TV
Had heard of brand (average for 6 brands advertised on TV)	51%	74%	40%	43%
Correctly identified brand name with product (average for 6 brands advertised on TV)	41	65	28	34
Correctly identified trade mark (average for 7 brands advertised on TV)	34	57	25	31
Correctly identified slogan (average for 6 brands advertised on TV)	45	77	35	43
Rated brand "very good" (average for 6 brands advertised on TV)	22	31	18	21
Bought average TV-advertised brand	18	24	16	18

point out on this list where you noticed this advertising for (brand)?" Before local television, the results were similar (as might be expected) for the people who ultimately acquired TV sets and those who later remained exposed to television; afterwards there was a striking difference, as Table 82 shows.

Coffin measured daytime television's sales effectiveness in another study for the National Broadcasting Company, late in 1956. 2,218 women in eleven geographically scattered cities were interviewed twice, about their product purchases, brand preferences, and television viewing habits. In this study Coffin matched individuals exposed and unexposed to the advertising, on the basis of their product usage at the time of the first interview. He was thus able to measure how many users of each product were still using it at the time of the second interview, and how many non-users had become users. It was then possible to calculate the rate of change for both viewers and non-viewers, and to determine whether exposure to television advertising resulted in more favorable patterns of "preservation" of existing customers and "generation" of new ones. Not surprisingly, the pattern was consistently favorable.

The NBC studies represent the most elaborate and thoughtful efforts yet made to measure the sales effects of any advertising medium. They offer by no means the only solid evidence in support of television's claim to a successful selling record. The scrapbooks of networks, stations and advertising agencies are filled with success stories —even though there are also notable instances of failure, or at least disenchantment.

Despite their patient grappling with the problems of adherence to scientific standards of controlled comparison, the NBC studies are vulnerable to one major criticism: that they measure the effects of advertising, rather than of television advertising as such. Apply the handsome budgets of television to any other medium, say the critics, and you will get equally handsome results.

TABLE 82

Awareness of Television as an Advertising Medium

(Source: NBC Fort Wayne Study)

Place Where Advertising Was Noticed (Average for Three Products)	Before Local TV		After Local TV	
	New TV Buyers	Unexposed Non-Owners	New TV Buyers	Unexposed Non-Owners
Television	9%	2%	85%	5%
Newspapers	25	21	14	26
Radio	41	39	9	35
Magazines	14	12	9	15
Billboards	6	6	4	6
All Others	6	5	3	4

These studies certainly do not provide a definitive basis for comparing the effects of television with those of other media. This would have entailed a much more elaborate study plan, in which the actual scheduling of advertising in a number of media could be experimentally controlled. Such a study, had it been made, might still have raised questions.

Few advertisers today would question the value of television as a marketing force. There is little question that, dollar for dollar, television advertising can produce more sales than any other medium can—for particular products and to meet particular marketing problems. But every medium can make this claim for individual fields. Today advertisers increasingly seek to differentiate among media and (U) to use each to best advantage in accomplishing specific tasks.

11. THE POLITICAL EFFECTS OF TELEVISION

As a political medium, television goes far beyond any other existing form of communications. Already it has been a major factor in two presidential elections. In the 1952 election, $6,000,000 was spent on broadcasting campaigning by the political parties, and this figure reached $10,000,000 in 1956.

(A)

Television has helped to bring to national prominence new and politically powerful personalities, some of them transient figures, some of them men whose stature and impact on the American scene has been considerable. Far more than radio, television has permitted the public to become—or at least to feel itself—familiar with national figures.

Television has played an equally important role in deflating other political personalities. Telecasts of congressional hearings and investigations have made millions of viewers eyewitnesses to the reactions of public figures in situations of extreme stress, an unparalleled historical development.

(B)

The appointment by President Eisenhower of screen and television actor Robert Montgomery as his television advisor, and Eisenhower's careful study of effective techniques of presentation reflects the importance which this medium has played and will play in the future. The theory has been advanced that, as political figures are increasingly required to appear on television programs, personal appearance and qualities of showmanship may have more to do with the selection of candidates for public office, and with their success or failure in that office, than the traditional qualities of success in politics.

Television can add to the lustre of a political candidate by permitting him to display his charms in thousands—or millions—of living rooms. It can also launch a political career by creating a public personality overnight. Rudolph Halley, a formerly obscure lawyer, was elected to the Presidency of the New York City Council, after his TV appearances as counsel to the Kefauver crime investigating committee. If Halley's initial success illustrates television's ability to turn an unknown person into a familiar figure, the failure of his subsequent efforts to win the Mayoralty suggests that other elements than familiarity remain important in the political picture. The close scrutiny of the television cameras can lead to disenchantment as well as to infatuation on the part of the viewers.

John Crosby, discussing the 1948 Republican convention, in the New York *Herald Tribune* of June 23, 1948, made a prophetic observation:

"The intimacy of television is going to be a problem both to candidates and to the reporters. We got spectacular close-ups of the faces of delegates who choose our Presidents, many of them frightening, others —to be honest—reassuring. A glimpse of Speaker Martin with his shy, predatory smile, saying: 'Of course, no one could refuse a summons like that.' Governor Dewey, radiating confidence, his smile firmly pinned on, sidestepping questions put by Joe Thorndike, managing editor of 'Life' (even one as to what he planned to do with that front porch on the White House). Young boy delegates gazing brightly into the eyes of young girl delegates with dawning and wholly unpolitical interest. Senator Vandenberg, scratching his cheek and trying valiantly to summon up some interest in Governor Green's keynote address."

The demands which television makes of a political candidate are far more exacting than those required by traditional forms of campaigning. In the political meeting, the candidate is usually at some distance from most of the spectators; on the radio they can hear only his disembodied voice. But television exposes to view every minute gesture and every nuance of expression. Discussing the 1952 presidential race, in the New York *Times* magazine of November 2, 1952, Robert Bendiner makes an appropriate comment:

"Repetition . . . is the life of politics, as it is of advertising, but it makes extremely poor television. If you happen to be at the railroad station when your candidate's train stops at Wappingers Falls, you expect to hear from him the same catchwords and stock arguments you have already absorbed from your newspaper reading, from billboards, and from campaign literature . . . But if, on your TV screen you should subsequently hear and see your candidate put on precisely the same show at Yaphank, Owl's Head and East Sciatica—the same trumped-up air of spontaneity, your enthusiasm would chill in short order."

Spontaneity and conviction are the qualities which TV most urgently requires in a candidate. But these are traits which can be cultivated by the skilled technician. Vice-President Richard Nixon, talking to the Radio and Television Executives Society, three years after his famous broadcast of September 23, 1952, observed that his address was put off by several days to permit time for thorough preparation, and to create suspense.

"An efficient 'off-the-cuff' appearance on television, creating the illusion of intimacy so desirable to win the viewers, according to Mr. Nixon, entails many hours of preparatory work," reported the New York *Times* of September 15, 1955. "He implied that there was, in fact, very little done or said that could be termed genuinely impromptu." (C)

The presence of the television camera tends to modify or even transform events, rather than merely to depict them. Political observers have noted that participants in televised spectacles are strongly aware of the camera and often act up to it (much like the studio audience which waves or smiles when it knows or imagines itself to be the focus of attention).

When a group of Southern delegates bolted the 1948 Democratic convention in Philadelphia, they were asked by the television operators to tear off and throw away their badges as a dramatic gesture of defiance. When the cameras turned elsewhere, many of these delegates rummaged through the pile of discards to get their badges back.

Televised Hearings

Televised sessions of Congressional hearings have in a few notable instances produced an atmosphere in which all the participants were as highly conscious of the unseen audience as of those in the same room. Perhaps the first important demonstration of this point occurred when gambler Frank Costello, called before the Senate's

Kefauver Committee, refused to testify in front of the cameras. Instead of his face, viewers saw the eloquently nervous gestures of his hands, and the reactions of committee members and spectators.

A Gallup poll conducted after these hearings found that 70% of the voters considered it a good idea to televise the sessions of Congress itself. Although proposals of this sort have met with strong opposition from Congressional leaders, a number of state legislatures have had their proceedings on the air. Wendell Barnes, an Oklahoma state representative, gave his impressions of the results in an interview with the New York *Times:*

"The most outstanding effect was on the Legislature itself. Whenever it knew the cameras were running, it stuck strictly to business. During that hour, you wouldn't see a single pair of feet on a desk on the House floor; not a single House member was reading a newspaper while someone was speaking, and attendance was excellent. Sure, there was some ham acting, obviously for the benefit of the TV audience, but you must expect things like that."

The *Times'* television editor, Jack Gould, has referred to the prospect that in the future, television might require all politicians to be actors (to a greater degree than heretofore) with personality superseding competence as the main criterion of public judgment. Gould notes TV's influence in electing John D. Butler, a handsome bachelor of "youthful and fresh appearance," as mayor of San Diego, over the opposition of a less attractive older man.

Televised public hearings have been hailed as a source of fresh vitality for democratic institutions. They have also been viewed as a possible threat. In May, 1954, a subcommittee of the House Committee on Un-American Activities held televised hearings in Lansing, Michigan. Percy Tannenbaum, interviewing a panel of 68 persons before and after the hearings, found that those who had seen the proceedings on TV increased their information about the hearings substantially more than did the unexposed. They also became less favorable in their opinion of the presiding Representative, Kit Clardy, and of congressional investigating committees generally. The viewers became slightly more critical of the use of the Fifth Amendment, and somewhat less favorable to the general idea of televising such hearings.

President Truman, while still in office, expressed his misgivings over the tendency of television to turn hearings into "Roman holidays" in which the rule of reason might be superseded by the emotions of a public untrained in the evalution of evidence and inclined to accept proferred charges as an indication of guilt.

Governor Thomas Dewey, while a candidate for the Presidency, has also described televised proceedings as being

> "of very doubtful legitimacy. To use the power of government to subpoena individuals, put them under the piercing glare of kleig lights and question them smacks too much of the Russian method to fit in with our institutions and respect for the dignity of the judicial process and the rights of individuals."

The political consequences of TV's penetrating powers were vividly demonstrated in May, 1954, when the Senate subcommittee on investigations heard the conflicting testimony of Senator McCarthy and Secretary of the Army Stevens and their aides. Day after day, as the proceedings picked their way through the naked trivia of the case, the viewing public saw the participants not only in their public poses but in their less guarded conversations and reactions. As the TV eye swept back and forth across the tables of the hearing room, the principles under discussion appeared to become more and more obscure, and the fascination, for the viewers, lay in the riddles of motive and the clashes of ambition exposed on the television screen.

The Army-McCarthy hearings provided a unique spectacle of widespread public concentration on a political subject. A study conducted in the New York City area by Advertest Research at the time of the Army-McCarthy hearings found that 51% of the adult public in TV homes had seen one or more live broadcasts of the daytime proceedings. Two-thirds of these viewers also watched one or more of the late evening rebroadcasts of the hearings. In addition, 26% of the public watched the filmed evening versions although they did not see the live sessions in the daytime. In all, over three-fourths of the television public had watched the hearings at one time or another.

The normal daytime television audience was increased by 55% as the result of public interest in this special event.

A CBS psychologist, Gerhart Wiebe, in a perceptive analysis of thirty interviews conducted two months after the hearings, finds it disturbing that the personalities of the protagonists were the main focus of interest rather than the issues involved in the controversy. His respondents thought of the principals in intimate terms, as though these were people whom they actually knew. They took sides as they might in a neighborhood quarrel, in which the participants would be judged on the level of face-to-face contact.

In Wiebe's judgment, only television, among the mass media, approaches the "intimate frame of reference" of vivid immediacy. As a result television caused viewers to change their feelings about the figures in the case, much as though there had been continuing personal contact. One lower-class housewife, who turned against McCarthy, said:

"I don't know just what it could be that changed my feelings about him, I just started to know more about him really and saw him in action as a lawyer and I became afraid of such a man, that the power he had was terrible to make other men feel uncomfortable."

Because McCarthy, Stevens and the others were perceived in such intimate terms, they aroused strong feelings of loyalty or distaste. This was not like an entertainment, put out of mind when it was over; it pervaded interest and discussion throughout the day. A shoe-repair shop owner described it this way:

"There was nothing that I can remember that had all the people talking and taking sides over so long a time as this. When they came into the shop they didn't discuss the weather like they do now till I wish they wouldn't mention it again but they always had some angle to tell about and ask how you felt about it, you just had to take a stand and there was no way to say you didn't care. That isn't so good for business but it wasn't like local politics where they wouldn't come in and trade any more, this seemed far away enough to make it exciting and very emotional for men and women and we surely listened and talked it and the only way we got away from it was to get to bed."

The Political Role of the TV Broadcaster

The television audience, for all its illusion of being on the spot to judge for itself, sees any political figure through the eye of the camera, and what the camera sees is itself controlled by technicians, directors and commentators. By their presentation of the political scene the broadcasters wield an enormous influence over the public's view of current events.   (D)

In the opinion of some observers, the turning point in Senator McCarthy's political fortunes was the television spotlight turned on his activity by Edward R. Murrow's program, "See it Now". This broadcast made extensive use of film clips that showed the Senator badgering witnesses, sniggering at effusive testimonials, and otherwise exposing himself to candid view. McCarthy asked for and got the opportunity to present his rebuttal to Murrow's report, but his own appearance before the television cameras may only have heightened the impression left by the original broadcast.

Some uneasiness has been expressed over the ability of a television commentator like Murrow to step into the arena of public debate and exercise a powerful force on the formation of public opinion. For years, radio news analysts have injected a personal note into the interpretation of the political scene. Television therefore does not raise new questions about the role of broadcast commentary on controversial issues. However, as a more powerful medium, it raises the old questions in a more compelling way. If a good reporter like Murrow can use his prestige, his air time, and his command of television technique to help change the prevailing image of a major political figure, could not the same be achieved by a broadcaster who was *not* on the side of the angels?

One comment on this subject, by the columnist John Crosby, makes an assumption that people can not really be influenced on important political subjects by a TV personality:

> "It seems to me that Murrow has influence simply because he doesn't misuse it, and the minute he tried to, he wouldn't have it. Perhaps I'm over-optimistic, but I feel strongly that the American public not only cannot be gulled, but would violently resent any attempt at persuasion

on matters they hold dear. They will buy the toothpaste, they will laugh at the jokes, they will tune in by the millions. But these are matters of no moment. The moment you get into areas where they feel deeply—the farm problem, foreign policy, public office—skepticism mounts.

"In fact, it might be stated as Crosby's Law that the more important the subject is, the less influence the guy with the mike has. In matters of the most profound importance to the individual—say, religion—I doubt that the Murrows, or Godfreys, the Winchells or anyone else could sway a single soul a single inch."

While this opinion is reassuring, it is hardly the last word on the matter. What reduces the influence of any individual broadcast commentator (or of any newspaper columnist or magazine editor) is the fact that in a democratic society his is one voice among many. Even though people tend to select publications and programs which jibe with their own attitudes, they are still in the normal course of affairs exposed to a great many different points of view. These contradictory influences do not altogether cancel each other out, any more than the competitive urgings to buy different brands of toothpaste or soap. A residue of change is always being left by the opinions expressed in the mass media as well as by those absorbed in interpersonal contact. Where the mass media speak with one voice and dissent is stilled, then their capacity to mold the public view on "matters of the most profound importance to the individual" is most clearly and terrifyingly exhibited.

The importance of maintaining a balance of broadcast opinion is recognized in the Federal Communications Act, which provides that "if any licensee shall permit any person who is a legally qualified candidate for any public office to use a broadcasting station, he shall afford equal opportunities to all other such candidates for that office in the use of such broadcasting station." The practical effect of this is to restrict political broadcasts to those actually paid for by the parties, and to virtually eliminate direct, face-to-face debate over campaign issues. Dr. Frank Stanton, President of CBS, has recently proposed that this provision be amended, so that free air time can be given to the representatives of the two major parties without making it necessary to include all the lesser ones, such as the American Vegetarian Party and the Prohibition Party.

James Reston, in the New York *Times* of May 26, 1955, raises an objection to this proposal: "The ability-to-pay principle is not just in a democracy, and . . . the injustice is likely to increase in direct ratio to the rise in TV costs, but the problem cannot be solved merely by changing the rules to give the Democrats and Republicans free time and blocking out all others. For while this might not produce injustice in national presidential elections, it could easily do so in state, Congressional and municipal elections. For example, Fiorello La Guardia's successful Fusion party campaign in New York City some years ago would have been handicapped by discrimination in favor of the major parties."

Reston notes still another problem in the increasing use of television by the Executive branch of the government, and the advantage this might give an incumbent administration which decided to increase the frequency of its televised press conferences in the months preceding election.

The problem thus posed is one of the neutrality of the television medium. An objection to televised presidential press conferences before election time implies that the way in which these conferences are depicted on TV works to the benefit of the incumbent party. The camera work, the commentary and the general direction will be such as to support the dignity of the office and reinforce an impression of the competence of the individual who holds it. Yet that individual and his fitness may at the same time be the object of strong attacks by the other political party, in the heat of the ongoing election campaign. Again, the apparently reportorial function of the television broadcaster may, on scrutiny, prove to be strongly partisan.

The most penetrating study of this question was made by Kurt and Gladys Lang during the 1952 political conventions. Their analysis focuses on the way in which the televised version of an event, by the method of its handling, produces a certain kind of impression on the part of the audience. Three TV networks pooled the video coverage of the proceedings, but each provided its own commentary. Ten analysts, all roughly equivalent in personal background and political persuasion, monitored the content of these broadcasts. Their reports, as evaluated by the Langs, indicate that very different interpretations of the same events were made by viewers of each of the three networks. This in turn reflects an unconscious bias arising from the different ways in which the three networks judged the audience. Since all the networks carried virtually the same *visual* content throughout, differences in the meanings the monitors ascribed to the same events apparently arose from differences in the three separate broadcast *commentaries*. That is, the three commentators differed in the inferences they made when they linked up the various episodes flashed on the screen.

For example, the Langs found that one network (Network A) stressed the action and sounds of the convention itself. In reporting a series of parliamentary maneuvers at the Democratic convention, centering on the question of seating the Southern states whose delegates had refused to sign a "loyalty pledge," Network A focussed on Chairman Sam Rayburn. Since the rulings of the Chairman were left inadequately explained, the viewers were left with "impressions of sinister forces, at work outside of the range of the television camera."

Network B's commentary carried an even greater impression of confusion, with the commentator frequently implying that he shared the viewer's bewilderment at what went on, and hinting vaguely that invisible pressures were being exercised.

Network C, on the other hand, tried to make sense of what went on, identifying and explaining everything that took place, so that the proceedings seemed far more rational to the monitors. All the details of maneuvering were brought into focus as part of a political contest, and the viewer was continually being reminded of the underlying issues of debate.

This contrasted with the commentary of Network A, which supplied a minimum of political interpretation, and which accordingly tended to make the proceedings seem mysterious. "The B commentator deliberately shared the viewer's imputation of dark forces lying behind that which they could not fathom . . . Any huddles caught by the camera were repeatedly taken as a sign that something was afoot, something that was not quite cricket."

The Langs observe that monitors hearing each of these highly different commentaries drew different interpretations of what was happening, even when they were highly critical of the commentary itself.

In their handling of the Republican convention the three networks again differed substantially in the impressions they created of the role of Governor Fine of Pennsylvania. In this case Network A actually shifted its camera view from the convention floor to the Pennsylvania delegation's caucus room, thereby focussing attention on the Governor, and turning him into a vivid personality for the viewers. In spite of general knowledge that the Governor had decided to throw his delegation's support to Eisenhower, Network A chose to present him as a "mystery man" up to the point where he officially declared himself. But the viewer was in no position to realize that the Network's handling of the matter had made Fine seem more important than he actually was.

Similarly, many viewers carried away the impression that Harry Truman had been the "kingmaker" of the Democratic convention, because TV emphasized his presence in Chicago, particularly during a break in the proceedings just before the Stevenson forces began to make better progress.

The Langs suggest that there are several ways in which public figures may be judged as television personalities: They may be judged for the appropriateness of their performance for TV, on their political role, or on the personal image they project of themselves.

A particular individual is not necessarily judged in the same way on all three of these counts. At the 1952 Republican convention, for example, a well-delivered speech by Senator Dirksen was appreciated regardless of whether viewers agreed with what he said and regardless of whether they thought it was politically effective. The dissociation of these elements in the viewer's mind may lead, the Langs warn, to a tendency to regard the proceedings as a show or spectacle.

Viewers interviewed after the Republican convention were vividly consciously of Thomas Dewey as a dominant figure whom they cast as a hero or villain depending on their own predispositions. But at the same time, he did not come across as a definite personality. As the Langs describe it,

"Monitors did note that he appeared cocky or confident or happy or calm, but they always looked for the reason. Dewey might be smiling, but the implication that Dewey smiling was always smiling about something could not be avoided. He never was seen to smile just for the hell of it. He was a man with a mind set on political goals, and with his feelings warmed or chilled as these goals were approached or temporarily put off . . . Being viewed in a political role, Dewey had to take the consequences. His praise was sung or he was vilified according to respondents' political views. If he was viewed as competent, this only made him all the more hateful to his opponents."

By contrast, Democratic convention Chairman Sam Rayburn appears to the Langs to have come across to the viewers as a fully-rounded personality, largely because when his conduct of the proceedings was challenged at a critical moment, the camera closeups gave the viewers an opportunity really to judge for themselves the manner in which he defended himself, and to form their own "estimates of whether or not there were tears in Rayburn's eyes, whether he had a temper and could keep it in check, where he was courageous and firm." Other leading figures at the conventions, upon whom the cameras also focussed in close-ups, but not in moments of spontaneous response to crisis, came across simply as stereotyped "functionaries."

The Langs conclude that the most important determinant of a political figure's television personality is what he stands for in the viewer's eyes, rather than what he says or how he says it. An individual's personality is most apt to come across, distinct from his political role or from his performance, when he is shown under circumstances where his partisan position is not relevant.

In seeking to answer the question of what kind of candidate can make best use of television, the Langs point to two conditions. (1) When the major issues of a campaign center on means rather than ends, the competence or suitability of a candidate assumes importance. (2) When politics and politicians are generally held in low repute the character of a candidate may appear to be particularly important. Under such circumstances the viewer is influenced not only by the sense of affinity he feels with the candidate, but by his appraisal of how close the candidate is to him. Since the politicians themselves believe that TV is an intimate medium, they tend to project social issues through the use of personalities. Accordingly the Langs see a danger in the political use of television because it converts political reality into an essentially irrelevant affair of drama and human interest.

Intensive interviews with 47 viewers, both before and after the conventions, provided further evidence for these observations. As the Langs describe it, the TV broadcasters covering the conventions endowed the viewer with "omniscience," with "a near limitless ability . . . to orient himself in a multiplicity of roles." The viewer saw everything—even what many delegates to the convention could not see. Accordingly the viewer had the illusion that he was seeing things for himself, even though he had to define the situation in terms of his own existing information or prejudices. He reduced the confusion of what he saw to a meaningful pattern, by paying minimum attention to things he considered unimportant (like the activities of the managers or evidence of pressures on the delegates) and he tended to simplify the proceedings into a race between top contenders.

The viewer limited his attention, among the range of impressions available to him, in terms of his existing political notions. For example, he could accept (1) the "sinister" notion that everything had been settled before the convention, (2) the "backroom" notion that politicians were making deals at the convention, (3) the "heroic" notion that the qualities of the candidates were being matched, or (4) the "representative" notion that the orderly democratic process was at work.

For the Langs, viewers' reactions to the Stevenson "draft" were highly revealing of the basic political assumptions by which they interpreted what they saw. The same events were used by persons who started out with different notions to illustrate very divergent reports of what had taken place. Viewers who started out with a sinister notion of politics naturally assumed that relatively few important decisions or events were taking place before the TV cameras, and they greatly limited the meanings they drew from what they saw. Viewers who accepted the heroic notion of politics focussed their attention on the few personalities whom they considered the real powers.

To a certain extent, the convention broadcasters may have encouraged the tendency of some viewers to interpret the proceedings as controlled or manipulated.

Because the television cameras could not really be everywhere, though the viewer wanted to feel that they were, there were often gaps in sequence which left the viewer feeling he had been left out of things. He sometimes even felt that way when the networks tried to take him behind the scenes. One respondent said:

> "I saw that caucus. They let us in on one state. I don't know which one now—South Carolina or Texas—or one of these, I think. They wouldn't let the press in. It was down in the Hilton, led by the big bosses.—You couldn't tell how the decisions were made. You couldn't hear anything. You could just see men standing around talking and saw just the backs of them."

In commenting on their own analysis, the Langs warn of the possibility that political telecasts may stimulate people to see more of the same thing on TV while possibly discouraging their actual political participation, since they have the illusion of being "supra-public participants", and are thereby divorced from "the social net-

(E)   work in which political action occurs."

Television and the Vote

(F)   Before the days of television, Paul Lazarsfeld, Bernard Berelson and Hazel Gaudet, analyzing how voting decisions were reached in Erie County, Ohio, found that radio was described as the most important source of information on the election by 38% of their respondents, while newspapers were named by 23%. However the two media were named with equal frequency as "most helpful" in arriving at the final decision.

Republicans, being better educated, were found to turn more frequently to newspapers, Democrats to the radio. The newspapers being predominantly Republican and the radio impartial, Republicans found the newspapers more consistent with their own ideas, while radio was more congenial for the Democrats. Curiously enough, the Republicans thought the newspapers were more impartial and closer to truth than the radio, while the Democrats thought the opposite. Voters who were in the process of shifting their loyalty toward the Republican side were more apt to mention newspapers as an influence, while those leaning toward the Democrats were more likely to mention the radio.

Berelson, Lazarsfeld and McPhee, analyzing the influences on voting in the 1948 election campaign, refuse to accept the notion of a cause-and-effect relation between exposure to the mass media and changes in political attitude. Instead they view the media as indispensable elements in the complex process by which people form opinions and arrive at decisions in our society.

"The familiar question as to whether the mass media 'influence' elections is, on the surface, an absurd question. In the first place, it is dubious whether any decisions at all would be possible without some mass device for enabling the leaders to present their proposals to the people. Second, typical debates about the role of the media too often imply a simple, direct 'influence'—like a hypodermic stimulus on an inert subject—and that is a naive formulation of the political effects of mass communications. Third, another common notion—that any influence of the media is somehow suspect, as if 'interfering' with the rational deliberations of the voters—implies an autonomously operating electorate. Such an image is also unrealistic."

The last point provides an effective answer to those observers who fear the capacity of television to interfere with the traditional or "normal" way in which the voter makes up his mind.

At first thought it might seem that television works in much the same manner as radio did in previous years, since like radio, television is required to be impartial in its treatment of the news and in its allocation of time for political speeches. From this it might appear to follow that television as a medium might provide an effective counterpoise to the overwhelmingly pro-Republican influence represented by the American press.

This may not be the case at all, for television, with its enormous production costs and greater complexity, presents a very different problem for the Democrats than radio did. In radio, the financial disadvantage of the Democrats at the national level did not pose an inordinately serious handicap. With television, the high cost of air time can easily lead the less affluent party to limit the number of its political broadcasts at a point where it is not effectively competing with its opposition. Moreover, there could be differences in the quality of the full-time talent and television experience which the two parties could afford to bring to the production of their programs and spot announcements. This might well be sufficient to make each Republican minute on the air more effective than each minute the Democrats have.

Goldberg, interviewing TV owners in New York before and after the 1948 party conventions, found that nine out of ten had seen at least one of the conventions on TV. When asked which convention had held interest most as viewed on television, most people selected the convention of their own political group. It appears, therefore, that voters use television in much the same way that they use newspaper reports on the speeches of political candidates: to buttress their existing political opinions.

The 1952 political conventions were viewed or heard in nine out of every ten American homes, according to data supplied by the A. C. Nielsen Company. This estimate covers the entire audience accumulated over a period of time. At their peak of interest, the conventions did not draw the same audiences as the more popular regular entertainment features. The highest Hooperating received by the Republican convention in New York was 36, the low 17. At the same time, "I Love Lucy" hit 62. The political speeches in October got ratings of 10 to 15.

Television appears to have made the conventions more interesting and alive than radio could. Virtually every television family watched the conventions, for an average of 26 hours per home. Only half as much time, on the average, was spent by the much larger number of families who listened to the proceedings on the radio.

The 1956 conventions were viewed, at least in part, by nearly 34,000,000 homes (93% of all TV homes), for an average of 16 hours and 18 minutes per home, according to A. C. Nielsen data. Both conventions reached the same number of homes—32,000,000 each. The Democratic convention, with its more dramatic open races for both presidential and vice-presidential nominations, drew audiences for longer periods of time than did the Republicans. The average home which watched any part of the Democratic convention spent 9 hours and 39 minutes, while the Republican convention was watched for 7 hours and 22 minutes by the average viewing home. Daily audiences ranged from 23 to 27 million homes, indicating a great deal of day-after-day tuning. 17,800,000 homes watched the ballotting for the Democratic presidential nomination, and 15,400,000 tuned in for Adlai Stevenson's acceptance speech. Slightly larger numbers watched President Eisenhower's arrival in San Francisco (19,200,000) and his acceptance speech (18,300,000). When the Democratic convention debated civil rights into the wee hours, a substantial part of the TV audience stayed up with it. 4 million homes were viewing at 2:30 a. m. during this part of the proceedings.

TABLE 83

	Listening to and Viewing of 1956 Political Conventions	
(Source: A. C. Nielsen Data)	*Democratic Convention*	*Republican Convention*
% of all TV homes viewing, at least in part	88%	88%
Number of TV homes reached	32,120,000	32,120,000
Hours per home reached	9 hrs. 39 min.	7 hrs. 22 min.
% of all radio homes listening, at least in part	44%	33%
Number of radio homes reached	21,000,000	15,600,000
Hours per home reached	6 hrs. 1 min.	3 hrs. 23 min.
% of all radio homes listening or viewing	87%	84%
Number of homes	40,930,000	39,500,000
Hours per home reached	10 hrs. 44 min.	7 hrs. 20 min.

(G)

In a national survey on voting behavior in 1952, Angus Campbell, Gerald Gurin and Warren Miller asked 1714 persons of voting age about their exposure to election campaign information through the four major mass media. At the time of the study only 40% of the homes in the United States owned television, yet 53% of the re-

spondents "paid attention to the campaign" on TV. More people
followed the campaign in the newspapers (79%) and on radio (69%),
fewer through the magazines, (40%).

Although fewer people saw the campaign on television than
heard it on the radio or read about it in the press, television was
most often named (by 31%) as the source of most information on
the campaign. (27% named radio, 22% newspapers, and 5% maga-
(H)   zines, in this connection.)

Persons of upper income, who were most apt to own television, named it most often as their main source of election information. However, Table 84 shows that at every income level, college
educated persons were more apt to mention newspapers or magazines, and less apt to mention TV, than persons of less education.
(This finding jibes perfectly with the observations made in an earlier
chapter about television's relatively greater impact at the middle and
lower educational levels.)

TABLE 84

Choice of Most Important Source of Election Campaign Information, By Education and Income

(Source: Campbell, Gurin and Miller 1952 Survey)

Most Important Source	Less than $3000			$3000 to $4999			$5000 and Over		
	Grammar School	High School	College	Grammar School	High School	College	Grammar School	High School	College
Television	13%	27%	10%	37%	40%	29%	49%	45%	33%
Radio	40	37	27	26	22	20	14	20	19
Newspapers	20	15	43	25	25	28	18	20	25
Magazines	2	6	7	2	5	7	4	5	13
More than one	9	9	10	6	6	15	10	7	9
None of the four	16	6	3	4	2	1	5	3	1
Total	100%	100%	100%	100%	100%	100%	100%	100%	100%

While men and women rated television equally high, men
mentioned newspapers more often than women, and women named
radio more than men did. There is some suggestion in this study
that television worked to Stevenson's benefit. As Table 85 indicates,
the percentage of persons who voted for Eisenhower was about the
same among those who named TV as their main source of campaign
information as among those who mentioned other media, whereas
there were relatively more Stevenson voters in the TV group.

TABLE 85

Voting Preference and Most Important Source
of Campaign Information
(Source: Campbell, Gurin and Miller 1952 Survey)

Voting Choice	*Most Important Source of Information*			
	TV	*Radio*	*Newspapers*	*Magazines*
Eisenhower	43%	40%	44%	54%
Stevenson	38	25	33	22
Did not vote	19	35	23	24
Total	100%	100%	100%	100%

In a further analysis of the findings from this survey, Morris Janowitz and Dwaine Marvick find that among those who considered television their main source of information about the campaign, 47% believed in an Eisenhower victory, whereas the proportion was 66% among those who relied mainly on newspapers. This difference they ascribe to television's neutrality of presentation in contrast with the Republican bias of the press. Among those individuals who changed their allegiance from Eisenhower to Stevenson in the course of the campaign, 43% mentioned television as their information source, whereas among those who switched from Stevenson to Eisenhower the proportion was 32%, also suggesting that TV worked to the advantage of the Democrats (though not strongly enough to win them the election). The regular Democratic voters (41%) and the regular Republicans (37%) did not differ so markedly in their television exposure, though the effect took the same direction.

Janowitz and Marvick observe that about a fifth of the electorate were under some concerted pressure from friends or associates to vote in a particular way; these were also the same people who were most exposed to the media. Those television fans who were subjected to personal pressures in the campaign, tended, like radio and newspaper fans, to conform to the political opinions of their associates. Among the TV fans who were not subject to personal pressure, the Stevenson vote was 45%, but it was 29% among the radio fans and 35% among the newspaper readers. "In short, television did provide a vehicle for the relatively unknown Democratic candidate to bring before those who actively followed the campaign his version of the issues and his personal qualifications. But it should be noted that Stevenson got almost no backing from television fans who were subject to concerted pro-Eisenhower pressures from daily associates.

A detailed analysis of the 1952 election results in Iowa produces no evidence that television shifted the political balance in favor of one party or another. Herbert Simon and Frederick Stern, analyzing the breakdown of the vote in Iowa for the elections of 1944, 1948 and 1952, on a county-by-county basis, were able to compare the total voting turnout and the percentage of Republican votes in areas with high and low degrees of television penetration. Controlling for the normal fluctuations in voting behavior from one election year to another, no indication was found of any direct influence from television. The authors suggest that the explanation might lie in the intense interest generated by the 1952 campaign through the other media, which left relatively little room for television either to attract new voters or to switch their votes.

Regardless of its ultimate effect on the actual vote, there is some evidence that television influenced the public image of the candidates. "The Influence of Television on the Election of 1952" was the subject of a study directed by Joseph Seibert of Miami University with the financial aid of the Crosley Broadcasting Service. This survey employed a battery of nine mail questionnaires directed at a panel of voters in fourteen counties of the metropolitan Cincinnati and Dayton areas, including the rural regions. The first questionnaire was sent out just before the political party conventions; the last one went out the week after the election. Nearly 1000 questionnaires were returned on the average wave of the study.

Perhaps the most significant finding of this research was its documentation of television's capacity to bring a candidate's message to voters inclined to the opposite side. In this predominantly Republican area, the Republican television programs were seen more often than the Democratic programs. However, people who ultimately cast a Republican vote were more apt to view Democratic programs than Democratic voters to view Republican programs. Because the greater part of the voters were pro-Eisenhower, it was easier for the Democrats to reach an audience in the opposite camp than it was for the Republicans. In fact, there were more Republicans than Democrats among those who viewed over 70% of Stevenson's speeches.

Because Republican speeches were viewed more than Democratic ones in this area, Seibert concludes that television was "of greater quantitative influence to the Republican cause." Eisenhower's early evening acceptance speech was seen by half the panel, Stevenson's by a third—but Stevenson had the disadvantage of making his acceptance speech at midday, and his speech of welcome after midnight.

This Republican advantage persisted throughout the campaign; their programs and speeches came at peak viewing times, whereas a substantial number of Stevenson's speeches were scheduled at off-hours, and many of them took place in September and October, when political viewing was at a low point. In general, political viewing fell off after the conventions and did not revive until ten days or so before election—a period in which much of Eisenhower's television effort was concentrated, notably the speech in which he promised to go to Korea if he won.

During the summer and early fall, audiences for political telecasts attracted less than 10% of the panel, some around 5%, while viewing of entertainment continued as strongly as ever. The greatest interest during this period was attracted to Republican vice-presidential candidate Nixon's explanation of his financial affairs after these had been the butt of Democratic charges.

The bulk of the Republicans' television impressions were made at precisely the times when voters were making up their minds. Voting decisions were made primarily during the convention period, and secondly, in the final week of the campaign. Seibert found 53% of his panel members making their selection of candidates at these two periods, while only 19% made up their minds during September and October, in the heart of the campaign. 6% decided in mid-summer, and the remaining 22% acknowledged that their minds were made up from the very start.

But if television was a powerful weapon for the Republicans, it also proved to be a major asset for the Democrats in their effort to turn the formerly unfamiliar Governor of Illinois into a figure capable of competing on the national scene with the well-known General. Both at the beginning and at the end of the campaign, Eisenhower outranked Stevenson on every trait of personality on which the members of the panel were asked to rate both candidates, except for "humor" and "speaking ability." However, Stevenson's position relative to his opponent improved between the beginning and end of the campaign on every trait except "humility" and "aggressiveness." With respect to humor, Stevenson's rating more than doubled among the TV viewers, and his ratings for "friendliness" and "sincerity" almost doubled. Eisenhower also showed gains, especially on the trait of "humility," but also for "intelligence," "sincerity" and "aggressiveness."

The notable increases in Stevenson's scores appeared to be the direct result of his television appearances, for they were found to be greater among the TV audience than among the panel members as a whole. However, it must be recalled that it was easier for Stevenson to show gains, since his original ratings were lower than Eisenhower's.

With respect to campaign issues, the television audience proved to be better informed than the panel as a whole, but this was probably because they represented a somewhat select group in education, and accordingly, in political interest. Among those panel members who termed television their main source of information about the election, many reported that they were spending more time with newspapers than before the campaign. The newspapers, Seibert points out, were a major source of information on the issues of debate while the campaign was at its peak—a time during which relatively few political broadcasts were scheduled. By contrast, television gave the biggest play to political speeches, and got the biggest audiences for them, during the periods when they were most full of generalities, — at the start and finish of the campaign.

Analysis of the panel's response led Seibert to conclude that

> "the election decision lay more in the realm of personalities than in any differences in platform planks or candidate proposals . . . Some panel members 'feared a change,' but most believed 'a change was needed.' To effect this change furthermore they placed faith in the personal characteristics and abilities of Eisenhower . . . They especially liked his sincerity, his friendliness, and his humility. Since these were traits which the television medium helped in an important way to project, it appears reasonable to conclude that it was in these areas, rather than in the area of issues, that television contributed the most to the final election results."

A rather different evaluation of television's influence emerges from a study of the political opinions of 1800 students in three California colleges, conducted by Ithiel Pool a week before the 1952 election. Both candidates were regarded very favorably by adherents of both political parties when rated on 38 personality traits. To focus on the role of television, Pool isolated from his larger sample two small groups of people who had not seen either candidate in person or in the movies. One group had seen the candidates more than once on television. The other group had heard them on the radio more than once, but had not seen them on television.

Both the viewers and non-viewers had a remarkably similar image of the candidates; on most traits they rated them about equally. However, the television viewers rated Eisenhower more favorably than the non-viewers on the traits of sensitivity and modesty, and rated Stevenson less favorably as conceited, snobbish and domineering.

It is not readily apparent why, in this study, television seems to have worked against Stevenson, while in Seibert's research it appears to have worked in his favor. Since Pool did not submit his questionnaires repeatedly, as Seibert did, the influence of television can not be traced through time. It is possible that his TV-watching students came from higher-income (hence Republican) homes, and were therefore less favorable to Stevenson from the start.

Conclusions similar to those reached by Seibert are stated by Bendiner in analyzing the 1952 campaign. He cites three major achievements of television:

"First, it enabled Adlai Stevenson, until the eve of the Democratic convention virtually the Great Unknown of American politics, to establish himself in three months as a figure of authentic stature. Politics aside, his eloquence, wit and unique personality, all conceded by the opposition, were impressed on the country to an extent that would hardly have been possible in so short a time by any other means, radio included.

"Second, television must be rated a major factor in the remarkable comeback of Richard Nixon, after revelations concerning his private finances seriously threatened to force him off the Republican ticket. Radio alone might have saved the day for Nixon, but there is no question that he proved himself a master of television technique and that the new medium counted very heavily in his rescue from impending disaster.

"Third, though there is no way of proving it, television should probably be given a good share of credit for the unexpectedly high registration throughout the country. Not only did TV indirectly stimulate a big turnout by the political interest it aroused, but, along with radio, it very directly pounded away at the theme through spot announcements, 'Get Out the Vote' shows, and other devices."

This last observation, it should be noted, contrasts with the Langs' warning that television, by turning politics into pure spectacle, might generate apathy toward direct political participation. Most of the signs seem to point toward a heightened interest and familiarity with all phases of the political process, as a result of TV's growing influence.

The significance of television was recognized by both parties in planning the 1956 election campaign. Presidential and Congressional campaign broadcasts in 1956 cost the Republican Party over $4,000,000, three-fourths of it for television. The Democrats spent nearly $3,000,000, of which over $2,100,000 went into television. Sponsors of the convention and election eve broadcasts reportedly spent $15,000,000 to bring them to the public. Nonetheless Robert Sarnoff, President of the National Broadcasting Company, estimated that the conventions cost the broadcasting industry $17-18,000,000 in lost revenues.

Brief spot announcements figured strongly in the campaign. Focusing on one key segment of the electorate, the Republican party bought about 150 spot announcements per market on Negro radio stations for the 9-week period preceding election day. The Republicans wound up their campaign on election eve with an 11:00 p. m.-Midnight program on all the networks, while the poorer Democrats had 45 minutes earlier on only a single network.

One important innovation was the shortening of regular half-hour entertainment programs to 25 minutes, permitting the last five minutes to be sold for political purposes, and avoiding viewer resentment at elimination of their favorite shows. These short units held the audience at the same rating level as the preceding entertainment. This so-called "piggy-back" schedule, in the words of

Richard Guylay, the Republican public relations director, was "the biggest bargain ever purchased in any campaign. Why, we were 'hitchhiking' on the big network programs—these shows delivered built-in audiences for us."

Guylay also credits television with the achievement of allaying public concern over Eisenhower's pre-election illness. "After 20 million people saw the President on TV, any talk of his health as an issue vanished as the campaign progressed."

In response to criticism, a Republican spokesman denied the charge that President Eisenhower was being "sold like toothpaste." This criticism, it was pointed out, confused the copy approach with the choice of media. A 20-second speech, according to this position, need not be any less "hucksterish" than a one-hour speech.

Sponsor Magazine of July 9, 1956, offered the following description of one of the Republican TV campaign items, a 15-minute show entitled "These Peaceful Prosperous Years."

> "The script of this 15-minute film deals with 'an average American family going about their daily living under a Republican era of peace.' Against a soft musical background, a family of four moves about in an American home fully equipped with the most modern conveniences. The narrator talks about what the Republican Administration means to each member of the family—'to you, Mom . . . to you, Junior . . . and to you, Sis.'
>
> "The drama ends with a voice saying, 'Give Ike a Republican Congress,' and the film then shows President and Mrs. Eisenhower singing 'God Bless America'."

The political effects of television underwent less systematic study in the 1956 election than in 1952. Voting preference and viewing of TV campaign broadcasts were studied by Irving R. Merrill in a four-wave panel study conducted in Lansing, Michigan. Initial interviews were held in March, 1956 in 2300 homes, repeated in April in 707 homes and again in September and after the November election, among those households with incomes of $4-7000.

High political participation was found to be related to heavier viewing of political broadcasts. Individuals who identified with a party viewed more political programs than did the independents. Strong Democrats viewed more Stevenson broadcasts than did weak

Democrats, and a similar pattern was found for Republicans. Moreover, people who identified with one party were more apt to remember programs of their own party than to remember non-partisan
political programs, or opposition broadcasts.

The sum of the evidence suggests that people "use" television
as they "use" other media, interpreting everything in terms of their
existing biases and expectations, but as in the case of other media
the information and impressions left by television are absorbed into
the ongoing stream of experience through which opinions are formed
and modified. What promises to make TV a more potent political
force than radio or the press is (1) its relatively close resemblance
to face-to-face persuasion, and (2) its ability to command vast quantities of the public's time.

12. TELEVISION AND THE JUVENILE AUDIENCE

Television has fascinated children since the first ancient Krazy Kat cartoon cavorted over the air waves. It has shown its power to generate fads and to create popular heroes among children on a scale which no other mass medium had previously been able to do. The most epic example of this was the startling overnight success of the Davy Crockett characterization created by Walt Disney on film for a showing on the Disneyland TV program of December 15, 1954.

While the Davy Crockett craze was in large part the product of clever promotion and publicity, it also appeared to correspond to a great need on the part of the juvenile public for a hero who symbolized all the virtues of an era as remote from the present as that of the space cadets who had been in vogue several years earlier. Within a few weeks the theme song of the Crockett film had soared to heights of popularity, and the coonskin cap had become the indispensable costume of the younger set. By the end of 1955 retail sales of Davy Crockett merchandise had reached the $300 million mark. Coontails, which had formerly sold for 25 cents a pound, rose to five dollars a pound in value, and caps were also manufactured in quantity from all possible furry substitutes.

Even in the epoch when more TV viewing took place in the tavern than in the home, a modest amount of programming was directed at the juvenile audience. This proportion grew as television became an accepted part of family life and as the typical station's broadcast day extended into the afternoon.

Families with children were from the start most susceptible to the lure of television. This fact was proclaimed with striking indelicacy in a full page advertisement placed in a thousand newspapers in 1950 by the Television Manufacturers Association. The illustration showed two unhappy children, and the headline ran, "There are some things a son or daughter won't tell you." The text sought to rouse feelings of extreme guilt in the breasts of parents who had not yet equipped their homes with TV. Their unfortunate offspring bore a "bruise deep inside"; they were set apart from their contemporaries.

"Our daughter holds us in contempt for not buying a set," one upset mother told Paul Witty, who questioned the parents of 2100 Evanston elementary school pupils in 1950. However, this point of view seems to have been extreme. Only 5% of the non-owners in Witty's survey said they were under pressure from the children to buy a set.

Children in non-television homes became familiar with the medium as quickly as their parents did. The guest viewing which was a familiar phenomenon among adults in television's early days was perhaps even more prevalent among children, since they move in and out of each others' homes more frequently and with less ceremony.

The extent of this guest viewing may be seen in a survey among students in a Junior High School in Stamford, Connecticut, described in the New York *Times* of March 6, 1950 79% of the high school students interviewed reported "regular" TV viewing, although only 50% had sets at home.

TABLE 86

Daily Time Spent Watching Television, by School Grade

(Source: Witty 1950 Evanston Study)

	Owners	*Non-Owners*
First Grade	2.85 hours	1.17 hours
2nd	3.01	2.03
3rd	3.42	1.44
4th	3.32	1.68
5th	3.15	1.03
6th	3.71	1.90
7th	2.91	1.95
8th	2.71	2.35
Daily Average	3.13	1.69

In Witty's Evanston survey also, children who did not have television at home reported half as much television viewing on the average day as did those in television homes. Among the eighth grade pupils (who probably produced more accurate estimates of viewing time than the younger children) the gap between TV and non-TV owners was only about twenty minutes a day. (See Table 86.)

Time Spent Viewing

From Witty's study it appears that the average child in a tele- **(A)** vision home spends something over three hours a day viewing. The heaviest viewers are children of about 11, in the 6th grade, who are at the set nearly four hours a day.

After his first survey in Evanston, Witty conducted similar studies in four successive years, first branching out to include other Chicago suburbs, and finally to the city itself. While his samples are therefore not quite comparable from year to year, the trends they reveal are nonetheless interesting to follow. Between 1950 and 1954 the proportion of pupils with TV sets at home grew from 43% to 96%. In that period, the weekly hours of viewing reported by grade school pupils in television homes remained about the same—21. (Witty began surveys of high school pupils in 1951; they reported 14 hours of weekly viewing in that year, and the same amount of time in 1954.) By contrast, the parents of the children surveyed showed a steady decline in weekly viewing hours, from 24 in 1950 to 16 in 1954. This is in accord with the trend, measured by the nationwide rating services, which showed a decline in the overall average as less interested persons acquired television sets.

Philip Lewis, questioning 1100 children in a Chicago high school in 1951, found that those who had had their sets longest spent the least amount of time viewing. Children who had owned sets for over three years reported 14 hours of weekly viewing; those who had owned sets between one and three years watched 16 hours a week; the new set owners who had acquired a set within the preceding year watched 17 hours a week. These figures suggest a wearing off of television's "novelty effect," which appears more striking in the case of these youngsters than for adults (on whom we reported in Chapter 4). There is a possibility that the children of the media-minded parents who bought TV first may have reacted against their elders' heavy use of the set, and turned to other pursuits themselves. Another explanation is that the growing child, whose world is constantly changing, finds it relatively easy to reduce the amount of time he spends with the medium as new activities and interests swim into his ken.

In Stewart's Atlanta survey, of the persons who had owned television for some time, 43% felt that their children's viewing interest decreased with time, though an equal number felt there had been no change. Only 15% reported that as time went on the youngsters actually watched TV more than formerly. These answers, are in keeping with those obtained in surveys of adult viewing patterns.

A mail survey of *Better Homes and Gardens* subscribers, described in an article by Ann Usher (1955), asked parents to report on their children's viewing habits in the first few months after the television set was acquired. In the initial period, according to this account, young children spent two or three hours a day viewing, older ones as much as five hours a day during the week, and up to seven on weekends. As the set lost its novelty appeal, viewing dropped down to 1-3 hours daily.

Surveys among school pupils in other cities have documented the extent of television's hold over leisure time.

1. In his study on Long Island in 1948, Coffin found children devoting 24 hours a week to TV in television homes. A year later, W. G. McGinnis, surveying pupils in the elementary schools of Perth Amboy, New Jersey, found they were watching between 15 and 25 hours a week.

2. The Stamford High School students reported on by Gould spent virtually as much time every week watching television (27 hours) as in class.

3. Walter Clarke reported in 1951 that the average 12 or 13 year old child in Cincinnati spent 3.7 hours a day before the television screen, or 30 hours a week.

4. Catherine St. John Mahoney submitted questionnaires to 500 third grade and 500 fifth grade pupils in both parochial and public schools in metropolitan Boston (1953). Third grade pupils averaged 2½ hours a day of viewing, fifth grade pupils 3 hours a day. On Saturdays and Sundays many children watched TV 8 or 10 hours a day.

5. Stanley T. Kaplan questioned 324 pupils in a Washington suburb in 1955 and found the average pupil spending 14 hours and 35 minutes on Mondays through Fridays watching TV, plus 5 hours 22 minutes on Saturday and 5 hours 8 minutes on Sunday, for a total of 25 hours and 5 minutes a week.

6. A survey conducted in 1957 (by the local chapter of the American Association of University Women) among nearly 10,000 school children in Falls Church, Virginia, found that nine out of ten watch television programs after 9:00 p. m. on weekday evenings. The proportion was only slightly less for the younger fifth-grade children than for the seventh-graders.

7. May V. Seagoe, asked 323 Los Angeles children how often they went to the movies or listened to the radio. One answered succinctly, "Only when the television isn't working."

Studies which try to estimate the amount of television viewing done by children on the basis of their parents' testimony have produced more conservative figures. Sweetser's 1950 study in Boston found that (according to their mothers) young children aged 3-6 watched TV 8 hours on Monday through Friday, and youngsters from 7-20 watched about 12 hours.

TABLE 87

Weekly Hours of Television Viewing, by School Grade

(Source: Battin 1951 Ann Arbor Study)

	Boys	*Girls*
First Grade	11 hours 54 minutes	15 hours 41 minutes
2nd	16 hours 35 minutes	14 hours 59 minutes
3rd	14 hours 34 minutes	17 hours 49 minutes
4th	19 hours 17 minutes	19 hours 28 minutes
5th	17 hours 28 minutes	23 hours 10 minutes
6th	25 hours 35 minutes	22 hours 31 minutes
7th	27 hours 34 minutes	21 hours 28 minutes
8th	23 hours 16 minutes	23 hours 21 minutes
9th	20 hours 18 minutes	21 hours 28 minutes
10th	19 hours 39 minutes	19 hours 8 minutes
11th	19 hours 21 minutes	17 hours 56 minutes
12th	19 hours 3 minutes	19 hours 2 minutes

Ann Fitzhugh Bell distributed questionnaires to the families of 1,853 school children in Palo Alto, California, in May, 1953. (At this time four out of five of the families responding had a television set.) From the parents' reports, 71% of the children in this predominantly upper middle class university community average one to two hours of TV viewing each school day. 20% watch more than two hours (and up to six), 9% average less than an hour. Boys and girls did not differ significantly in the amount of their viewing, but children between 6 and 10 years appeared to watch television most. Television viewing began to decline for girls at the age of 13, for boys about a year later.

T. C. Battin, questioning 1100 children in the schools of Ann Arbor, Michigan, in 1951, found the heaviest viewing to occur in the sixth, seventh and eighth grades. At the younger age levels, girls appear to watch TV slightly more than boys do, but at the high school level there is not much difference.

TABLE 88

Daily Hours of Television Viewing, by School Grade*

(Source: Koch 1952 Columbus Study)

	School Days	Saturday	Sunday
Kindergarten-Second Grade	2 hours 20 minutes	3 hours 16 minutes	3 hours 36 minutes
Fourth-Eighth Grade	2 hours 56 minutes	4 hours	4 hours 25 minutes
Tenth-Twelfth Grade	1 hour 57 minutes	2 hours 26 minutes	3 hours

* No data shown for third or ninth grade students.

One interesting by-product of Battin's survey is that it supplies some evidence by which we may judge the accuracy of children's reports of their own viewing habits. Battin first asked the children in his sample to estimate the number of hours they spent watching television each week. He then gave them a seven-day diary in which their actual viewing was recorded as it occurred at home. This diary was filled out as a classroom assignment. The diary reports were within one or two hours of the original time estimates in 86% of the cases; in only 1% was there a discrepancy of more than 4 hours. These findings add to the believability not only of his figures but of those obtained in the other local studies reported here.

The finding that children in the upper grade school age group spend more time viewing than those older or younger is corroborated in a study made in 1952 in twelve schools in the area of Columbus, Ohio. The results of this survey, directed by Freda Postle Koch, are summarized in Table 88. Of the 905 children questioned, 88% had TV at home.

A national survey of high school students directed by H. H. Remmers, R. E. Horton and R. E. Mainer, of Purdue University in March, 1953, found that the average teen-ager with a television set at home spends about three hours daily in viewing. Of the total 3000 students sampled, 63% watch television in their own home, 22% occasionally watch television in the homes of friends or relatives and 15% had no opportunity to see television (largely because they lived outside the reception area).

TABLE 89

Hours High School Students in TV Homes Spend Watching TV on Average Day, as Related to Mother's Education

(Source: Remmers, Horton and Mainer High School Survey, 1953)

Average Daily TV Viewing	Grade School	Education of Mother — High School	College
Less than one hour	11%	16%	22%
One to two hours	26	30	33
Three to four hours	28	27	27
Five to six hours	14	12	7
More than six hours	21	15	11
	100%	100%	100%

Remmers and his associates found no significant difference in the amount of TV viewing time between teen-agers who had had sets in their home for more than a year and those who had had it for less than a year. Since no additional breakdowns were made, it is hard to say whether or not this contradicts Witty's finding about the wearing off of the novelty effect. The amount of time spent viewing television was found to be closely related to social status. Where family income is high and the mother has been to college, students spend less time watching TV than where income is lower and the mother has had only a high school or grade school education.

While there is no exact agreement in the hourly viewing figures produced by all these studies, made at different times and places by different methods, they clearly demonstrate the extent to which television has become an influence in the lives of American youth.

Changes in Program Preference

Although children spend somewhat different amounts of time with television at various age levels, these differences are small compared with the changes that take place, as children grow, in the pattern of their program preferences. These shifts in taste reflect the child's growing maturity and breadth of interest. As he ages, he transforms the roles in which he imagines himself, the persons with whom he identifies, and the whole character of his fantasy life.

Katherine M. Wolf and Marjorie Fiske have traced the progression of children's preferences in comic books. In the "funny animal" comics the very young child first finds his primitive brightly-colored sharply etched desires, dreams and impulses acted out in the adventures of human-like but non-human creatures. By the age of 10 and 11 the child is too sophisticated for Chicken-Licken, Peter Rabbit or even Mickey Mouse. He is ready to explore and conquer the world, and "fantastic adventure" comics of the Superman variety allow him vicariously to achieve the impossible. At the age of 12 "true" and "classic" comics have a greater appeal. The vivid frank exercise of personal fantasy seems childish; the youngster is ready to cope with the real environment.

The changing pattern of preferences can be seen in the reasons which children of different ages advance to explain why they like their favorite TV shows. Battin, questioning children in Ann

Arbor, found that in grades 4-6 children want shows that are "filled with action." At grades 7-9 they stress variety and suspense. In high school, grades 10-12, they have incorporated adult values; they stress the educational or informational aspect of the programs they watch, and comment on the quality of writing or production.

An analysis of children's viewing habits, made by the American Research Bureau, presents some additional evidence along the same lines. Table 90 shows the percentage of children at various ages

TABLE 90

How Children's Viewing Differs, by Age Level

(Source: American Research Bureau, January 1952)

	Per Cent Viewing Programs in Each Age Group					
	6 & Under	7-8	9-10	11-12	13-14	15-16
Captain Video	11%	27%	20%	15%	14%	8%
Howdy Doody	43	50	48	20	16	11
Super Circus	15	20	17	17	10	3
Gabby Hayes	19	16	17	8	9	4
Roy Rogers	11	27	20	23	11	8
I Love Lucy	5	16	25	25	29	28
Hit Parade	1	1	2	4	5	14
Toast of the Town	4	6	7	7	10	9
Milton Berle	8	23	27	25	25	25
Fireside Theater	3	16	13	17	22	18
Playhouse of Stars	2	6	10	9	10	5
What's My Line	5	12	12	8	10	9

who watched individual programs—children's and adult—during one week in January, 1952. "Howdy Doody," a marionette show, had a very high appeal for children under ten, and then dropped off sharply in interest. (The marionette or puppet, like an animal, stands in the mind of the young child as a representative of emotions and wishes which he cannot attribute to a human actor.) Although children of six and younger do considerably less viewing than older ones, "Howdy Doody" was seen by 43% at the time of this research. Captain Video, a science fiction serial in the time-tested tradition of Buck Rogers, was at the height of its popularity among children of seven and eight,

and then held a steadily diminishing interest. Super Circus, essentially
a children's variety show, held a remarkably constant level of interest
through the age of twelve and then dropped sharply. Two cowboy
programs, Gabby Hayes and Roy Rogers, had a somewhat similar
pattern. Hayes, being a "funny" character, was interesting to younger
children, and had little appeal to those of eleven or twelve. Roy
Rogers, who plays the game straight, developed high interest for
seven and eight year olds but was already too juvenile to attract the
sophisticates of 13.

TABLE 91

Children's Viewing at Different Age Levels,
for Average Program of Various Program Types

(Source: American Research Bureau, 1954)

	6 & Under	7-8	9-10	11-12	13-14	15-16
Science Fiction	9%	17%	15%	14%	11%	7%
"Kid Shows"	14	19	18	11	7	4
Western	10	18	15	15	8	6
Situation Comedy	4	15	16	15	15	10
Music	2	7	5	5	6	9
Comedy Variety	5	15	18	15	15	16
Variety Music	2	5	5	4	5	4
Drama	1	7	8	9	11	5
Audience Participation	3	5	8	5	7	5
Daytime	4	5	4	3	4	3
Mystery	1	5	6	6	8	4
Average of all types	5	11	11	9	9	7

Perhaps the most interesting aspect of this table is that it
shows how early in life children begin to look at programs directed
primarily at adults. A popular comedian like Milton Berle was over
the heads of children 6 and younger; moreover they were apt to be
in bed by the time he came on the air. By the age of seven, one
child in four had stayed up to watch him, along with the other members of the family. A somewhat similar pattern held true for a situation
comedy program like "I Love Lucy." Although a dramatic program
like the "Fireside Theater" or a quiz show like "What's My Line"

attracted fewer viewers—adults as well as children—the children appeared to be watching them with the rest of the family by the time they were seven or eight.

In a more recent analysis of children's viewing habits, the American Research Bureau shows (in Table 91) how *average* programs of various types are viewed by children at different ages. The percentages in this table represent the proportion of all children in the particular age group who watch the average program in each category shown. (From this table it appears that the greatest amount of viewing is done by children between the ages of 7 and 10. The school studies we have already cited suggest that viewing is heaviest at 11 and 12. This discrepancy may most easily be explained by the fact that the American Research Bureau bases its figures on diaries in which the adult members of the family are asked to record the viewing done by younger children. By the time children reach the age of 11 or 12 their parents may expect them to fill out the diaries themselves, and it seems reasonable to suspect that they may be somewhat lax in doing this.)

As in the analysis of individual shows, the breakdown of average program ratings shows that the "kid shows" aimed at younger children (like "Kukla, Fran and Ollie," "Howdy Doody" or "Rin Tin Tin") begin to lose their attraction beyond the age of 10, whereas Westerns and Science Fiction continue to hold interest through the age of 12 before the audience starts to drop off.

The first adult programs which children begin to watch (strongly by the age of 7) are comedy shows of either the situation or variety types. From the available evidence, it does not seem as though other types of programming fare arouse large audience interest among children at any age up to 16.

In the light of this information it is not surprising that when 1200 New York City school children were asked in 1955 (by the New York *Herald Tribune*) to name their favorite programs, family-type shows were named more often than programs aimed specifically at children. In the survey of *Better Homes and Gardens* readers, children aged 5 to 9 had four juvenile programs and one situation comedy among their top five favorites, while those aged 10 to 14 named adult shows more frequently. Older teen-agers, aged 15-19, naturally selected adult shows, including plays as well as comedy and variety programs.

Similarly, a survey conducted in England by Mark Abrams (1955), among 1500 children aged 8-15, found that more had watched adult programs on the preceding day than had watched children's shows. "Tea-time viewing is at best a mere warming-up, a preliminary flexing of the eye-muscles, before the main diet starts at 7:30 PM." Only a third of the mentions of three favorite programs went to children's shows.

Programs which are not aimed primarily at children are nonetheless not necessarily "adult" in their appeal. In particular, the comedy and variety programs to which children first gravitate as part of the family viewing group generally are, in subject matter, style and manner of presentation, pitched at a level which is both within a child's comprehension and attuned to his range of interests. The producers of such programs commonly assume that they are reaching a "family audience," and this is kept very much in mind in the writing and direction.

Shows of this type are distributed throughout the evening hours, and are not concentrated in the early evening when most youngsters are watching television. At the same time, programs of other types, which are also distributed through the time schedule, do not attract large numbers of youthful viewers. Dramatic programs in particular have relatively few children in their large audiences, because they commonly deal with adult problems, conflicts and emotions.

TABLE 92

Popularity of Television Program Types Among Teen-Agers

(Source: Remmers, Horton and Mainer High School Survey, 1953)

	Per Cent Who Watch Very Often, by Income Level		
	Low	*Medium*	*High*
Plays	55%	54%	53%
Sports	48	40	38
Mysteries	63	55	49
Family comedy	62	61	54
Quiz shows	33	29	27
Variety shows	56	56	49
Western movies	39	27	25
Opera	8	10	13

By the time youngsters reach high school age, their program preferences are very close to the adult pattern. This may be seen, for example, in Table 92, which shows the popularity of various types of programs among the high school students questioned by Remmers, Horton and Mainer. With the exception of opera, westerns and quiz shows, most program types are "watched very often" by roughly half those queried, suggesting the kind of continuous and relatively indiscriminate viewing we described in Chapter 4.   (B)

There is one interesting by-product of this analysis, and that is the suggestion that teen-agers of different social backgrounds have remarkably similar viewing preferences. To be sure, some differences exist, and they are of the expected variety: pupils from high-income homes are most apt to watch opera, least apt to watch mysteries and situation comedies; pupils from low-income homes are most apt to watch Westerns, quiz shows, and sportcasts. But on the whole, these variations are far less than might be expected, in the light of the known disparities in adult tastes and life styles among people at different social levels. This suggests that television-viewing is so deeply embedded in the group culture of the present-day teen-ager that it can create a high uniformity of preferences and interests, quite apart from the traditional influence of the family and its particular position in society.

A survey of nearly 5,000 teenagers made in 1955 by Eugene Gilbert and Company for the Bureau of Advertising of the American Newspaper Publishers' Association finds that 70% evaluate television as the most entertaining medium, while only 17% rate it as "most practical." (Magazines receive 54% of the mentions on that point.) The youngest teenagers are most apt to name television as the medium which they would find hardest to be without, but the proportion declines with increasing age (from 55% of the 13- and 14-year olds to 18% of those 18 and 19). On the other hand the percentage mentioning newspapers increases (from 18% in the 13-14-year age group to 39% among those 18 and 19) and so does the percentage mentioning radio (from 23% to 36%). Partly this shift may represent changing tastes and media patterns that accompany growing maturity of interests; partly it may reflect the development of a new generation conditioned to television from the very earliest years of its life.

The Child as Consumer

(C)   Children's television programs, like most others, are commercially sponsored, and advertisers are highly aware of the importance of youthful family members as purchasers of certain commodities. Products like cookies, candy, soft drinks and breakfast foods are widely advertised on children's programs. Advertisers are not only concerned with products that are actually consumed by children. They are also interested in the child who himself does a good share of the family shopping for groceries, or in the child who accompanies his mother to the store and helps to fill the shopping basket with items whose brand names are familiar through advertising.

Even very young children learn to imitate jingles or announcements on television or radio, much as they imitate the entertainers who emerge as significant heroes in their lives. To the youngster it appears just as natural to sing a song extolling the virtues of a detergent or headache remedy as to hum a nursery rhyme.

The products with which children become familiar in this way are not necessarily healthful ones like canned peas or shredded wheat. Several years ago, Florence Brumbaugh asked 400 children, aged 6-12, to list as many television-advertised products as they could in fifteen minutes. The youngest children wrote down an average of twenty items; the eleven-year olds named fifty each. Fifteen brands of beer and thirteen brands of cigarettes were named, as well as numerous brands of drugs and cosmetics. One detergent received 110 mentions. Almost all the brand names were spelled correctly, even though many of them were much harder than words on school spelling lists.

The extent to which such advertising makes an impression is also shown in a survey of teen-agers made in 1955 by Advertest Research. Among these youngsters 13-19 years old, 65% had a "favorite brand" of cigarettes, 57% a "favorite brand" of beer. There is nothing surprising in this, of course, for young people, like adults, are apt to base their impression of a brand on the images created by its advertising rather than on their actual experience with it. It is not at all unlikely that television has a strong influence on the specific brand choices which children make of products that are essentially intended for adult consumption. Yet the juvenile consumer, like his parents, will decide among the various conflicting advertising appeals and claims on the basis of his own predispositions and tastes.

It is not at all certain that television actually induces a youngster to begin smoking or drinking at an advanced age, in response to the exhortations of the TV announcers. When he begins is far more likely to depend on the standards set in the youngster's own family or in the crowd of his contemporaries. For some time there has been a steady increase in the proportion of smokers and drinkers in the population as a whole. This can be attributed primarily to fundamental changes in the American style of life induced by urbanization, higher income, the change in work pace and in the standards of female propriety.

To some extent advertising has contributed to this general tendency, not so much by stimulating the appetite for tobacco and drink as by making tobacco and drink seem commonplace and therefore acceptable. Television advertising may have some influence in this sense. Television entertainment, like motion picture entertainment, also works in the same direction, if only in that it makes the standards of deportment of Broadway or Hollywood familiar to millions of other Americans. Edward R. Murrow, casually smoking a cigarette while he conducts an interview on a program sponsored by an oil company, may be encouraging the smoking habit just as much as any TV announcer for a tobacco firm, in the same way that Clark Gable, sipping a highball in Cinemascope, helps to make moviegoers feel that this is a perfectly natural accompaniment to a conversation and not at all sinful.

TV, Children and Parents

The family viewing situation is reached by the contemporary American child only after several earlier phases. The infant coming to the dawn of awareness in the television age sees the set as an integral part of his natural environment. The sights and sounds that emanate from it are part of the blur and the whir that make up the total image of the home, which the child gradually learns to differentiate into separate objects with distinct functions. Television finally emerges as a distraction from the background as an occasional change of picture or sound, or the appearance of an interesting or familiar sight like a dog or an apple, calls for a sudden brief flurry of attention.

Between the age of 2 and 3 the child begins to follow sequences of plot and story. By 3 he can watch the set for a substantial period of time (a half hour) without losing attention. He has strong program preferences, and utters loud protests when these are ignored. Hero worship has set in, and the daily arrival of the beloved announcer or master of ceremonies is feverishly awaited and greeted with cries of ecstatic delight. By 4 the child is turning the set on by himself. He is now (within the bounds set by parental controls) a free agent exercising free choice as a consumer of entertainment and information.

At the earliest stage the infant may be aware that the set is a competitor for his parents' attention. At a later stage the set may be used deliberately by the parents to divert the child's attention away from themselves. In this sense the set serves the same purpose as any device intended to "keep the child out of mischief" (a euphemism for "out of the parents' way"). As a distraction, television has a strong technological advantage, in that its ability to retain the child's attention and interest is considerably greater than that of a picture book or a toy.

The extent to which television is used by the busy housewife to divert or occupy her children and keep them out of mischief while she tends to her chores is shown by Ripley's 1955 telephone survey of TV viewing in Columbus, Ohio. At every time period of the day, he found that set usage was higher in homes with young children than in childless homes. Between 8:00 AM and 4:00 PM it was almost twice as high, and it was over three times as great between 4:00 and 6:00 PM. (No such difference existed in the case of radio.)

There would seem to be some potential dangers in the common practice of using TV as a baby sitter, if the net effect is to reduce the amount of direct attention the child receives from his parents, or the extent to which he participates in family life. However, it is difficult to trace any damage done to the child's emotional well-being in this respect, for if TV is interposed between children and parents this usually reflects attitudes and behavior expressed by the parents in other ways as well.

Conflict over a choice of programs often occurs among the children in a family, especially if they are of different ages. In the

Better Homes and Gardens survey, three out of five families reported some bickering over what to view in cases where there was an age difference of five years or more between the children. Conflicts are generally resolved either by rotating choice, by giving the older child priority, or by letting the younger child have his way during the earlier time periods before he goes to bed.

The choice of programs may be a bone of contention between children and parents, as it may be among adult members of the family. A fifteen-year-old girl told Koch, "My mother likes Ed Sullivan while I prefer the Comedy Hour. So we compromise. A half hour of each on Sunday nights."

Television becomes a point of conflict between parents and children not only when they want to watch different shows at the same time, but also as parents attempt to enforce their views of what the child should and should not be viewing. Parental discipline has two aspects: (1) control over the total amount of viewing, and over the times in which viewing is to be done, and (2) control over the selection of individual programs.

Half the Washington children questioned by Kaplan answered "yes" to the question, "Do parents and child ever disagree on any types of programs?" A third answered "no." Only 6% reported that their parents select programs for them to view.

Where parent-child conflict occurred over the choice of programs, a third of the parents questioned by *Better Homes and Gardens* said they usually kept the upper hand, but 10% said the children usually had their own way. Actually, fathers and mothers differed more in their choices of favorite programs than did parents and children.

These parents reported that mealtime and bedtimes were periods of particular difficulty. One family in three permitted the child to watch TV while he ate supper. As one parent described it, "the family supper table has become a lap meal." In only a small minority of these predominantly upper-middle-class households were children allowed to stay up as late as they wanted to watch television. Virtually all those parents with childen in school reported stiff competition between television and homework. In this case only a handful of extremely permissive parents let their children watch television and do their homework at the same time, while the rest insisted that the set be turned off or that the child do his work in another room. One family in three reported conflict between television and outdoor play or household chores.

The "time-consuming" character of television was the single most important objection voiced by parents in this survey. Two parents in five said they disapproved of some of the programs their children wanted to look at, but a majority reported that the children followed their guidance in the choice of programs. One in four said they insisted on their youngsters watching certain special programs— either special events, educational broadcasts, or other shows they felt were especially suitable.

From Koch's survey in Columbus, it appears that parental control over children's TV entertainment is drastically curtailed after the child finishes grade school and enters high school.

TABLE 93

Parental Control over Children's Viewing, By School Grade

(Source: Koch 1952 Columbus Survey)

	Kindergarten-Second Grade	4th-8th Grade	10th-12th Grade
Per cent whose parents always let them choose the programs they watch	17%	13%	36%
Per cent whose parents sometimes let them choose the programs they watch	73	76	54
Per cent whose parents have rules on watching	59	61	29
Per cent who disagree with parents on some programs	42	47	26

As Table 93 indicates, there does not appear to be any difference between the controls reported by grade school children of different ages, but there is a distinct difference between them and the high school pupils. One reason why the high school teen-agers receive less supervision in their TV viewing is that their program tastes apparently are considerably closer to those of their parents; at least they reported much less disagreement over the choice of programs. The programs on which disagreement was most frequently reported are murders, mysteries and detective stories, and— in the case of the youngest group—cowboy programs.

Koch also found an age difference in the restrictions reported by those whose parents have rules on watching. The parents of the youngest children exercise control mostly over the times and conditions of viewing, whereas the parents of the older grade-school and the high-school pupils restrict viewing as a punishment for bad conduct.

It is interesting to note that parents set rules primarily in terms of the amount or timing of TV viewing, rather than in terms of content. Of those children who reported parental controls, only a fourth of the children at the grade-school level and virtually none at the high-school level said their parents restrict their viewing of certain kinds of shows.

Parents' attitudes toward television resemble those they have expressed toward radio in previous years. In his survey of radio listening in television areas, Politz found that most people (68%) believe that on the whole radio is more good than bad for children. Only 5% believe that it is more bad than good. Opinion is even more favorable in households which have one or more children under the age of 15. Those who think radio is more good than bad for children said that it is educational and informative (mentioned by 45%). An additional 25% cited radio's entertainment capacities. On the other hand, those who feel that radio is more bad than good cited bad programs and ideas, crime stories, etc., in most cases (57%).

Studies of parents' reactions to TV have, in general, uncovered opinions along the lines summarized in the April 24, 1954, issue of *Information Service,* a publication of the National Council of the Churches of Christ:

"The arguments against children's use of television run in general like this: television is a spectator activity which leaves little play for the child's creative imagination (as compared with radio or books, for example); it takes time that would otherwise be spent in pursuits that are physically, mentally, and socially more constructive; it interferes with meals, family schedules, and home study; the available programs introduce the child to crime and violence and to questionable tastes and values; and it is used by the parent as a substitute for intelligent and loving supervision. Against these the proponents of television say that this medium is a 'window on the world' of incomparable value; that the minds and imagination of this generation are given an unprecedented outreach through this new medium; that there are after all a number of 'good' programs to choose from; that episodes of crime and violence are an outlet for rather than a stimulus to aggression; and that television is making the home once again the center of American family life, reversing the centrifugal forces that have been dispersing the family in recent decades.

"Somewhere in between these two groups stands another set of opinions to the effect that television programs, like fairy tales or comic books, are in themselves neither 'good' nor 'bad' for children, but are simply one more addition to the vast complex of stimuli the world presents to the growing child, and that the child's response is determined by his character, temperament, emotions and family and group experience far more than by the content or format of the program."

In his first study of television's effects on school children (1950), Witty submitted questionnaires to 1736 parents. Since the research was done in the upper-income suburban community of Evanston, Illinois, these responses were not as favorable to TV as those obtained in some of the studies already reported. Yet only 13% of the parents disapproved outright of children's programs on TV, while another 25% disapproved of some programs but liked others. 55% expressed general approval. The parents who spoke approvingly of television echoed the opinion that it had brought the family closer together.

"TV has increased our happiness at home."
"It has given the children a happier home where they can laugh."
"My two 16-year-olds like to stay home now. I am so glad, as I would not know where they were otherwise. They have been backward in school. But television has helped them a lot."

Four out of five of the television-owning parents did not think their children spent too much time watching television, and this was true whether or not the children were very young.

The parents who disapproved of television, either wholly or in part, had two major grounds for criticism: They felt there was too much violence and sensationalism, especially in Western films, and they also felt that television, as a passive activity, interfered with wholesome physical development.

A third of the television-owning parents reported that TV created problems at home, principally in getting children to go to bed, eat their meals, or do their chores on time. One mother who said she had "no difficulties at all" explained that "we adjust our schedule to television." As Witty continued to question both parents and teachers in later years, he continued to get reports of difficulties in behavior or adjustment which were attributed to television: nervousness, fatigue, eyestrain, disinterest in school work, and impoverishment of play.   (D)

In his 1950 study in the Boston area, Sweetser found the mothers of grade-school children in TV homes overwhelmingly (94%) of the opinion that television is good for children. Four out of five cited its educational value, a third said it kept the children occupied and out of mischief, and smaller numbers mentioned its entertainment value, said it helped children to relax, or said it kept the children at home with the family.

Three-fourths of those interviewed cited undesirable aspects of television for children. Half criticized what they felt was an emphasis on "horror"; about a third said it was hard to get their youngsters to go to bed on time. ("White-collar" mothers were more critical than those in working class families.)

Stewart's Atlanta survey also found parents to be generally favorable in commenting on TV's effects on their children. A third reported that television had changed the bedtime hour for the youngsters, but most of them felt there had been no change in attention to study, performance of school tasks, or school grades. About three out of four parents felt there had been no change, since TV, in the kinds of games the children played, or in the size of the play group, but only half thought that TV had not changed the amount of exercise the children got. All but a few parents felt that television was *not* making their children more tired by the end of the day.

There was a sharper division of opinion in answer to a question on whether TV had affected the child's attentiveness to his household chores. Only a third thought there had been no change, while the remainder split between those who said their children required more prodding and those who said "they hurry to get done now" so they can watch TV. (Clearly the differences in these responses reflect differences in the routine of different families and in the use of threats and rewards to gain obedience.)

Nine out of ten parents said they had noticed the children "imitating" something they had seen on television—usually either cowboys in western movies or the dancing and singing of variety shows. Puppets, comedians, acrobats and commercial announcers were also mentioned as objects of imitation. As a source of new ideas or mannerisms, the parents interviewed considered TV most important. Only seven out of ten had noticed their children imitating something they had heard on the radio. A third had seen the children imitating comic books characters, and half had been aware of the children imitating the parents themselves. This capacity of TV to serve as a source of new experience for children apparently aroused approval rather than apprehension. One mother said, referring to her child:

> "It has made him smart. He is learning by sight—recognizes ads and names he sees on TV. Learned a lot of new words. It has taught him a lot as well as amused him."

According to the Palo Alto parents questioned by Bell, 53% of the children are reading less than before TV, 24% are less apt to "make things" and only 13% play less in groups. 51% reportedly stay at home more.

69% of the parents reported that their children discuss the programs, with parents in 56% of the cases. 65% of the children were reported to watch television with their parents during meals. Two parents in three feel that television draws the family together in a common interest. Two in five said that television helps them to discipline their children and to get household chores done. Three in four said that they help their children choose programs.

An elaborate analysis of parents' attitudes toward television was made in 1953-4 in metropolitan New Haven, under the auspices of the Broadcasting and Film Commission of the National Council of the Churches of Christ and the Yale University Divinity School.

In this study, directed by Everett Parker, questions were directed at 650 TV families with children (out of 3,559 households originally contacted). An overwhelming majority of the parents interviewed (69%) indicated that they generally favored children's programs as they were. 26% were generally disapproving, and the remaining 5% had mixed sentiments.

These over-all proportions obscured a tremendous difference in the outlook of persons at different social levels. Parents whose income was above average divided almost evenly pro and con in their opinion of children's TV, while parents of below average income were generally favorable, four to one. These differences are completely consistent with the findings of earlier studies of the public's attitudes toward broadcasting.

(E)

In general, people of higher social position, income and education are more critical of existing fare in radio, television and the movies, while those at the lower end of the social scale are more ready to accept what is available. There are probably several reasons for this: Since mass-media content tends to be geared at the level of the common denominator, the better educated are more apt to feel that it fails to come up to their own standards of value and taste. Moreover, persons of higher-than-average social standing are in general more articulate and self-confident; on most surveys they feel freer to express their opinions even when these are unpopular or when they seem to imply some questioning of established authority.

Parents of children between the ages of 4 and 15 were somewhat less favorable to television than were parents of very small children (for whom TV viewing had not yet become important) or those of older teen-agers (whose viewing habits resembled those of the adults). However in homes where there were children in *both* the 4-9 and 10-15 year age brackets, parents were more favorable than in homes where the children were of the same age group. The researchers suggest that these may be larger families in which TV is more useful to the parents in keeping the children out from under foot.

About a third of the unfavorable comments about children's programs involved objections to their general character and content. A fourth of the criticism related to the violence which many parents felt was rife on children's TV. Other objections were made to the scarcity of educational and religious programs on TV and to poor scheduling of children's broadcasts.

The principal object of concern on the part of those who complained about the types of programs broadcast were the Western films which, to the parents, seemed to loom in the forefront of their children's viewing. One mother expressed her sentiments this way:

"He drives the family crazy with this bang-bang! Bang-bang from early Saturday morning until late Sunday night."

Parents reported that 34% of all regular program time viewed by children was on Westerns, compared with 45% of the program time which was spent on children's variety shows, 7% on children's drama, 5% on children's educational or religious programming, and 9% on adult programs. However, Parker and his associates believe that "Westerns undoubtedly bulk larger in children's viewing than the statistics would indicate, simply because there are so many Westerns available that parents could not identify them by name." The authors also note that parents greatly underestimated in reporting the amount of time their children spent in viewing adult programs.

"Practically no parents reported that their children watched evening crime drama shows; yet a considerable number were worried about their effects on the children."

It therefore seems that parents' anxieties over children's viewing practices are not only reported directly in their objections to TV programming but also reflected in their embarrassed distortions of reality in describing to an interviewer what their children view. This suggests a point of view which we find again and again in examining public opinion about television, and which is especially important in analyzing attitudes toward children's television. There is a feeling, never stated in so many words, that the set has a power of its own to control the destinies and viewing habits of the audience, and that what it "does" to parents and children alike is somehow beyond the bounds of any individual set-owner's power of control.

Television's most important benefits for children are educational, in the eyes of the parents questioned by *Better Homes and*

Gardens. Parents of children up to the age of nine believe that TV helps to build the vocabulary. Others mentioned that it creates a liking for music, or that it develops imagination and awareness of current events. Most parents do not believe that TV has encouraged their children's interest in reading, though only 13% said that it had actually interfered with reading. Parents frequently cited as an advantage of television the fact that it kept their children quiet or "off the streets." 23% of the parents feel that television has helped improve their children's moral standards and only 3% feel it has been harmful in this respect. 54% believe that television has not had any effects on morals, good or bad.

Jaye Niefeld, working through Eugene Gilbert's field staff of student interviewers, interviewed the mothers of 2270 children aged 6-14 in New York, Chicago and Los Angeles. 55% of the mothers said they disapproved of certain programs for their children, but this proportion rises to 75% of the mothers of the 6 and 7 year-olds, and drops to only 38% of the mothers of children 11-14. 47% of the mothers of 8-10 year olds expressed disapproval of some programs. The mothers of the younger children objected to programs which tend to excite children or "make them act silly" whereas the mothers of older children were concerned more with "love stories" or "immoral stories" unsuitable for adolescents. At every child age level, but especially for the 8-10 year olds, mothers objected particularly to violence, crime and murder, as program elements.

The younger the child, Niefeld found, the higher the percentage of mothers who actually controlled its TV viewing. 62% of the mothers of 6 and 7 year old children decide what programs the youngsters can see; the proportion drops to 39% for the 8-10 year group, and to 25% for the 11-14 year olds.

John R. Thayer questioned parents of 1452 Columbus, Ohio schoolchildren (1957) regarding the rules they imposed on viewing. For 5-7 year olds, the principal rules were "must sit at specified minimum distance from TV set" and "may not allow TV to interfere with regular meals." For children aged 8 or more the main rule was "must finish homework or chores before watching TV." Two-thirds of the parents encouraged viewing of particular programs. One-third discouraged viewing certain programs.

In summary, the evidence seems to indicate that most parents think of television as a mixed blessing. On the whole, they approve of TV for their children, much as they like it themselves, because it has opened up new opportunities to pass time pleasurably. This feeling seems to be rationalized by comments that television keeps children at home or out of mischief, or that television represents an important educational influence.

At the same time many parents, especially middle class parents, are concerned about possible harmful effects. Some see TV as a monster engulfing the child's leisure time to the loss of other activities, more "normal" for the pre-television era in which they themselves grew up. Still others are worried primarily over the content of television programs, and its effects on the child's moral and cultural values and on his psychological well-being.

(F)

TV and School

(G)   Even more than most parents, educators have been concerned with the question of whether television has interfered with schoolwork. A number of studies have dwelt on this point.

Lewis, interviewing Chicago children in 1951, found that 69% of those in television homes did their homework before they watched TV. 8% watched TV first, then did their homework, 7% did homework between programs, and 2% acknowledged that they had the set on while they did their homework.

In Ann Arbor, Battin found that a fifth of the children admitted that television interfered with homework. In these cases, either homework was speeded up so that they could catch their favorite programs, or TV actually distracted them while they were trying to do their work. Four out of five felt that television caused no interference.

A third of the children questioned felt that television had influenced their reading habits, but two-thirds said there had been no change in the number of books and magazines they read. While TV did not appear to have changed the amount of reading, it does appear to have had some influence on the kind of reading done. About 12% said that television had stimulated reading interest in new subjects. Another 10% said that it had changed the type of reading done, since programs they had seen suggested books which they might otherwise not have read.

While only a small percentage of these youngsters said that television had reduced their hobby interests, over a third of them said television had stimulated new hobbies. Four out of five said they had learned new things by watching television. Of the boys, a third had learned "how to make things," 13% said TV had shown them how to take care of pets. The girls had learned mostly about cooking or other aspects of home economics, or how to improve their personal appearance.

Witty, questioning Evanston youngsters in 1950, found that 31% said TV helped them with their schoolwork, while 67% said it did not. A higher percentage of sixth graders (the heavy viewers) than of younger or older pupils felt that television was helpful. However, the answers given in response to Witty's question may not all have been the ones he was seeking. One child explained that television was the reward to which she looked after completing what was essentially a disagreeable chore.

"Makes me want to do my homework so I can watch TV."

In a later survey (1954) Witty found pupils reporting that TV had caused a decline in reading activity; of every five pupils, two were reading about the same, two were reading less, and only one was reading more.

Witty found many teachers, as well as parents, critical of television. In his first (1950) survey, half the teachers interviewed expressed dissatisfaction; one out of four thought that some improvements were needed. One teacher commented,

"The programs most appreciated seem to be those of sub-standard quality. As a result, children today are not amused or entertained by anything offered in a classroom unless it parallels this low standard."

Another teacher's remarks suggest just the opposite, namely that television entertainment sets too high a standard of attractiveness.

"Competing with Hopalong Cassidy, Milton Berle, or the Lone Ranger for the interest of pupils is a formidable problem."

In his studies Witty attacked a problem which had been raised before with reference to the motion pictures—namely the relation between media exposure and school achievement. In the Payne Fund series, Mark May and Frank Shuttleworth had compared children who were light and heavy moviegoers and had found the latter group to average lower in school grades, and in deportment ratings. They were also rated lower in reputation by their teachers and received fewer mentions for popularity by their classmates. While May and Shuttleworth at the time drew a cause and effect relationship, it seems reasonable to suppose that other factors might have been involved. For example, the children whose poor school and social performance might have been a sign of personal maladjustment might also have been the ones with the strongest impetus to seek solace in the movies' fantasy world. Or moviegoing may have been heavier in the homes of children whose parents were lower on the social scale and who for that reason were also less apt to do well in school.

These explanations might also apply to Witty's findings in relating the amount of TV viewing to the academic records of children in grades 3 to 6. The bottom fourth, from the standpoint of scholastic attainment, spent 26 hours a week watching television, while the top fourth watched 20 hours a week. However, Witty found no relationship at any grade between the amount of television viewing and the intelligence quotients of the youngsters.

Similarly, no conclusive findings were obtained in a study of 544 sixth grade public school children and 454 parochial school seventh graders who were questioned by Xavier University in Cincinnati in 1951. In both cases, the children in TV and non-TV homes were matched for mental age, and then compared by their scores on the Metropolitan Reading Test and the Arithmetic Proficiency Test. The children in television homes were further sub-divided according to the amount of control their parents exercised over their TV habits. The degree of parental control was measured on the basis of the bedtime hours, the extent to which "undesirable" programs were viewed, the amount of over-all viewing, and the existence of restrictions on the viewing of some programs.

The results of the analysis showed that in reading and arithmetic proficiency there were no significant differences between the children whose parents exercised strong control and those who were controlled only lightly. There were also no differences between the children of TV homes and those whose homes had no television.

In Remmers' survey, of the teen-agers who had television at home about two in five believe it interferes with their schoolwork, either "somewhat" or "very much." This is true of about one in five of those who watch television outside their own homes.

The students who watch television most (five hours or more a day) were less apt to say it interferes with their school work than were those who watch television between one and four hours. It might be thought that the heavy viewers are in families where homework seems less important, but this does not appear to be true.

The proportion who report that television has interfered with their schoolwork is exactly the same regardless of the mother's educational attainment. It therefore appears that reports of TV interference with other activity simply reflect attitudes toward the medium, which in turn are reflected in the amount of time spent viewing.   (H)

Television, Violence and Delinquency

From the very beginning, television programming has been   (I)
under attack on the grounds that it is heavily loaded with violence and sadism and that it therefore encourages and stimulates aggressive impulses in the juvenile audience.

A nationwide survey conducted by George Gallup and released in November, 1954, reports that 70% of the adults questioned place at least part of the blame for "the upsurge in juvenile delinquency" on crime-type comic books and on mystery and crime programs on television and radio. A fourth of those who blame either the comic books or television and radio programs said they contribute "a great deal" to teen-age crime. Men and women did not differ at all in their responses on this question, although older people were more apt than younger ones to ascribe the blame to the mass media.

Nearly half the Palo Alto parents interviewed by Bell reported that their children had been emotionally disturbed by programs, especially the 6 to 7 year olds.

Young people themselves are less likely to feel that TV has threatened their welfare. In Remmers' survey of high school students' opinions the question was asked, "Some people claim that too many television programs show things that young people shouldn't see, such as crime and improper behavior. How do you feel about this?" Two-thirds of the television-watching teen-agers replied that such programs are not harmful. Those who never watch television gave this response slightly less frequently, indicating that familiarity with TV creates acceptance of it. Interestingly enough, the children of high income TV families were no more apt to describe its effects as harmful than the youngsters from middle and low income TV families, even though other studies have shown their parents to be more critical. This again seems to support the notion that TV creates its own standardized tastes and values among children, cutting across social class lines.

The charges which have been raised about television closely resemble those which in former times have been raised in turn against each of the mass media as it has mounted to popularity with both adults and children.

In the early 1930's, Henry Forman's book "Our Movie-Made Children," which summarized the Payne Fund studies of the motion pictures, had on its jacket the following description:

> "Here is a book showing the movies for what they really are—a monster Pied Piper, with marvelous trappings, playing tunes irresistibly alluring to the youth of the present day. They have become, in fact, a sort of superimposed system of education for the young, a system with which established social institutions, such as the School and the Church, cannot compete, in attraction or appeal."

The President of Columbia University, Nicholas Murray Butler, asserted that

> "daily broadcasting of the passions and caprices and adventures of men and women in plays and on the screen, interpreted by ill-equipped authors and directors, cannot but be destructive of ideals that have proved to be wholesome and worthy of preservation."

Edgar Dale, studying 500 films in 1920, 1925 and 1930, found that four-fifths of them dealt with "love, crime, mystery and sex." Although criminals were often portrayed as unattractive, they were frequently shown to be "gay, jaunty, adventure-loving and courageous." In 115 pictures Dale reports that 43 crimes were attempted and 406 crimes actually committed. He asks: "How otherwise can this scarlet procession of criminal acts or attempts be described than as a veritable school for crime—especially for certain types of boys and girls."

Herbert Blumer and Philip Hauser, studying the relationship between motion pictures and juvenile delinquency and crime, found that movies were a source of harmful ideas. They saw the motion pictures as a powerful experience for young children, a wellspring of imagery and a subject for daydreaming. They report an "excruciatingly realistic attitude of the child toward the picture. To the adult it may be good art or bad, it may be clever mechanism, good photography, effective direction, successful or unsuccessful story telling, a good movie, or hokum and trash. To the young child it is reality itself."

In the opinion of these authors, the great power held by the motion pictures over the emotional life of a child made them a model for delinquent or criminal behavior.

M. I. Preston in 1941 reported on a study of the reactions of 120 boys and 80 girls, aged 6 to 16, to movie and crime stories. 76% of the children "habitually exposed" to radio and the movies evidenced "increased nervousnesss," compared to 40% of those not "habitually exposed." Sleeping disturbances occurred in 85% of the heavily exposed group and in only 19% of the control group. More of the habitual radio listeners and movie goers were nail biters. Up to the age of 12, they commonly exhibited such reactions as "retiring to the mother's bed for comfort and reassurance, screaming, pulling bed covers over the head, burrowing the head under the pillow, or diving under the covers, there to spend an uneasy night plagued by vivid recollections."

As reported by the *Journal* of the American Medical Association, "as early as the seventh year it was noted that habitual exposure of young children to crime and horror programs often produced a callousness to the suffering of others and an atrophy of sympathy and compassion toward those in distress."

Radio, too, drew the same sort of charges. Azriel Eisenberg, reporting on "Children and Radio Programs," describes a report in the New York *Times* of February 27, 1933, which tells of children who had nightmares "directly attributable to lurid radio bedtime stories," of others who would break down and cry in the middle of a radio story, or who would "scream in fright and turn off the radio or stop their ears until reasonably certain that the danger was passed."

Eisenberg questioned 3000 pupils in 18 New York City schools and analyzed 2610 compositions submitted by the children. He found that a third of the children reported that they sometimes dreamt at night about the things they heard on the radio. 27% reported that they lay awake in bed thinking about what they had heard. One child wrote the following in a composition:

> "A program that frightens me is the Witch's Tales. If it were in the afternoon it wouldn't seem too ghostly, but it is on at a pretty late hour of the night when everything is still and sometimes I think that a witch could walk right into the room, grab me, then take me to an undergound den, and torture me there. After the Witch's Tales, which ends about ten-thirty p.m., I try to fall asleep. Then comes the sad part of it. If I do fall asleep I dream of ghosts, goblins and witches and many other fairy tale folks, which frighten little folks. From now on, when the Witch's Tales comes on the air, I won't listen in, unless it comes on the ether earlier."

An occasional parent also echoed the problem posed in the preceding quotation. One mother reported that she disconnected the radio, on the advice of her son's teacher, when his schoolwork began to suffer. The boy continued to listen to his favorite programs, at the homes of friends or in radio stores. The mother defined her problem (and Eisenberg is not disposed to question this) as a conflict between herself and the radio, rather than between her and the boy:

> "How can I prevent my boy from listening to programs that are not good for him? He simply will not take my advice. I wish they were off the air entirely. These programs are not only a hindrance but they

corrupt my boy's morals. He tries to imitate and repeat certain words. He talks about guns and gangs, usually saying 'stick 'em up.' "

Robert Zajonc, studying what types of radio characters children identified with, found that success was the most important element in determining whether a character was accepted and admired, or rejected. In other words, children were more apt to identify with a strong bad character than with a weak good one.

Television has raised much the same kind of discussion that had formerly raged over other media. In the Christmas, 1949, issue of the *Saturday Review of Literature,* the editor, Norman Cousins, listed the following instances of TV's pernicious influence:

"In a Boston suburb, a nine-year-old boy reluctantly showed his father a report card heavily decorated with red marks, then proposed one way of getting at the heart of the matter: they could give the teacher a box of poisoned chocolates for Christmas. 'It's easy, Dad, they did it on television last week. A man wanted to kill his wife, so he gave her candy with poison in it and she didn't know who did it.'

"In Brooklyn, New York, a six-year-old son of a policeman asked his father for real bullets because his little sister 'doesn't die for real when I shoot her like they do when Hopalong Cassidy kills 'em.'

"In Los Angeles, a housemaid caught a seven-year-old boy in the act of sprinkling ground glass into the family's lamb stew. There was no malice behind the act. It was purely experimental, having been inspired by curiosity to learn whether it would really work as well as it did on television."

Walter Lippmann wrote in one of his columns:

"There can be no real doubt, it seems to me, that the movies and television and the comics books are purveying violence and lust to a vicious and intolerable degree. There can be no real doubt that public exhibitions of sadism tend to excite sadistic desires and to teach the audience how to gratify sadistic desires. Nor can there be any real doubt that there is a close connection between the suddenness in the increase in sadistic crimes and the new vogue of sadism among the mass media of entertainment."

The New York *World Telegram and Sun* (June 10, 1952) quoted

Dr. Frederic Wertham to the effect that "the TV programs, the sexy-minded radio shows and the comic books are helping to build these fires in the kids of today who will be the potential rapists of tomorrow." Wertham feels

> "it is a wonder there are so few rape cases as we have now," since "the average young boy is shown, or told, that it's proper and glamorous to hang, punch, rip clothes off, kick or spank a woman. He gets it from all sides—movies, TV, radio and comics. Only last week I had a case of a 13-year-old boy who assaulted an 8-year-old girl, tying her hands above her head. Where did he learn that? He saw it on TV, or heard it through a propaganda medium."

Dr. Joost A. M. Meerloo, a well-known psychiatrist, describes television as a habit-forming addiction, and warns of its "hypnotizing, seductive action." He cites the example of a fifteen-year-old girl who "showed every sign of television addiction," skipping school, or showing a sabotaging attitude toward her school work.

> "A psychologist had made the diagnosis of schizophrenia, based on the increasing symptoms of apathy and a lack of mental contact. First, I tended to agree with this diagnosis. But gradually I found that she was more willing to relate to me when we started to talk about the television programs. Then the girl became vivid, showed interest, told about her wishes to take part in the programs, and so forth. It took several sessions of psychotherapy to make her better aware of the fact that she had completely surrendered to fantasy life."

Similar charges were brought before a special Senate subcommittee to investigate juvenile delinquency which held hearings on the influence of television, in 1952, 1954 and 1955. The report of the subcommittee (headed by Senator Kefauver) points out that

> "Television crime programs are potentially much more injurious to children and young people than motion pictures, radio, or comic books. Attending a movie requires money and the physical effort of leaving the home. So an average child's exposure to films in the theater tends to be limited to a few hours a week. Comic books demand strong imaginary projections. Also they must be sought out and purchased. But televi-

sion, available at a flick of a knob and combining visual and audible aspects into a 'life' story, has a greater impact upon its child audience."

Arthur W. Wallander, former police commissioner of New York City, declared in a statement to the subcommittee:

"Crime programs on TV and radio have long glorified the criminal and the 'private eye' type of detective. Almost all of the programs have the 'private eye' put it over on the cop. They glory in making the policeman look dumb. Not only the child but the parents themselves tend to lose all respect for the very man they are supporting as their front line defender against crime. This breeds not only a sort of disrespect in the child even to the point of making him a cop-fighter in aggravated cases, but it makes the parents cop-fighters in the mental sense too."

Opinions of psychiatrists and child psychologists, solicited for presentation to the subcommittee by the National Association for Better Radio and Television, predominantly supported the viewpoint that televised portrayals of violence and crime led to violence and crime in actual behavior. In many of these statements (as in Lippmann's column), television was lumped together with the other mass media as a source of difficulty or actual danger: A noted psychologist, Charlotte Buhler, wrote:

"It is a well-established fact that audio-visual learning is one of our finest tools in education. To have television defeat this purpose by presenting to the children assorted negativistic attitudes some people have toward life and presenting this in dramatic form cannot help but have its repercussions, particularly with those children who are already hostile to society and can be so easily led into delinquency roles. These children identify themselves with the criminal and generally miss the point of Crime Doesn't Pay, which its sponsors profess to be the sole purpose of these programs. In actuality these children are intrigued by the technique they see the criminals use, but visualize themselves as more intelligent than these criminals and would outsmart the law-enforcing agents. For children who are not insecure, disturbed and hostile such programs are a waste of time and offer no constructive or creative stimulation."

A child psychiatrist, Arthur R. Timme, concluded that

"Television crime programs have a very deleterious effect on the minds of growing children. I have seen their ideations so colored by witnessing violence, killing, shooting, cheating, outwitting, conniving, etc., that they grow up with a completely distorted sense of what is right and wrong in human social behavior."

Another psychiatrist, Edmund Bergler, echoed the same point:

"Although all movies and television plays make the concession of showing that the criminal is eventually punished, this climax has no effect on the real or potential criminal; he classifies such retribution as a vow to prevailing mores; and dismisses it. The criminal (actual or potential) also believes that he, unlike his counterpart on the screen, will be too smart to be caught."

Still another psychiatrist, Edward Podolsky, wrote Senator Kefauver as follows:

"It has been my experience that presenting crime, violence, sadism and illicit sex in an attractive and adventurous form in the mass media of the movies, television, radio, fiction and the comics has a very definite and decided effect in quite a few cases of initiating and sustaining a social and criminal activity in juveniles and adolescents. The human mind in these age groups is quite impressionable and easily conditioned. By constant and repeated presentation of undesirable and criminal activity in mass media, many children and adolescents in time accept these as an attractive way of living."

Sheldon and Eleanor Glueck, in their classical studies of juvenile delinquency, do not refer to the role of the mass media as a possible contributing cause. Questioned by the subcommittee, Glueck remarked:

"We may say that a consistent hammering away influence of an exciting or salacious crime, day in and day out, must have an erosive effect on the mind of the youth."

In the ongoing discussion of TV and children, much attention was placed on the findings of the Smythe studies already discussed in Chapter 3, which showed the extent of violence in TV programming at the hours of peak child viewing. To pursue this analysis further, members of the staff of the Senate juvenile delinquency subcommittee monitored 42 program hours of each Washington, D. C., station during September, 1954. The programming during this period was found to be similar to that listed on the daily TV schedules for a dozen other widely dispersed American cities.

About a fourth of the total viewing time on the four Washington stations (38¾ hours of the potential 168) was devoted to programs concerned with themes of crime or violence, in the judgment of the subcommittee's investigators. They point out that the child viewer often has little choice except between two crime programs. Between 6:15 and 6:30 PM, on September 14 and 16, a child could choose between a western thriller, "Black Phantom," a crime film in an oriental setting, or "Hoppity Skippity," which is a puppet show suitable only for very young children.

The acts of violence telecast during this period appear to a large extent to have occurred in feature films rather than in programs prepared directly for television. Some of the scenes from these films, as summarized in the subcommittee report, read like a veritable chamber of horrors, though they are in fact the common garden-variety of grade C Hollywood fare. The following synopses are typical:

" 'River Patrol.' In one of the scenes, a member of the gang of smugglers was shown as he carefully prepared to strangle a suspected informer. It was then shown how the murderer proceeded to kill his victim by garroting him from behind, illustrating the technique of crime. Another scene showed the leader of the gang brutally striking a witness and threatening him with dire consequences if he reveals what he has seen. Another scene showed the leader of the gang drawing a concealed sword from a cane and impaling his next victim through the abdomen with the weapon. In another extensive fight sequence a brutal scene is shown in a closeup shot of the gang leader crushing the hand of a police investigator by stepping on his outstretched fingers on a metal stairway. Another closeup shows the expression of agony on the officer's face as he elicits an agonizing scream . . .

" 'The Crimson Ghost' included the following scenes: (a) The Crimson Ghost overpowering a girl during a violent struggle in a warehouse.

(b) A member of the gang striking a young criminologist over the head with what appeared to be a metal stool during a fistfight. (c) A member of the Crimson Ghost gang swinging a shovel at the prostrate criminologist as he is about to reach for his pistol. (d) A truck being driven through a warehouse wall, over a pier and into the water carrying to his death an unconscious man who is in the cab of the truck. (e) A scene showing an agent of the Crimson Ghost about to be executed by electrical remote control for revealing gang secrets. He clutches at a metal apparatus around his neck and while the following scene did not show the actual execution, a puff of smoke is seen rising into the air with the sound effects indicating that the man had been 'fried.' (f) The criminologist's secretary being tortured by gangsters in an effort to obtain information. One scene shows the girl in anguish as her arm is twisted behind her and forced upward and another shows the girl's hand being crushed in a drawer by her interrogators. (g) A member of the gang being pushed from a window to fall to his death on the pavement several stories below. A sequence shows the body as it falls and lands, facing the viewer, on the concrete."

Commenting on the findings of the subcommittee staff, Ralph Banay, a research psychiatrist from Columbia University, observed that "if the proverb is true that prison is college for crime, I believe for young disturbed adolescents, TV is a preparatory school for delinquency." Banay points out that juvenile delinquency is largely a matter of emotional health or disturbance. Widespread exposure to TV violence on the part of emotionally disturbed children therefore has a considerable effect and contributes to delinquent tendencies.

To add substance to these remarks, it is pointed out by the subcommittee report that a sample survey of the school population of the United States, conducted in January, 1955, by David Abrahamsen, found approximately 10% of the school population, or about 2 million children, to be emotionally disturbed. In some schools as many as 60% of the pupils enrolled were experiencing some sort of emotional difficulty. It was apparent from these data that even if only a minority of all children were susceptible to harmful effects from such programs, their numbers were far from few.

Robert M. Goldenson, surveying 18 authorities on the question, "Are television programs responsible for juvenile delinquency?", found that a majority answered "no," but Goldenson points out that, while delinquent acts cannot be attributed to any mass medium, this does not mean that the over-all effect of television is not harmful.

Many of the clinicians whose opinions were solicited by the Kefauver committee were extremely cautious in drawing connections between exposure to violence in television programs and the occurrence of violence in actual life.

For example, Professor Otto Billig of Vanderbilt University reported:

"My clinical experience has led me to believe that television programs, movies, etc., have a very limited influence on the child or juvenile. We have performed rather exhaustive psychiatric and psychological studies on juvenile delinquents. Most youngsters do not seem at all influenced by such outside factors. The well adjusted personality can resist them without difficulties. A very occasional case was triggered into some delinquent act and possibly received specific ideas on how to carry out a crime. But only the emotionally disturbed and insecure individual appears susceptible to outside forces. Other outside pressures have probably greater significance, such as recognition by neighborhood gangs, inadequate or lack of group activities, etc.

"There is little question as to the disturbing educational or artistic value in the poor taste of the mentioned programs, but I would consider as disadvantageous and even detrimental to the problem of juvenile delinquency to blame them as the actual cause. In doing so we would avoid the main issues. We need to focus our efforts on the principal causative forces rather than on surface appearances. Our clinical experience has shown us that insecurities in the individual family play a major part in juvenile delinquency."

Dr. Frank Coburn, of the State University of Iowa, presented a similar sentiment when he said:

"The primary and most important factor in the production of juvenile delinquency in my opinion is a disturbed family relationship in the home of the child who is considered a delinquent. These disturbed relationships with or between parents produce in the child problems which he tries to solve. Sometimes his solutions are realistic, sound and acceptable. At other times the solution is not acceptable to the community and the child is considered delinquent. It would appear likely that certain criminal and delinquent solutions for the child's problem

are suggested by what is seen on the television and movie screens and
I think it is fair to say that a certain number of children choose these
solutions who might not otherwise choose them had they not been exposed to this example. More important, however, than its role in the
causation of juvenile delinquency, I believe that the screen and television provide directions for the delinquent's behavior to take. Directions
which even the fertile mind of the adolescent would not have thought
of had he not seen them elsewhere."

Still another psychiatrist, Dr. Louis H. Cohen, made this observation:

"I believe that though these bad programs are always rather silly
and in bad taste, the degree to which they are actually influential in determining juvenile crime is so vague and probably statistically impossible to evaluate that it would be quite foolish to ascribe to such programs the weight of a causal factor sufficient to justify any thundering
campaign against them on this basis. I am personally convinced that
they should not be produced, but only because they encourage a de-
graded taste for a kind of knowledge which is unnecessary for healthy
social life."

James L. Caddigan, Director of Programming and Production of the Dumont television network, pointed out that the way in
which a juvenile program is presented on television may have a good
deal to do with its acceptability to adult viewers. He described complaints received by station WABD over a block of western films
which was being run. The format was changed. An announcer dressed
as an Indian introduced the western as part of "The Great Record." As
Caddigan reported it, "the westerns thus became stories that his
father had told him. We interwove Indian lore background into his
what we call 'bridges' between the segments. We ran the same westerns that we had received complaints on and now we received letters
of praise for good programming."

Virtually all of the expert testimony submitted to the subcommittee, on both sides of this controversial subject, was based on
professional judgment rather than on actual research evidence.

There was one notable exception. In testimony before the
Senate subcommittee, Eleanor Maccoby reported on several experi-

mental studies undertaken in the Boston area. She took issue with the theory that the frustrated child, seeking "escape" as he watches television *reduces* his aggressive impulses by identifying himself with the violence he sees on the TV screen. She suggested that aggressive feelings might be increased rather than reduced by aggressive scenes: The aggressive content of television programs may actually deter the child from aggression if the scenes depicted are coupled with warnings about the consequences of violent behavior.

> "The child may learn that aggressive action is permissible under certain conditions (for example, in battle, when the action is directed against an enemy), but can also learn that unprovoked aggression against members of one's own society will bring retribution. It becomes important, then, to know not only how many killings a child sees on TV programs, but to know who does the killing, why he does it, and what the outcome is."

Maccoby points out that

> "The very children who are presumably using the movie as an outlet for their aggressive feelings are the ones who carry away the aggressive content in their memories."

The child's tendency to imitate what he sees on the television screen may lead him to positive as well as negative directions.

This suggests that the media content merely sets off impulses which are already latent in the situation. For example, Maccoby cites the example of two boys who did something which might have been extremely dangerous to their brother after seeing a motion picture.

> "That motivation to deal harshly with their brother was already present before the boys saw the movie. The movie simply added to their repertoire of possible things to do to their brother and triggered off activity which already had strong potential behind it."

In her research, Maccoby focussed directly on the problem posed by these observations. She sought to find out what the circumstances were under which television was likely to produce the most profound effect on the child's imagination. More specifically, she asked herself whether the child's appetite for TV fantasy was in some way connected with the frustration he suffered in his daily life.

Two-hour interviews were conducted during the winter of 1951-52 with 379 mothers, all with a child in kindergarten. The typical child in this group spent an hour and a half a day watching television. Maccoby began with the premise that in watching television programs the child was exercising a need for fantasy which could be related to the restrictions and controls he experienced from his parents. On the premise that fantasy was a response to frustration, she predicted that the heaviest viewing would be by children who were most restricted.

In her conversations with the parents, Maccoby tried to classify their treatment of the child in terms of nine characteristics which could be related to the degree of control the child experienced at home. She then related these characteristics to the amount of television viewing done by children at both the upper middle class and lower class levels.

The upper middle class children ran true to the prediction that the child would spend more time watching television, the more frustrating his home experiences were.

At the lower income level, however, the reverse appeared to be true. Children who were punished physically and who were especially restricted in the sphere of sex were heavy television viewers. But those who were restricted only in the sense of "being required to be neat, quiet and mannerly, and go to bed at a rigidly enforced bedtime" did not watch television as much as the children whose parents were most permissive on these points.

Maccoby suggests that the explanation for this class difference lies in the patterns of adult viewing at these two social levels. The upper middle class parents spend less time with TV. Their children, when frustrated, are apt to watch television, an activity in which their elders do not particpate. At the lower income levels, the parents are heavy TV viewers. The lower class child, if frustrated, turns toward television for his fantasy life. If he is not frustrated he still imitates his parents and wants to spend time with them, watching television. The difference between restricted and unrestricted children is not evident at this social level.

In a later study on the same problem of fantasy and frustration, Maccoby tested the hypothesis that children would be more sentitive to the aggressive content of films if they had been frustrated just before they saw them. Her experiment was made with five classes of fifth and sixth grade children in suburban Boston schools. The experimental "frustration" in this case consisted of a spelling test before the films were shown; the "non-frustrated" children were given easy words to spell, while the "frustrated" children were given extremely difficult words. The non-frustrated children remembered the general content of the films somewhat better than did the frustrated children. However, the frustrated children remembered more of the aggressive content and less of the neutral material. A repetition of this research, with children in two upstate New York semi-rural schools, failed to replicate the findings.

Emotionally disturbed children are particularly susceptible to the impact of violence, not only in films, but in television, radio, comic books, or any other communications medium. In 1954, a group of teachers in the Chicago area made a special study of those pupils whowere exceptionally heavy TV viewers. As reported by Witty, many were well adjusted and good students. While there were also some problem cases most of these could not be related to television alone, but rather to poor home conditions or to a lack of interest or display of affection on the part of the parents.

One little-stressed danger which television holds for the child is in the area of what Joseph Klapper calls "premature maturity." A psychiatrist, Eugene David Glynn questions, "what will be the result of such constant stimulation from such early ages? Will it result in the need for ever increasing stimulation as the response to the old stimulus becomes exhausted? . . . One wonders: Will reality match up to the television fantasies this generation has been nursed on? These children are in a peculiar position; experience is exhausted in advance. There is little they have not seen or done or lived through, and yet this is second-hand experience. When the experience itself comes, it is watered down, for it has already been half lived, but never truly felt. The fate of Emma Bovary may become the common fate."

Concluding Observations

What assessment should be made of the sharply contrasting body of opinion which exists on the subject of this chapter, on which so many experts are aligned on opposite sides of the fence? While a great deal of informed and intelligent judgment has been expressed on the effects of television on children, there is actually very little real research to support either one viewpoint or the other. One reason for the scarcity of empirical evidence is that it is very difficult to trace back the specific influence of televised violence and relate it to actual delinquent or disturbed behavior.

In most discussions of TV's effects, two separate problems are interwoven or confused. First there is the question of whether television actually incites children to commit acts of violence, through its illustrations of the techniques of crime. The second question goes farther than the first and concerns the over-all effect of television on the every day values, beliefs and behavior of children in the mass.

It is relatively easy to make an independent assessment of the first and more dramatic charge, that television is actually a "school for crime." Few persons would dispute the point that a child who is already seriously disturbed may be stimulated by television to turn his aggressive impulses in a particular direction, or to imitate a previously unfamilar technique of aggressive behavior. The seriously disturbed individual, child or adult, may borrow from any aspect of his experience in devising the form of an anti-social act. He is just as likely to put ground glass in his father's cereal because he saw this done on television or in a motion picture or read about it in a comic book as because a friend had mentioned the idea in conversation, or because he has read about a similar case in the newspapers. The isolated criminal episode which can be directly linked to a specific television performance is certainly no basis from which to generalize.

The real sources of aggressive impulses or other disturbances arise primarily out of a child's interpersonal relationships, particularly with his parents and peers. Television does not create psychological problems, though it may influence the way in which they find expression.

The child uses all his experiences as a source of stimulation and fantasy, including those from sources which seem to be most harmless. At the age of 2½, the writer's daughter was very much struck by an illustration in a delightful little nursery story (with the usual advisory board of educators and child psychologists) which described the adventures of some children who went on a wonderful trip to far off places in a bed which flew through the air like a magic carpet. The picture of the two children, with their dog and toy animals, merrily sailing through the clouds on this bed produced only terror in my daughter's heart. She required assurance for several evenings that her bed would not fly away.

If television cannot really be blamed for turning children into criminals or neurotics, this does not imply that it is a wholly healthful influence on the growing child. A much more serious charge is that television, in the worst aspects of its content, helps to perpetuate moral, cultural and social values which are not in accord with the highest ideals of an enlightened democracy. The cowboy film, the detective thriller and the soap opera, so often identified by critics as the epitome of American mass culture, probably do not represent the heritage which Americans at large want to transmit to posterity.

In this respect, television is no different from any other popular art. It has become the focus of recent discussion because it is both the newest mass medium and the one with which children spend the greatest amount of time. The problem, as far as children are concerned, is much the same as for society at large, though its impact is greater in the formative years of life. In the case of children's TV programs, as with those for adults, the content characteristics which are most decried by the critics are the very features which attract the audience. This is the principal dilemma faced by the broadcasters themselves, and is discussed further in the following chapter.

13. FRONTIERS OF TELEVISION

Before another half-dozen years have passed, the television set will be as universal a feature of American homes as radio is today. TV's growth will continue as new stations are opened in outlying areas (improving both the quality of reception and the choice of programs) and as the growing number of obsolescent small-screen sets brings the price of a receiver within the purchasing power of even the lowest income.

The television set of today is as different from the television set of the future as the radio of a generation ago, with its awkward horn-shaped loudspeakers, is different from contemporary portable receivers. TV sets will be lighter and more compact as transistors replace vacuum tubes, and printed circuits replace wiring. Picture tubes will be flatter and permit a larger screen area than at present. The television set of a few years hence may be shaped like a picture frame and hang on the wall, operated by a small chair-side control box. Another possible development is projection television to create pictures of even larger size. In either case the television set will lose some of its present characteristics as a bulky immovable piece of furniture that occupies a dominant position in the family living room. It will become less obtrusive and more portable. The increasing number of obsolete sets scattered throughout the rooms of the house will help to make television a more accessible, more personal medium.

(A)

A technical development of major importance was the announcement by Ampex of an efficient television tape recorder, in April, 1956. This new device permits programs to be rebroadcast at a far higher level of picture quality than was possible with the use of kinescope films. The kinescope required about three hours for processing after the original program was sent out over the wires. This made for an inevitable and substantial time differential between programs broadcast live and in the kinescope version. Using the tape recorder, a program can be rebroadcast almost immediately. This has particular importance for news telecasts, since for the first time it makes it possible for locally originated news programs to be as fresh in their national and world-wide coverage as the network shows.

Color Television

Color TV broadcasting on a regular basis was begun by the major networks in 1954. By the spring of 1957 only 150,000 sets were in operation, of which a good proportion were located in television stores, taverns and restaurants—the very kinds of public places in which TV itself first made its debut. As in the case of black and white television, the high cost of color TV sets will come down as mass production becomes possible. As the market for black and white sets diminishes, manufacturers will be willing to make the necessary investment in advertising and to absorb initial production losses, in order to encourage the growth of a market for color TV. (B)

The addition of color does not change the attributes of television as a medium, but it gives it a more realistic and natural character, and at the same time heightens the possibility for esthetic artistry in the presentation of entertainment—especially variety and dramatic shows. Color also holds out exceptional promise to advertisers, for whom it makes possible more vivid demonstrations and better product identification. (From this standpoint, color makes television a more effective competitor with magazines.)

Commercial tests conducted by the Schwerin Research Corporation showed that the average color TV commercial tested has higher sales effectiveness than the typical black and white commerical, though its specific content was less well recalled. Women seem to be more susceptible than men to color advertising.

Once color acquires popularity, it will hasten the obsolescence of existing sets. This in turn will stimulate the development of a used set market which will accelerate the spread of TV to the lower income segments of the population and also hasten the trend to multiple set ownership.

Color TV was sanctioned by the Federal Communications Commission only after a preliminary period of bitter debate over two rival systems, one advocated by CBS, the other by NBC and its parent company, the Radio Corporation of America. The CBS system was perfected earlier, but the RCA system had the advantage of permitting existing sets to receive color signals in black and white without the need for an expensive adapter (which the CBS method would have required). At present, color broadcasting uses the same channels employed in ordinary black and white transmission.

International TV

Outside the United States television will continue to grow at a rapid rate for many years to come. Before World War II, some European countries were ahead of America in the technical development of television, but in the postwar period TV was impeded in these countries both because of the need to recuperate from the devastation of war itself and because the relatively high price of a television set makes it a luxury item in countries where incomes are lower than in the U. S.

In spite of these handicaps, television has already become part of everyday life in many parts of the world. By the summer of 1957, there were 18,500,000 television sets in use outside the United States. By the end of the year there are expected to be 460 stations in 48 countries. (Just as in the United States, many stations in a country may transmit the same programs.) The broadcast day is generally much shorter than it is in America.

Great Britain had 7,500,000 receivers in operation by the middle of the year, and Canada had 2,700,000, putting them closely behind the United States in density of saturation. The Soviet Union, with transmitters in 29 cities, was reported to have 3,000,000 sets. Seven other countries had over 300,000 sets each, for a total of about 4,125,000: Brazil (600,000), Cuba (300,000), France (600,000), West Germany (1,100,000), Italy (575,000), Japan (650,000), and Mexico (300,000). Belgium, Colombia, Czechoslovakia, East Germany, Holland and Venezuela each had between 100,000 and 200,000.

(C)

The number of sets is not a direct indication of the size of audience as is true in the United States, where viewing today typically takes place in the family unit. In many countries a large proportion of the sets are in cafes and other public places where substantial numbers of people can watch. In French small towns, there is the institution of the Tele-Club, through which a set is collectively bought and installed in the school or town hall to permit group viewing.

As a powerful and growing medium of communication, television has become a major instrument in the cold war. At recent international trade fairs, such as those in Djakarta, Bangkok, New Delhi and Karachi, live television displays and demonstrations have been a major attraction of the American exhibits and their popularity has prompted the Soviets to set up rival displays of their achievements in the medium. The U. S. Information Agency prepares documentary films on American life and news features for release on television stations in many countries overseas.

Television holds out unique promise as a means of spreading ideas and information across national boundaries. Radio broadcasts addressed to different countries necessarily have to be in different languages, which convey different nuances of expression and meaning. Television eventually will offer the opportunity of simultaneously broadcasting the same visual image to many different countries at once, with commentaries dubbed in the local language.

Actual transmission of TV programs across national borders has already taken place in Europe. The "booster" transmitters required to amplify signals and relay them on to another country will in a few years be replaced by coaxial cables which will link stations in different European countries, and make international television networks an everyday reality. At the moment trans-Atlantic television is not possible, except through the use of kinescope films or tape recordings, because of the restricted range of diffusion of TV signals. However, ways may be found to overcome these limitations through the use of relay planes or ships, or through the use of a different type of transmission system than is employed at present (the "scatter system" of diffusion). In the United States airplane transmitters have been used to relay TV signals from the Bahamas to Florida and thence to a national hookup.

American television programs have had considerable success in other countries, especially in Britain, where they have been widely used by the new commercial television system, and where the language-dubbing problem does not exist. In the winter of 1955-56, the top ten shows in popularity among homes that could receive

British commercial TV included "I Love Lucy," "Dragnet," "Robin Hood," "Gun Law" and "Roy Rogers." Conversely, TV film package producers in the United States have increasingly made use of programs shot in Europe with (lower cost) local talent and authentic ("continental") settings.

One technical difficulty which stands in the way of international television is the fact that the standard of broadcast definition employed in different countries is not the same. Slight differences in the transmission systems of different countries call for a different number of lines to make up the television image, and a different number of picture frames broadcast per second to provide the visual illusion. This means that broadcasts transmitted by one system cannot be received by receivers geared for another system, unless these receivers are especially adapted. The line definition employed in U.S. TV broadcasting, for example, does not produce as fine grained a picture as that of Italy, which in turn uses fewer lines than France. At some point in the future it will probably be even more important than at present for all TV stations to adhere to some universally accepted standard definition.

Commercial broadcasting of TV as it is known in the United States is practiced in Latin America, Japan, Thailand and the principalities of Luxembourg, Monaco and the Saar, whose transmitters get into the nearby larger countries. Commercial TV was also established in Australia in 1956. Other nations have carried into television the system they employed in radio broadcasting, with stations operated either directly by the government or by an official but autonomous agency (like the BBC in Britain). The BBC exclusively dominated British television during its early period of growth. After long and sharp debate the establishment of the Independent Television Authority in 1954, and the start of its broadcasts in November, 1955, marked the beginnings of commercial broadcasting in Britain. To bring in the new channel on existing TV receivers a converter is necessary, and conversion has proceeded at a rapid pace.

The British system of commercial broadcasting differs from that in the United States in that the programs themselves are not under the control of sponsors. Companies merely buy the rights to commercial time and their spot announcements are sandwiched at intervals between the programs. The timing of the announcements is rotated to give all the advertisers equal adjacency to the more popular shows. The Independent Television Authority was not limited by the civil service salary scales of the BBC, and was therefore able to attract a substantial amount of production talent. The competition for viewers appears to have placed the BBC on its mettle, with resulting improvement in the general quality of British TV.

TABLE 94

How TV Time Breaks Down on BBC, ITA and New York

Source: Paulu's British Broadcasting

	ITA	BBC	NY TV Stations
Light entertainment	37%	16%	53%
Children's programs	15	17	11
Sports events	18	16	3
Documentaries, talks	7	15	12
Drama	11	11	10
News, newsreels	7	10	8
Serious music	1	3	1
Religion	1	1	2
Other broadcasts	3	11	0
	100%	100%	100%

Commercial television was introduced into Britain amidst a divided public opinion and against considerable parliamentary opposition. Gallup polls conducted in 1952 found an even division of opinion on the question "Do you approve or disapprove of the plan for television to be sponsored by advertising?" By the fall of 1957 however, commercial TV was firmly established. Over a fourth of British homes had sets capable of receiving a commercial channel as well as the BBC, and these homes gave three-fourths of their viewing time to ITV.

Commercial television in Britain has borne the strong impress of American methods and American programs. As Table 94 indicates, its program content bears more of a resemblance to the American formula than to the BBC. Light entertainment is the staple fare, and sports events receive even greater emphasis than on the BBC, and considerably more than in the United States.

It is of some interest to note that in Britain as in the United States, the widening of viewer choice has not changed the extent to which TV is used as a medium. In his definitive study of British Broadcasting, Burton Paulu reports that in early 1956 the average viewing level for adults was 40% among those whose TV sets could get only BBC, and also 40% for those with the choice of BBC or ITV.

Educational Television

(D)   Television is a natural medium for teaching purposes. It permits visual demonstration and illustration which radio could not provide. It allows the extraordinarily good teacher to influence a great number of students instead of confining him to a single class at a time. It permits teaching techniques to be standardized at a high level. It can correlate, with the smoothest of transitions, many different teaching devices: direct personal lecturing and demonstrations, motion pictures, slides, specimens, drawings and charts. As George A. Kelly describes it:

> "The viewer is brought up close to the speaker's face. No longer is the pupil seated at a desk 30 feet away from his shrill-voiced teacher; he is taken up and seated on the teacher's lap, and she speaks into his ear with the soft voice of understanding. Now, for the first time, he catches the twinkle in her eyes, senses the lines about her mouth as she speaks, hears the overtones of gentleness in what she has to say. No longer is the blackboard a shiny black expanse on the far side of the room; instead, what he is expected to examine is brought up to reading distance and set down before him at the center of his attention."

The potential importance of educational television must be viewed in the context of a growing demand for higher education, and an increasing shortage of qualified instructors. In 1957 there were 8,900,000 young people aged 18-21. Within the next ten years the number is expected to grow to 13,700,000. While 36% of those who reach college age currently seek admission to colleges, the proportion is expected to rise to 46% within a decade.

Closed circuit (non-broadcast) television is a valuable tool of instruction which has already found many uses. It has been used, for example, by an instructor in a teachers' college to observe a student teacher in front of a class and to comment on her performance before a group of other students. Closed circuit television has been employed to permit physicians to observe the progress of a delicate operation. It has been used in business to permit company officials to address meetings of employees or salesmen gathered at widely scattered points. In industry, closed circuit television may become an important adjunct to automation, since it permits the observation of processes in manufacturing and materials handling which no human eye could view directly because of dangerous conditions. It is a labor-saving device; a single inspector or operative can simultaneously watch several television screens whereas normally a separate inspector would be required to observe each phase of the operation.

These instructional advantages are by no means limited to closed-circuit TV. Educational TV stations have broadcast operations to home audiences of physicians. One (WCET in Cincinnati) has broadcast dramatized business and office situations for the management training programs of industrial establishments in its area.

Summarizing existing research on TV's use in education, George J. Wischner and Ivan H. Schier conclude that TV "can teach."

"Within the range of subject matters and student groups investigated, TV groups generally learn as well as regular instruction groups. In some instances TV groups achieve significantly better than their controls. With respect to retention measures, TV groups do as well as regularly instructed groups . . . Absolute score differences between TV and regular instruction groups for the most part have been relatively small . . . TV is particularly suitable for teaching material involving small parts and their interrelationships. This is probably due to the closeups which TV makes possible."

In one series of experiments on the use of TV in instruction, Robert Rock, James Duva and John Murray compared the effectiveness of lessons taught by means of live television, kinescopes (motion pictures of film programs) and direct instruction. Their subjects were reservists at nine naval air stations. Three experimental groups, each of approximately 100-120 men, were taught by one of the methods, all allowed the same amount of teaching time. Questions were answered afterwards, by a local officer in the case of both the live and filmed instruction, and through a special telephone connection to the television instructor. Television teaching by highly qualified instructors was found to produce better results than live local instruction, in about half the cases. Among the (better educated) officers, only 13% learned more from live instructors than from TV, whereas among enlisted men (who may have required more individual treatment) 27% learned more from direct instruction. Filmed recordings of TV programs were found to produce only slightly less satisfactory results than live television.

In subsequent studies made for the Army, the same authors found that three out of four men who had been shown a televised training exercise said they preferred it to the usual classroom method of explaining the same problem.

A continuing experiment on the use of closed-circuit television in teaching had been conducted since 1955 at the State University of Iowa, under the direction of Dean Dewey B. Stuitt. In this case, discussion sessions were conducted by means of a two-way system, through which the instructor could observe and listen to the students, as well as the other way around. Students taking an American Government course by this method described it as "much more interesting" than other courses by a slightly larger margin than did students taking the same course in the conventional manner. The TV students also spent more time in their preparation for the course. Unfortunately there is no way of knowing whether this heightened interest was in some respect accounted for by the experimental nature of the project.

There was no evidence that the TV course succeeded in imparting more information or stimulating more thought than with the ordinary teaching method, either from the students' own observations or from their achievement examinations. Courses with different subject matter seemed to arouse somewhat different degrees of favorable and unfavorable response, but in general students seemed to equate the efficacy of the two types of instruction. On the other hand students who had not had any experience with closed-circuit television teaching tended to believe that they would learn less from it than from an ordinary course. In general, TV proved to be successful as a substitute for face-to-face teaching, inhibiting neither the ιstructor nor the students to any important degree. However, the important question of evaluating TV's utility for lectures and discussion, respectively, was not answered by the research.

Enthusiastic hopes have been voiced over the possibility that non-commercial television stations, operated by universities or municipalities, might help to raise the level of popular taste to a point where commercial programming would have to improve. (This philosophy also has underlain "Omnibus" and other ventures of the Television Workshop of the Ford Foundation.)

In its original allocations, the F.C.C. provided 242 (later 245) channels for non-commercial or educational broadcasting purposes. But it takes more money to set up and operate a TV station than most universities or boards of education can afford. By the fall of 1957, an estimated 30 million dollars had been spent to promote educational TV, yet only 26 non-commercial stations were on the air (a number of them on UHF). The earliest of these was station WOI-TV at the University of Iowa which has carried commercially sponsored network programs to help pay its own way. The slow growth of educational television stations is reminiscent of the history of educational radio, as reported by Llewellyn White.

> "From 1921 through 1936, no fewer than 202 educational station licenses were granted, the majority of them before 1927. During the same period, 164 licenses were permitted to expire or were transferred to commercial interests, most of them prior to 1930. It is significant to note here that 50 of the 164, or 30.5%, were held for a period of less than one year; 85, or 51.8%, for less than two years; 109, or 66.46%, for less than three years; and only 55, or 33.54%, for three years or more."

The university operated TV stations (like university operated radio stations) have been an important training ground of technicians and talent for the broadcasting industry. A number of TV stations, commercial and non-commercial, have offered regular credit courses on the air as part of university extension programs. But probably the greatest successes of educational television are programs broad-

cast over the commercial TV networks, like "Omnibus," Frank Baxter's Shakespeare broadcasts, the child care program of Dr. Benjamin
Spock, "Meet the Press," "Adventure," "The Search" and 'Wide
Wide World." Most of these programs were conceived and planned
by the networks themselves.

A mail survey of 260 public and parochial school systems in
towns or cities in which commercial or educational TV stations were
operating was made in November, 1955, by David C. Stewart of the
Joint Committee on Educational Television. He found a steady increase in the number of hours of school-sponsored programming on
both commercial and educational stations. Interestingly enough, for
every two hours of programming produced for actual instruction
purposes in the schools, there were five hours of programming produced with the general public relations purpose of acquainting parents
and other citizens with interesting aspects of the school system.

> "Many school systems report a special emphasis upon interpreting
> special training such as dramatics, industrial arts, student government,
> music, physical education, and journalism . . . Some of the most effective
> programs were on the responsibility of the schools in the training of
> handicapped children; programs on speech correction, blind children
> demonstrating Braille, etc. Demonstrations of school counselling services
> were also rated high in effectiveness."

J. Stacy Adams has compared the characteristics of 50 viewers
of the University of North Carolina educational TV station and 58
non-viewers (1956). By the conventional criteria (e.g. education,
economic status, total amount of TV viewing) he found the two
groups to be virtually identical. However the viewers were more
"culture-oriented." They read more magazines and newspapers (particularly editorials); they were more favorable to education in general
and particularly to educational TV. Of the viewers, 88% disagreed
with the statement "Television is for entertainment and relaxation,
not for education," while only 47% of the non-viewers disagreed.
Similarly 84% of the viewers, but 60% of the non-viewers disagreed
with the notion that "poetry, classical music and opera are just for
highbrows."

The major challenge faced by the educational broadcasters is
to make informational programming interesting enough to attract an

audience. Few teachers are also great entertainers, and the happiest results are achieved when there is close cooperation between those who know a subject well and producers who are skilled in the craft of presentation.

Leland Baxter, writing on "Educational Television" in the *Atlantic Monthly* of November, 1955, cites seven "delusions" which have inhibited the growth of educational TV:

1. "That all television must be entertaining."
2. "That education is not entertaining."
3. "That every television audience must be large."
4. "That educational television must compete with commercial television and will therefore fail, because where would the money come from for another Ed Murrow show, or, for that matter, another Ed Murrow?"
5. "That charitably supported television should not, if it could, compete with commercial television."
6. "That commercial television with its public service time will provide ample opportunity for cultural offerings if only the educators have the wit to grasp the nettle."
7. "That people will not give money for what they can get free."

While Baxter believes these assumptions to be more or less unfounded, his optimism over the future of educational television is not shared by other observers. Max Wylie, a TV writer who is enthusiastic about the possibility of using the talents of fine teachers in regular programming, offers this sharp comment on educational TV:

"A smothering truth about American educators and educational groups (it would be fairer to say 'spokesmen for groups')—in their earlier relations with radio—is, in too many chapters, a story of empty enthusiasm, committee chairmen, and waste. Right now in television this same quality of empty enthusiasm (because the 'romantic appeal' of television is so much stronger) is urging entire groups of educators to permit themselves to be photographed, as it were, at the foot of Mt. Everest before their assault on the summit has begun, even before their equipment has arrived . . .

"The professor, when sitting before his first microphone or before his first camera, is a lonely man. For years he's enjoyed the uncertain serenity but the certain authority that faculties could fire students.

"He is now in the presence of a student body that can fire the faculty: and a student body that does so.

"This is a truant body, and though never beyond the reach of interest, forever outside the law. These truants tune him in, sample him, tune him out.

"Here's the awful lesson the educator has to learn: nobody has to listen to him any more, and nobody will if he's dull."

An important distinction must be made between educational TV stations operated by universities or governmental agencies and educational television in a larger sense. The number of non-commercial stations will probably increase as more colleges offer advanced training programs in TV production and as more school systems begin to use television teaching as part of the regular curriculum (much as motion pictures gradually came to win a place). But there is no reason to believe that these educational stations will ever achieve a dominant place in the leisure-time viewing habits of the mass audience.

In its broader definition, educational television encompasses all the programming on commercial TV which in some degree teaches as well as amuses its viewers. The extent to which the broadcasters extend their interest in this sphere depends less, perhaps, on the activity of educators than on the changing appetites of the audience.

The UHF Controversy

The future of the ultra-high-frequency channels is dependent in part on decisions yet to be made about the future of "pay-as-you-see" or subscription television. Both of these subjects have aroused extreme controversy and are at the time of writing in the hands of the F.C.C. for solution.

The debate over UHF television has its origin in the fact that, in the early period of television channel assignments, the Commission and the industry underestimated the rate at which television would develop as a medium and the number of transmitters that would be required. A television channel takes up an enormous amount of room on the electronic spectrum—far greater than that used up by a voice radio signal. The twelve channels assigned in 1945, two through thirteen, were originally considered adequate by the F.C.C. to accommodate the expected number of TV transmitters, allowing for the fact that the same channel could not be allocated to stations within 190 miles' distance of each other, to avoid interference. The post-war TV freeze was imposed when it became apparent that the existing twelve very-high-frequency channels would not be sufficient to take care of the demand for stations. In lifting the freeze, the Commission opened up a band of 70 additional channels, numbered 14 through 83, in the so-called ultra-high-frequency band. By the spring of 1957, one television station in five was on UHF, mostly in small and middle-sized cities.

In the TV broadcast spectrum, the length of transmission distance and the quality of reception decline the shorter the wave length. Channel 2 on the very-high-frequency band reaches farther than Channel 13 because it operates on a longer wave length. By contrast with the VHF stations, the UHF transmitters have a smaller reception area, with a typical viewing radius of about 40 miles as opposed to 60 or 70 for VHF. To produce a signal of a given strength, the UHF stations require more power than an equivalent VHF station. They are also subject to technical difficulties; their signals are more prone to interference from the landscape.

The most serious handicap faced by UHF stems from the fact that its signals cannot be received by the ordinary television receiver without special adjustments or the installation of a converter. The cost of converting a normal VHF set to UHF reception ranges from $10 to $15 for the installation of a metal strip that enables it to get one UHF station to $40-$60 for a special all-wave converter that picks up the whole UHF band. Conversion usually means not only adjusting the set but installing a special antenna at further cost to the owner.

In the few areas, like Portland, Oregon, where a UHF station was the first to be established, conversion presented no problems because sets earmarked for such regions were usually specially equipped by manufacturers. But in areas where VHF stations had already been established, or where there was fringe reception from VHF stations in other cities, new UHF channels had a difficult job to win acceptance. Manufacturers were slow to get all-channel receivers on the market. Difficulties and delays were sometimes caused by the inexperience of television service men in installing converters, with the result that the pioneer UHF fans in some cases had faulty reception. Word-of-mouth reports caused others to desist from getting their sets converted too.

Studies by the American Research Bureau and Videodex indi-

cate that within the reception areas of UHF stations the percentage
of sets converted to receive the signals ranged from 5% to 96% in the
spring of 1956.

The slow rate of conversion in many UHF markets made it
more difficult for the new UHF stations to secure advertising, particularly network advertising. A kind of spiral process set in. Low
rates of set conversion caused national advertisers to prefer established VHF channels rather than UHF outlets. This in turn meant
that the UHF stations found it difficult to get the well-known programs of the two major networks, and had to be satisfied either with
"package" programming on film or with the less popular shows of
the ABC and (in the earlier period) Dumont television networks.
Since the UHF station often did not carry the big-time shows there
was less incentive for TV owners to convert their sets.

An analysis of the amount of network programming carried
by new (post-freeze) television stations was made by the F.C.C. for
the week of March 14-20, 1954. In the smaller cities, with less than
250,000 population, the newer VHF and UHF stations carried about
the same median number of network hours—15 and 14 respectively.
However in the larger cities, the new VHF stations carried twice as
much network programming as the U's—37 hours weekly, on the
average, compared with 19 for the new UHF stations in the larger
markets. The two major networks made no bones about their preference for VHF, and in several cases they shifted their affiliation from
UHF to VHF channels as these were established in the same markets.

The net effect of these difficulties was a high rate of mortality
among UHF stations—about one in three. Other holders of UHF
allocations failed to proceed with the building of stations. The problem was alarming in itself, but it also caused concern in some quarters
of the broadcasting industry on grounds of general policy. Opinion
was expressed that only through UHF, with the tremendous number
of channels that it opened up, could television develop to a point
where viewers would have the same wide choice as in radio. The
ideal of having local TV stations serving many small scattered communities in the manner of radio is largely contingent upon the
development of UHF. The future of educational broadcasting, and
other non-commercial stations, is also closely related to the course of
progress on the UHF band. But this band is doomed to remain

dormant as long as America's TV receivers are not equipped to tune into it.

The entire subject of UHF was explored at length in May, 1954, by the Senate Subcommittee on Communications. The hearings of the subcommittee served to highlight the arguments on both sides of the controversy and left the industry, the public and the Congress better informed, but they did not in themselves result either in legislative action or in changes in the rules of the F.C.C. At these hearings, the UHF broadcasters gave an eloquent report of the difficulties they faced. An official of the UHF station in the St. Louis area summed up the problem with the following anecdote:

> "A few weeks ago an operator of a North Carolina UHF station, who numbers among his stockholders several wealthy associates, came to me and asked what difficulties we were having in operating a UHF station in the St. Louis market. We had quite a lengthy conversation. At the conclusion this very fine southern gentleman turned to me and said, 'Mr. Tenenbaum, I know how we're gonna cure our U troubles; we're going to buy us a V.'"

In the course of the hearings, F.C.C. Commissioner Frieda Hennock charged that virtually every community with an existing or prospective UHF station would also be in range of VHF from other cities, thus making the position of the UHF station operator virtually untenable. She pointed out that the F.C.C. itself was increasingly permitting "drop-ins" of additional VHF channels in communities which either had a UHF station or were slated to have one.

Thomas P. Chisman, Manager of a station in Hampton, Virginia, described an example from his own area, the Norfolk region, of the use of a "phantom city" as a device for winning a new VHF allocation:

> "Princess Anne, Va., is a literal crossroads, in effect marking the place on an automobile map where two roads meet. Princess Anne has a population of about 250 persons. It has, however, a country post office. Having found a post office, some Norfolk people have now proposed to the Commission that this post office should be used as a basis for assigning VHF Channel 13 to the Norfolk area on the ostensible basis that it is assigned to Princess Anne . . . If Channel 13 is added to the Norfolk area on the pretense of being assigned to this phantom community of 250 per-

sons, UHF in the Norfolk area will be dealt what may well be a death blow."

Ben K. McKinnon, General Manager of a UHF station in Greenville, South Carolina, made this observation:

"The Commission has, in my opinion, shut its eyes to its own requirements that a TV station in Gastonia, N. C., be a Gastonia station and not a Charlotte station, that a Spartanburg station be a Spartanburg station and not another Greenville station, regardless of the desire for transmitter relocation to obtain network affiliation. Any station which is allocated to and located in a relatively small community is going to try to locate its transmitter and to so program as to serve and take advantage of the larger market area. Obviously, therefore, the competition to stations in the larger community is going to be increased. Unfortunately, due to a combination of other problems and their growing pains, the first station to suffer and suffer the most is the UHF station."

A rebuttal came from W. Theodore Pierson, a spokesman for a number of the established VHF stations. Pierson stressed the unique capacity of VHF to provide service to the "remote and gulley areas" of the nation which could not be covered by UHF's shorter signals. He attacked

". . . the temerity of a group of people who can come here and excite this committee about the threat of a monopoly or lack of competition, and then make proposals designed to prevent anyone from competing with them. I would like to illustrate that with the Greenville (S. C.) situation. In Greenville there are two stations, a VHF and a UHF station. A representative of the UHF station appeared here and asked this committee or the Commission, or both, to take action to prevent a station that was allocated to Spartanburg, a few miles away, from rendering service to the people of Greenville. They also went on to say that they did not want any stations outside of Greenville to render a service to the people of Greenville.

"Now I can understand the private interests that would dictate a desire of that kind. I can understand why these two operators would like to have this cozy and comfortable situation for themselves, but I am wholly incapable of understanding how they can say that that promotes competition, or how they can say that that is in the public interest of the people of Greenville for this committee or the Commission to say to them you can never have more than two signals . . . If the Greenvilles, the Atlantic Cities, and the other markets in the same situation have only two stations operating in their area, by law or by Commission regulation no station outside of those markets can serve it, I want someone to tell me how under those circumstances we can have more than two national networks."

Frank Stanton, CBS President, pointed out in his testimony that the VHF broadcasters had also taken great risks and suffered great losses in TV's early days. Aggregate operating losses of networks and stations were $48 million in the three years 1948-50, and $27,500,000 was borne by the networks and their stations.

Stanton was critical of suggestions that control over the choice of individual station affiliates be taken away from the networks, in order to discourage their preference for VHF. He expressed the opinion that any proposals to regulate network affiliations would

"present extremely serious threats to television networking as we know it . . . For if the advertiser finds that no network can give him substantially full circulation on a national basis, he will either turn away from television altogether, or he will turn to film programs placed on a spot or market-by-market basis, simply choosing in each market that station which will give him the largest circulation. This will hardly help the weaker stations; the business will flow more swiftly to the stronger stations."

Stanton pointed out that sustaining live programs by themselves cannot economically justify the maintenance of a network. He argued that proposals which limit an advertiser's potential circulation will raise the cost per thousand and therefore "critically hurt" all of television advertising. This would have a serious effect on the development of color TV, since it costs a station $25,000 to $30,000 to adapt itself to network color broadcasts but many times as much to originate color broadcasts. Stanton maintained that the networks could hardly afford the tremendous investments required for color TV if the proposals to regulate network affiliations cut down on advertising revenues.

Frederic J. Ball, a spokesman for Zenith Radio Corporation, proponents of pay-as-you-see television, argued that the unsuccessful UHF stations would have had most of the same difficulties if they had been VHF.

"They are not in the wrong bands, but in the wrong towns, at least from the networks' point of view, who are guided by the economies of national advertising."

This opinion was echoed in an analysis prepared in October, 1955, by Sidney S. Alexander, CBS economic advisor. He concludes that "only about 600 of the over 1,800 channels allocated by the F.C.C. can be economically supported as program originating stations under the conditions likely to hold over the next few years." In this analysis the problem of UHF stations was sidestepped in order to place emphasis strictly on the number of stations that might be supported by markets of specified sizes as indicated by current experience. To afford four stations, with minimum annual revenues of $500,000 per station, a market requires a minimum of 125,000 TV homes, according to Alexander. By contrast a market requires 20,000 television homes to support one station with revenues of $200,000 a year. On this basis Alexander finds that 78 markets can economically support four stations. An additional 30 have between 83,000 and 139,000 TV homes, and can therefore support three stations each. 57 markets have between 50,000 and 83,000 TV homes, and are therefore in the two-station class. 52 smaller markets can support one station apiece.

Since between a fourth and a third of the homes assigned to the one and two-station markets fall within the range of stations in the larger cities, Alexander believes that his estimate of the number of economically viable stations is high rather than low. He estimates that 79% of all U.S. families would be within a 75-mile reception radius of the four-station TV market areas as he defines them. Three and four-station markets together would cover 86% of the homes. Two or more station markets raise the figure to 92%, one or more station markets to 95%. If 70 satellite transmitters (not originating programs) were added to his basic list of 588 stations, 96% of the families would be within the 75-mile range.

The main point of this analysis is the inference that the real problem of the UHF stations is not set conversion, reception quality or network affiliation, but the fact that they are largely located in smaller markets in which television stations would find it difficult to operate under any circumstances.

"The great bulk of the unsuccessful, or unapplied for, UHF channels could not be successfully operated as program originating stations now or in the near future, even if they were, by some miracle, transformed into VHF channels."

The most serious problem in TV broadcasting economics, Alexander points out, is that of stations in markets within the shadow of larger cities, within reception range of the bigger stations. The only hope he holds out to them is the possibility that as time goes on the minimum cost of operating a station may go down and (the rather likely) probability that local advertising revenues will increase. Since the latter possibility seems very likely to come to pass, over a five or ten-year period, Alexander's analysis must be regarded as more applicable to the immediate future than to the long range.

A number of solutions have been advanced for the difficulties of UHF, ranging from proposals to eliminate VHF television (immediately or as color comes in) over to the opposite extreme of proposals to eliminate UHF broadcasts. Eliminating VHF would in the long run deprive the public of the technical advantages of broadcasting in this band, and cause enormous confusion and expense in the short run, since it would make set conversion a universal problem and curtail reception in many fringe areas.

Eliminating UHF would also cause hardship in areas where it is well established. More important, it would defeat an important and long-standing objective of the F.C.C.—to make possible the development of truly local community television stations, and to eventually permit the audience to select from a wide variety of competitive programming.

Other proposals have been made which would have the practical effect of eliminating UHF, by adding a small number of additional channels to the VHF band at the expense of FM radio or radio short-wave bands now used for military, aircraft and miscellaneous communications purposes.

It has also been suggested that present allocations be adjusted so that certain markets are all-UHF while others are all-VHF. This would eliminate the present "intermixture" of stations on these two bands broadcasting from the same cities.

The F.C.C. has indicated its belief that transfer of all TV to the UHF band represents the optimum solution to the problem. The F.C.C.'s final decision will be reached only after a program of research and development has been launched to explore methods of improving the technical quality of UHF broadcasts, and a long period of transition would permit broadcasters and set owners to prepare for any ultimate shift to UHF. As an interim measure the Commission moved to end intermixture in 13 markets. During 1957 several Congressional investigating committees continued to probe UHF, along with other problems of control in the broadcasting industry.

(E)   The debate is by no means over.

"Pay" Television

(F)   Another controversial development relates to "pay-as-you-see" or subscription television. Several pay TV systems have been suggested. The essential principle is that a scrambled image is sent out over the air. It can be unscrambled only by a special converter keyed to a predesignated code. The viewer unscrambles the image by inserting the proper coins into a collection box (working much like the old fashioned gas meter), or it might be possible to record his viewing with the aid of a punch card, which would permit monthly bills to be sent out. The companies which advocate pay-as-you-see television (of which Zenith and Skiatron are the leading proponents) start from the premise that specialized audiences exist for some types of entertainment which cannot for one reason or another be handled on commercial television. They envision pay broadcasts covering two distinct types of programming:

1. Works of high cultural merit which appeal only to a limited group of the population (like chamber music recitals, or operatic performances). The advocates of pay-as-you-see argue that such programs would never win an audience large enough to make them attractive to a sponsor in a prime evening viewing period. However,

a large enough audience could be attracted at the rate of 25c, 50c or even a dollar a performance to make such programs economically feasible from the broadcaster's standpoint.

2. Certain types of entertainment now barred from commercial television, because of the fear that television will interfere with box-office receipts. A world series game, a world championship heavy-weight match, a performance of a first run Hollywood film or a Broadway play—these might all be barred from commercial TV in spite of their broad popular appeal. While an advertiser might not be able to compensate the promoters or producers for the box-office losses which television might cause, the pay-as-you-see audience would offer a considerably greater take than the live spectators.

The argument for pay-as-you-see television rests on the assumption that it will add something new to the programming fare which is currently offered. The proponents of pay TV say that they would be competing with the existing television stations only for viewers and not for entertainment talent, since they would be presenting programs that would not be available under ordinary circumstances. They contend that pay-as-you-see television would make it economically feasible to cater to minority tastes and at the same time satisfy a broad popular demand for extraordinary spectacles which would normally be seen by only a limited number of spectators in a single city, and which have already proven their ability to attract large paying audiences through theater television.

The opponents of pay-as-you-see television, primarily the networks, do not find the above argument convincing. They point out that commercial television does allow room for the expression of cultivated minority tastes. They cite an impressive list of high-calibre telecasts: performances of classical operas and Broadway shows, and of plays and operas written especially for TV by outstanding figures like Robert Sherwood and Gian-Carlo Menotti. They refer to the huge audience attracted on TV to the American premiere of the film "Richard the Third," and mention outstanding documentary broadcasts like Chester Bowles's report on "Assignment: India." Such evidence of their good intentions and positive accomplishments is offered by the networks as evidence that commercial television not only can appeal to the elite but that it can bring high-calibre programming within range of the broad mass of viewers who might not be moved to pay a fee for the same type of entertainment.

The critics of pay-as-you-see TV see it not as a supplement to existing commercial television but as a threat to its very existence. (Frank Stanton, paraphrasing Lincoln, holds that television cannot exist "half free and half fee.") In their opinion, new movies, prize fights and other special attractions would not long be sufficient to program pay-as-you-see TV. To attract a regular audience it would be necessary to have a full schedule of regular programming that could compete with commercial TV. The pay-as-you-see television stations would have to develop their own programs, and they would therefore have to compete with commercial television for the talent that has won great audiences.

The economics of pay-as-you-see TV are such, say its critics, that once established, it could outbid commercial TV in competing for star performers. Pay-as-you-see revenues would be greater than any that might be obtained from advertisers. With commercial TV, a sponsor may pay $25,000 a week for the talent on a half-hour variety show with an audience of 25,000,000 people, and a similar amount for broadcast time charges. However, an audience of a mere 400,000 people paying 25c a head would pay the same costs and at the same time leave a 100% profit margin. On this basis, since they could easily afford to offer higher fees, the pay-as-you-see stations would gradually establish a monopoly of major talent. They would book the top Hollywood and Broadway stars, and thereby quickly attract large numbers of viewers. Once they had audiences of sufficient size, there would be nothing to prevent pay-as-you-see television stations from introducing sponsored advertising messages. As a result, the public would soon find itself with commercially-sponsored TV at the same time that it would have to pay for the privilege of viewing.

The preceding argument rests on the assumption that entertainers could be lured from commercial to pay-as-you-see television by higher salaries. In fact many performers might be dissuaded from making such a move both because of the structure of income taxes and the lure of the largest possible audience. The very fact that an artist is widely known permits him to command a high return for his talent. Commercial television can probably continue to create its own stars as long as it has access to new performers and can put them under contract. Pay-as-you-see television, if it arrives, will attract part of the audience away from commercial TV, and also certain specialized kinds of programming and talent, but there is no reason to believe that it will inevitably shake the foundations of the present system, as predicted.

Both parties in the pay-as-you-see dispute have used research to bolster their positions. An operating test of pay television was made early in 1951 by the Zenith company among a panel of 300 Chicago families. The programming consisted of first-run Hollywood motion pictures. In the first month of the test the average family watched 2.1 films a week, but this dropped to 1.5 in the second month and 1.6 in the third. Over the test period the average expenditure per family was $1.73 a week. As many as 60% of the panel homes watched some films; as few as 8% watched others.

Most of the surveys on the subject are not actual tests of pay television in practice, but polls in which people are asked their opinions of the *idea* of pay television. Thus the manner in which the questions are posed has a great deal to do with the results. It seems evident from most of the available findings that the public is fairly apathetic on the subject.

A reader poll conducted among readers of the *Saturday Review* (which has been highly critical of television) found 65% of those replying (a group not necessarily representative even of the readers) in favor of subscription TV. A survey by Tele-Census among 2600 Los Angeles set owners also found two out of three in favor of pay-as-you-see. However, a reader survey made by the New York *Herald Tribune* early in 1955 found that three-fourths of the 1650 persons who submitted questionnaires said they would be unwilling to pay for special television programs. Many of the remainder qualified their response, especially with the observation that they wanted no advertising. A survey made by the California Poll late in 1955 found that three out of every four persons in the state had heard of pay-as-you-see TV. Half thought it was a bad thing, a fourth thought it was good, and the remainder had mixed opinions or none at all. Sentiment in favor of toll television was highest among those persons who were most critical of present television programming.

A survey of public reactions to the idea of pay-as-you-see TV was made in February, 1955, by Elmo Roper and Associates for the Columbia Broadcasting System in Columbus, Ohio, a three-channel market. A majority of the 449 television owners who were interviewed were satisfied (70%) with the kinds of programs they now got on television, and not interested (62%) in pay television when it was explained to them. The heaviest TV viewers were most receptive to the idea of getting "the best Broadway plays, the newest moving pictures, championship fights, opera, and other things you don't see now" at a charge of 50c to $1.25 a show. Those who were not interested in such a scheme said that they were generally satisfied with present programming, or that they did not watch TV enough to make a pay system worthwhile. Some also complained of the expense, or remarked that they preferred to go out to see shows of special interest.

As the next step in the study, the respondents were shown a sample program for three stations, one of which represented a pay-as-you-see program schedule. When asked how much time they would spend watching each of the stations, 45% said they would not watch the pay station at all (compared with 13% and 16% respectively who would not watch the other two). The average number of hours the pay station would be viewed was estimated at 1.8 weekly, compared with 3.4 and 2.3 each for the other channels. (This suggests that the pay station might draw nearly as large an audience in total hours as one of the free stations with its present program.)

When the respondents were asked whether they preferred the "test" station to adopt the special pay-as-you-see programming or to retain its present free programming, 70% said they preferred it to remain the way it was. However the ones who preferred pay programming indicated that if a charge was made for *all* evening televison programs (including those on the present networks), they would be willing to pay nearly twice as much for the special programming of the "test" station as for the regular programming on the other two channels. 55% of this pro-pay TV group indicated they would oppose pay TV if it meant paying for the programs that were now available free of charge.

In summary, only a hard core of persons (preponderantly above-average in income), representing 9% of the total sample of television owners, would favor pay television regardless of the possibility that it might mean an end to free programs. On the other hand, as many as 55% indicated that they would watch at least some pay programs if these represented a supplementary service, with no threat to the free character of existing programming.

When asked whether the government should authorize pay television, 65% replied that it should not, but this question came at the end of a series which raised the point that pay-TV might pose a threat to free programs.

The findings of a survey made for *Look* Magazine in 1956 by Alfred Politz Research suggest that willingness to pay for a television program of one's choice is not at all in ratio to the amount of money charged. In this study people were first asked to indicate which of nine types of television programs they would like to see. A third of the respondents were later asked, for the same list of program types, which they would be willing to pay 25 cents to see. Another third of the sample were asked whether they would be willing to pay 50 cents, and the remaining third whether they would be willing to pay a dollar. While 64% of the respondents say they would be interested in seeing a variety show when no cost figure was mentioned, 28% would be willing to pay a quarter to see it, and the proportion goes down to 17% when the price is raised to a dollar. Similarly, the percentage interested in a free showing of "a film never shown in movie houses" is 48%; 21% would pay 25 cents to see it; 13% would pay a dollar. 43% would be interested in a free performance of a leading current Broadway play; 22% would pay 25 cents to see it, and 15% would pay a dollar.

Sports telecasts are far less sensitive to price changes. About half as many people (21%) would pay 25 cents to see a heavyweight boxing championship match as would want to watch it free (41%). But these prospective viewers represent a hard core of active fans; 19% would pay a dollar to see the same broadcast. Similarly the proportion who would pay a dollar to see a world series baseball game is almost the same (23%) as the percentage who would pay a quarter (25%). Lovers of the fine arts show the same zealous interest. 7% would pay a dollar to watch a performance of a leading opera company. At a 25 cent rate viewing would go up only slightly, to 9%. For the performance of a leading ballet company the number of prospective viewers remains about the same—at 5%—at either the higher or the lower price.

A year later, Politz again asked the same questions of a national sample, on behalf of *Look*. He found that public interest in watching most of the nine types of free TV shows had declined somewhat, but that public willingness to pay for the privilege of viewing had increased for almost all of the shows, regardless of price.

None of the findings from the research thus far conducted seems sufficiently conclusive to present the policymakers with a clear-cut mandate. The suggestion that pay-as-you-see television be introduced on a test basis may very well be the entering wedge by which it is established in peaceful co-existence with commercial TV, which seems destined to occupy the dominant role for some time to come. If pay TV uses a closed-circuit wired system (as some of its advocates wish) the conflict between the two methods may take an even different form.

The Dilemmas of TV Policy

The pay-as-you-see controversy raises a basic question about the merits of the U. S. system of commercially-sponsored broadcasting. This system has the general approval of an overwhelming majority of the American public, as a number of opinion surveys can attest.

In Field and Lazarsfeld's report of the 1945 survey made by the National Opinion Research Center on public attitudes toward radio, it was found that people who were critical of radio also tended to be critical of other social institutions. (Only 35%, in this study, said they prefer radio without advertising.) Heavy listeners to radio were most favorable to the present system of broadcasting. In Lazarsfeld and Kendall's review of a repeat survey in 1947, similar findings are reported.

Asked their opinion of present television programming, 39% of the people questioned by the California Poll in late 1955 described themselves as "very much satisfied," and an additional 49% said they were "somewhat satisfied." Only 6% reported they were "not at all satisfied."

This public support reflects a general readiness to accept the merits of established and familiar things. Apart from public opinion, there are few objective standards by which the American system can be compared with the government-operated broadcasting systems of other countries.

The situation in television is somewhat different than it is in radio. The American radio, with its four networks and numerous independent stations, offers listeners a greater variety of program content than can be obtained in any other country. The British Broadcasting Corporation, which is held in universally high regard for the quality of its programs, operates three radio services of which one, the Third Program, is pitched well above the average level of taste and has only a small minority of regular listeners. British television viewers had no choice of programs at all before the establishment of the Independent Television Authority.

American television, like American radio, is probably as free and as lively as any broadcasting system in the world. Yet U. S. radio has faced serious criticism, and television has from the start of its life undergone similar attacks. As Cousins described it in TV's early days,

> "Out of the wizardry of the television tube has come such an assault against the human mind, such a mobilized attack on imagination, such an invasion against good taste as no other communications medium has known, not excepting the motion picture itself.
>
> "In the one year since television has been on the assembly-line basis, there has been mass-produced a series of plodding stereotypes and low-quality programs. Behind it all, apparently, is a grinding lack of imagination and originality which has resulted in the standardized television formula for an evening's entertainment; a poisoning, a variety show, a wrestling match. All speculation over the future of television must begin with the hard truth that right now it is being murdered in the cradle."

At heart such a severe condemnation of television represents an indictment of the popular arts, of which television is the most recent and the most time-absorbing. In the character of its content TV represents no radical new departures; its subjects and themes are virtually identical with those of the other mass media of entertainment. In fact the most serious charge that has been made against television—that it is a disturbing influence on children—is really an attack on another medium. Criticism has centered not so much on the children's programs produced especially for television as on the old Hollywood films (particularly Westerns) presented to fill the gaps of programming time. It does not reduce the sting of the criticism to observe that it applies equally well in other fields, but it does support the argument that TV represents no regression from any previously established high-water-mark of popular culture.

Wylie, a writer who believes that "all the shooting and rough-riding and fist-fighting in all the Westerns and kid shows in the whole history of television never hurt a flea," points to a fallacy in the critique that television represents a gigantic public waste of time.

> "It might not receive sociological sanction to suggest that what our forefathers did with their leisure time when they were themselves youngsters was to waste it whenever they could; and that when they grew older, and sat around the stove in the general store, they heard very little that was important, improving, or culturally provocative. But it would be closer to the truth."

Yet this observation, shrewd as it may be, does not meet the objection that any medium must be judged by its own opportunities rather than by the standards of the past.

One of the problems which besets television, like any other mass medium, stems from the fact that production facilities are highly centralized. The communications arts are concentrated in the few big cities where there are large reservoirs of specialized skills and talents. Television, like radio, has become centered in New York and Holly-wood, with their large reserves of actors, writers and craftsmen in the allied arts of theater and film. This has led to the charge that broadcasting has lost its touch with the broader American public. Not only the broadcasters' values, but their private gossip are spread to a thousand towns across the nation. John Crosby, writing in *Life,* November 6, 1950, has stated the point pungently for radio, but it might be applied even more strongly to television, where local programming plays an even smaller role.

> "Another reason why radio so profoundly misunderstood the American people can be ascribed to its points of origin. At the start, some of

the best radio programs emanated from Chicago, Cincinnati and a host of other communities. When radio grew rich and successful it settled immovably in New York and Hollywood, two of the least characteristic cities in the country . . . About 70% of the costliest and most important programs emanated from Hollywood, a city so far removed from the main stream of American life that the listener had to have a special frame of reference to understand the jokes. The smog; the irresponsibility of the Los Angeles motorists; Cucamonga. That was the stuff of which radio spun its dreams. It was not only trivia; it was local trivia."

But the big-town provincialism of the broadcasters, if it exists, goes well beyond the subject matter of their jokes; it may affect the fundamental nature of their programming. Llewellyn White, in his book on "The American Radio," makes this point, implicitly, when he writes:

"No two broadcasters have quite the same problem, or quite the same responsibilities. A man with a little 250-watt local station in an agricultural community may not have to worry so much about diversity of interest as a man who broadcasts from a 50-kilowatt clear-channel station to city-dwellers, miners, dairy farmers, automobile workers, and small-town folk. A network's responsibility toward residents of New York City, who can tune in the other three chains and nearly a score of independent stations, will not be the same as its responsibility toward the thousands who must depend upon it for the only radio fare they get."

It is true that the planning and production of network TV programs takes place in New York, Los Angeles, or Chicago — cities where viewers have a wide variety of program choices. The planners and producers inevitably see the medium from the perspective of these large centers. The programs to which they tune in their own homes help to form their image of the medium in which they work. Yet the decisions they make professionally affect people whose viewing opportunities and needs are radically different from their own.

The relation between network and local programming has become an even more serious issue in television than in radio. The audience for local programs is restricted by the terms of the network affiliation which any local station must eagerly seek in order to get the big-time shows which attract the viewers. In exchange for the opportunity to carry these network programs, the affiliate grants the network the option rights to its time at certain specified periods. Since these include the peak viewing hours of the middle evening, local shows must be fitted into other times, when the number of viewers is generally less.

While some alarm has been expressed over the power of the networks to control the best viewing hours of their affiliates, it is not easy to prove that the public interest would be better served if locally originated programming had greater prominence. Programs of outstanding merit, when carried by the networks on a sustaining basis, are often ignored by the individual affiliates, who prefer to put on local shows for whom a sponsor can be found. Some of TV's best shows, well-known in the big cities where there are network-owned stations, are beyond the reach of millions of viewers in smaller towns.

The sharpest criticism of American television comes from those who deplore the commercial sponsorship of television programs. At bottom, the attack is one on advertising as such, but TV advertising is more ubiquitous than any other form. The underlying thought is that the constant procession of commercials proclaiming the merits of one product after another tends to make Americans materialistically-minded, thereby posing a threat to their moral, spiritual and cultural values. The public itself does not appear to share this unfavorable opinion of broadcast advertising.

In Lazarsfeld and Kendall's 1947 study, four out of five persons believed that radio stations were fair in giving both sides of public questions, compared with only three out of five who believed that newspapers were fair. Over half the people who thought newspapers were not fair blamed their owners, compared with only one in four who blamed the station owners for unfairness on radio. A third of those who thought radio was unfair blamed advertisers, while only 7% blamed advertisers for unfairness in the press.

The broadcasting industry itself may be more readily inclined than the general public to blame the advertisers and their agencies for the deficiencies of their medium. *Broadcasting* magazine surveyed radio station managers in 1946 on the question, "Which of the following do you feel have done the most to retard improvement in programming?" Advertising agencies were named by 47% and advertisers by 44%, while only 21% mentioned the local stations. 23%

placed the blame on the Federal Communications Commission, 21% on the rating services, and 10% on the listeners themselves.

At the first radio conference held in Washington, Secretary of Commerce Herbert Hoover remarked, "It is inconceivable that we should allow so great a possiblity for service to be drowned in advertising matter." From that time until the present, the relation of broadcasting to advertising has been a matter of vigorous debate. In the F.C.C.'s *Blue Book* a former president of the American Tobacco Company is quoted as saying,

> "Taking 100% as the total radio value, we give 90% to commercials, to what's said about the product and we given 10% to the show . . . I don't have the right to spend the stockholders' money just to entertain the public."

This more or less innocent description of the relative selling impact of the commercial message and the program has been cited by a number of critics as an illustration of the typical sponsor's outlook on the content of broadcasting. Much has been made also of those instances in which advertisers have clearly exercised pressure. John Crosby reports that the late George Washington Hill, a storied figure among the advertisers of the 20's and 30's, required the president of the National Broadcasting Company to dance in his presence to the music of the Lucky Strike Dance Orchestra, in order to make sure that the tempo was right.

But times have changed since broadcasting has become big business, and today it may be the advertiser, eager for better programming and time availabilities, who dances to the network's tune.

The best answer to the critics of broadcast advertising is that commercial sponsorship provides an economically feasible way to provide a relatively high quality of television service with less pain to the consumer than a set license fee, or any other form of direct taxation.

A more sophisticated charge against commercially-sponsored television runs somewhat like this: The advertiser necessarily looks on the audience from a marketing standpoint. He is interested in programming only to attract attention for his commercial messages and thereby increase the chances of making a sale. The advertiser is understandably interested mainly in the cost-per-thousand viewers he reaches. He wants to spread the total cost of broadcasting over as many people as he can possibly attract. Programs must be pitched at the lowest common denominator of popular taste in order to insure that the audiences will be as large as possible. The net effect of this, so runs the argument, is that commercial television degrades the cultural level of the American public, since people become accustomed to the kinds of programs that are made available to them.

A kind of endless spiral process can be described. Because of the commercial character of the broadcasting industry, careful research on program audiences has been done for the past 20 years as a basis for showing advertisers what they have bought or what they can buy. This means that the criteria which are commonly used in judging programs are not the esthetic canons of the critics but the criteria of dollar and cents return on investment as represented by the number of homes reached and the cost of reaching them. The demand is first of all for higher ratings and only secondarily for higher standards of artistic accomplishment or informativeness. The public gets more and more of what the majority likes.

Spokesmen for the broadcasting industry have often pointed out that their sensitivity to ratings makes their operations highly democratic, since the public gets what it wants. Seen in this light, the critics are intolerant snobs who merely want the majority to bow to their superior taste. Sometimes even the most incisive of critics (like White) leaves himself wide open to such a charge:

> "There may be, numerically, more 'bobby-soxers' than lovers of good drama, good music, sprightly conversation, and stimulating discussion. However, the latter pay the larger share of taxes, and it is just possible that they have a larger voice in shaping the future of our society."

Victor M. Ratner, in an unpublished paper on "Intellectuals and the Popular Taste," defends the public's right to "cultural democracy."

> "Today, television and radio more often than not bring into our home programs which were never designed for us but for *other* people. Culturally speaking, we now live on a public highway. Other people's

programs come to us automatically following a program we like, or while we're searching for a program we like. In this way, many an intellectual has, for the first time, been directly exposed to mass tastes.

"He is shocked. He reacts, as almost any of us do, to sharp variations from his own standards. He is also indignant at this invasion of his privacy. He does not say: 'This program was intended for other people, not for me.' He says: 'This is a *bad* program. Why do they put it on?'

"It is a knotty question. Whose standards should apply? . . .

"Freedom of thought is one of our most profound rights. Yet judging from the anguished criticism of mass media one sees so often, many of us are not yet prepared to defend freedom of *taste*—when it is someone else's taste set against our own. We will fight hard for religious democracy and political democracy, but what might be called 'cultural democracy' is still something of a new concept. Whether we are educated or uneducated, we haven't yet been made to doubt our self-assurance that of course we know what is 'good' or 'bad' — unconsciously projecting *our* tastes as a standard for the community.

"I suggest this may be so because it is only recently in history we have been brought directly into contact with the cultural tastes of an entire nation, instead of the narrower tastes of our particular group in society. We have been far quicker to criticize these 'other' tastes than to understand them; one reason, perhaps, why our criticism has had so little effect."

Robert Kintner, in an address before the National Association of Radio and Television Broadcasters, has taken a similar stand:

"The regular presentation of half-hour programs on radio and television are the basic ingredients of our business that entertain millions of people every week. I realize it is fashionable, even in a section of our own business, to decry standardized programming, but the fact remains that the great bulk of our watchers desire to see and hear familiar faces and familiar voices. I see nothing wrong with catering to this basic public taste."

From the standpoint of the critics this is a spurious argument, since it fails to recognize that the broadcasters not only respond to and express popular tastes, but also create them. What goes out

over the air becomes familiar and what is familiar has a good chance
of being liked. Gilbert Seldes has stated the point this way:

"If the mass media merely serve their audiences, the measurement
of size is a sound business practice; if they go further and create audiences for themselves, the conclusions they draw from their statistics
become important to society at large . . . The broadcasters . . . began
to sample the audience, to submit programs to carefully selected groups
before putting them on the air. It seemed a natural way to ensure against
failure; it was harmless and necessary. But the very act of sampling indicated that the broadcasters already had a definite picture of the audience
in their minds, and that this picture was colored by their own statistics
on the size of the audience. The figures were so impressive that broadcasters began to believe they were serving the majority of the people.
As one of them said, 'There is a lunatic fringe that doesn't listen to
radio.' He meant, it seems, that only very few people never listen at
all, but he expressed graphically the conviction upon which broadcasters
act: that there is a vast heartland of listeners, around which, like a glacial
fringe, are dotted the insignificant, inattentive few. If the broadcasters are
right, they can be criticized only insofar as they have failed to meet their
obligations to their majority; if they are wrong, the serious charge against
them is that they have had the privileges of a true mass medium and have
served only a large minority . . .

"So long as mass media are considered as private entertainments, with
negligible effects on those who enjoy them, and with none whatever on
those who pass them by . . . the mass media will consistently try to increase the numbers of their patrons and at the same time will steadily
undermine the capacity to question, to criticize, and to protest . . .

"The entertainment arts have a public as well as a private character,
. . . pleasures taken individually have profound social effects. Nothing
effective can be done so long as the old concept of a purely personal
relationship between the citizen and his diversions remains unchallanged.
The justification for public pressure is public danger."

Dallas Smythe, discussing "A National Policy for Television"
in 1950, gives the following answer to the argument that research
expressed the democratic will of the mass audience:

"Whatever may be the merits of market research as a guide to
production of commodities, it by no means follows that the same tech-

nique is altogether valid for the entertainment and information agencies. In the former there usually are some standards of comparison. But the same is hardly ever true in the latter. The absence of standards, and the consequence of programming according to the present public preferences in the field of radio and movies, is indicated by an illustration borrowed from The Magnificent McInnes, a novel about public opinion polling. The author has one of his characters answer this same question by telling this familiar anecdote. Have you ever, in putting a child to bed, been asked to tell a story? You ask, 'What would you like to hear?' The answer, like as not, is 'The Three Bears.' (How could the child ask for a story he had never heard?) And before you get to the end of the familiar story the child is asleep . . .

"To generalize this a bit further: the American people expect and respect sincerity, diversity and freshness in their entertainment. And they expect more than entertainment from their communications agencies. As one distinguished communications scholar puts it, 'There is a large, presently untapped reservoir of seriousness in the American people.' How else could one explain the enormous audiences that 50 years ago thronged to hear 'orators' and 'chautauquas.' It will be evident from a little reflection that deep in our mores is the attitude that the responsibilities of the agencies which serve our minds and our souls is on a much higher level than the responsibilities of the agencies which supply us soap and razor blades."

White similarly feels that there is an irreconcilable difference between the outlook of commercial broadcasting and the demands of a democratic society.

"It must be fairly obvious that not everything that the average American requires to enable him to understand and perform his increased duties as a citizen will, in terms of radio programs, sell goods and services . . . Let us be frank about it: What we have here is a continuing contest between two diametrically opposed approaches to the problem of public service in radio—one based on long-range citizen need as the criterion, the other based on Hooper ratings and sales charts."

The responsibility of the broadcasting industry to serve the public interest first and foremost has been stressed by the Federal Communications Commission and accepted by the broadcasters themselves since the beginnings of commercial radio in the United States, on the *quid pro quo* principle that the industry has been granted access to the public domain (the air waves). This implies that it has an educational, almost missionary, function of lifting the level of popular taste by making programs available of a type which most people might not be particularly interested in at first blush.

Sometimes the attempt to classify broadcast output as public service leads far afield, as White points out:

> "A network executive submits that Bob Hope renders 'public service' (because the comedian has urged people not to cash their War and Victory Bonds). The educational director of a chain insists that 'Amos 'n' Andy' does (because Andy, the amoral one, always 'pays' for his deviousness) ... A few (broadcasters), extolling the 'citizen-building' qualities of crime-does-not-pay programs, appear not to understand the temptation to every youth to copy the culprit's techniques, omitting his one 'fatal' mistake. So-called 'children's' shows that, week after week, portray the triumph of unpunished brats over idiotic caricatures of parents are offered as 'public service' . . . News, of course, any and all news—news that is integrated and evaluated to give the listener some idea of what is at stake for him, as well as news that pours out in a steady, unrelated mind-numbing stream—automatically 'rates' as 'public service.' "

Yet the broadcasters can point quite proudly, and properly, to outstanding programs like "Omnibus" or "See It Now." Ratner remarks:

> "The program structure *already* favors the side of serious programming, not light programming; . . . more of such material is already offered in total than its numerical size of audience warrants. This happens in mass magazines and newspapers as well.
>
> "Such weighting in favor of serious and cultural programming takes place for a variety of reasons: the 'importance' of the minority audiences, the prestige value of such programs, the desire of media to discharge their responsibilities for balanced programming and 'cultural leadership' . . .
>
> "What we can expect, I think, as the audiences of our time continue to grow, is the creation of more and more *great art cast into the language of ordinary people*—the same insights into truth, expressed for majority rather than minority audiences . . .

"What seems like a swift lowering of our cultural standards may be only the slowing up of a train as it takes on many millions of new passengers—who ultimately will be carried to those higher plateaus of culture where only a small fraction of the human race found itself in the good old days."

Kintner similarly decries the "myth that the American broadcaster is 'tasteless.'"

"A relatively few, but very articulate, critics of radio and television report that the lowest common denominator is always aimed at by our business, with the result that programming is generally crude and at an average level. The facts are that radio and television have contributed greatly to the public's enjoyment in the field of entertainment, by making more familiar classic material, as well as creating new art forms . . . Whether it is in the field of drama, music, documentaries, news or information, a close study of our business over the past fifteen years will prove, without question, that we have equaled, if not exceeded, other media in both presentations of past and contemporary material and in experimentation in new art forms.

"Radio and television have an enviable record in drawing upon creative sources throughout the world, whether they be writers, directors, actors or other types of talent, but even more important, particularly in television, they have set up procedures whereby new and untried creative forces of all types — whether from the church, entertainment or information world—have been channeled into direct contact between the cold transmitter and the warm human personality."

The televised film version of Shakespeare's "Richard the Third" was seen by far more people than had ever seen the play performed since it was written. However, the broadcasters can by no means maintain that programs of this calibre are in any sense typical of the day-to-day output of American television stations or that the numbers of viewers they attract compare in size with the vast audiences reached by programming of more dubious cultural value. When people are offered their choice of a social documentary and a comedy program a greater percentage will generally select the comedy. But the choice is far more often one between two middle-brow or low-brow programs than between the two programs of unusual merit.

In an article in the Autumn, 1951, issue of the *American Scholar,*

Lyman Bryson, of Columbia University and the Columbia Broadcasting System, writes sympathetically of the broadcasters' dilemma:

"The fact is that most people are more interested in advertising and sports gossip, and comics, than in serious matters.

"Broadcasting judged by high standards is wasteful. Printing judged by the same standards is more so. . . . The point of this is that the differences between popular taste and cultivated taste are much the same in all the arts that have been amplified by mechanical processes. . . .

"There are several difficulties in making the truth of this point prevail. One is the inexpugnable illusion of people of developed taste that they know what the public wants. I am quite ready to admit that the commercial broadcaster also does not know what the public wants. The field is littered with costly mistakes. The point is that his mistakes do cost him money. He does his guessing with the benefit of market research, which is quantitatively indicative, and is not trusted as anything else. He works in a system of lethal competitiveness where most scholars could not breathe. He make his guesses in the teeth of his rivals, not before a silent and subservient class or his admiring colleagues. He frequently goes wrong. But it seems a little irrational to suppose that he is always wrong on the main point, and that the intelligentsia, with not even their reputations at stake, are always right.

"[Broadcasters] may, incorrigibly, still hope for large numbers of auditors when they put on frankly highbrow shows. When large numbers do not listen, the programs often stay on the air if they please even a small and not very responsive part of the public . . .

"The most popular hours are still taken up by the most popular programs. The broadcaster cannot do much about this. He has only a front page to offer at any moment and when more than 40% of all the receiving sets are tuned in, at nine in the evening, he tries to capture a good share of that fabulous audience."

Essentially, the debate between defenders and critics of present-day television arises out of a basic disagreement over the social function of mass communication. Are the media to be seen primarily as sources of influence on the ideas and values which people hold, or are they rather a means by which people can pleasantly pass their ever-growing leisure time? The two philosophies cannot be said to be mutually exclusive. Those who consider television viewing as essentially a pastime still want and expect it to be an influence on consumer behavior. Those who are concerned mainly with TV's impact on beliefs and mores generally acknowledge the necessity of conveying information in palatable and entertaining form.

The broadcasters, especially the networks, are in the cross-pressure of these two opposing viewpoints. Their first inclination is to program for entertainment. This is the way to capture the large audiences on which depend not only their advertising revenues, but also their feelings of professional accomplishment. However, they are highly sensitive to charges that they are shirking their responsibilities as mass communicators. Partly this sensitivity arises out of craftsmanly pride and common decency, partly out of anxieties (common to all big businesses) of governmental investigations and possible controls.

In their handling of controversial subjects, the broadcasters bend over backwards, in an effort to be scrupulously non-partisan. They are less partisan politically than magazines and newspapers. Sometimes the fear of being branded unfair is inseparable from the fear of offending any sizable segment of viewers, and then controversy may be avoided altogether. (The widespread use of the "Red Channels" blacklist of Communists and alleged pro-Communists comes under this heading.) Still, the subject matter of television programming has increasingly been extended to cover sensitive topics. The critics of television drama can show its limitations of quality, but it would be hard for them to demonstrate that these stem from any narrowness of themes.

Almost everyone connected with the broadcasting industry prefers to produce good programs rather than bad ones. If programs are not always as good as they might be, this is usually not because of an assumption that the public wants bad programs, but often because it is not easy to produce good ones. Moreover, people would not stop watching television if the available programs came closer to fulfilling all the demands of the serious critics. This would be true provided that there was improvement in the over-all level of competing programs, and not just in the programs of one network. However, stations, and networks are not likely to forego any competitive advantages by engaging in collusion or collaboration on their total programming.

The principal problem in upgrading the quality of television programs is the prodigious appetite of the medium itself for talent of every sort. There is actually a greater demand for people to write, direct, produce and act in programs than there are people with the necessary genius to make every show on the air an esthetic success. A number of highly popular radio and film comedians have been fazed by the prospect of turning out weekly programs that meet their own self-imposed standards, and have chosen to go on the air only once a month—or even less frequently. If the whole TV industry were to follow suit, and present on the air only programs with which its producers and directors were fully satisfied, the number of hours in the broadcast day would have to be substantially reduced. There are dim prospects for any such curtailment.

The rate at which television consumes new material will probably increase for some time, though repertory programming will necessarily be introduced too. (Already some oustanding TV series have been rerun not only once but several times, continuing to attract large numbers of new viewers. Exceptional documentaries and TV plays like Rod Sterling's "Patterns," which won great critical success, have been repeated successfully.)

In an average week, the number of hours a viewer can spend profitably viewing good television programs, if he exercises discrimination, is probably greater than the time he can spend seeing good new films, or reading worthwhile fiction in current magazines. But if he watches TV three hours every night, its treasures will be readily submerged. The habit of selective viewing has not as yet been built up among the American TV audience as a whole. The audience discriminates among TV programs only up to a point. We have seen that people tend to stick with a channel, and to continue watching television—regardless of the particular programs offered or of the number of different competitive programs available. Perhaps one reason for this lack of discrimination is the relative scarcity of serious newspaper or magazine criticism of television programs, comparable to serious criticism of motion pictures, plays, concerts or art shows. Television is covered in most of the American press through gossip columns and publicity handouts. The scarcity of intelligent, continuous and widespread commentary on individual TV programs promotes complacency on the part of the broadcasters. At the same time it encourages the public to accept programs unquestioningly and to suppress the occasional inclination to turn off the set altogether.

In its brief history, television has become the American people's most important source of ideas, apart from interpersonal contact. It has changed the position of the other mass media, and profoundly affected the way in which we spend our time with our families, and outside the home. It has influenced our outlook on the world and our political decisions, and it has an ever greater potential for doing this.

Yet television has wrought no violent revolution. It has not destroyed conversation or revived the intimacy of Victorian family life; it has not converted Americans from an active people into a passive one; its psychological effect on the young has not always been for the best, but at the same time it has not produced a generation of delinquents. Americans continue to work, play, make love, and raise children. Our world, in the age of television, is still the same world. But we experience it in new and different ways.

APPENDIX: THE STATUS OF TV RESEARCH

Research on television, like most research on the mass media, has a curiously divided character. Large sums have been spent to study television's audiences, mostly by the practitioners of commercial market and media research. However, some of the most interesting studies of the subject have originated in the universities. These studies start with a different set of objectives than those of the commercial researcher.

The audience surveys conducted for the broadcasting industry, or for advertisers and advertising agencies, are akin to other types of business research. They represent an attempt to make marketing decisions on the basis of hard and fast calculable data, much as other types of business judgments are made with the aid of production statistics or sales and cost figures.

Measurements of audience size represent actual or potential sales figures for a broadcaster; they are as vital to him as measurements of the market to the production plans of a manufacturer. Program ratings provide the television advertiser with an index of his show's popularity. More important, they tell him how large an audience he is reaching with his advertising messages in exchange for the money he has spent as a sponsor. This permits him to examine the trends of the program itself, and to compare its performance with those of competing companies.

The essential characteristic of commercial broadcast measurement is that it must be done by a standardized method and on a regular repeated basis. Great amounts of data must be systematically gathered, processed, analyzed and reported at the highest possible speed.

Apart from the rating services, commercial research is

oriented to immediate and specific problems. Ordinarily, the researcher cannot permit himself the luxury of theorizing or looking for generalizations. He must stick to the task in hand and come up with a fast and workable solution to the problem his client puts before him. Each research project tends to be undertaken from scratch, and there is therefore a certain amount of duplication with similar research undertaken at other places and times for other clients. Wariness of competitors means that research findings are usually kept confidential.

The commercial researcher commonly deals with generous quantities of data but rarely has the time to explore them in depth. By contrast, the academic or university researcher usually has only limited resources, and handles them more intensively. He starts with a broad interest in the communication of ideas. He is interested in television because it has influenced established ways of behaving and thinking, because it has become a force in public opinion and the political process.

In a few cases, television studies on a substantial scale have been made under academic auspices with the aid of grants from business. More often, the academic studies have been made in college communities, using small and not very systematic samples. It is often possible to draw conclusions from such studies only from the fact that they are in general agreement. The figures that emerge from any single study usually cannot be projected to the wider population.

Researchers in the universities were quick to recognize the importance of studying the social impact of television, but they were for the most part without resources adequate to match the scope of the problem. Only in very few instances were they able to conduct surveys, even on a local scale, with adequate samples and detailed analyses from which firm conclusions could be drawn.

Unfortunately, no research group — commercial or academic — undertook, while there was still opportunity to do so, a systematic study, over a period of time, of the social changes which television brought in its wake. To describe American life before television, we must reconstruct it from memory or from documents; we can no longer observe it firsthand. For practical purposes, life without television no longer exists in the United States except in a few remote and untypical areas. Almost all the households which lack television are still somewhat subject to its influence. Lacking television, they are by definition different from the rest.

Many great studies of radio's social influence were underwritten by the broadcasting industry and conducted as university projects. Few such joint studies have been made of television. The heyday of radio research occurred when the industry was fully developed and on the lookout for additional advertising. Research was used to persuade advertisers of the value of the medium, and for general public relations purposes. In the case of television, there was no great need to persuade advertisers that the medium could sell; they were already convinced of its merits. The problem for the broadcasters was one of providing facilities to meet advertisers' demands.

During TV's early years, the networks conducted their business at a loss. Research seemed like a dispensable luxury when it went beyond the essentials of measuring audience size, particularly since it was not essential to win advertising support. As television approached maturity its continuing success meant that there was no special urgency about major studies apart from those which demonstrated that its heavy costs to advertisers paid off in sales. Of course many of the fundamental questions faced by the broadcasters had already been answered. Much of the research on radio was applicable to television, because TV was similar to radio in its programming formulas. There was already much information about the differences in program preferences and tastes among different social groups, and about the psychological gratifications which people derive from various types of shows.

Television research's emphasis on the statistics of audience measurement has left it weak on the qualitative side. There have been relatively few intensive case histories of individual TV programs or program types. Few studies have used non-statistical techniques to describe or understand television's impact.

Theoretical Origins of TV Research

Research on television and other mass media has its roots in several distinct tendencies in social science.

1. The outlook of one group of scholars stemmed from the nineteenth-century tradition of reformism in social science. The social scientist was seen as the man who studied society in order to change and improve it. The preoccupation with social reform expressed itself in an interest in such symptoms of social disorganization as mental illness, family conflict, juvenile delinquency or crime. Scholars concerned with the influence of the mass media on young people tended to fit the problem into this context: movies and radio were considered, like slums, to be a breeding-ground of social disturbance.

Perhaps the leading illustration of this type of research is the notable series of studies of the effects of motion pictures on children, conducted under the auspices of the Payne Fund during the early depression years. A great variety of methods (surveys, essay contests, intensive interviews, psychological experiments, content analysis) were used to appraise the impact of the films on youth. In later years, other researchers starting with much the same perspective have looked in turn at radio, comic books, and recently television. These studies represent the American sociologist's concern with the problems and dislocations which the mass media, like any other new invention in a complex society, create in their wake.

2. The study of public opinion by means of the survey method began to acquire general acceptance at about the same time that radio grew to pre-eminence as a medium of

communication. This new growing medium fascinated the early practitioners of opinion research. The studies initiated by Paul Lazarsfeld at the Office of Radio Research at Princeton University (and later continued in what became the Bureau of Applied Social Research at Columbia University) brought a fresh research approach to the study of radio's effects on society. These studies primarily used the opinion survey method, though they also included analyses of program content and of intensive interviews.

The progress of opinion research indirectly reflects the political developments of the thirties and early forties. With the growth of Communism and Fascism, social scientists became fascinated by the great mass movements that could win the loyalties and sway the minds of millions of people through the skillful use of propaganda. In the control of such cynical and talented practitioners as Goebbels, the mass media became means by which public opinion could be deliberately manipulated.

World War II stimulated a great development in the systematic study of communications content. Harold Lasswell and his associates, many of them working for government agencies, pioneered in the application of psychological concepts to analysis of political propaganda output.

3. With the developing interest in propaganda, the focus of opinion research moved away from what it had been in the first days of polling, when the major aim had been to describe what people thought. Now emphasis shifted to exploring the reasons why people thought as they did, and the influence of specific communications in shaping attitudes.

New attention was paid to the motivations which attract people to one form of communications content rather than another. By studying the origins of audience tastes and preferences it was possible to explain the hold which the media had won over the masses of listeners and readers.

The growth of clinical psychology and psychoanalysis had provided a better understanding of the unconscious workings of the human mind and emotions. Sigmund Freud and his early followers (notably Carl Jung and Otto Rank) had been intrigued with the creative process in art. The artist's selection of symbols to convey experience, and the audience's response to them, reflected the workings of the unconscious in a way which was particularly amenable to exposition and interpretation. The popular arts were later subjected to similar types of analysis. At first the effects of specific radio programs, like soap operas or quiz shows, were judged only on the basis of psychoanalytical observations and insights. This was not very remote from the humanistic tradition of art criticism, in which a work is discussed in terms of the patterning of its content, and the critic's subjective interpretation of its meaning. Later these subjective means were supplemented by empirical research, using intensive interviews to get a description of listening as an activity, and (in some instances) projective techniques to arrive at a description of the respondent's personality and motives.

4. Another source of interest in the study of communications effects came from the experimental tradition in psychology. The behaviorist psychologists started with the scheme of "stimulus-response" in studying learning and conditioning effects in animals, and then applied the same concept to the study of human behavior. The response to a specific stimulus was determined by measuring the relevant characteristics of the subject before and after the experimental element was introduced. L. L. Thurstone was perhaps the foremost of those who applied this method during the twenties and thirties to study the effects of communications on attitudes. A high point for this type of research was reached in the massive series of experiments undertaken by the Army during World War II by Carl Hovland, Samuel Stouffer and others. In these studies, the subjects were no longer regarded as passive recipients of the communication. Differences in effect were related both to variations in the content and form of communication, and to variations of attitude before the experiment.

Measuring the Audience

At the same time that these developments were taking place, notable strides were being made in the audience measurement techniques undertaken for the radio broadcasting industry. Commerical research was concerned primarily with the number of people who listened to particular radio programs. It employed such methods as telephone surveys, personal interviews, or diaries kept by listeners. As time went on, the broadcasters overcame their preoccupation with the mere number of people in their audiences. They became interested in the kinds of people who listened to particular programs, and in the flow of the audience from one program to another in the course of an evening of listening. They tried to find out what listeners liked and disliked in a program, in order to make improvements that might raise the level of attention and interest. They also sought to determine the comparative effectiveness of programs, as measured by the ability of listeners to recall the sponsor and as measured also by "sales effectiveness tests," in which listeners and non-listeners were compared with respect to their purchases of the advertised brands.

Television research emerged full blown from the study of radio. The radio rating services (Nielsen, Pulse, Hooper) turned to television with little or no changes in their measurement techniques. Several new organizations (the American Research Bureau, Trendex, Videodex) emerged to measure television audiences, but these adopted methods which had already been used for radio. Radio research had become important only after radio itself had won a place in the overwhelming majority of American homes. By contrast, television research was begun when television was still a youthful medium.

Radio underwent no major changes during the years it was being intensively studied, but the television researchers, from the very start, had to apply a great proportion of their energies and budgets to the mere task of keeping track of

TV's constant growth and transformation. The rising number of sets and stations, the changing program schedules and viewing habits as TV took shape meant that there were an almost infinite number of immediate jobs for research to perform. The broader-gauge psychological or sociological problems connected with the medium tended to be ignored, since they were not pertinent to the main function of winning and holding advertisers.

From the very beginning of radio advertising, the measurement of audiences has presented problems for research. In the early days of radio, great stress was laid on listener mail as an indication of audience size and distribution. Later it was determined that more accurate measurements would be obtained by going out and asking people about their listening habits or by reaching them on the telephone and finding out what they were listening to at the moment. The next step was to get people to keep a diary record of their listening. More recently, mechanical means of recording set tuning activity have been developed.

Audience Mail. It was realized rather early in radio's history that the volume of mail received by a program is not an accurate indication of audience size. The flow of letters can always be augmented by special appeals or requests from the performers on the program. Also the format of certain programs (for example, any musical request program or listener quiz) evokes more communications from listeners than others do. Programs directed at some sections of the population are more apt to arouse a good listener response than programs directed at a less articulate group. Finally, fan clubs and other pressure groups can support their favorites by turning out an exceptional quantity of mail.

In radio's pioneer days, mail was sometimes used as a means of getting some general hints about the *character* of the listening public. For example, geographic breakdowns could be made, although these were somewhat unreliable because listeners in some areas were more responsive than others. Letters were analyzed by the sex of the writer, and conjectures were even drawn about the social background of the writer, based on the style of composition, the quality of the paper and so on. Such rough indicators have been superseded in U.S. domestic broadcasting by more systematic methods of audience measurement, but analysis of listener mail is still an important source of information about the audiences for many radio stations overseas and in international information programs, such as those of the Voice of America, the BBC, Radio Free Europe, and so on.

One value of audience mail is that it provides some clues as to audience reactions, where no other hints are available. Unfortunately, mail is not a reliable source of information on such questions, any more than on the question of audience size, simply because mail does not come from a representative sampling of the audience. It is easier to signify disapproval of a program by flicking the dial than by writing a letter of complaint, so that even the writers of critical letters must be considered fans.

A program's strengths and weaknesses can far better be assessed by means of such a technique as the Lazarsfeld-Stanton Program Analyzer, in which groups of listeners or viewers are assembled. As the program is played for them, their minute-by-minute reactions are obtained as they press pushbuttons to signify their approval or disapproval of what is happening. These responses are recorded on a tape synchronized with the timing of the show, so that a "profile" of liking and disliking can be obtained and the high and low points located. Questionnaires and discussion interviews are also employed to get the full picture of audience reaction.

The Program Analyzer has fallen into disuse as exclusive program sponsorship by advertisers waned, though variants of the original methodology continue to appear. In the 1960's it became fashionable to substitute physiological measures for interviewing, since these were more responsive to the minute second-by-second changes in response to the commercials, which (rather than the programs) were the real objects of research.

Audience Studies Inc. has used a psychogalvanometer, which measures skin conductivity, in order to gauge the level of emotional response to changing TV-commercial content. An eye camera developed by Eckhard Hess and used by McCann-Erickson measures pupil dilation as an independent, involuntary expression of emotional arousal.

The testing and pretesting of television commercials has become a bigger and bigger business, but it has not contributed significantly to our understanding of TV as a medium, although it has produced many ingenious techniques. For instance, cable TV has been used on a "split-cable" basis by organizations like Ad-Tel to compare commercial performance in different halves of the same market.

Listener and Viewer Surveys. Broad-scale public-opinion-type surveys are an established means of studying habits and preferences in listening and viewing. Surveys using a standardized questionnaire administered by trained interviewers can produce highly detailed information that lends itself to thoroughgoing statistical analysis. Such surveys are employed for the following purposes:

1. Penetration Studies. These provided a basis for estimating the actual extent of television (or radio) ownership, and the distribution of sets in different regions, among different types of households, and in different parts of the house.

2. Coverage Surveys. These define the geographical area in which people actually view or listen to a particular station with a measurable frequency (for the average day, weekly and in four weeks). In such surveys *"circulation"* is defined as the actual number of homes that view or listen to a station with specified frequency.

The American Research Bureau has divided all the counties of the United States into 207 "Areas of Dominant Influence" in which stations located in a particular market have over half of the viewing audience. Nielsen has an almost identical arrangement, with 198 "Dominant Market Areas." This classification has the convenience of assigning every county in the United States to a specific TV market against whose total population ratings can be projected. At the same time, the designation of market boundaries often disguises the realities of overlapping coverage from transmitters in different cities.

3. Program Popularity Surveys. Cross-sections of the public are sometimes asked about their liking or viewing of specific programs (or types of programs). The resulting figures are indicators of program popularity, and *not* precise measurements of actual viewing (or listening) habits. Recall of viewing is hard to measure exactly after a lapse of days or weeks, and particularly when a question is phrased in general terms (like "What television programs do you watch regularly?"). The results tend to give the few shows with the largest audience a disproportionately large share of the total.

TvQ is the name of a service, affiliated with the Home Testing Institute, which produces a monthly report of program popularity based on questionnaires returned by 2,500 families. The service measures the changing preferences of different population groups and is not considered to be a measurement of audience size.

Mail Surveys. Mail surveys are useful where it is important to get samples so large that personal interviewing would be prohibitively expensive. They have been used mainly in set-ownership and coverage surveys. The Standard Audit and Measurement Service (and the Broadcast Measurement Bureau in former years), in its 1952 survey of radio-station coverage, employed a massive-scale mail ballot.

The Broadcast Rating Services

Why do the radio and television ratings produced by different measurement services often fail to agree? The answer is that each service uses a method somewhat different from its competitors. The results are not strictly comparable because different things are being measured in each case.

On the whole, the rating services agree rather well, at least in ranking network programs by popularity. Few major programming decisions based on one rating service would have to be reversed if another rating service were used. In selecting individual stations for a network line-up or a spot schedule, however, it is sometimes possible to be drawn in one direction by one rating service and elsewhere if another is followed.

The user of ratings must always keep two things in mind: (1) No service is perfect; each method of measurement has its own limitations. (2) Small samples, used by most rating services, leave a margin of statistical error around every reported rating percentage. Differences of a few percentage points are usually not significant. Why are the samples not larger? Because advertisers will not foot the bill.

The Roster Method. The roster recall method of measuring audience size most closely resembles the field survey, for it is based on direct interviewing of a large cross-section of the population. It is used to measure radio audiences by The Pulse, Inc., and was formerly used by them to measure TV.

Pulse presents respondents with a list of programs broadcast over local stations during the four- or five-hour period immediately preceding the one in which the interview takes place (they are questioned in the afternoon about their morning listening, in the late afternoon about their early afternoon listening, and in the evening about their listening of the evening before). Interviews are conducted during the first week of each calendar month and the report is available approximately four weeks afterward. The sample size in each radio market ranges between 400 and 1000 for each measurement period. Pulse has been providing measurements based on this method since 1941. Pulse discontinued its TV ratings in 1963, but the roster method is still employed for TV in other countries.

The main advantages of the roster recall method are three: (1) It is less expensive than some other rating services, because it gets audience information for a sizable block of time. (2) It records listening and viewing for late and early hours during which it is not feasible to conduct telephone interviews. (3) The questionnaire includes more detailed audience classification information than other rating services can offer, so that it permits elaborate marketing analyses.

The main limitation of the method is that the use of the lengthy roster may discourage a discriminating response. People may exaggerate the amount of listening or viewing they do by giving a uniform answer for a station over a substantial time period, instead of pointing selectively to individual programs. This becomes a special problem in the case of daytime radio programs, particularly musical ones of which detailed recollections are apt to be blurry.

The Coincidental Telephone Method. This method employs brief telephone interviews in which respondents are asked what they are actually listening to or watching at the moment, and, often, about their viewing during the previous half hour. Albert J. Sindlinger Research conducts such studies on a customized basis. Trendex and C. E. Hooper, Inc., formerly produced regular reports by this method, but Trendex now concentrates on special tests of commercial recall, while Hooper, after merging with Daniel Starch and Staff, discontinued its rating service in 1970.

The Diary Method. This method requires the active cooperation of a sample of the listening or viewing public. Each family that agrees to be part of the panel receives a diary to be kept by the TV set (or sets). They are asked to list, by time period, all the programs they watch or listen to for a specified period and to indicate who is in the audience.

In general, the diary method has the following advantages: (1) It permits a continuous record to be kept, for a full reporting period, of the listening or viewing habits of a constant sample, thus putting all the ratings for one report on a uniform base. (2) Like the roster and coincidental telephone methods (but unlike the mechanical recorder method), it records actual viewing rather than tuning. It need not provide any suggestions or cues to the respondents, as the roster method does. (3) It permits inquiries on related marketing subjects, and detailed classification of audience characteristics.

"Open-ended" diaries require the respondent to write in the programs viewed, and thus produce lower ratings than diaries which have a roster of programs listed.

The disadvantages of the diary method are: (1) The original sample undergoes some attrition from people who refuse or neglect to cooperate or who submit incomplete or unusable diaries, so it may not be as perfectly representative of the population as it was originally intended to be. (2) It is possible (though this is only conjecture) that people who keep a diary over a period of time tend to become more self-conscious in their listening or viewing, so that they are no longer altogether typical. (3) Since many diaries tend to be filled out hours (or even days) after the program is heard, there may be some memory losses, particularly for less distinctive or less popular shows or for shows listened to by children (or other nondiary-keeping members of the family).

In the case of family-viewing diaries like those that Nielsen and the A.R.B. use for their local ratings reports, the final returns are from only a part (generally between 40% and 60%) of those who agree to cooperate when they are first contacted, and these are only a part of those in the original sample. (The actual percentages that the respondents represent are a trade secret.) It must be noted also that family diaries tend to be kept by the housewife, who is not always an accurate reporter of what other members of the household are viewing. The results from such family diaries tend to run somewhat higher than the results from viewing diaries separately kept by individual members of the family.

The American Research Bureau and the Nielsen Station Index both employ the diary method to produce local ratings for individual markets. TV homes are first contacted by phone to get promises of cooperation. Further telephone calls are made after the diary is delivered, to insure cooperation and to answer questions. The diary is kept for the first week in the month, and a new sample is drawn for the next month. The A.R.B.'s sample ranges in size from 600 to 1,800 cases per city, and Nielsen's ranges from 500 to 2,500. Local reports are issued approximately three to four weeks after the measured week. For all but the biggest markets, reports are produced three times a year by both services, covering all the "Areas of Dominant Influence" and "Dominant Market Areas."

The Mechanical Recorder Method. This method differs from the others described thus far in that it measures program audiences not by asking people what they have watched or heard, but by impersonal means of recording the tuning activity of their receivers. The Nielsen Television Index employs a national panel of 1,200 cooperating families. The panel is maintained indefinitely.

A device known as an "audimeter" is connected with each of the radio and television sets in the household. This device automatically clocks and records, minute by minute, the wave length (or channel) to which the set is tuned. The recording tapes are sent to Nielsen by the panel members every two weeks. The tapes can then be matched against known rosters of stations and programs to arrive at national ratings for network programs.

Nielsen provides several different types of measurement:

"Homes using television" indicates the proportion of all television homes in which a set is actually in use.

"Share of audience" figures indicate what percentage of the sets in use are tuned to a particular program during the average minute it is on the air.

"Average minute audience" measures the percentage of sets within reception range of the program that are tuned to it during the average minute it is on the air.

The *"Nielsen rating"* measures the percentage of sets in the reception area who are tuned to the program for 6 minutes or more.

Nielsen's rating reports are issued about 2½ weeks after the close of the period covered. Nielsen's audimeter data are coordinated with information on the characteristics of individual program viewers obtained from a national panel of 2,300 diary households to produce the Nielsen National Survey.

In addition to national TV ratings, Nielsen also issues a popularity report for television cities where all three network programs are broadcast (the "Multi-Network Area" report).

The outstanding advantages of the Nielsen television index derives from its use of a mechanical recording device. This permits programs to be rated for every week in the year except four. The continuity of the panel means that ratings are highly comparable week after week. Because all tuning is measured, it is possible to trace the flow of the audience minute by minute and from program to program and to measure the accumulation and duplication of audiences from week to week. This makes them useful for detailed analysis and diagnosis of program strengths and weaknesses.

The limitations of the national Nielsen rating service emerge, as do its merits, from the use of the mechanical recorder. The service is a costly one to operate, and to subscribe to. Because ratings are based on tuning rather than on personal reports of listening or viewing, there are no data on listeners or viewers per set or on audience composition (except from home characteristics). Although unattended but operating sets are measured by Nielsen, this probably is of very slight importance for evening shows.

At the start of 1958, A.R.B. also placed in operation a rating system, "Arbitron," which offers instantaneous measurements of tuning at 90-second intervals, using an automatic reporting device on the set hooked to a central point by private telephone lines. The Arbitron reports are available only for New York City.

In addition to the syndicated television-rating services, two other services rose to prominent use in the late

1960's, the Brand Rating Index and the W. R. Simmons Media Service. Both studies provide annual reports on consumption patterns and on exposure to *all* the major media. Simmons uses a two-week individual viewing diary to measure and describe television audiences, while B.R.I. uses a roster of programs, which the respondent marks to show the number of times he has watched each one within the past month. These studies in no way substitute for the ability of Nielsen and A.R.B. to trace program-viewing trends from week to week and to show these trends in individual cities. The large amount of information they provide on magazine readership and product usage, however, makes them especially useful to advertising planners, who prepare computer analyses of how media "mix" together to provide efficient coverage of the most likely customers.

As television viewing changes from a family activity to an individual one, the relevant measurement of television's audience also undergoes change. While laymen (and even a good many TV professionals) think of a program rating as "the percentage of people watching a program," it has in fact traditionally reflected (as measured by the leading rating service, the Nielsen Television Index) the percentage of television households in which a set was tuned to the program for more than five minutes. As more and more households acquired more than a single set, Nielsen's standard measurement changed from "sets in use" to "homes using television." The problem of what to do when more than one set in a household was being used was resolved by the simplest expedient: treating each set tuned to a program as though it were located in a separate household. This has the inevitable effect of inflating program ratings relative to households using TV; as the proportion of multiset homes continues to grow, this inflation will be increasingly perceptible.

More significant, however, has been the decline in the number of viewers per set, which steadily increases the disparity between the proportion of homes using television and the proportion of people watching. (These proportions could not of course be the same unless everyone in the family were always at home and always watching at exactly the same time.) Accordingly, emphasis in the field of television ratings has moved steadily toward the measurement of *individual* viewing by people with different social characteristics (and presumably different marketing value to the advertiser). But to perform such measurements accurately is a tougher proposition than the automatic metering of set tuning, since it requires reliance on the cooperation and memory of a broad cross-section of the public.

Simmons compared program ratings based on the personal coincidental interviews he conducted for his national media study in 1966 with those obtained for the same programs from his usual diary technique. The latter were 32% larger. Another experimental study by Simmons (in 1968) used a coincidental measure to establish who was viewing and then went back to the same people a week later with detailed questions using a storyboard to get a recall measure of the same programs. In only about half the cases did the answers agree.

A Congressional inquiry in 1963 had produced a flurry of concern over the accuracy of the ratings. Hearings and investigations produced evidence that made it seem doubtful that one or two of the minor local rating services conducted field work at all. Even such reputable organizations as the A. C. Nielsen Company were confronted with individual cases of fraudulent field work, though there was never any intimation that these reflected any widespread problem. Far more pertinent was the criticism that the rating services presented their estimates of audience size as though they were engraved on tablets of stone, and that they failed to provide adequate explanations of their methods and sampling errors within their reports. As a result, every major rating service underwent changes in method and reporting procedures, and the broadcasting industry established a Broadcast Ratings Council to provide a continuing research evaluation. A study of radio ratings methodology, conducted under the auspices of this Council in 1966, compared a number of commonly used measurement techniques and found variations ranging up to 100% in the size of the ratings they produced for the identical programs.

The precision of the national TV audience statistics underwent fresh scrutiny in 1966, when the Politz research organization conducted a national survey in 12,000 households, using the "personal coincidental" method. The survey found 41% of the homes using television in evening time, in comparison with a level of 55% reported by Nielsen. Moreover, Politz found fewer viewers per household, with a total of 24% of the adults watching prime-time TV, compared to 41% estimated by Nielsen, a comparative difference of 71%. The broadcasting industry dismissed the Politz results because of the high proportion (35%) of households in which no one was at home. A follow-up study sponsored by *Life* magazine checked out Politz's interview technique, using an electronic device that detected the presence of a working TV set, and found virtually no discrepancy. The broadcasters riposted with a series of experiments using coincidental telephone surveys.

Contam (The Committee on Nationwide Television Audience Measurements), a broadcast industry research consortium, compared television usage levels as measured by meters and by coincidental telephone surveys in two studies in 1967 and 1968. Meters produced results that were 8% or 9% higher. By increasing the number of attempted dialings and by letting the phone ring longer, the coincidental method yielded a higher response, and hence a higher reported level of set usage, closely similar to that obtained from Nielsen's audimeter sample.

The critics responded by observing that residential listed telephones did not provide the same accurate sampling basis for projectible statistics as personal interviews might: 89% of U.S. households have telephone service; 11% of residential phones are unlisted, though in some cities the proportion is as high as 33%. There is no clearcut basis for distinguishing residential and business phones in developing telephone samples. In any case, the critical question involved the extent of viewing by individuals and not by households. (The broadcasters reported nothing on this point, although it was a logical by-product of their basic questions.)

Although the issues involved in this continuing debate are somewhat technical, they are by no means academic, since they concern the fundamentals of TV's return on the economic investment made by advertisers. The essence of the measurement problem is that it is far easier to get accuracy from a single, one-shot survey in which elaborate and expensive methods are used in sampling and interviewing, than it is to get representative results repeatedly from the same sample of people. Repetitive contacts are essential in order to provide the broadcasting business with the continuity needed to compare ratings from one period to the next. Yet repetitive contacts also inevitably cause an attrition in the rate of return, and the less cooperative respondents are also apt to be different (and generally lighter) in their viewing habits. It takes repeated efforts before Nielsen can find a family willing to accept an audimeter, and not every audimeter household remembers to send in a usable record of its viewing every two weeks.

C. E. Hooper, Inc. conducted a coincidental telephone survey in 1968, in New York, where both Nielsen and the A.R.B. had meter panels. They contacted the people originally interviewed and offered them $25 worth of gifts as an inducement to them to have their sets hooked up "undetectably" to a meter. The TV-viewing level in the homes of those who allowed the meter to be attached was only slightly higher than the level shown for the same period by the two other rating services, but it was over a fourth greater than viewing among those who had rejected the meter (about half the original sample).

The ratings services provide measurements that have become indispensable to the management of broadcast programming and advertising, and there is not one of them that would not be happy to enlarge its samplings and improve its techniques if the cost of such increased accuracy could be economically justified.

Frontiers of Television Research

With all the concentrated research to which television has been subjected, there is still much that remains to be learned. The commercial researchers still face unresolved problems. The fact that different rating services produce different results is a source of confusion in the broadcasting industry. Technical improvements in ratings can only come from more specific knowledge of the kinds of biases or distortions that arise from each of the various methods of audience measurement. But the real challenge to TV research is not in the area of accumulating more or better statistics on audience size.

Much is known about the audiences for various types of television programs, but remarkably little is known about the broadcasters themselves. Students of journalism have devoted a great deal of attention to describing the structure of the modern newspaper and the organization of its staff. The newspaperman as a social type is a favorite subject of sociological description and a well-known and romanticized figure in the public imagination. Leo Rosten and Hortense Powdermaker, in their studies of the motion-picture industry, have provided sharply drawn portraits of the film makers, and have discussed the values and folkways of Hollywood in much the same manner that the anthropologist uses to describe the organization and culture of a primitive tribe.

The only writings remotely analogous to these in the case of television are popular articles and books on such TV personalities as Arthur Godfrey, Jackie Gleason, and Liberace. Social scientists have not yet looked seriously at the social structure of the industry, and the relationships among its component parts: the creative personnel — performers and writers, the network program and production people, the local-station owners, the advertisers and advertising agencies. This is an industry that calls on the services of many types of specialists with differing interests and very differing conceptions of the objectives of television itself. Few systematic studies have described the way in which various elements in the industry think of the audience and its wants. We have only anecdotal accounts of which programming decisions are reached. No one has examined the role of research itself in the planning and production of programs.

The type of content analysis most commonly described to analyze television programming consists essentially of a systematic count of the number of times in which certain types of characters appear or actions occur. An analysis is made of the statistical incidence of various symbols or acts over the whole array of program output. No particular attention is paid to the inner dynamics or structure of particular programs.

In such notable studies of the movies as those by Siegfried Kracauer or Nathan Leites and Martha Wolfenstein, the unit of discussion is the individual film. This qualitative approach makes it possible to see a communication (like a film or a book or a television program) as a whole. It makes possible a meaningful interpretation of its appeals and effects, by showing what its content represents in terms of the audience's fantasies and aspirations. If this approach were taken toward television, case studies of the content of individual programs might be related to studies of audience reaction. It would also be highly useful if the statistical type of content analysis were applied to the programming of a wide group of stations and conducted on a continuing basis. This would permit the study of trends in the output of the several networks, and of the available TV fare in cities of different size.

To conduct the ideal study of the social effects of television, the researcher today would have to begin in a foreign country where TV has not yet been introduced so that the changes that take place can be traced through time. In a few years no such country will exist.

NOTES

1. Mid-Century America and the Growth of Television

(A)   The first voyage to the moon in 1969 was seen in 94% of all U.S. television households (some 53.5 million in all) and was watched an average of 15½ hours in each. The moon landing by Apollo 11 was seen by some 600 million people around the world.

(B)   By 1969, 46% of the work force held white-collar jobs.

(C)   In 1969, 56% of the population had attended high school, and 25% of those over 18 had been to college. 29% of the population was living in the central cities of metropolitan areas, and 35% in the suburbs. In 1970, 64% of families owned their own homes.

(D)   In 1970 the average work week was 37.1 hours.

(E)   In 1970, 83% of U.S. homes had refrigerators, 78% gas or electric ranges, and 70% electric washing machines.

(F)   In 1970, 43% of the women over 16 held jobs.

(G)   In 1969, 667 consumer magazines circulated 315,736,000 copies per average issue, and 1,163 industrial magazines circulated 30,843,000 copies. In 1971, 1,748 daily newspapers circulated 62,107,000 copies each day.

(H)   Radio is now in 93% of the cars on the road and still is estimated as being in 10,000,000 public places.

(I)   To all intents and purposes, virtually all inhabited parts of the United States are now within reception range of a TV signal, and 96% of all homes have a TV set.

(J)   By 1970 a cumulative total of over 173,000,000 TV sets had been sold in the United States.

(K)   Of the 4,500,000 black-and-white TV sets sold in 1970, 92% were portable and table models. By comparison only 50% of the 4,800,000 color sets sold that year were portable and table models, while the remainder were consoles. 11% of the black-and-white sets sold were 9-inch screen size or smaller, and 37% were under 12 inches in size.

(L)   In 1971, A. C. Nielsen estimated that 90% of the U.S. TV households could receive four or more channels and 57% could receive seven channels or more. (Only 3% could receive one or two stations.) The average household could receive 6.8 channels and this number is constantly increasing as new stations continue to come on the air. (It should be noted that these estimates do not evaluate the quality of reception for different channels; during peak viewing hours the true range of choices is apt to be less than the total number of channels that can be received, because of the duplication of network programs over stations in different cities.)

(M)   35% of the TV households, with 43% of the adult U.S. population, had more than a single TV set, at the start of 1971.

(N)   At the beginning of 1971 there were 818 commercial and 212 noncommercial stations on the air, as well as 2,385 CATV systems, serving approximately 6.5% of all TV households.

(O)   Since television arrived at the point of saturation coverage, it no longer makes sense to compare TV households with the small minority of households on the margins of society who are without TV. The most significant comparisons to be made are between single-set and multiset families, and between those who have color TV and those who do not. The growth in the number of multiset households is of course inseparable from the growth of color television, which by

1971 was present in 40.9% of TV households. (Differences in the characteristics of these households and in their viewing habits are discussed in the notes to Chapter 4.) Charles B. Riter found in 1966 that purchasers of color TV bought them essentially as replacements for black-and-white sets that were wearing out, but he also noted that "where the black-and-white set does not require extensive service, the customer would rather keep the set for convenience in lieu of the small compensation received as a trade-in."

(P)   William Belson found that in 1950, British TV families had more children and fewer elderly adults than nonviewing families and were also somewhat larger. In the earliest days of television, the number of small children under five was the same in both viewer and nonviewer families; as time went on more of those with children under five were in the viewing category.

Summarizing a study he made in 1954, Belson reports that "The viewers of this period seem to have been drawn somewhat more than nonviewers from those with a materialist outlook ... they tended somewhat to be people who associated themselves with or expressed themselves in terms of material pleasures, material welfare, and the possession of things. By contrast, the nonviewers seem to have tended more than the viewers to be people who could 'live within themselves' as it were." These differences, Belson points out, were not attributable to the effects of television, but reflected the selective nature of set acquisition.

Studies of TV growth in other countries parallel the American experience with respect to the attributes of early set ownership. In the underdeveloped world, the possession of a television set is a high-prestige matter. In Colombia, a survey found that a third of those who claimed to have a TV did not actually have one. In 1947, when only 0.2% of the United Kingdom's population had a TV set, 48% of the set owners were in the income group that represented the top 12% of the public. By 1951 (when 9% of the homes had TV), the top 12% in income accounted for 24% of the set ownership; by 1955 (when 49% had TV), the top income group accounted for only 14% of the total. By 1964, 91% of the homes had a "telly."

2.   Popular Culture and the Appeals of Television

(A)   In 1970 the networks began the practice of permitting critics to review films and tapes before their actual broadcasts, thereby permitting them to build the audience for programs by notices that appeared ahead of time.

(B)   Herbert Kay, who has done psychological studies of the audience appeal of many dozens of TV programs, concludes that "TV viewers pursue an active, intensive hunt for new programs and stories. Other things being equal, they favor the new, truly different program over the carbon-copy imitation. The big rub is that other things are often not equal. The viewer may have to choose between a well-produced carbon-copy type of show, and a new type which was unsuccessfully executed."

In the mid-1960's, 37% of the adult population in West Germany said their principal reason for watching television was to find out what was new. Only 24% said they viewed TV for entertainment, and another 8% to pass the time. 6% said they viewed it for educational or cultural reasons, and 2% out of loneliness. (Cited by Alphons Silvermann.)

(C)   Performers who appear regularly on television quickly grow accustomed to stares, smiles, and unsolicited conversations when they appear in public. But people who make guest appearances, such as quiz-show contestants, are often approached with a sort of puzzled familiarity by people who think they know them from someplace or have met them somewhere, but just can't place them. Often, a former quiz-show contestant once told me, the association is made to a very homey or intimate setting for the previous encounter, which did after all take place in the individual's own living room.

During the Security Council sessions that accompanied the Six-Day Arab-Israeli War of June, 1967, the television cameras often focused on the Council's president for the period, Hans R. Tabor of Denmark. As a result of the 51 hours of broadcasts of the debates, Tabor received 8,500 letters, mostly from women, and many of a highly personal nature. One fifteen-year-old girl addressed him as "My Dear Hans." Viewers sent him money and gifts, asked for photos and autographs, proposed marriage, and offered advice on his personal habits.

(D)   Leo Rosten has said, "When the public is free to choose among various products, it chooses—again and again—the frivolous against the serious, 'escape' as against reality, the lurid as against the tragic, the trivial as against the serious, fiction as against fact, the diverting as against the significant."

(E)   Suggestive though fragmentary evidence in support of the thesis that viewing is a passive experience compared to reading comes from an analysis by Herbert Krugman of brain-wave activity recorded by the EEG technique.

(F)   The "realism" of television may in part reflect the illusion projected in the small scale of the picture tube. This makes extraordinary subjects seem "manageable" because they are shown in smaller-than-life size, while they would be overwhelming if viewed on a motion-picture screen.

In an experiment using three groups of people divided into high-, middle-, and low-self-esteem categories, Howard Leventhal showed two scare messages involving automobile safety. In one film a shot of a car collision was shown. In the other the gory, mutilated bodies of accident victims were shown. In each case, half the respondents saw the same film on a huge 10′ × 15′ screen from a very close viewing distance, while others saw a small 2′ × 3′ image on the screen. The large image had an inhibiting effect on the low-self-esteem subjects. They were more likely to accept the message on automotive driving safety when the image was small and less threatening. They "reported fatigue when they were exposed to the big picture and said they could not or did not want to think of themselves as accident victims. It seemed that they tried to cope with the danger by avoiding the issue altogether. The impression given by the huge images was one of unalterable reality, so low-self-esteem subjects saw little reason to take action to protect themselves." On the other hand, the high- and middle-self-esteem subjects accepted the recommendations more readily with the large picture.

3.   The Content of Television Programming

(A)   Herman Land finds that program costs are about 60% of all television costs and are rising at the rate of 8% a year. He estimated (in 1968) that network programming accounts for 61.2% of the average station's schedule. 14.2% is locally originated programming, and 24.6% consists of syndicated programs and films. The cost per program hour per station is $309 for the average network program, $477 for a local program, and $147 for the average syndicated program.

The three networks spend between $10,000,000 and $15,000,000 a year for program development. According to Land, the average one-hour pilot cost $184,000 by 1965 and was up to $350,000 by 1968. For a half-hour pilot the rise was from $80,000 in 1965 to $250,000 (in some instances) by 1968. But only one third of the program ideas that filter through to the pilot stage get on the air. Of the few presented on television, two-thirds do not last through the first season.

The networks retain strong control over the selection of programs, but they themselves produce shows that fill only 10% of the 74.5 weekly hours of network prime time. Package producers fill 72%, and feature films 18%. Advertising agencies have virtually left the field of program production, though the reduction of network hours in the 1971 fall season has aroused a revival of their interest in this phase of the business.

One important aspect of TV content does not lend itself readily to objective quantification, and that is the *quality* of programming. Charles Sopkin, who spent "Seven Glorious Days and Seven Fun-Filled Nights" monitoring all six commercial television channels in New York City, disputed Newton Minow's characterization of TV as a "vast wasteland," and concluded that "gigantic garbage dump" was a more accurate description. He said, "I naively expected that the ratio would run three to one in favor of trash. It turned out to be closer to 100 to one." This is, of course, one man's opinion and not evidence.

(B)   In 1971, only 4% of evening network programming is broadcast live.

(C)   57% of all TV time is devoted to network shows. 10.1% of locally originated programming time is live, while the rest is in syndicated or feature films.

A survey of 235 TV stations, made by *Television Magazine* in May, 1964, found that of the locally produced hours, 25% were news shows, 29% children's shows, 11% educational or cultural, and 10% variety or panel programs.

(D)   A 1970–71 Nielsen classification of 74 prime-time television programs showed the following breakdown:

Situation comedy	37%
Variety	22
Suspense and mystery	15
General drama	12
Feature films	10
Western drama	4
	100%

(Not all the programs in each category were of the same average length. Half-hour programs accounted for less than a third of all network prime time. The 7:00 P.M. network news shows are not covered in this compilation.) The most notable change since 1957 is the rise of situation comedy and the decline in general drama.

Of 33 daytime shows on the network, 18 were serials, maintaining the glorious tradition of soap opera; 9 were quiz and audience-participation shows; 6 were situation comedies. The popularity of different program types continues to have a cyclical character. In 1960 there were 21 television Westerns; the next year there were 15, then 11, then only 5, then 11 again.

In the 1970–71 broadcast season, there were only seven network shows on the air that had lasted ten years or more, and another eight (excluding the "Tuesday Movies," the "Thursday Movies," the "Saturday Movies," and the "Sunday Movies") that had lasted for five years or longer. In the 1960–70 decade, between 29% and 46% of the programs on the networks in any given season failed to return to the air the following year.

(E)   A succession of more recent studies have examined the characterizations and action of TV programming as reflections of the national culture and expressions of the value system upon which television is itself a powerful influence. These analyses continue to find television presenting an assortment of people and settings that are atypical in their representation of the American scene.

Although Negroes were a rarity in TV's early days, the progress of the civil-rights movement in the early 1960's brought more of them on to the air. At least one Negro appeared in 21% of the half-hour programs monitored by Ernest Kinoy and Rita Morley in November–December, 1967, and reported to the New York City Commission on Human Rights.

A study of the portrayal of working-class characters in prime-time television was made by Frank Gentile and S. M. Miller in 1956. Only seven characters out of 122 could be identified as belonging to the "working class"; all were men, spoke poor English, and were rarely shown in a favorable light. Melvin De Fleur analyzed a sampling of the TV output of four channels in a Midwestern town during late afternoons and evenings on weekdays and between 10 A.M. and 11 P.M. on weekends. He found that the characters shown on TV were characteristically drawn from high-status occupations, though about a third were connected with law enforcement. Occupational roles tended to conform to stereotypes, but individuals in high-status roles were portrayed as more handsome, intelligent, and socially adept than those in less prestigious occupations. Power was associated with occupational status: foremen, ranch owners, and judges ranked at the top. A high proportion of the women shown on TV had occupations and were gainfully employed.

The most comprehensive study of television programming content in recent years was conducted by George Gerbner for the National Commission on the Causes and Prevention of Violence and later repeated for the National Institute of Mental Health. The study covered the period 1967–69 and included all television plays, feature films, and cartoon shows broadcast on the three networks in prime time and on Saturday morning: a total of 281 plays and 182 program hours. Three-fourths of the leading characters were single, male Americans, mature and upper class, and in the prime of life (a profile that is in interesting contrast to that which is most typical of those people who watch TV the most). Only 10% of the leading characters were children, adolescents, and old people, and 4 out of 10 had no visible occupation. In 1969 lower-class characters represented only 2% of the total. 95% of the American characters shown were white, while only 35% of the characters of other nationalities were white.

Otto Larsen, Louis Gray, and Gerald Fortis analyzed 18 prime-time network programs in 1963, including shows classified as interesting either to adults or to children or to both children and adults. They categorized the goals of the characters in these programs (reflected in their words and actions) as related to property, self-preservation, affection, sentiment, power and prestige, and to satisfaction of psychological drives. They also classified the methods by which the characters achieved goals as legal, nonlegal, economic, organizational, escape from the situation, and chance or accidental. Relating the goals to the methods, they concluded that these were roughly similar for programs directed toward children and for those aimed at adults. While the goals of characters on TV programs tended to be socially approved, they were often obtained by methods that were socially disapproved. The conclusion was that both children's and adults' programs projected the same view of a world in which unconventional and often underhanded methods were better instruments for achieving success than conventional means.

Since it is action that evokes the audience's interest, and since struggle is the essence of action, the subject of violence as a staple feature of television has aroused continuing concern. TV's nightly projection of violence as a common expression in human relationships has been linked to other tendencies toward increased violence in the culture.

The *Christian Science Monitor* assigned staff members to watch network television in the first week of the fall 1968 broadcast season. In 74½ hours of programming they found 254 incidents of violence or threatened violence, and 71 killings or suicides. It should be noted that violence and sex are prominent in the printed media as well as in movies and TV. Herbert Otto, comparing magazine content in the early 1950's and again ten years later, found a significant increase in the amount of violence and sex. He also found a substantial increase in the visibility of paperback books featuring such themes. Gerbner found about 8 out of 10 TV plays containing violence, with about 5 violent episodes per play and 8 per hour. Of the 762 leading characters, 7 out of 10 were involved in violence in 1967; 6 out of 10 in 1969.

While the overall level of violence remained the same by Gerbner's counts, there was a steady reduction in killings. In 1967, 2 out of 10 leading characters were involved in killings; by 1969 there was only 1 in 20, showing very clearly the conscious efforts being made by the broadcasters to reduce the level of violence following the assassinations of Senator Robert Kennedy and Martin Luther King.

Although there were fewer leading characters committing violence in 1969 than in 1967, there was no change in the overall amount of violence in which they were engaged. In about half of the violent episodes a weapon was used, and about half of the violence shown in cartoons was of a lighter, comic nature. Half the violence in 1967 and 1968 resulted in casualties, but only 1/6 of it in 1969. In fact, only half of all the violent episodes showed any painful after-effects. Violence tended to occur in settings that were remote and set in a time other than the present. Among the characters involved in violence, 5 out of 10 committed violence themselves, but 6 out of 10 suffered violence. On the other hand, a leading character was twice as likely to be a killer as to be killed himself.

Gerbner reported that a substantial proportion of TV violence occurred in cartoons. Of the 95 cartoon plays studied for the period, only 4 did *not* contain any violence. The average cartoon hour had nearly 6 times the rate of violence shown by the average hour of adult TV drama and 12 times that of the average TV movie hour. In 1969, cartoons represented 39% of all the programs analyzed, but 53% of all violent episodes. The psychological effect of "comic" violence in cartoons addressed to the juvenile audience obviously cannot be equated with that of more realistic representations of violence in TV drama and films watched by both children and adults.

(F)   Charles Winick found that of the censors' deletions, comments, and changes in scripts, 21% were related to sex; 12% to violence; 11% to advertising; 9% to racial or ethnic reasons; 8% to the spoofing of serious matters (such as mental illness); 8% to antisocial matters; 7% to special interests (such as disparaging references to the blind); 5% to religion; 5% to crude remarks; but only 1% to political matters.

4. Patterns of Television Viewing

(A)   The first comprehensive national survey of the American public's attitudes toward TV was conducted in 1960 for the Bureau of Applied Social Research. The survey, conducted by the National Opinion Research Center and Elmo Roper Associates, was taken of 2,500 persons over 18. The results were reported by Gary Steiner in his monograph *The People Look at Television,* which provides a fascinating look at television as it reached maturity.

Three out of five persons named television among the new inventions of the past 25 years that had done the most to make their lives more enjoyable. (The runner-up was cars, named by over one-third of the men, and washers, named by one-half the women.) Both men and women named TV ahead of any other appliance and invention as the one they would most miss if the clock were turned back. Only 5%, however, were less willing to do without a television set for several months than to do without a car, refrigerator, newspaper, or telephone. (In 1959 a Bruskin study found that the public named the television set ahead of the refrigerator and the stove as "one of the three most important things you have in your home.")

A comparison of TV, radio, magazines, and newspapers found TV rated far and away the most entertaining and as the medium that "creates the most interest in new things going on." Most people said it "seems to be getting better all the time" and "has the hardest job to do." It ranked roughly equal with newspapers on fairness and as "most important to you" and "most educational." Newspapers were far ahead on "complete news coverage" and also outranked TV on "doing the most for the public." The higher the ratings of television were, the lower the educational level of the respondents, and vice versa. Steiner concluded that the public at large found TV relaxing and entertaining and was not very critical of it. Viewing was regarded as a "lazy" activity, reading as an interesting one.

In a 1970 national survey which repeated many of Steiner's questions, Robert Bower found that television's position as a news medium had substantially strengthened during the decade of the 1960's. In 1960, 19% of the people named television for "the most complete news coverage," and 59% named newspapers. By 1970 the two media were neck and neck, 41% for television and 39% for newspapers. Television also went into the lead on "the fairest, most unbiased news" and even led radio 54% to 39% as the medium that "brings you the latest news most quickly." Bower, however, found an increase from 24% in 1960 to 41% in 1970 in the proportion who say that television "seems to be getting worse all the time." This was paralleled by declines in the proportions who rated television as "interesting," "relaxing," "for me," "important," "lots of fun," "exciting," "wonderful," etc. Although public attitudes toward television seem to have deteriorated when viewed in these general terms, the overall comparison of viewing habits and program preferences fail to show many important changes in the course of the decade.

Bower's 1970 survey, when compared with Steiner's 1970 study, concluded that while older people expressed themselves as personally more satisfied with television than younger people, there was no evidence that a new "television generation" had emerged with attitudes toward the medium that were significantly different from its predecessors.

A 1971 Harris survey found that 37% considered television better than ten years ago; 32% found it worse.

A series of studies conducted for the Television Information Office by the Roper research organization has found television steadily increasing its lead over newspapers as the medium people cite as their primary source of news "about what's going on in the world today." (TV news, in contrast to the local slant of newspapers, tends to be more oriented toward national and international events.) In 1959 newspapers were cited by 57%, television by 51%, and radio by 34%. By 1971 the proportions were: television 60%, newspapers 48%, radio 23%. The proportion naming television as the medium they would most want to keep, if forced to choose just one, went from 41% in 1959 to 58% in 1971, while newspapers went from 31% to 19%.

A 1964 study in West Germany asked: "If there were conflicting reports of the same event in the newspaper, on the radio, and on television, which would you believe?" 12% said the newspapers, 9% radio, and 42% television. 37% took no position.

A 1969 study by Sindlinger and Company found television rated two to one over newspapers on "fairness and objectivity" by a national telephone sampling. Newspapers and TV were neck and neck on "most thorough coverage," but television was rated by 47%, as against 35% for newspapers, as the news medium that people said they "most depend on." 66% named television for "fastest coverage," compared with 23% for radio and 7% for newspapers. Television was consistently rated higher among women, newspapers among men. Walter Cronkite was by far the favorite news commentator, substantially ahead of Huntley and Brinkley, his rivals at the time of the study.

A more involved national study by Opinion Research Corporation in 1967 had respondents rate 120 news items (culled in equal numbers from the four major media) for "the best way to find out." For the average item, newspapers were selected by 59%, TV by 29%, radio by 4%, and magazines by 8%.

The contradiction between this (newspaper-sponsored) study's findings and those of other (often TV-sponsored) research is readily explained. Questions framed in a general way evoked TV's associations with great news events, while specific questions about more typical news items produced responses that reflected TV's more limited coverage of the full range of daily news.

A survey made in 1969 by Martin Goldfarb and Associates for the Canadian Senate Committee on Mass Media found that while 43% of a national cross-section of Canadians said they were most interested in local news, and 55% in national and international news, only 30% wanted to see more local news, and 64% wanted more of the national and international. Newspapers were rated as the most important local news medium by 39%, TV by 25%, and radio by 33%, but for international news only 24% picked newspapers, 12% radio, and 56% TV. (The pattern for national news was similar.) Nine out of ten felt that media can affect people's thinking or way of life, and three-fourths of these named TV as the medium that had the greatest effect. Newspapers, however, were named by margins up to three to one over television as the best source of information on such matters as places to shop, consumer goods, taxes, economics, legal changes, labor, and national politics.

TV was rated by a majority (compared to radio and newspapers) as the medium "easiest to get information from," "most relaxing," and as one that "makes you forget," while a majority rated the newspaper first as "requiring most energy and concentration from the user," and as the medium that "makes you think," "gets below the surface of the news," "digs for the truth," and "tells the whole story." While radio was described as most immediate and newspapers as most private and personal, television was described as most exciting, influential, and sensational. People tended to turn to newspapers for facts, background, and news interpretation, but to TV for special events, entertainment, and relaxation. Two out of three chose television as the most powerful medium in its ability to affect people's thinking or way of life. While people were more reluctant to lose TV for a week than to go without newspapers or radio, TV and newspapers were evenly matched when people were asked what medium they were most reluctant to lose for a year.

A national survey of 2000 Americans made for the Bureau of Advertising by Opinion Research Corporation in 1971, found that 45% named television and 51% newspapers as the place "to find out all there is about...news you are very much interested in." Newspapers' lead grew to 35%, against 18% for TV, when the public was asked where they were "most likely to get enough facts" to fully understand very complicated news. The same study found 29% of the people saying they were watching TV more now than a few years ago and 29% saying they were watching less, while 40% said the amount of their viewing was unchanged. The people who reported more newspaper reading, however, were twice as many as those who reported less.

(B)   In retrospect, it no longer seems valid to lump all other media together in comparing their consumption with that of TV. When people are grouped into five categories of equal size (quintiles) according to the total amount of TV viewing they do, their total use of print media does not seem to be related to their viewing habits:

TABLE 95

TV-Viewing and Reading Habits

(Source: W. R. Simmons, 1970)

Amount of TV Viewing	Percentage Who Read One or More Newspapers Yesterday	Average Number of Magazines Read
Top 20%	78%	3.9
Second 20	80	3.9
Third 20	80	4.0
Fourth 20	80	4.0
Lowest 20	77	3.7

One could, of course, probe deeper to establish the fact that there were qualitative differences between the kinds of publications read by light and heavy viewers. The aggregate figures on magazine readership reflect the wide distribution of *TV Guide, Reader's Digest,* and *Life,* whose orientation is in the same tradition of mass popular culture as is that of the TV networks.

The concept of "media-mindedness" may better be narrowed down to that of its opposite: "media-avoidance." Below the level of the people for whom reading is a difficult or impossible task and who devote a correspondingly large amount of time to the broadcast media, are those who might be characterized as media isolates; many of them are the people who live alone, those in institutions, the eccentric and feeble-minded, and those whose extreme poverty or rural isolation make the media virtually inaccessible.

(C)   During 1970, Nielsen reports that the average television household had a set on for 5 hours and 59 minutes a day (for a seven-day average). The increase in set usage since the mid-1950's can be accounted for by the lengthening of the broadcast day, which made programming available almost everywhere from early morning until late at night. (In TV's earlier era many stations maintained only a restricted broadcast day.) The increase in set usage was also translated into longer hours of actual individual viewing. Nielsen estimated that in October-November, 1969 (heavier than average viewing months), the average housewife watched 29 hours weekly, the average man of the house 22 hours.

The expansion of viewing time occurred in Britain as well as in the United States. William Belson reports that the time given to television by adult viewers grew from an average of 13 hours a week in 1953 to over 18 hours a week in 1967. In U.S. cities with a high rate of unemployment in 1970, male viewing showed a substantial increase, especially in daylight hours, compared with similar cities with a low unemployment rate.

(D)   In 1971 Simmons reported that 77.5% of the adults over 18 read a newspaper "yesterday," and 33% of these readers read 2 or more dailies. The average time spent for each paper read, according to a 1967 study by Opinion Research Corporation, is 37 minutes. Reading time cannot properly be compared with viewing or listening time as an index of what is communicated.

(E)   The 1970 Simmons survey found the typical adult of 18 and over reporting 3.5 hours of viewing a day (averaging weekdays and weekends). But the heaviest-viewing quintile watched 6.4 hours a day, over 10 times as much as the lightest-viewing quintile, who viewed 0.6 hours. Altogether, the top 20% of viewers accounted for 42% of all viewing hours, the next 20% accounted for 25%, the middle 20% accounted for 18%, the next 20% accounted for 11%, and the lightest-viewing 20% did only 4% of the total viewing hours. There was just as much variability among men as among women, as the next table shows.

TABLE 96

Average Number of Viewing Hours per Week

(Source: W. R. Simmons, 1970)

Amount of Viewing	Total Adults	Men	Women
Top 20%	44.5	39.3	50.5
Second 20	27.3	23.9	30.6
Third 20	18.7	16.6	21.6
Fourth 20	12.4	10.3	14.0
Lowest 20	4.3	3.1	5.2
Total	21.6	18.7	24.3

In TV's growth period, the social differences between heavy and light viewers reflected, in part, the social differences between people who owned television sets and those who did not. Poor people, childless and older people, and rural people were the last to acquire TV and were, therefore, still included among the light viewers or nonviewers when the original text of this book was prepared. For this reason, the heaviest viewing at that time appeared to occur at the lower-middle-class level. But as TV ownership acquired virtual universality, some of the latecomers turned out to take the greatest advantage of it. The presence of the small percentage of non-TV owners accounts for the fact that viewing dips slightly when family income falls below the $3,000 mark and among people who have never gone beyond a grade-school education. But in general the evidence clearly supports the conclusion that the amount of viewing time is in indirect proportion to social status, as measured by education and income. (Kent Geiger and Robert Sokol concluded from a study of 500 Boston televiewers that the very fact that heavy TV viewing was considered socially undesirable made it a secret delight for many middle-class viewers.)

There are only minor differences in the amount of viewing in different geographic regions, although the proportion of the population in metropolitan and rural areas does vary from one to the other. Older people watch substantially more TV than younger adults. Single, widowed, and divorced individuals tend to view less than married people; they are more likely to go out for recreation and sociability. The evidence is shown in the next series of tables from the 1970 W. R. Simmons media-survey report.

TABLE 97

Weekly Average Viewing Time by Adults

(Source: W. R. Simmons, 1970)

Total Average Hours	21.5
Ages	
18–19	17.4
20–24	19.6
25–34	21.3
35–49	20.5
50–64	23.1
65+	24.5
Education	
Postgraduate	15.4
College graduate	17.3
Some college	18.5
High-School Graduates only	21.7
Some High School	23.8
No High School	23.5
Household Income	
$25,000 and over	16.3
$15,000–$24,999	17.6
$10,000–$14,999	19.6
$ 8,000–$ 9,999	20.7
$ 5,000–$ 7,999	23.5
$ 3,000–$ 4,999	25.5
Under $3,000	23.8

TABLE 98

Television Viewing by Age Group
(Sunday to Saturday 8:00 A.M. — 1:00 P.M.)

(Source: W. R. Simmons, 1970)

Men

Amount of Viewing	18–24	25–34	35–49	50–64	65 & Over
Top 20%	14%	15%	17%	26%	31%
Second 20	13	18	21	21	27
Third 20	28	23	19	18	12
Fourth 20	18	24	21	19	15
Lowest 20	27	20	22	16	15
Total	100%	100%	100%	100%	100%

Women

Amount of Viewing	18–24	25–34	35–49	50–64	65 & Over
Top 20%	16%	24%	17%	19%	24%
Second 20	14	18	18	24	25
Third 20	21	19	24	19	16
Fourth 20	23	19	21	22	14
Lowest 20	26	20	20	16	21
Total	100%	100%	100%	100%	100%

TABLE 99

Television Viewing by Family Income
(Adults 18 and Over)

(Source: W. R. Simmons, 1970)

Amount of Viewing	$15,000 & Over	$10,000– $14,999	$5,000– $9,999	Under $5,000
Top 20%	11%	15%	22%	27%
Second 20	15	19	22	20
Third 20	24	22	19	17
Fourth 20	25	23	19	16
Lowest 20	25	21	18	20
Total	100%	100%	100%	100%

TABLE 100

Television Viewing by Education
(Adults 18 and Over)

(Source: W. R. Simmons, 1970)

Amount of Viewing	Some College & College Graduate	High-School Graduate	Less Than High-School Graduate
Top 20%	13%	18%	25%
Second 20	16	21	21
Third 20	22	23	17
Fourth 20	23	20	19
Lowest 20	26	18	18
Total	100%	100%	100%

TABLE 101

Television Viewing by Marital Status
(Adults 18 and Over)

(Source: W. R. Simmons, 1970)

Amount of Viewing	Married	Single, Widowed, Separated, Divorced
Top 20%	21%	17%
Second 20	22	16
Third 20	20	20
Fourth 20	20	20
Lowest 20	17	27
Total	100%	100%

Television viewing of Negroes is slightly higher than that of whites. It is 24.4 hours a week for non-whites, according to Simmons, compared to 21.1 hours for whites. (As the Introduction indicates, this difference is largely a reflection of the social-class differential between Negroes and whites.) Bradley Greenberg and Brenda Dervin compared the media habits of 131 low-income Negro respondents, 150 low-income whites, and about 200 individuals in a cross-section of the telephone-owning public in Lansing, Michigan, in 1967. Although the low-income people who were interviewed watched substantially more TV and were more favorable toward TV than the public in general, low-income Negroes and whites were very similar in their viewing habits.

The socio-economic correlates of television viewing were evident in Communist as well as in Western society. A study by Boris Firsov of the audience for Soviet TV found that, among a Leningrad sample of 1,900 people, in most program categories ratings declined as education increased.

(F)   While audiences are generally greater in winter than in summer, climatic variations can cause exceptions to this pattern. In San Francisco, for instance, the audience for the "Beverly Hillbillies" was 50% higher in August, 1969, than in January, 1970, while in Cleveland the summer audience for "Gunsmoke" was only half the winter size. In January, "Gunsmoke" had a rating of 10 in San Francisco, but of 24 in St. Louis. In Columbus, Georgia, a two-channel market, the soap opera "Love of Life" had a rating of 10 (for a cost to the advertiser of $2.86 per 1000 households reached), while in one-channel Lafayette, Indiana, the same program had a rating of 4 (and a cost per 1000 homes of $24.00).

(G)   R. H. Bruskin reported in May, 1968, that 65% of the men and 56% of the women in a national study said that "there are one or more TV programs they enjoy so much that they almost feel they have to watch them week after week." The shows mentioned were primarily high-rated popular entertainment shows ("Bonanza," "Peyton Place," "The Dean Martin Show") and soap operas ("As the World Turns").

(H)   In 1968 H. W. Land Associates made an analysis of Nielsen data for the National Association of Broadcasters. They found no difference in the amount of set usage in areas with varying degrees of television choice.

Number of Stations	Percentage of TV Homes Viewing in Prime Time
2	58
3	60
4	60
5	59
6	59
7	61
8	58

(Incidentally, an analysis made by Pulse in 1966 found the same to be true of radio. Markets were grouped into those with fewer than 5 AM stations, those with 6 to 10, and those with 11 or more. Pulse concluded that tune-in levels were unrelated to the number of stations.) Herman W. Land also analyzed what happened to viewing levels after a third VHF channel was added to 2 existing channels. In 3 of the 6 examples there was a drop or no change at all. (A 1971 Nielsen analysis *did* find that in large families there was some increase in viewing when there were more choices—reflecting the fractionation of the multiset audience to which I referred in the Introduction.)

The inelasticity of TV audience size has been found in other countries as well. The Canadian Broadcasting Corporation, looking at viewing habits in seven cities before and after a new, privately operated station came on the air, found that there was no change in total viewing hours, though the government-owned station got a reduced share of audience in every case as a result of the new competition.

After Independent Television came to the United Kingdom the amount of viewing increased as the amount of broadcast time increased. As the broadcast week lengthened from 17 to 35 hours of evening programming, average nighttime viewing per person increased from 7 to 12. When the broadcast week stabilized, so did viewing time. As Land observes, "during any given year of the upsurge, the amount of viewing in band one to three (both BBC and ITA) was the same as the amount in BBC-only homes ... Those who could (and usually did) watch more than one channel did not watch television for any greater length of time than those who could receive only one channel."

During the Spring of 1970 Granada Television went off the air in Lancashire, England, as the result of a strike. During the four weeks of the strike, viewers in that area were left only with the option of watching the BBC channels; about half had access to only a single channel, and half could receive both Channel 1 and BBC 2 (which presented highbrow or quality programming). During the strike, BBC 1 audiences increased by about 80%, but the audience was consistently 15 points lower than might have normally been expected for that period. BBC 2 did not increase its ratings. When the strike ended, Granada and its BBC competition returned to their previous levels of audience, and total viewing was back where it would have been.

(I)   Recent statistics show that summer reruns average about two-thirds of the audience that is attracted during their original winter showings. Of those who see the average summer rerun, 45% are watching it for the second time.

(J)   Who watches the TV news? During the 1969–70 season, an analysis of Simmons data for the average evening found that 12% of those 18 to 34 had watched one or more of the early-evening network newscasts, compared with 36% of those 50 and over. A study of the TV news program viewing pattern in Britain (by Andrew Ehrenberg and I. R. Haldane) found that there was no special pattern of viewing the news; it was a direct and randomized reflection of the overall amount of viewing. This absence of a special following for news would not be duplicated in the United States, where the range of simultaneous viewing choices is greater than in the United Kingdom and the viewing pattern more complex.

An analysis was made by the American Research Bureau (for Katz TV) of February and March, 1967, ratings reports for 279 stations in the top 100 markets. Their analysis indicates that the major factors affecting ratings of early-evening local newscasts are network affiliation, starting time, and length. CBS and NBC affiliates came out virtually identical. There were minor differences by time zone. Average ratings were directly proportionate to the number of stations in the market. In a two-station market, the average share was about one-half; in a three-station market one-third; in a four-station market one-fourth; and in stations with five or more markets, it was under one-fifth. The later the starting time of the early-evening local newscast, the higher the rating. Half-hour newscasts outrated the longer and shorter newscasts. Local evening newscasts following a network show rated slightly higher.

An analysis made by MacManus, John and Adams in 1968 found that TV specials tended to attract light viewers of above-average education and income. A comparison of the ratings performance of news specials with the regular programming they replaced during the 1966–67 broadcast season, found a highly variable record, depending on the individual program. The specials tended to get a below-average rating, though a few did nearly as well as the regular feature.

The average "special" of particular merit attracts only a fraction of the audience watching television. A much-heralded four-hour Africa program, produced at a great loss by ABC, drew only 15% of the homes watching TV.

In general, documentaries on emerging nations (probably typical of most special public-affairs programs) drew audiences less than half those of the typical entertainment program in the same time periods. Nielsen does not report ratings on nonsponsored programs (which most special documentaries are) unless these are specially ordered.

A 1960 study by WHIO-TV in Dayton, Ohio, found that Sunday was preferred to other days of the week for "public-service" programs, thereby demonstrating that people tend to prefer what they are accustomed to getting.

John Robinson and James Swinehart point out that a TV interview with Walter Lippmann, drawing only 10% of the available audience, is still reaching more people than read an issue of *Time* magazine, and that most of them are not the *Time*-reading type.

The composition of the television audience reflects the daily time cycles of children, full-time housewives, and working adults. This means, as the text points out, that there are rarely startling differences to be found in the characteristics of viewers for shows broadcast in prime time and aimed at the general family audience. Viewing preferences, in contrast to actual viewing patterns, are far more responsive to social variations in taste. A 1965 TvQ analysis shows, for example, that "enthusiasm" for Westerns such as "Bonanza" and "Gunsmoke" was about 50% higher among people with under $5,000 income than among those earning over $10,000, while a comedy serial about a schoolteacher, "Mr. Novak," had about 20% greater "enthusiasm" from those with over $10,000 income than from those who earned less.

The same analysis showed that programs such as the "Walt Disney Show," the "Dick Van Dyke Show," the "Bell Telephone Hour," and "CBS Reports" ranked high in popularity among people of higher education, though they did not show up among the favorites of those with less schooling. It must be remembered that since people with higher education

and income watch less television, they are disproportionately underrepresented in the audiences of even
those programs that are most popular among them.

When we look at the percentages of homes at
different socio-economic levels actually viewing programs of different types, we continue to find the
expected variations in popularity. The next table
groups families by the education of the household
head. It shows that dramatic, mystery, and situation-
comedy shows principally appeal to the middle
levels of the population, where the head of the family
never went beyond high school. Variety shows increase their audiences as the social scale lowers, while
feature films have more appeal as the scale rises.
News and information programs reach the same proportions of viewing households at different educational levels. (It must be noted in passing that the
typical size and composition of the audience of individuals for different kinds of programs may not be at
all the same in different social classes, but this is
obscured in the ratings that show set usage.)

TABLE 102

How TV-Household Ratings Vary by Education and Program Type
(October, 1966)

(Source: A. C. Nielsen)

| | Homes Reached, by Education of Household Head | | | |
	At least Some College	High-School Graduate	Some High School	Grade School Only
General Drama	15.2	21.3	17.3	14.5
Mystery Drama	17.2	20.3	18.3	13.7
Situation Comedy	16.5	19.2	20.5	17.2
Western Drama	13.7	20.3	18.9	19.1
Variety	15.9	17.9	19.2	21.2
Feature Films	24.1	23.1	22.4	16.7
Informational	11.4	11.2	11.1	11.0

William Hazard interviewed 430 adult TV viewers in Austin, Texas, in 1966, and related their viewing
habits to their performance on a series of psychological tests. He found low social status to be linked with
symptoms of high anxiety as well as with a low level
of cultural participation (as measured by the reading
of books, visits to concerts, museums, and the like).
Low status was also associated with a preference for
television programming that dealt in fantasy. The
implication of this study is that the fictional fantasy
of television allays the anxieties of people at the bottom of the social heap, which helps explain their heavy
viewing. But the heavy viewing also reflects their lack
of cultural resources as well as their resistance to
active participation in the real world. The findings of
this research therefore tend to support the "catharsis"
theory that has been advanced to suggest that fictional
TV violence allays rather than provokes violence in
the real world.

Michael Maccoby, a social psychologist, interviewed mothers of 500 high-school children of Palo
Alto, California, and classified them as either "life
loving" or "death loving." Of the former group, 73%
were light viewers of television, watching fewer than
eight hours a week, and 6% were heavy viewers, watching fifteen hours or more. Among those whom he
classified as "death loving," only 39% were light
viewers and 30% were in the heavy viewing group.
He concluded that "people [who] feel lonely, bored,
and dead inside . . . seek TV for vicarious thrills."

L. I. Pearlin found that individuals who felt frustrated on their jobs were most likely to be viewers of
"escapist" TV shows. A master's thesis by James Smith
(reported by William Catton) found violent programs
preferred by individuals with poor driving records. A
1968 Simmons analysis found that Negro men were
80% more likely than white men to view violent pro-

grams. Unskilled workers were about 150% more likely to view them than were professional and managerial types. Men who had not completed high school were well over twice as likely to view violent shows as men who had been to graduate school. The addiction to the fantasy of televised violence was clearly in direct and inverse relationship to social-class position, and it was greatest among the heaviest viewers of TV.

James Carey, reanalyzing a national survey, conducted in 1963, of over 5,000 households, found Negroes reporting more weekend viewing than whites, and showing decidedly less preference for programs that depicted the intimacy of family life rather than "action." Alan Fletcher compared program preferences of about 250 Negro and 200 white children and found that Negro preferences were greater for those programs in which the main character was without a husband or wife.

The popularity of individual television personalities shows wide variations among different age groups of the population. A study of 2,400 viewers conducted by TvQ in 1968 found, for example, that two Negro performers, Bill Cosby and Sidney Poitier, were among the top 5 among people aged 12–34 but not among older persons. Familiarity with a performer was not a good indicator of his popularity.

Older people show more of a preference for comedies, Westerns, quiz, and variety shows and for news and information programs, and they are less apt to watch feature films. Children watch comedies and Westerns more than other types of shows, and teenagers like films on TV. (33% of the teenagers but only 15% of the adults questioned in a 1969 Harris Survey were classified as having a high preference for media violence.) An analysis of prime-time television-program ratings made by Foote, Cone and Belding in 1969 found that the average program had a rating

¼ higher among women over 50 than among those between 18 and 34.

TABLE 103

How Average Audience Ratings Vary
by Age Group and Program Type
(January, 1971)

(Source: A. C. Nielsen)

Types of (Prime-Time) Programs	Children 2–11	Teens 12–17	Men 18–49	Men 50 +	Women 18–49	Women 50 +
General Drama	7.1	11.9	11.1	12.1	15.2	14.6
Mystery Drama	9.5	12.2	13.4	14.6	14.5	15.3
Situation Comedy	14.6	12.6	9.7	12.2	12.2	15.3
Western Drama	12.9	13.2	14.0	26.7	15.5	26.8
Variety	7.6	8.5	10.7	17.3	12.1	21.0
Feature Films	9.6	16.3	16.6	9.8	16.2	11.9
Informational	4.6	5.1	6.5	15.2	6.9	15.4

TABLE 104

How the Proportion of Older Viewers Varies by Program Type

(Source: A. C. Nielsen, 1970)

	% over 50 (of adults 18 and over)
Total U.S. population	37%
All prime-time viewers	41%
Audiences for:	
Feature films	23%
Suspense and mystery	37
General drama	40
Situation comedy	40
Quiz and audience participation	46
Variety	49
Western drama	54

The Introduction has already made the point that the inexorable trend toward increased choice of channels and more sets in the home will lead to more individual, and hence more differentiated, viewing. This in turn is bound to divide the audience. The average minute rating for a prime-time network show had dropped to 17.0 by the 1969–70 season.

The most important new development in changing viewing patterns is the parallel growth of multiset and color-TV households. The initial effect of both these developments was easily interpreted as a great boost to total viewing. An early (1959) study by NBC of 4,000 color-TV homes and a matched 4,000 black-and-white homes found that the average color program rating was 80% higher in the color-TV homes, and there were a greater number of viewers per home.

In 1962, the American Research Bureau found that in Omaha, Nebraska, color programs reached nearly twice the audience in color-TV homes as in black-and-white homes; moreover, the one channel that broadcast in color at that time was getting, in color homes, a 44% higher rating for its black-and-white programs (exhibiting once more the tendency of the audience to carry over from program to program). Nielsen states that the addition of a color set yields nearly ten more hours of set usage per week; a second black-and-white set adds nearly thirteen hours to total set usage weekly. In 1971 color-TV owners spent 7% more daytime viewing hours on weekdays and 24% more on weekends.

The overall evidence requires some differentiation by program type, since for some shows the addition of color provides more of a new dimension than for others. In 1965 "Bonanza" secured a 56 rating in color-TV homes, while it was getting ratings in the mid-30's from the general audience. W. R. Simmons reported in 1967 that situation comedies, which at that time were all televised in black and white, showed a 36% lower level of viewing among women in color-TV households, while audience-participation and science-fiction programs had ⅓ higher viewing among men in those homes.

The complex relationships between color- and multiple-set ownership, demographic patterns, and social status give some indication of future trends.

A special analysis of data from the 1970 W. R. Simmons & Associates Research report provides comparisons of people living in black-and-white and color households, and of those in single and multi-set households. Information on set ownership and personal characteristics came from interviews spread between November, 1968, through October, 1969, among a probability sample of 15,322 people 18 years of age and over throughout the continental U.S. Television-viewing data were obtained from a self-administered personal diary filled out for a consecutive two-week period (between Oct. 12 and Nov. 15, 1969) by each respondent in a subsample of 6,834. This personal diary is a more sensitive measuring instrument than the family diary used by the major local syndicated TV-rating services.

Among people in color-TV families, 63% have more than one TV set at home, compared with 30% of those with only black-and-white TV. (Looking at it another way, of those with a single set in the house, 22% have only a color TV, while among those in multiset families, 51% have a color set. One-third of those in multiset households have 3 sets, making the average number of sets in those households 2.3, compared with the U.S. average of 1.5.) When there is a color TV at home but no children under 18, there is more than one set in 53% of the cases. This proportion rises to 78% in families with 3 children or more.

The desire for color TV, or for the second set, should obviously be greatest among those who are most TV-oriented and who were the heaviest viewers to begin with. Yet adult viewing in color-TV households is about the same as in black-and-white households, and viewing in households with more than one set is about the same as in households with only a single set. (The hours of weekly viewing covered all seven days, so that Saturday and Sunday contribute disproportionately to the total.)

TABLE 105

Viewing Hours per Week by Color and Number of Sets

(Source: W. R. Simmons, 1970)

	Men	*Women*	*Total Adults*
Color	19.1	24.9	22.2
B & W	18.9	24.3	21.7
One-set	18.9	24.1	21.7
Multi-set	19.0	25.1	22.2

We might surmise that the pressure to acquire a second set is greater, the larger the size of the family and the greater the demand on the existing set. The next table shows this is indeed the case:

TABLE 106

Multiset Ownership by Presence of Children in the Family

(Source: W. R. Simmons, 1970)

	More Than One TV
No children under 18	33%
One to two children	49
Three or more children	50

Since children under 18 are most often found where the family head is between the ages of 35 and 49, it is not surprising that the proportion of multiset households is higher in this group than where the family head is younger or older.

TABLE 107

Color and Multiset Ownership by Age of Family Head
(Source: W. R. Simmons, 1970)

	Color TV	More Than One TV
Under 35	32%	35%
35 to 49	38	55
50 and over	32	35

We might also assume that since the acquisition of an expensive color set or of any second set is a significant consumer expenditure, it would be linked to family income. The following table shows that color TV and the second set *are* more often found in families above the mid-point in income than in the lower-income brackets.

TABLE 108

Color and Multiset Ownership by Family Income
(Source: W. R. Simmons, 1970)

	Color TV	More Than One TV
Under $8,000	24%	26%
$8,000 and over	43	55

These findings might appear paradoxical in relation to our general knowledge of TV-viewing habits. As has been pointed out (and as in the case of radio in its heyday), the total time people spend watching television has been inversely related to their income and educational levels.

In the next table, we see that those with higher incomes watch less TV, regardless of whether or not they have color TV, and whether there is only one set at home or several.

TABLE 109

Viewing Hours per Week by Family Income
(Source: W. R. Simmons, 1970)

	Color	B&W	Multiset	One Set
Income under $8,000	25.9	24.3	26.5	24.0
Income over $8,000	20.5	18.6	20.4	18.2

A similar paradox may be seen when we look at viewing in multiset and one-set households according to the size of the family. We have already noted that the bigger the family the more likely it is to own color and the second set. But viewing among adults is *less* when there are children present, whether there is one set in the family or more than one. (Incidentally, the presence of children seems to have more effect in reducing the hours viewed by men than it does the hours viewed by women.)

TABLE 110

Viewing Hours per Week by Presence of Children under 18
(Source: W. R. Simmons, 1970)

	Multiset	One Set
No children	23.1	22.5
1 to 2 children	21.9	20.7
3 or more children	21.2	20.6

The same effect is visible when we look at the number of hours viewed by the age of the household head. Those 35 to 49 watch least, and those 50 and over (where there are least apt to be children under 18 present) view most.

TABLE 111

Viewing Hours per Week by Age of Household Head
(Source: W. R. Simmons, 1970)

	Multiset	One Set
18 to 34	21.8	20.3
35 to 49	21.1	19.4
50 and over	23.7	23.4

The evidence suggests that, as in the case of television's early years, the effects of color TV and of multiple-set ownership will become quite different as both phenomena become more extensive.

5.   TV Viewing in Its Social Setting

(A)   Toru Yamamoto's report on television's introduction into Japan notes: "In the initial stage of television service, those who jumped at the new invention in an attempt to use it for attracting customers were persons engaged in service trades, such as proprietors of restaurants and coffee shops. They put up signs at the entrances of their shops saying: 'Television playing.' These proprietors aimed at boosting business by attracting those who could not afford to buy television sets. Such restaurants and coffee shops were packed with customers, especially during professional wrestling shows."

In the early days of European television, viewing as a group activity became a major focus of interest for existing social clubs, and it also became the central purpose around which new clubs were created, especially in working-class, urban neighborhoods and in rural areas. In France, in the late 1950's, the "teleclubs" became a major social phenomenon and the subject of a UNESCO monograph.

In an effort to bring the fellahin into the mainstream of Egyptian life, the Egyptian government installed 1,000 communal television sets in village TV clubs to which farmers can belong by paying a token fee. In 1963, with 1,000,000 television sets registered in Poland, 12% were in villages, which held half the population. Farmers represented 5% of the individual TV-set owners, and rural TV clubs represented 8%. In a mail study of 1,030 rural TV clubs in Poland, Andrzej

Duma concluded that there were five times as many of these clubs as rural cinemas. Over half the clubs were located in villages that were close to larger towns. The longer television had been in an area, the greater the penetration of clubs to villages remote from the towns. Village schools accounted for one-third of the collectively owned TV sets. Other clubs were organized under the auspices of state and cooperative farms and machinery centers, of local social groups, and of workshops and factories.

Over half the clubs conducted other activities (entertainments and lectures) as well as providing a place to watch TV. The number of viewers per set ranged as high as 48, with Sunday by far the most popular viewing day and early evening the time of peak viewing on weekdays. Feature films were the most popular programming, with "a sensation crime story" in second place. Asked about the changes that had occurred under the influence of TV, one-fourth of the respondents referred to "better manners and human relations." One percent said that television increased "initiative for new forms of cultural and educational work." Some of the verbatim responses were highly revealing:

> "Boredom is passing away; men are visiting saloons less frequently."
> "I meet now at the TV set persons who used to spend their nights drinking vodka or wine."
> "Young people spend their time by the TV set; they do not stand on street corners as before."
> "Viewers' vocabulary has become richer."
> "Television brings individual farmers and workers from state and cooperative farms closer together. Local antagonism between the newcomers and old villagers is waning."
> "All people in the village have a feeling that they are linked with the wide world."

"The world seems closer to us and easier to understand. We see the life of people in other continents. On the TV screen we recognize state officials, scientists, famous men in Poland and abroad."

"Television brings a man closer to contemporary life."

"Television in the country is a revolution in a man's life; this is the end of the old world and the beginning of a new one. This is the end of prejudice and superstitions."

"Our workers came for the first time in contact with the theatre, concerts, music halls through television. Otherwise, they would never try to visit these places during their trips to town, considering them not worthwhile spending the money."

(B)   A survey made by A. J. Wood Research in 1965 among 620 persons in thirteen large cities found that 89% of the color sets were in the living room, compared with only 69% of the black-and-white sets. Portable (black-and-white) sets were more often found in bedrooms than in living rooms. When two sets were in use at the same time in a household, adults and children tended to split up. In fact, the opportunity for parents and offspring to watch separately was cited as an advantage of having a second set by those who had one; one in four said it prevented family arguments. One-fourth of the two-set families said both sets had been on simultaneously within the past 24 hours. A study made for the National Association of Broadcasters in 1966 found that upper-income (over $10,000) households (more likely to be equipped with dens, rumpus rooms, and furnished basements) were less likely to have a TV set in the living room (63%) than the public at large (77%). Although Negroes as a group have lower incomes than whites, they were less likely to have TV in the living room (67%) and more likely to have it in the bedroom. The explanation may be simply that in many lower-income families the living room serves multiple uses, including that of a children's bedroom.

(C)   Gary Steiner (1963) found that television owners named the evening as the part of the "typical weekday" that they most enjoyed, while nonowners were more likely to mention other times of the day. (About one-third of those who preferred the evening named TV as a reason for enjoying it.) In an interesting comparison of the reasons respondents gave for why "I" view and why "most people" view, Steiner concluded that the least acceptable reasons for watching TV were when there was nothing else to do, when viewers felt lonely, when they were reluctant to miss "something good," for escape, or just because everyone else was watching.

About three out of four parents queried by Steiner said they thought children were better off with television than without it. About one-third could give an actual example of where a child had benefited from TV, whereas one-fourth could cite a harmful instance. Better-educated people were more likely to cite TV's educational values for children, whereas those with less schooling stressed its baby-sitting aspect. Two out of five said they enforced rules over the children's TV viewing.

When Steiner asked a national cross section to "describe most of the television programs on the air today," twice as many voiced favorable comments as critical ones. Far more people wanted TV programs to be enteraining than to be "creative," tasteful, or serious. While Steiner concluded that "most people like most programs," he found that people who were most critical of TV in general were also most positive about the programs they specifically liked. Although a majority said TV did not have enough educational programs, a plurality also agreed that TV should "concentrate on providing the best entertainment possible" rather than "more in the way of providing informational material."

In a comparison of New York programs watched against programs available, Steiner found that entertainment accounted for about 67% of the hours presented and for 67% of those viewed, news for 20% of the time available but for 29% of the time watched, and public affairs for 15% of the air time and only 5% of the viewing. Steiner found that an overwhelming majority of viewers — including those who complained that TV did not offer enough information or food for thought — chose to watch entertainment rather than information programming when both were available at the same time.

A variety of other studies have examined the public's perceptions of TV's effects upon the society. An F.C.C. Broadcast Bureau analysis of complaints received for January, 1968, found 640 aimed at TV programs and 176 at commercials. Of the programming complaints, 160 were directed at specific shows and 88 were general criticisms. Seventy-five expressed concern with crime and violence; 63 complained of program cancellations; 19 alleged subversive Communist influences, and 3 charged cruelty to animals. Only 2 (in that month) criticized news coverage.

Seventy-five percent of a national cross section interviewed for the Eisenhower Commission in 1968 said that TV likely or possibly plays a part in making America a violent society, and 86% thought it might trigger violent acts from maladjusted or mentally unstable people. Only 34% thought it likely or possible that TV supported and strengthened traditional American values. A nationwide survey of 2,400 persons by R. H. Bruskin for the Television Information Office found that 21% of the public spontaneously named television as one of the causes of increased violence.

A survey in England by Research Services Limited found in 1964 that the public volunteered very little spontaneous criticism of TV violence but that a majority agreed when presented with a statement that there was too much violence on television. Before this, William Belson, working with BBC, got British viewers to state in group discussions and in correspondence some of their ideas about the effects of TV. The conclusions may be summarized as follows:

1. Television brings the family together in the home and makes its members cooperate in getting household jobs done; the interests and standards of family members become more alike as time passes. TV, however, makes members of the family less interested in each other and makes the house a quieter place. Television reduces sociability, visiting, and entertainment. But through TV, "The nation is being drawn together."

2. Television reduces interests, specifically cinema-going, reading, and attendance at football matches. It makes people passive and lazy. It reduces their initiative and imagination and leads to a feeling of futility or failure. On the positive side, it reduces boredom and irritability and improves thinking habits.

3. Television interferes with children's studies, though it is educational.

4. Television cuts down juvenile delinquency, but it spoils manners and lowers moral standards.

5. Television makes people lose sleep and is bad for the eyes.

Belson reports that a 22% drop in adult-education class attendance in London was blamed on television. He quotes a clergyman as saying, "Television is potentially one of the world's greatest dangers," and refers to another statement about bringing "the demoralizing influences of the music hall right into the home."

Belson's own notable series of researches on

TV's social effects in Britain began as a test of the validity of these ambivalent public assumptions. Among other things, he found that the effects of programs were often quite different from those intended by their producers. "The presentation of an American talking proudly about certain technical developments in his country was regarded by some members of an English audience as another case of American 'big talk.' A policeman shown being tough with a young criminal was regarded by some viewers as brutish. A woman, seeing some hot and enticing soup in a television advertisement by Bloggs, failed to think of it as Bloggs' soup but thought instead of the other brand she happened to have in the cupboard."

Belson reports on a before-and-after test of a TV series "Bon Voyage," "designed to teach the viewer, in an interesting way, some French words and phrases and some general facts of the kind likely to be of use to the English visitor to France." He found that the program did indeed produce a "slight increase in viewers' knowledge of the words and phrases and of the facts presented, but that this was accompanied by an increase in viewers' apprehensions about language difficulties and, in general, about visiting France."

(D)   The "family" nature of TV has always imposed certain restrictions on its content, though the standards of censorship have progressively eased to the point where off-color innuendoes are a commonly accepted feature of late-evening variety shows.

Robert D. Kasmire, an NBC vice-president, commented to *The New York Times* (April 29, 1968) on the effect of greater permissiveness in the mores: "When we got a letter of protest, we calculated it represented the feelings of thousands of viewers. Now we consider a complaint as the viewpoint of a single person. There are always some people who see a phallic symbol in the test pattern." Daniel Melnick, a producer, asks, "Which is more frank: a blue joke, a suggestive movie, or TV films of Marines fighting the Vietcong?" (As a matter of fact, a Canadian study of a TV documentary on Vietnam found many viewers disturbed by the war scenes, but 90% agreed that they should have been shown on the air.)

(E)   A national Harris survey conducted in 1968 for the Eisenhower Commission on Violence found that 43% of adults said they most often chose TV when they wanted to relax and get away from daily tensions; 19% chose books, and 12% radio. Among the teen-agers 32% chose TV, 26% radio, and 22% books.

(F)   A 1969 survey by the National Opinion Research Center classified a cross-section of the U.S. public on a "political activity" index and found that it ranged from a low of 1.3 hours for those who watched 4 or more hours daily to a high of 2.2 hours among those who watched 1 hour or less. (It was 1.5 hours among those who watched no TV, a group that included the marginal minority of nonowners, about whose special characteristics I have already commented.) The same pattern was found when viewing was examined within homogeneous racial, religious, economic, and educational groups: "The more hours a citizen spends in front of his television, the lower are his rates of (political) participation. This holds true even when all other social characteristics are held constant."

John Robinson's 1967 examination of trends in time budgeting leads him to conclude that visiting has stayed at the same level since 1950. Game-playing, dancing, eating out, and adult-education activities appeared to show increases.

William Belson conducted four separate surveys involving nearly 9,000 viewers and matched non-viewers in different locations in the United Kingdom during the mid-1950's. He concluded that television did not affect the overall amount of time that a family spent at home but somewhat altered its distribution during the day, slightly reducing the time at home during the morning and early afternoon and slightly increasing the time at other periods of the day. He concluded that while television tends to keep younger (and especially childless) couples at home together, it has reduced the degree to which large families are at home together. Belson found very small if "not negligible" differences in the home-centered activity of TV and non-TV owners. There was slightly less joint activity in the homes of the viewers in three out of the four surveys, but after several years of set ownership the differences tended to disappear.

Belson found that during the first year of set ownership, there was a sharp reduction (14%) in viewers' outside interests and that this was maintained during the second year. Thereafter, however, activities associated with these outside interests tend to move back toward the pretelevision level and to regain it after four to six years. The principal loss, Belson says, is in the most intensely pursued interests. "One of TV's effects has been to render interest more passive, for the loss in behavior is greater than that in 'strength of interest.'" Belson compared activities that related to interests featured in TV programming and other activities. He concludes that "treatment of interests in TV programs makes up to only a small degree for the reducing effect which the process of continued viewing exerts on such interests in that longer period when they are not being so featured."

Belson found a 21% drop during the first year of set ownership in "acts of initiative" that a separate sample had selected from everyday life. ("Like when my transport was running late, I used another means of transport," or "I corrected some member of the public who was acting badly.") These reverted to their original level after the first year.

Comparing matched samples of viewers and nonviewers in London in 1958 (at a time when TV was in three out of five British homes), Belson found a significant reduction in such activities as theater-going (down 44%) and balletgoing (down 21%). He also reported a 7% drop in social activities and in visits to places of historic importance. Home-oriented activities, gardening, and membership in associations and clubs underwent very little change. But television increased attendance at painting exhibits, particularly after a broadcast featured televised presentations of art.

(G)   A 1964 newspaper interview (cited by Tomoo Sato) reports on television's effects on the Japanese family: "'Even without television we have so little time for enjoying conversation together with all members of the family ... and yet, television has its own advantages,' says Mr. Yamaguchi. He mentions as an example that there are many husbands who come home early when there is a night baseball game on or a boxing match on the television screen. 'This can be easily seen if you go to a bar of medium or inferior class. The bar people do not expect from the outset that they can have many customers on a night when there is a telecast of a night baseball game.' After the baseball program on the television screen is over, the family may enjoy talking together at home. This is more likely when the wife and children also like baseball. They can discuss the game they have just watched on the screen, says Mr. Yamaguchi."

A survey of French worker and peasant tele-viewers was conducted in 1966 by Renaud Sainsaulieu and Annette Suffert (reported by Michel Crozier). Sixty percent of the respondents said that television had greatly changed their lives, though three out of four denied that it had influenced people's opinions. Many of the same individuals who denied that television could influence opinions reported that their own view of the world (particularly of foreign countries) was profoundly changed. Television was also considered to have expanded interpersonal contacts, and 57% said it was a useful subject of conversation. Many (24%) said they knew people who had been pushed toward more active participation in outside activities by TV. Forty percent of the workmen, however, and 59% of the peasants reported some difficulty in understanding broadcasts; the peasants largely complained of words and ideas that were over their heads, the workers complained that programs were sometimes directed at a different social class.

(H)   A study by Clara T. Appell of Brooklyn College found that 60% of the families sampled had changed their sleep schedules, and 55% their eating patterns. 78% reported using TV as a baby-sitter.

(I)   A 1964 study by Barbara Wand, of about 200 households in Ottawa, found that some two-thirds of the programs people watched were shows they had earlier indicated interest in watching. A sixth of the viewing was of programs in which they had not previously expressed interest, and another sixth was contrary to the program choice they had previously expressed.

In the days of the one-TV set family, at least, regularity of viewing seems to have depended on family consensus over the merits of various programs. Wand found that families did not tend to view programs as a group unless there were common program choices made by parents and children. When parents and children differed in their choices, the parents tended to dominate the final selections. When the conflict of interests was between either parent and a child, mothers and fathers seemed to have roughly equal say. But on the balance, the social structure of the individual family seemed to determine the form that television viewing actually took.

A study conducted by the Bureau of Advertising in 1965 found that in a good many cases, members of the television audience were "along for the ride" on a program selected by another family member. These individuals (17% of the total in a study of 1,003 people in three cities) were evidently less attentive than were those who had themselves selected the program (their recall of commercials on those programs was 50% less). The same kind of difference in attentiveness between "primary" and "secondary" viewers was found when people who were watching a program alone were divided into those who deliberately intended to watch it and those who said they were just flicking the dial or who had stayed with the station after watching another show. (Of the "primary" viewers 19% remembered the last commercial; of the other, 11%.)

A study by J. Walter Thompson of five daytime television programs found that 14% of the housewives counted in the audience were actually out of viewing or hearing range, 28% were in hearing range only and were not watching the set, and of the remaining 58% in viewing range, 31% were engaged in activities other than viewing.

Simmons reported in 1967 that viewer "attentiveness," or interest in the program as a whole, averages around 61% for all programs, but ranges between 53% for daytime game shows and 78% for soap operas. Simmons found that attentiveness to television programs increases as the evening progresses; it is higher among women in evening hours than it is in the daytime when household chores intervene. It is higher among older people than among younger ones and among poor people compared to wealthy ones. It is higher when there are no children at home.

In a report in 1968, Simmons found that among adult men viewers the percentage paying full attention was 83% of those watching Westerns; 81% of those watching movies, dramatic, and quiz programs, and 74% of those watching family situation comedies and science fiction. Among women, full attention was being paid by 83% of those watching drama programs, 80% of those watching quiz shows, and 68% of those watching situation comedies. It was only 49% of those watching daytime situation comedies and 51% of those watching daytime variety shows.

The 1969 Starch study of TV viewing in Atlanta found that among people who reported viewing the average half-hour program, 64% had viewed the full half-hour, and 21% watched for fifteen minutes or less.

(J)   In July, 1969, a couple in Queens, New York, quarreled over whether to watch the New York Mets playing baseball or a soap opera, "Dark Hours." The quarrel ended with the husband beating his wife to death. On one occasion four inmates at the Federal House of Detention in Manhattan were slashed with razor blades in a fight in the institution's TV room over whether to watch a baseball game, a film about a deer, or a program about zoologists in Tanganyika.

6.   Radio Listening in the Television Age

(A)   Because of television's present universality, data on the small minority of "radio-only" homes are no longer available.

(B)   Nielsen's radio ratings were discontinued in 1964. The last available figure that is comparable with those in Table 38 is 2.2 hours (for 1963), unchanged since 1956. Since it has been generally accepted that household usage of radio is no longer a meaningful measure, radio listening must now be estimated on the basis of individual behavior. Unfortunately, the radio ratings services measure specific program and station audiences rather than total listening patterns over the span of a full day. The 1964 All-Radio Measurement

Survey, conducted by Audits and Surveys for the radio industry, estimated daily listening at 2 hours for men, 3 hours for women, and between 3 and 5 hours for teenagers. From the 1970 Simmons survey it is possible to make a liberal estimate of 2–4 daily listening hours among persons over 18. Gilbert Youth Research, in a study for the Bureau of Advertising in 1970, found average radio listening to be 1 hour and 48 minutes per day among high-school children, and 1 hour and 56 minutes among college students.

(C)   By 1971 the number of radio homes had grown to 62 million, virtually all the households in the nation. Ninety-five percent of the people tuned in at some time or other in a typical week. A Brand Rating Index survey in March, 1970, found 22% of the people over 12 listening during the average quarter hour between 6:00 and 10:00 A.M. Between 10:00 A.M. and 3:00 P.M. 15% listened in the average time period, and this level held at 16% between 3:00 and 7:00 P.M. Between 7:00 P.M. and midnight, 10% of the people were listening to radio during the average quarter hour.

TABLE 112

A Comparison of Radio Listening and Television Viewing in Two Cities
November, 1970

(Source: American Research Bureau)

New York

Average Quarter Hour Exposure in Hour Beginning	% of Adult Men		% of Adult Women	
	Listening to Radio	*Watching TV*	*Listening to Radio*	*Watching TV*
6 A.M.	19%	Under 1%	16%	Under 1%
7	30	2	36	3
8	25	1	34	3
9	21	Under 1%	29	4
10	20	3	26	5
11	18	4	22	8
12 Noon	19	4	19	9

TABLE 112 (Cont.) A Comparison of Radio Listening and Television Viewing in Two Cities
November, 1970

(Source: American Research Bureau)

New York

Average Quarter Hour Exposure in Hour Beginning	% of Adult Men		% of Adult Women	
	Listening to Radio	Watching TV	Listening to Radio	Watching TV
1 P.M.	18	6	18	12
2	17	6	17	13
3	18	5	16	13
4	19	7	17	12
5	20	11	18	15
6	18	23	18	25
7	14	28	13	33
8	11	35	10	40
9	9	38	8	44
10	9	36	9	41
11	8	22	8	21

Chicago

	Listening to Radio	Watching TV	Listening to Radio	Watching TV
6 A.M.	22%	1%	22%	Under 1%
7	29	3	35	4
8	21	2	31	5
9	17	3	26	6
10	16	3	22	9
11	15	4	20	11
12 Noon	15	5	18	14
1 P.M.	13	4	16	15
2	14	3	16	13
3	15	4	17	11
4	18	6	16	13
5	19	16	18	18
6	15	25	14	29
7	10	31	10	38
8	8	36	9	42
9	8	38	8	44
10	8	28	7	32
11	6	17	5	20

The largest network radio audience ever recorded in the United States was on the occasion of the boxing match between Cassius Clay and Sonny Liston on February 25, 1964, which drew over 75,000,000 listeners.

There are no exactly comparable measurements for radio and TV on a national basis, but a Pulse All-Media Study in New York in 1967 found a third of the people over 12 listening to radio between 7:00 and 8:00 A.M., when only 2% were watching TV. The same study found more people listening to radio than watching TV for every daytime period. Between 6:00 and 7:00 P.M. the radio and TV audiences were approximately equal, and after that time the radio audience dropped as TV viewing soared. Between 9:00 and 10:00 P.M., when TV viewing was at its peak, 12% were listening to the radio.

The evidence shows that radio is not used as a substitute for TV. A 1967 study by the Brand Rating Index found that radio listening time was not very different among the heaviest-viewing fifth of the public than among the lighest-viewing fifth. Moderately light viewers of TV spent somewhat less time listening to radio than other viewing groups.

(D)   Of all AM radio stations 40% are now network-affiliated, and network programming accounts for 18% of radio listening between 6:00 and 10:00 A.M., for 16% between 10:00 A.M. and 3:00 P.M., for 15% between 3:00 and 7:00 P.M., and for 8% between 7:00 P.M. and midnight. Both network and locally originated programming have undergone tremendous changes in the past dozen years. The Arthur Godfrey Show was the last regularly broadcast half-hour network show surviving. Regular network output consists almost entirely of five-minute newscasts and features, supplemented by sportscasts and special events. Local radio programming, as the reader well knows, is devoted largely to musical recordings, with stations increasingly specializing their selections to aim at the tastes of a particular sector of their home markets. (To illustrate the growth of specialization, BRI announced in 1971 that users of canned dog foods prefer "good music" radio stations.) A national survey in 1967 for the Bureau of Advertising found that 73% of the adult public said they usually kept their radios tuned to a specific favorite station.

(E)   There are now some 321 million radios functioning in the United States, or an average of 5 per household. This included 100 million portable sets and 80.5 million car radios (93% of the cars on the road have radios, and radio-equipped cars have the radio turned on 62% of the driving time, according to the Radio Advertising Bureau).

In a single year, 1969, over 51 million radios were sold. Twenty-seven million of them were portables, 12 million were car radios, nearly 8 million were clock radios, but less than 5 million were table radios and consoles. The number of stations serving this vast quantity of receivers had mounted to 4,382 AM and 2,308 FM stations. FM stations get 25% of the average radio audience in the eight largest markets, according to an American Research Bureau study, but this share inevitably must be less in smaller cities where FM is less fully developed. In the nine top markets the proportion of households with an FM radio increased from 41% in 1964 to 74% in 1969.

7. Television and Reading

(A)   William Belson found in England that the number of books read for pleasure or relaxation was 23% less among TV viewers than among matched nonviewers, and the strength of interest in book reading was 9% lower. There were also declines in nonfiction reading for information purposes. Belson found less reading about politics, international and world affairs, about people in other countries, and about developments in science.

(B)   Reading books is not a direct reflection of book-buying, which reflects affluence as well as the distribution of leisure time. In the United States, dollar sales of books soared during the TV era, reflecting the expansion of the educational system and of the textbook market, as well as the phenomenal growth of paperback books. In 1969, hard-cover book sales amounted to $2.8 billion. In the same year, 360,000,000 paperback books were sold, at a sales value of $214 million.

(C)   In 1950, 11,000 new trade books (exclusive of texts and technical and religious books) appeared in the United States, of which some 2,400, or 22%, were works of fiction, poetry, and drama. By 1970 the number of new titles in the field of creative writing had grown to 4,600, but this represented only 13% of the 36,000 new trade books that appeared. Creative writing accounted for a diminishing proportion of the expanding book business, perhaps because of the limited supply of talent and perhaps because of the competitive attractions of TV as the major medium of fantasy entertainment.

(D)   Library circulation grew from 235 million volumes in 1953 to 560 million in 1968.

Edwin Parker (1963) compared the public library circulation figures for Illinois communities in which television had been introduced before and after the F.C.C. "freeze" of 1950. By examining the pattern during the freeze and after it was lifted, he concluded that in the TV areas, library circulation was less than it would have been in the absence of TV, especially for fiction.

(E)   Of magazine sales, 37% are now in single copies, no significant change since 1954.

(F)   According to the Magazine Publishers Association, the average adult today buys 1.68 magazines per

week or month (depending on the frequency of issue).
At the end of World War II, the figure was 1.23. The
total number of magazine copies (per issue) circulated
rose to 223,000,000 in 1970.

Because the huge-circulation mass magazines
such as *Reader's Digest, Life,* and *TV Guide* are essentially in the same tradition of popular culture as
TV entertainment, their readership is spread rather
evenly among heavy, medium, and light viewers of TV.
TV Guide's circulation reached 15,420,000 in 1970.

(G)   The trends described on this and the preceding
pages have continued in more recent years. During the
decade of the 1960's the *Saturday Evening Post* ended
publication. The circulation of *Life* and *Look* (before its
demise in 1971) grew by 33%. The news magazines
grew 81%, the women's magazines 39%, and men's
magazines 75%, due almost entirely to the phenomenal
growth of *Playboy* from 1 million to 5.3 million. The
Reporter ceased publication, and the combined circulation of *Harper's, Atlantic, Commentary, The Nation, New
Republic,* and *Commonweal* grew by 65%. Television's
appeal to young people wrought particular havoc with
the sale of comic books, whose annual circulation hit
a peak of 600 million around 1952 and dropped to
half that amount in 1969.

(H)   A 1967 survey by Opinion Research Corporation shows that reading time for each daily newspaper
read still averages 37 minutes. Comparisons of TV
and non-TV owners are of course no longer appropriate. Perhaps reflecting the competition of TV cartoons,
readership of Sunday comics by adults dropped from
79% of Sunday-newspaper readers in 1950 to 60% in
1970, according to Carl Nelson Research.

In England, Belson found that "television appears to increase somewhat the number of people who
spend time looking at press advertisements," and that
a third of the viewers claimed that seeing a commer-

cial caused them to notice newspaper ads for the same product. He found that viewers read as many different items in the paper as they did before the advent of TV.

(I)   Studies of the comparative appeals and functions of TV news and newspapers have already been commented on in the notes to Chapter 4. The evidence seems to support the proposition that the media complement each other and that the growing audience for television news has not been built at the expense of newspaper reading. The comparative importance of the media as sources of news may be better sought in audience statistics than in attitude surveys. A 1967 study by Opinion Research Corporation found that 60% report watching a TV newscast "yesterday," while 55% heard a radio newscast. Within a two-week period, Simmons reports that 47% of the adult public watch one or more of the early evening network newscasts, but the proportion of daily-newspaper readers (four out of every five people) is the same among the regular TV-news fans who watch nearly every night, among the occasional and infrequent viewers, and among those who watch none of the news programs in a two-week period.

An analysis of the 1970 Simmons survey shows that 22% of the public over 18 watch one or more of the early-evening network newscasts on the average weekday. The proportion however, drops to 11% among those aged 18–34 and rises to 34% among those over 50; it is 29% among those with incomes under $5,000 and drops to 18% among those with incomes over $10,000, thus reaffirming that news viewing is essentially a reflection of the overall pattern of TV viewing, with a wide variability by social class.

Galen Rarick, interviewing about 400 readers of the Salem, Oregon, *Capital Journal,* concluded that prior exposure to a broadcast news item increased readership of newspaper items about the same event.

(J)   Daily-newspaper circulation (62 million in 1971) is at an all-time high and long kept pace with the growth of the active adult population between the ages of 21 and 64. The number of papers circulated per 100 households has fallen to 99, reflecting changes in family composition as well as a probable drop in the proportion of people who read several papers a day. The 1971 Simmons survey finds 77½% of the adult public reading at least one newspaper every day, and 33% of these reading two or more. Although the total number of newspapers published has held steady, consolidations and mergers and failures have reduced the number of big metropolitan papers as new suburban dailies have begun publication. As noted in the Introduction, the complex economic difficulties of big-city dailies would be evident even without the competition of television, and newspaper failures and mergers have been characteristic of the postwar period in other parts of the world, including countries (such as France) that had not permitted broadcast advertising. Belson found that in the United Kingdom television had actually slowed a decline in the circulation of the popular press, while, at the same time, it also slowed an expected increase in the circulation of serious or "quality" newspapers.

8.   Television and the Movies

(A)   By 1960 weekly attendance had declined to 41.1 million, and by 1970 it was down to a level of 19.2 million. Since the population grew 31% in this same period, this is equivalent to a 67% decline in the per-capita rate of moviegoing. The total number of motion-picture houses remained relatively stable since 1953, though they served fewer patrons and had changed location. By 1971, the number of enclosed motion-picture theaters was 10,800, but there were also 3,900 drive-ins.

William Belson has noted that there was a substantial decline in British moviegoing after 1946, before the arrival of TV, though his data indicate that movie attendance continued to drop steadily between 1948 and 1960 as television penetration moved from zero to the 80% level. Belson concludes from his surveys that TV reduced movie attendance on the part of viewers by one-third and the strength of interest in attending the movies by one-fifth.

(B)   A national survey of U.S. moviegoing habits, made by Daniel Yankelovich for the Motion Picture Association in 1968, found that 61% of the public still considered films "more satisfying" than TV, though 30% preferred television. Eighteen percent of those over 16 could be categorized as "frequent" moviegoers, since they attended films at least once a month. They accounted for 76% of all the admissions. Of this group 54% were between the ages of 16 and 24, but there was a sharp difference between the single and married young people. Sixty-three percent of the single, but only 22% of the married, went to the movies at least once a month. The same study also found that 30% of the public never attend films, and another 18% almost never go.

(C)   As early as 1957, a Politz study found that nine out of ten New Yorkers watched television movies at some time or other over a four-week period. NBC was first to inaugurate a movie night, in 1961. The first telecast of "The Bridge on the River Kwai" in 1966 drew an estimated audience of 60,000,000 viewers.

By 1970, some 13,600 feature films were available for TV broadcasting, and films of ever more recent vintage were being shown. Movies were outdrawing regular TV programs in the evening ratings. Films dealing with the themes of prostitution

("Never on Sunday") and adultery ("The Apartment")
—themes that would have been unacceptable to the
old Hays office—became acceptable fare for family
viewing on the home screen. "Of course," said one
producer of pornographic films, "if the picture is too
good, people won't notice the sex." TV viewers did
not, however, see most films in their original condition. Of all feature films shown for television, 81%
are cut.

By 1968 NBC was running three movie nights
each week, so that it became possible for a viewer to
see a first-run feature film on at least one network
every evening of the week. United Artists received
$116,000,000 from NBC for a package of 94 films.
Such movies as "The Long Voyage Home" have been
shown in New York more than 75 times over the years.

One factor that encouraged the marriage of television and the film industry was the reduction of financial risk that normally accompanies a strictly theatrical
venture. The knowledge that a film will receive a certain return from television makes its box-office performance less vital to its financial success. Networks
are paying an average of $800,000 for two or three
showings of new feature films. They showed 134 films
in prime time during the 1969–70 season.

Studies released in 1968 by the Home Testing
Institute reported that a film's performance at the box
office in theatrical showings was no indication of its
ability to attract the TV audience, or vice versa.

9.   Television's Effects on Spectator Sports

(A)   A study conducted by the Bureau of Advertising
in 1963 found that three out of four men reported
watching baseball telecasts four or more times within
the previous twelve months; two out of three had
watched four or more professional football matches,
and the same proportion had watched baseball four

times or more. Half had watched the same number of basketball games; half had watched bowling; two out of five had watched wrestling four times or more, and a third had watched that many golf matches.

The TV audience of the typical sports event is composed of 45% men, 31% women, and 24% of what in the language of the ratings specialists are termed "non-adults." Average audience ratings in 1969–70 were 8% of the TV households for regular baseball games, but went up to 21% for the World Series. The typical NBA basketball game drew 9% and the average college football game on ABC had 13% of the homes tuned in. The average audience for a typical pro football game on CBS was 15% of the TV households, and 9% on NBC, but the Super Bowl game was pegged by Nielsen at a 39.4 rating, or an estimated audience of 70,000,000. (On network television, professional football games continue to be blacked out in the home team's city.)

Professional football matches have consistently generated larger TV audiences than college football. The TV audiences for football and for golf have tended to be especially popular among younger, higher-income men in metropolitan areas, while baseball has more appeal to the smaller towns. An analysis of Simmons data for the fall, 1967, football season found that 49% of the most faithful TV football fans had been to college, compared with 21% of those who watched no TV football at all.

Wrestling turned out to be a somewhat ephemeral phenomenon on the TV screens of the 1950's. The audience became disillusioned with the simple-minded, fake gymnastics of its heroes and villains. By the early 1960's TV wrestling had become an occasional event rather than staple nightly fare.

(B)   In England, William Belson concludes that TV led to an 11% increase in attendance at sports events. He found a 17% increase in attendance at major soccer matches by London viewers, and a 47% increase in attendance at horse races! The reports of change in activity were closely paralleled by the changes in the level of interest.

While pro football in the United States outpulled college football as a TV attraction, actual attendance at pro football games was limited by the comparatively small number of teams and games. Almost 9 million spectators attended professional football games in 1969, while 27.6 million saw college games. A one-minute commercial on the Super Bowl game cost $200,000.

Although the initial impact of TV was adverse to the major baseball leagues, by 1969 attendance was back to 27.2 million. Compared to the fast-moving pace of football, televised baseball was apparently less successful in holding the attention of viewers or of building passionate interest in live attendance at the sport. Nonetheless, during racial unrest in San Francisco on September 27, 1966, a special telecast of the San Francisco Giants-Atlanta Braves baseball game was credited with keeping people off the streets and therefore calming the nervous city.

(C)   Attendance at minor-league baseball games fell from 42,000,000 in 1949 to 10,000,000 in 1969, and the number of clubs fell from 448 to 127 in the same period. The competition of big-time baseball on the TV tube was clearly too much for the grass-roots teams.

(D)   In 1971, the major-league baseball clubs were paid about $24 million for telecasting rights. (The large sums paid by the networks for broadcasting rights do not include the additional expenses of actual coverage. A single World Series game requires the presence of a sixty-man crew.) Broadcast rights to the 1972 Olympics in Rome cost the American Broadcasting Companies $13,500,000, while the winter games in Japan cost NBC $6,400,000. In 1970 professional football received some $46,000,000 from the TV networks. The American Football League was created to meet the needs of television.

The National Football League established a film subsidiary to promote a variety of programs that appeared on TV not only in the football season but throughout the year, featuring background material on the players and the game. The salaries paid to professional athletes have soared, in keeping with their new status as television stars.

Advertising on sports telecasts commanded a premium price, because of the high proportion of men (and in advertisers' minds, of younger, better-educated, higher-income men) in the audience. In the last three months of 1969, advertisers paid the networks $293 million for the right to air commercials on sports broadcasts. On one occasion (the 1967 Super Bowl game), the kickoff of the second half had to be redone after it was discovered that it had taken place while a commercial was still being shown.

10.   TV and the Advertisers

(A)   By 1970 advertising had grown to the $19.7 billion level, with $12.3 billion going into the five major media. Television advertising had reached $3.66 billion. Newspapers were at $5.85 billion, radio and magazines each at $1.3 billion, and outdoor had grown modestly to $237 million. The ratio of advertising to consumer sales remained constant at about 3.5%, raising the fascinating question of how long an expanding economy could continue to overload the absorptive capacity of the consuming public with a steadily rising number of commercial messages.

(B)   In 1970, TV advertisers invested $3.6 billion, while the viewing public spent $5.2 billion for purchase and maintenance of their sets, a 40–60 ratio. Advertisers spent $1.3 billion for radio, and radio owners

$.9 billion, a 59–41 ratio. In the case of magazines, advertisers spent $1.4 billion, and readers $1.5 billion, a 48–52 ratio. Newspaper advertisers spent $5.7 billion and readers spent $2.4 billion, a 70–30 ratio.

(C)   Average ad noting in magazines was about 35% to 40% in 1967–68, according to Starch. Among the five major media, TV received 30% of the total advertising investment in 1970, while newspapers had 47%, magazines 11%, radio 10%, and outdoor 2%.

(D)   In 1970, broadcast advertising expenditures broke down as follows (in millions of dollars):

	Radio	*Television*
Network	$58.0	$1,715.0
Spot	355.0	1,255.0
Local	865.0	690.0
Total	$1,278.0	$3,660.0

Local radio advertising was 68% of the total for radio, local TV advertising 19% of the total for television.

(E)   In 1969, 187 national advertisers used network radio, but the format of network radio had drastically changed. Only one half-hour daily network program (Arthur Godfrey's) remained on the air, and regular network time was confined to five-minute units (with a few ten-minute units among them), made up primarily of news, with some sportscasts and other background or "accent" pieces. In addition, live radio reporting of sports and special events added to the networks' share of broadcast time. In 1971, Godfrey announced his retirement from regular broadcasting.

(F)   The number of network-radio advertisers grew from 130 in 1957 to 197 in 1966.

(G)   NBC and CBS now have television coverage of virtually all U.S. households, and ABC has about 96%.

(H)   Since radio today tends to reach an individual listening privately on his own transistor set, the cost per thousand homes reached is no longer a meaningful measurement. In the 1969–70 season (according to

Batten, Barton, Durstine and Osborn) "drive time"
spot radio (6:00–10:00 A.M. and 3:00–7:00 P.M.)
reached 1,000 adult men for $2.45 and 1,000 women
for $1.85, while network radio in the same periods
cost $1.65 per 1,000 for men and $1.40 per 1,000 for
women. Between 10:00 A.M. and 3:00 P.M. ("housewife time" in the radio salesman's argot), women could
be reached at $1.70 per 1,000 on spot radio and $1.40
on the network. Daytime spot TV cost $3.00 per
1,000 women, and daytime network TV was $2.15
per 1,000.

(I)　　　In 1970 McCann-Erickson estimated that national (and regional) advertising accounted for 58.4%
of all advertising, and for 48% of the advertising in the
five major media. It was 81% of TV advertising, 32%
of radio, 18% of newspapers, 100% of magazines, and
66% of outdoor.

(J)　　　In 1969, the number of national advertisers
spending over $25,000 in magazines had declined
to 2,502.

(K)　　　By 1969, the number of network television advertisers had risen to 434, but the number of national
and regional spot-TV advertisers had fallen to 1,564,
reflecting the economic constraints set by rising TV
advertising costs as well as the growing concentration
of American business.

(L)

TABLE 113

Top Ten Television Advertisers (1969)

(Source: TvB: McCann-Erickson, Inc.)

		Total TV
1.	Procter & Gamble	$176,333,000
2.	General Foods	88,179,300
3.	Colgate-Palmolive	82,698,600
4.	Bristol-Myers	76,955,100
5.	R. J. Reynolds Industries	63,024,000

TABLE 113 (Cont.)

Top Ten Television Advertisers (1969)

(Source: TvB: McCann-Erickson, Inc.)

		Total TV
6.	American Home Products	62,310,400
7.	General Motors	53,625,100
8.	Warner-Lambert Pharm.	51,359,400
9.	Lever Brothers	50,487,300
10.	Sterling Drug	48,695,700
	Total Top Ten	$ 753,667,900
	Total National TV	2,931,000,000
	% Top Ten of Total	26%

Network advertising accounted for 47% of all television investments in 1970 ($1.7 billion). Spot advertisements placed on a station-by-station basis by national advertisers accounted for another 34% ($1.2 billion), and local spot advertising placed by merchants, car dealers, and other retailers and local services represented 19% ($690 million).

(M)   The extent to which television has increased its share of four major categories of national advertising is clearly shown in the following table:

TABLE 114

How Different Kinds of Advertisers Spend Their Money (1969)

(Sources: Media Records, Inc.; PIB; BAR; RAB; LNA; McCann-Erickson, Inc.)

	Food	*Industry Appliances*	*Gasoline and Oil*	*Automotive*	*All National Advertisers*	*All Advertisers*
Television	68%	54%	51%	35%	50%	30%
Radio	5	3	23	9	7	10
Newspapers	12	16	17	35	18	47
Magazines	10	25	6	18	23	11
Outdoor	5	2	3	3	2	2
Total for Five Media	100%	100%	100%	100%	100%	100%

(N)   The following revision of Table 73 shows that
           the sources of television advertising revenues have
           somewhat more diversified, with food, soap, and auto-
           motive advertisers accounting for a somewhat smaller
           share of the total than was true in the past.

TABLE 115

Sources of Network Television Revenues by Major Industry Classifications

(Source: BAR, 1970)

	% Share of Total
Toiletries & toilet goods	18%
Food & food products	15
Drugs & remedies	11
Soaps, cleansers, & polishes	9
Smoking materials	9
Automobiles, automotive accessories & equipment	8
Household equipment & supplies	5
Confections & soft drinks	4
Jewelry, optical goods, & cameras	2
Gasoline, lubricants, & other fuels	2
Apparel, footwear, & accessories	2
Beer, wine, & liquor	2
Radios, television sets, record players, & musical instruments	1
Office equipment, stationery, & writing supplies	1
Household furnishings	1
Industrial materials	1
Miscellaneous	8
	100%
Total	$1,732,910,700

(O)   The steady process of inflation in the 1950's and
           1960's, the expansion of population, and the changes
           in the basic ways in which media are sold make long-
           term comparisons of media rate changes difficult. The
           short-run picture, as the following table shows, is for
           prime-time network TV to keep pace with rate in-
           creases in the other media and for spot TV and day-
           time network TV to raise rates at a faster pace.

TABLE 116

Changes in Advertising Costs, 1965–1970

(Sources: BBDO; Bureau of Advertising)

	Rate Changes	Cost of Reaching 1,000 Households
Network television—daytime	+ 36%	+ 26%
Network television—prime time	+ 20	+ 11
Spot television	+ 43	+ 27
Network Radio	+ 26	+ 12
Spot radio	+ 23	+ 9
Newspapers	+ 19	+ 15
Magazines	+ 21	+ 4

The increased number of TV households accounted for only part of the rising cost. Actual costs per 1,000 people reached rose faster than costs per 1,000 homes, for reasons already explained. The increasing number of commercials, and their trend toward shorter lengths, progressively reduced the levels of commercial recall. Studies by Grey Advertising reported a 26% decline between 1965 and 1969 in the recall scores of commercials whose performance was checked by the agency. Overall this resulted in a 45% increase in the cost of reaching the same number of people able to recall the average commercial.

(P)   Program production costs have continued to soar. This may be illustrated by considering two shows that maintained their format virtually unchanged over a number of years. The production budget for a single broadcast of the "Ed Sullivan Show" went from $90,000 in 1958 to $185,000 in 1968. "Bonanza" went from $110,000 in 1960 to $211,000 in 1970. The highest estimated program production cost on record was for the March 18, 1970 broadcast of "David Copperfield" on NBC—$1,800,000. (Only half of this sum was recouped from the sponsors.)

TABLE 117

Average Production Costs of Prime-Time
TV Programs (1970–71 Season)

(Source: *Variety*)

First-Run Movies (2 hours)	$750,000
Westerns (1 hour)	205,000
Variety (1 hour)	192,000
Situation Comedy (½ hour)	104,230
Adventure Drama (1 hour)	205,000
Game Shows (½ hour)	35,000
Variety (½ hour)	100,000
News (1 hour)	140,000

(Q)   The cost of sponsorship and participating sponsorship of network programs can no longer be divided into production and time charges, since the two are combined into a "package" price. Since the characteristics and numbers of actual viewers vary from program to program even when the number of households reached remains the same, the comparative cost per 1,000 homes is no longer as meaningful a measure as it once was.

TABLE 118

Comparative Efficiency of Different Types of TV Programs

(Source: BBDO)

Program Type	Cost of Reaching 1,000 Homes with one Minute of Sponsored Commercial Time 1971
Prime Time	
Variety	$ 8.50
Drama	10.40
Live Events	7.25
Documentary/News	8.75
Travel/Adventure	8.90
Child/Animated	5.40

TABLE 118 (Cont.)

Comparative Efficiency of Different Types of TV Programs

(Source: BBDO)

Program Type	Cost of Reaching 1,000 Homes with one Minute of Sponsored Commercial Time 1971
Daytime	
Serials	2.00
Game	1.35
Comedy	1.45
Fringe Time	
Early News	3.05
Late-Night Talk	3.50
Sports (average)	5.55
Professional Football	5.45
College Football	5.95
Basketball	4.60
Baseball	5.15
Golf	8.15
Hockey	4.85

At the end of the 1960's, the rise of the new media buying services revived the emphasis on cost-per-thousand. The buying services competed with advertising agencies in their claims to make more efficient buys of spot TV. They often did this by dealing in "distress merchandise" — time that a station had been unable to sell at the regular rates and that was available on a last-minute basis at a cut price. This tendency (with which the agencies were forced to compete) meant that the earlier emphasis on audience characteristics no longer applied. "Box-car figures" based on aggregate audience size and price resumed the same significance they had enjoyed in a less sophisticated era.

Commercial production costs have also gone up to the point that they represent a substantial expense. The cost of producing a 60-second black-and-white commercial rose 83% between 1963 and 1968. The price of an average 60-second color commercial was $16,000–$18,000 in 1968, according to Gordon Webber, vice-president and director of TV commercial production, Benton & Bowles. He has commented that "the $50,000, $100,000, and even the $300,000 spot is not uncommon." Film processing was $150 for a black-and-white commercial in 1959. In 1968 a color commercial cost $1,390 to process. Production costs for the average commercial, based on one day of shooting inside a studio, increased from $6,000 in 1959 to $10,500 in 1968. Increased hourly costs for production crews accounted for part of the difference, as the following table shows:

TABLE 119

Minimum Daily Wages for TV-Production Crews

(Source: *Madison Avenue*)

	1959	1968
Cameraman	$113.95	$197.87
Director	125.00	163.00
Director Assistant	50.00	85.00
Scenic Designer	70.98	79.83
Hairdresser	40.00	55.00

(R)   In 1960, 50% of network programs were exclusively sponsored by national advertisers who developed some identification with the programs and their personalities. By 1966 this proportion had dropped to 25%; in 1968, 5% of the programs had sole sponsors, and 7% alternate sponsors. By 1971, rising costs, multiple sponsorship, and the widespread use of "scatter plans" to disperse commercials over a broad audience resulted in the virtual elimination of direct program sponsorship—down to 7%.

(S)   The vast increase in the number of new products and brands introduced each year produced an additional impetus for more advertising positions and for shorter commercial units. The N.A.B. Code, revised in 1968, increased the permissible number of consecutive announcements from three to four within programs and from two to three at the station break. The Code permits 10 minutes of commercials per hour in prime time and 16 minutes at other hours. (To place this in some perspective, Lebanese television permits 25% of air time to be devoted to advertising, and on one program sponsors ran the same commercial three times in a row in Arabic, French, and English.)

Eighty percent of national spot messages are from multiproduct advertisers. Spot-television advertising shifted in emphasis during the decade of the 1960's, with early evening becoming progressively more important and daytime progressively diminishing in its share.

In the first year after 30-second commercials appeared (1968), there was an increase of 27% in the total number of commercials aired. Between 1966 and 1970 the number of prime-time commercials increased by 33%. In that same period, the proportion of prime-time commercials of 30-second length or less increased by 70%, from 47% of the total to 80%. On September 22, 1968, the ABC-TV network presented the motion-picture premiere of "Zorba the Greek." Between 9:00 and 11:42 P.M. the progress of the motion picture was interrupted by no less than 43 commercials, some presented in sequences of as many as eight at a time.

Time magazine of July 12, 1968, reported on an especially delightful collection of TV commercials:

1. A woman, responding to the call, "Where's the Open Pit?" dashes across the lawn with a bottle of Open Pit barbecue sauce — and disappears into an open pit.

2. A baker, having carelessly forgotten his Vicks Cough Silencers, tosses pizza dough into the air, coughs, and catches it — splat — in the face.

3. A mousy little guy, sploshed with Hai Karate after-shave lotion, brutally chops down a scent-crazed female on the make.

4. Marilyn says: "I'll tell you what your problem is, Gloria. You have bad pizza. Bad pizza!" After Gloria switches to Jeno's, Marilyn tries another tack: "Now I'd like to talk about your deodorant." Gloria: "Marilyn, how would you like a nice belt in the mouth?"

Broadcast advertising, since stations are subject to Federal regulation, has been unusually sensitive to categories of products that are freely promoted in print. Liquor, for example, has not been advertised on the air. For a period of several years, stations were required by the F.C.C. to carry anticigarette commercials, which the tobacco companies considered very effective. There was longstanding criticism of cigarette commercials on the grounds that they influenced children to smoke. Finally, after the Surgeon General's report on cigarettes' effects on health, these commercials were banned from the air in January, 1971. A new subject of controversy loomed as public discussion of narcotics addiction raised questions as to whether proprietary "medicines" advertised on TV made young people receptive to trying illegal drugs.

Senator Frank Moss told a Congressional Committee in September, 1970, of one woman's experience: "Last August I chanced to see a commercial for a stimulant called Vivarin on the CBS network.

My children saw it also. The next day at rest time my then three-year-old daughter said if I gave her a Vivarin she would not have to stay in bed."

A Federal Trade Commission study of 500 television commercials in 1969 found that "a typical theme running through these commercials is to hold the product out as the pathway to success and happiness and the antidote to what is otherwise a drab, boring, or lonely life." Commissioner Mary Gardiner Jones infers that "to the viewer, these ads convey the message that the setting and people of the television commercial represents the real world with real products available to the viewer if he follows the prescriptions of the TV message."

E. B. White (in the *New Yorker* of December 3, 1960) once proposed that the ideal format for commercial television would be to have parallel screens, one for the programming, the other for regularly scheduled advertising: "On the advertising screen Zsa Zsa Gabor would be giving the news of underarm security; on the editorial screen the Secretary of State would be giving the news of national security. The viewer could decide which presentation, which person, seemed the more attractive or instructive."

Film Director Stanley Kubrick has observed that a feature film made with the same care as the typical commercial would cost some $50 million. Paul Goodman says, "The only part of television which has fulfilled its promise at all is the commercials. It is the only part that has any aesthetic validity.... Apparently all the creative artists are in the advertising agencies who make the commercials.... It would be much better if we dropped the programs and stretched the commercials to half an hour. It would be far more authentic. It's authentic because it's about something; namely, someone wants to make a buck. It's for real."

Over the years, a variety of studies have found

the public generally more critical of TV commercials than of other forms of advertising, primarily because it is the form of advertising that people find most intrusive and of which they are most aware. At the same time, a majority clearly continues to feel that commercials represent the necessary cost of maintaining the programming they enjoyed. Two weeks after limited TV advertising was introduced in Holland, 48% of the TV owners said they liked TV better with advertising, and 18% said they liked it less. A year later the question was repeated, with identical results.

Gary Steiner (1963) found that most Americans had both positive and negative things to say about commercials; the most common positive response was to their entertainment qualities; the criticism was of both their content and of their frequency. Three out of four agreed that "commercials are a fair price to pay for the entertainment you get." By 1964 a Roper survey for the Television Information Office found 81% agreeing with this statement. Forty-five percent said that advertisers had the most to say about what kinds of programs got on the air (27% named the television industry and 26% the public). In another study, Steiner (1966) found that few televiewers expressed any reactions to commercials, pro or con, while they were actually viewing in a normal home setting.

Reanalyzing data from Steiner's 1960 study of 2,500 people, Meyersohn concluded that commercials were not salient when TV was discussed in general. Most people, however, expressed clearcut feelings about commercials when the subject was brought up, and these feelings tended to be negative. The frequency of interruption was most irritating to high-school-educated (and presumably middle-brow) viewers, whereas college-educated viewers were most likely to criticize content. The entertainment character of commercials was most often mentioned on the positive side, with their informative values next. Heavy viewers were generally least critical, reflecting their lower social and cultural position.

Raymond Bauer and Stephen Greyser did not find television advertising, or for that matter, any form of advertising, salient as a subject of public discussion or as a cause for annoyance in a 1964 national survey. They did find that people who were least favorable toward advertising were most prone to exaggerate the amount of evening television time devoted to commercials. In general, the intrusiveness and inter- ruptions of broadcast commercials were the most often stated reasons for disliking advertising. People displayed far more conscious awareness of TV ads than of those in any other medium; TV commercials accounted for 65% of all the advertisements recorded and classified in a special half-day count of conscious "exposures." (By comparison radio contributed 16%, newspapers 10%, and magazines 7%.) Of the TV commercials, 27% were categorized as "annoying" — a far higher proportion than for print ads — but 38% were classed as "enjoyable," and 31% as "informative."

Of 2,518 persons interviewed for the National Association of Broadcasters in 1966, 58% charac- terized TV commercials as annoying, as compared to 31% who thought them enjoyable (the proportions were reversed for print ads). In a mail survey of 1,026 people, conducted by Warwick and Legler in 1967, those who said television programs were getting worse were twice as many as those who said they were getting better, while more thought commercials were getting better than thought they were getting worse.

Of the Canadians interviewed by Goldfarb in 1969, 63% named television advertising as the kind that influenced them most. The proportion that agreed they were influenced by advertising a great deal or somewhat was about equal to the proportion who said they were not at all influenced by it or fought it. Seven out of ten agreed that advertising is an art form, three out of five preferred humorous advertisements, but only one in three agreed that television commercials were sometimes more interesting than the programs.

A Bruskin survey in 1971 found 66% of the U.S. public picking television as the medium that carries the most "interesting" advertising; 16% named magazines, and 13% newspapers. An Opinion Research Corporation study made for the newspaper Bureau of Advertising in 1971 found only 10% naming television, compared to 14% for magazines and 25% newspapers, as the place where they were "most likely to find advertising that can be trusted"; TV was named by 32%, newspapers by 13%, and magazines by 8% as the place where they were least likely to find such advertising.

A 1970 study by Foote, Cone & Belding found 71% of the adults reporting that they viewed television "last night." while 8% actually did not remember whether they had watched or not. Of those who watched television, 68% claimed to have been in the room for all the commercials, but only 44% said they had paid attention to all of them. These people were disproportionately concentrated among the older, less affluent, and less educated.

As the number of commercials has increased and as they have become shorter, advertising research has devoted more attention to the effects of position and length. The results obtained have varied with the degree of aid to recall by the respondent. Since commercials are today almost always on film or tape and are repeatedly shown, the levels of recall can often be quite high, particularly when the viewer's memory is jogged.

A New York study of about 400 people, conducted by Blair Radio in 1966, found that about 7 out of 10 correctly identified the visual element of the typical commercial. NBC tested a series of well-known TV commercials in 1967, and after interviewing some 700 people on the telephone, found that about 7 in 10 could report on the prime visual elements just by hearing the audio portion. NBC concluded that less expensive radio versions of TV commercials could be effectively used by advertisers. In these two studies, however, the people interviewed were given cues to remember what they saw. In 1967 Baber Advertising of Toronto made four separate surveys in London, Ontario, to measure both unaided and aided recall of three commercials. Next-day unaided recall ran between 2.6% and 6.2%.

Studies made by the Richmond Newspapers between 1956 and 1966 found that 24% of those viewing the average program could name a sponsor or product type advertised. Simmons found in a 1968 coincidental telephone survey that 42% of those paying full attention to a program during the previous half-hour period could correctly name the product or brand advertised, and 19% recalled two or more products. The percentage among those paying less than full attention was 21%. Recall of the brand name was 31% among those paying full attention; 13% among those paying less than full attention.

Oscar Lubow reported that an analysis of "over 500,000" television commercials measured over the years by the Starch and Hooper organizations found a decline in recall levels between 1960 and 1970— from about 42% to about 23%. Both in 1960 and 1970, a fourth of those who reported "noting" a commercial could not associate it with an advertised product. Misidentification rose from 10% in 1960 to more than double that proportion in 1970. The "clutter" of commercials succeeding each other at station break time was widely blamed for this loss of effectiveness.

A study conducted in 1962–63 by two advertising agencies — Foote, Cone and Belding, and Needham, Louis and Brorby — found that spot and in-program commercials performed equally well among housewives in daytime. Commercials that appeared at the beginning or end of programs performed as well as or better than those embedded in the middle. The type of program did appear to influence recall of the commercials within it. Studies made by Herbert Kay for Television Advertising Representatives found that various television programs differed widely in their attraction for viewers who were susceptible to brand switching in different product fields, or in various other attributes. (Curiously, "The Doctors" and "Children's Doctor" both scored well below average on "health concern.")

A study made by Norman, Craig & Kummel in 1959 had noted that sponsor identification was higher for commercials placed in nonviolence programs than in violence ones. In a 1968 Hooper study, commercials in science-fiction programs averaged only a 14% score, while those in musical-variety shows had a high of 49%.

The same study reported that the average prime-time network commercial was correctly recalled by 19% of those over 12 who reported watching the program in which it appeared. Scores were lower for commercials in low-rated programs, suggesting that they were less able to hold the attention of their viewers. Recall scores averaged 17% for commercials spotted in "scatter plans," compared with 36% for those in sponsored programs. Piggyback commercials (the selling of two products in succession) averaged a score of 13%, compared with 23% for single-product messages.

Research conducted by BBDO in 1969 concluded that the content and character of the commercial had more to do with its recall than did its positioning. Commercials placed in the second half of a "clutter" sequence, however, did better than those shown first. (Dodds Buchanan, in a study of 149 New York women, also found that first position in a series of commercials was best.)

BBDO used its Channel One facility in the early 1960's to pretest pilot versions of commercials by inserting them into a regularly scheduled program on a Utica, New York, station. They concluded, in a report issued in March, 1964, that thirty-second commercials were generally about two-thirds as effective as those of one-minute length and that a thirty-second commercial presented in piggyback form got variable but generally somewhat lower effects than the same commercial presented in isolation. The same series of studies found that the awareness of a commercial could be increased by 75% by placing a brief promotional "billboard" for it at the outset of the program.

An observational study by Gary Steiner (1966) found "no visible penalty" attached to the half-minute piggyback compared to the one-minute commercial. Nor did he find either half of the piggyback superior, though the second of two one-minute commercials back-to-back did get less attention than the first.

A 1967 study by Schwerin of some 1,500 television commercials rated 30-second commercials nearly as effective as the one-minute variety. Short commercials were better liked than one-minute ones. A weak beginning to the first of a pair of back-to-back commercials affected response to the second of the pair.

A 1967 study made by Daniel Yankelovich for Corinthian Broadcasting compared 30-second and 60-second commercials for the same six products in a laboratory experiment with matched groups of people —a total sample of 417. Comparing responses before and after exposure, Yankelovich concluded that there was no difference between the shorter and longer versions in communications value, involvement, or empathy. The shorter commercials had 92% the level of brand recall. He concluded also that the effectiveness of a 30-second commercial was the same regardless of whether it occurred in an isolated position within a program or was piggybacked with another commercial of the same length. A critique of this study, by the Advertising Research Foundation, discounted the conclusions on the grounds that the conditions of forced exposure in the test may have created a heightened response to all the advertising and thereby minimized differences that might be significant in real life. In spite of this authoritative criticism, the Yankelovich study was widely used as a sales tool by the television industry in justifying the move toward 30 seconds as the basic unit of television advertising (at time charges that represented some 60% of the former 1-minute standard length).

An experimental Starch study of 1,840 commercials broadcast during one four-week period in Atlanta in 1969 found that recall increased among those who reported watching the channel from 24% in the case of 10-second commercials, to 28% for the 20-second, to 32% for the 30-second, and to 39% for 60-second commercials. (The use of a recognition approach [using interviews on the following day with still photographs of the commercials] raised the overall level of recall among program viewers to 33% for the 10-second commercials and to 42% for the 60-second commercials.) For 10-second commercials misidentification was as great as correct identification, for the 20-second, the ratio was one and a half right to each incorrect one, for the 30-second it was two to one, and for one-minute commercials three to one. The same study found that correct identification and "noting" both declined as the number of commercials per half hour increased, but that the position of the commercial within the program had little effect on the level of recall.

(T)   Television's ability to sell is not limited to the products of commercial sponsors. The line "Look that up in your Funk and Wagnalls'" on Rowan and Martin's "Laugh-In" is assumed to have been the cause of a 20% increase in sales that put the dictionary into an extra printing.

Analyzing 67 television campaigns in which sales patterns could be traced and related back to advertising, Schwerin concluded in 1964 that "dollars spent on advertising provide only a comparatively small part of the explanation for sales changes," and that the quality of the commercials was far more important than the actual dollar expenditures.

(U)   During the 1960's, the sales effects of television — and of other media — have been subjected to an increased amount of investigations, which tend to confirm the original statement that TV is the best medium — for certain purposes, as every medium can claim. A major study by General Foods in 1970 compared the return from TV and magazines and found the results a standoff. A study conducted by Opinion Research Corporation for the Bureau of Advertising in 1969 similarly found TV and newspapers roughly equivalent in their sales productivity per dollar expended in advertising. The task of selecting or mixing the right combination of media, and of using them persuasively to best advantage, must be faced afresh with every new marketing problem.

11.   The Political Effects of Television

(A)   TV and radio advertising by all candidates in 1968 totaled $59,200,000, according to the F.C.C.

Median expenditures on broadcast advertising in 1970 were 9¢ to 10¢ a vote for gubernatorial candidates, 8¢ to 9¢ a vote for Senate candidates, and 1¢ to 2¢ a vote for Congressional candidates. Twelve of the 79 candidates for governor spent over 20¢ a vote.

(B)   The effective use of television announcements by wealthy candidates whom it catapulted from obscurity to prominence (and in many cases to high office) prompted, in 1971, the introduction of Federal legislation to limit campaign spending.

A Gallup study conducted for Foote, Cone and Belding in 1970 found that 65% of the public favored controls on political advertising. A large majority felt that television was influential in affecting voting choice. A Roper survey for the Television Information Office in January, 1971, found that 21% of the public thought there should be no limits on political campaign spending, while 42% thought that there should be limits but that the candidates should be permitted to use media as they wished. While 10% thought TV spending should be curbed, 7% wanted curbs on sound trucks, 7% on radio, 6% on billboards, and 5% on newspaper ads.

(C)   The televised "great debates" between Nixon and Kennedy were the highlight of the 1960 presidential campaign, and may have had a decisive influence on the outcome of that closely fought race.

No less than twenty-two different survey organizations were involved in attempted assessments of the "great debates." Elihu Katz and Jacob Feldman concluded that "the debates were more effective in presenting the candidates than the issues." The first debate obtained ratings substantially higher than the subsequent ones, but this reflected its more advantageous timing. Since these debates were on all three networks, they dominated viewers' choices and received approximately the same size of audience as the programs they had preempted. An examination of the ratings for all network political broadcasts during the 1964 campaign found that they averaged around 9, compared with 14 for the typical entertainment programs they had preempted.

Nielsen reported that viewing of political broadcasts in the 1960 campaign averaged 4.5 hours per home, compared with 2.7 in 1956. In 1964, without the benefit of the "great debates," the average went down to 2.9.

(D)   The manipulation of tape and film can create a picture of a public figure that does not conform to reality. Candidates for state office have "campaigned" through TV commercials based on film footage clipped and manipulated to eliminate signs of infirmity. Before they were broadcast President Eisenhower's press conferences were recorded on film and edited to remove his malapropisms.

A mail survey conducted by the N.A.B. in 1963 found that about a third of commercial TV stations editorialized, about 50% of them on a regular daily or weekly basis. Local subjects were the concern of 90% of their editorials; only 25% of the stations ever dealt with international themes. Only 6% said they ever editorialized on behalf of political candidates.

(E)   The political role of television has been vividly apparent not only in election times but at moments of great national crisis, such as the Kennedy-Khrushchev confrontation over Cuban missile sites, and on other occasions when presidents have addressed the public to win sympathy and support for controversial courses of action. The unique ability of television to serve as a powerful integrative political force at a critical moment has never been more dramatically demonstrated than on the occasion of President Kennedy's assassination.

The TV reportage of the Kennedy assassination was tuned in to by 96% of the households. At 1:30 P.M. on the Friday the President was shot, 19,000,000 persons were watching TV. Fifteen minutes later, or five minutes after the report of the shooting, there were 24,000,000 watching, and an hour later, 37,000,000. By 6:15 in the evening there were 81,000,000 viewers. The initial report of the event was given by word of mouth to 49% of the public, who then turned to radio or TV for confirmation.

In a telephone study of 419 people in San Jose, Bradley Greenberg found that "earliest knowers" (those who knew in the first 15 minutes) were most apt to have gotten their information from radio and TV, whereas those who found out beyond that time had learned of it by word of mouth.

Nielsen found that between that Friday and the funeral on Monday the average home had had a receiver tuned to the Kennedy report for a total of 31.6 hours. A survey by the National Opinion Research Center found that people estimated spending 8 hours Friday, 10 hours Saturday, 8 hours Sunday, and 8 hours Monday watching the story on TV or listening to it on the radio.

Paul Sheatsley and Jacob Feldman, in reporting on the above NORC study, note that even political opponents of Kennedy shared the general grief and sense of personal loss. The reactions of most people were like those at the death of a close friend or relative: they "followed a well-defined pattern of grief familiar to medical practice," with all of the usual symptoms of sleeplessness, fatigue, and loss of appetite.

Fred Greenstein noted Irving Janis' observation of similarities between the intense TV viewing on that weekend and the "compulsive staring" at disaster sites. One student he interviewed said, "I kept waiting for something that would make me more hopeful or feel better about it. It never came, of course, but you're tied to the TV set in hopes that it would." Another remarked, "After the TV went off last night, I thought about . . . why I had spent the whole day and it struck me that I was waiting for somebody to explain why this happened."

William Mindak and Gerald E. Hurst found evidence of television's functions in remarks like: "I was right there when it happened." "It brought you there as if you were one of the close spectators— closer than had you been on the street watching what was taking place." "It was better than being there. You could see more than you could if you were there, I'm sure." "I would like to have seen more of the first of it when he was shot. They should have had a camera on that motorcade, I should think."

Walter Cronkite and the other well-known TV newscasters whose reports on the assassination continued on a marathon basis for those grueling days provided an element of familiarity and reassurance that gave viewers the feeling that matters were under control and that calm strong people were in charge of the nation's institutions. TV's explicit images also provided relief from the anxieties of uncertainty about what was happening: "I think it actually made us feel better, if we could have felt better, because we knew exactly what was happening." "It only made you more depressed, but it helped you realize things were okay and you could get it out of your system."

The grim events of 1963 were repeated in 1968 when Senator Robert Kennedy was assassinated. By the afternoon of the day following the killing, 97% of a national cross section of adults interviewed by the Sindlinger telephone poll knew what had happened. Fifty-seven percent said they had first heard on the radio, 20% on TV, 18% by word of mouth, and 6% had first seen the news in the newspaper. Nielsen's

Instant Audimeter service in New York showed that 15.9% of the TV homes in the area were watching television at 7:00 A.M. Wednesday morning — as against 1.6% at the same hour on the preceding Wednesday. By 8:00 A.M. 25.6% of New York area homes were using television, as against 8.2% a week earlier.

(F)   NBC's president, Julian Goodman, has claimed that voting in presidential elections jumped nearly 30% after TV appeared on the scene. Actually, 51.3% of the civilians of voting age voted for a presidential candidate in 1948 and 62.6% in 1952 (an increase of 22% during a period when television rose to a 37% penetration level). Between 1956 and 1968 the proportion voting has fluctuated between 60% and 64%, although almost all U.S. homes have at least one TV set.

Whether or not TV has directly raised the level of voting, it has clearly demonstrated its capacity to increase the visibility of campaigning candidates and of the whole electoral process. Maxwell McCombs, reanalyzing the University of Michigan Survey Research Center data from three presidential election campaigns, found a remarkable growth between 1952 and 1964 in the exposure of Negroes to the media, which parallels the growth in political participation by Negroes. A substantial part of this change (with all of its attendant political, cultural, and economic implications) came about as a result of TV's arrival on the scene. The effects were especially marked at the lowest educational level.

In the 1959 British general election, John Trenaman and Denis McQuail found that TV made voters better informed about the policies of the parties but concluded that watching the candidates did not change attitudes toward the parties, or voting behavior. In the 1964 election, Jay Blumler and Denis McQuail conducted a series of interviews with a panel

of 750 voters in two districts in Yorkshire. They rein-
terviewed 390 individuals of the original 1959 study
and found that those who owned TV watched election
broadcasts substantially more than the TV owners in
1959, while the small, hard-core, non-TV group
watched less, reflecting their remoteness from the
world of politics.

The importance of television to the electoral
process was shown by the high proportion of people
who rated it first over other media as a source for
political news. Sixty-one percent called it "most helpful
for weighing up political leaders," 50% said it was
"most helpful for understanding political issues,"
and 45% thought it the "most impartial." It was second
to the press, however, in giving the "most full account
of political events."

When respondents were given a list of reasons
to explain why they occasionally avoided party election
broadcasts, 37% chose to answer, "because my mind
is already made up." Blumler and McQuail conclude
that a "mild dislike" of political broadcasts is quite
common, and they note that a good part of the audience for such broadcasts is made up of people who
lack political interest but who are still curious to
become better informed about their "political environment". A majority of those interviewed felt that there
were too many political broadcasts, and most of those
with opinions disliked the arrangement of having both
TV networks carry the programs at the same time,
leaving them no option on what to view.

Blumler and McQuail found (not unexpectedly)
that habitual usage of political television was lighter
among heavy TV users, but they also found that
exposure to the political broadcasts was greater among
the people with the strongest political motivations.
People who looked to the programs for voting guidance got more information from them than did less

motivated people who actually watched more of the broadcasts. Although television appeared to have had little net effect on the two major parties, Blumler and McQuail conclude that it did shift votes toward the Liberals, whose broadcasts gave them unusual visibility among the least motivated and most persuasible voters. Although the Liberals had 13% of the vote, they had received 60% as much air time as each of the major parties. The results of this study therefore carry interesting implications regarding the role of television in enhancing the position of minority candidates with guaranteed access to air time.

Broadcasting of U.S. election returns has become a major annual event on TV and arrives at a high point every four years at the climax of each presidential race. Straightforward bulletins on the actual balloting have been supplemented, especially in the 1960 and 1964 elections, by computer projections of the returns in hand to statewide totals. (This has been done with estimating procedures that relate the population characteristics and historical voting record of each district to the available returns, leading to fast—and occasionally incorrect—forecasts of the outcome for a given state.)

Because of the time difference between Eastern and Western states, election news returns have been on the air for hours before polls close on the Pacific Coast, Alaska, and Hawaii, thereby raising the inevitable question of whether the voters are influenced by the foreknowledge of how the election seems to be going. (CBS's Frank Stanton has suggested a uniform national voting period to meet this problem.) A University of Michigan Survey Research Center study found that only 5% of the voters in 1964 had seen any election returns before they voted, but in a close election this 5% could spell a critical difference.

Harold Mendelsohn interviewed approximately

1,700 California voters both on the day before the 1964 election and again after the polls had closed. Only 1% who disclosed their voting intentions in the first telephone interview later reported switching from one presidential candidate to another. There was no evidence of a bandwagon effect occasioned by TV reports on Election Day (to which, in fact, only 12% of the sample had been exposed before they voted), nor evidence that foreknowledge of the returns kept people from voting. Since most voters had planned ahead of time when they would go to the polls, and since only 11% of the voters who made their decision on the last day watched election returns before casting their ballots, Mendelsohn concluded that the broadcasts could not be considered a significant factor. He did, however, find that last-minute election-eve campaign appeals on television by the candidates represented an important influence on many of those who were undecided at the time of the preelection interview. But these appeals were among a battery of persuasive efforts that both sides used at the last moment.

Kurt and Gladys Lang conclude from their study of the same election that the outcome of the voting was not affected by the TV newscast, but note that this did not mean there were *no* effects. The Langs interviewed 347 California voters after the election as well as 109 in Ohio for purposes of comparison. More of the California voters felt that the computerized projections of the results killed the fun of watching the election returns.

Feelings about the importance of the election's outcome did not seem to be closely related to whether of not people watched the returns before they voted.

The proportion of voters who watched the election results on TV before they voted was no different among those who thought the presidential and Senate races would be close and those who did not, but those who watched the returns before voting tended to be above average in political interest and in party loyalty.

Those people who became certain of the results early in the evening were more likely to attribute their certainty to computer projections than were those who formed their conclusions later when they saw the actual returns. The computer was thought to be "most helpful" when its predictions were best accepted.

The Langs inferred that the early returns affected voters' perceptions of the outcome only in relation to other information from polls and other sources to which they had been exposed before Election Day. Long before TV, Harold Gosnell had shown that intensive campaign activity could get out the vote in local elections that were essentially uncontested. The Langs find this congruent with their own observation that "the crucial social-psychological factor is the voter's long-term commitment to participation in the electoral process."

In California the Langs found no evidence that from hour to hour, as the returns came in, there was any defection of voters from their original choices or any dissuasion from voting itself. The later the vote cast, the more likely the voter was to have some notion of how the election was going, but Johnson's majority among the very last voters was not related to whether or not they had watched the TV reports.

The Senate race was closely matched, unlike the presidential election. In this case the election returns did seem to increase people's eagerness to vote, especially if they leaned toward the underdog.

The Langs note that both in Ohio and in California, most of the voting decisions actually related to local issues and candidates, about whom voters were less likely to have made up their minds in advance than about the presidency. There was no evidence that the broadcast returns might have produced *both* a bandwagon effect *and* a shift to the underdog that cancelled each other out.

Another study in 1964 also found differences between the national and local effects of TV election news. Douglas Fuchs interviewed about 2,700 voters in Seattle and in Southern California during the week before the 1964 election and again in the week after the election. He found that voters who went to the polls after they had seen election returns were slightly more apt to report a switch in their original presidential choices. They reported somewhat *less* switching, however, than other voters in their choice of candidates for state office.

In 1968, Coffin and Tuchman conducted a before-and-after study among 2,000 voters, three-fourths of them in the Pacific Time Zone and the remainder a control group in the East. The first interview was held in the three days before Election Day and concerned voting intentions, preferences, and interests; the second interview, conducted in the two days after the election, asked about what had actually happened. The West Coast respondents were divided into two groups, according to whether or not they had been exposed to TV election news broadcasts before they voted or decided not to vote. Of the voters in the West, 62% voted before the news reports first came on the air at 3 P.M., and only 6% saw the broadcasts before their vote (or decision not to vote). Four percent of the Westerners, compared with 7% of those in the East, reported last-minute changes in their plans to vote. In the East 6% switched candidates at the last minute — the same proportion as among the Westerners who had not been exposed to the election news. Among the small number of exposed Westerners, only 7% reported a change in voting preference — in effect, no significant difference. Considering the extreme closeness of the 1968 election, Coffin and Tuchman concluded that advance knowledge of election returns from TV broadcasts had no detectable influence on voter turnout or on the actual choice of candidates.

In summary, the evidence seems to suggest that no national election to date has been affected by the telecasting of returns, but there is at least some indication that people who watch the returns before voting are not identical with other voters in their subsequent actions. The possibilities of influence remain sufficiently important in their implications to warrant further research.

(G)   During the 1968 campaign, the Democratic convention was viewed in 90% of the television homes for an average of 9½ hours, while the Republican convention was viewed in 84% of the TV homes, an average of 8 hours. Convention planners actually adapted the timing of their sessions to coincide with the maximum hours of viewing.

During the 1968 conventions, ABC, unlike its two major competitors, broadcast only a daily 90-minute summary of the proceedings in preference to live coverage. It enjoyed a huge jump in ratings for its regular programs as a result.

(H)   In the course of the 1958 New York gubernatorial election, a study of 537 voters by Cunningham and Walsh found that newspapers and television were mentioned equally as the main source of information about the candidates. Two out of three voters reported seeing both candidates on television, but Rockefeller made a much more forceful and positive impression than did Harriman.

12. Television and the Juvenile Audience

(A)   Preschool children continue to be heavier TV viewers than those of school age. A Nielsen analysis for January--February of 1970 finds the average child between two and five watching 30 hours and 41 minutes a week, while the child six to eleven years old watches 25 hours and 49 minutes. The difference, as might be expected, is most apparent during school hours and is far less visible in the evening and on weekends. It is worth noting that in the "children's hour" between 5:00 and 7:30 P.M. on weekdays, 43% of the preschoolers and 38% of the six--eleven age group are watching during the typical time period, but the proportions rise to 45% and 54% respectively between 7:30 and 9:00 P.M., when the programming is presumably directed to adults.

Wilbur Schramm, Jack Lyle, and Everett Parker secured data from some 6,000 schoolchildren and 2,000 parents, as well as from hundreds of teachers and other officials in the United States and Canada, between 1958 and 1960. They found that even in "Radiotown"—a town without TV (in Canada in the late 1950's)—children and adults did not live in a "pretelevision era" but were highly conscious of the presence of TV in the larger culture. Comparing this town of about 5,000 with another town of the same size with TV, they found grade-school children in Radiotown spending about 15 minutes more a day on homework, going to four or five times as many movies a month, listening to substantially more radio, and reading more comic books.

Schramm, Lyle, and Parker found children first exposed to television at age two and coming to use it actively a year later. Picture magazines also become important to them at that age; between three and six they become acquainted with radio and with the movies. At the age of four 67% of the children were using TV; by the age of five the proportion was up to 82%, and by six it was 90%. (44% were using newspapers at age seven, and 71% by age nine.) Mass communications usage reached a peak in the sixth grade. In San Francisco, televiewing reached a peak at about 23 hours a week in the eighth grade and thereafter showed a decline. There was no particular difference between boys and girls in the amount of viewing, though sex differences in program preferences were manifested early.

Among young children, the more intelligent ones watched more TV, but between the ages of ten and thirteen they left the ranks of the heavy viewers. Overall, children of better-educated and upward-mobile parents watched less TV than did other children.

Jack Lyle and Heidi Hoffman studied the viewing habits of several thousand first-, sixth-, and tenth-grade youngsters in the Los Angeles area in 1971, and they concluded that children were spending more time in front of the TV set than they did at the time of Schramm, Lyle, and Parker's research ten years earlier. They comment, however, that attention is not to be equated with being in the presence of a set, and that other activities are often in progress at the same time. They also note a greater hostility toward commercials and more skepticism about the programming in general. (Because of the limited scope of the study it is difficult to accept the authors' generalizations.) Half of the first-graders said they sometimes or often modeled their play activity on things they had seen on TV. Forty percent of the boys and 60% of the girls acknowledged that they had been frightened by what they had seen on the tube, although the authors observe that "children do seem to enjoy being frightened to some degree."

At the sixth- and tenth-grade levels, children who watched a great deal of TV violence reported more conflicts with their parents. The brighter students watched more television than the others, though they were also more active participants in their other activities.

In the mid-1950's, Hilda Himmelweit, A. N. Oppenheim, and Pamela Vince conducted a landmark series of studies of television's effects on children. The research involved two matched samples of 1,854 children in London and three other cities. Children with TV at home were paired (on the basis of sex, age, intelligence, and social class) with others in the same classes who did not have TV and did not regularly watch it. The opening of a new TV transmitter in Norwich made it possible to supplement this main study with a before-and-after survey among 370 children in that city. The researchers used a rich variety of techniques: questionnaires, diaries, personality tests, and teacher ratings. In addition, they conducted a number of other surveys and analyses of the content of TV programs.

Himmelweit's findings in England paralleled the findings in the United States in many respects. She found, for example, that the first people to acquire television were those with an established dependence on the outside stimulation of radio and club activity and with narrower reading tastes. In two-thirds of the households the set was left on for the evening, though most children turned away from the set when they did not like what was on.

Children of higher intelligence and more active interests tended to be lighter viewers, but in general children's viewing patterns followed those of their parents. Children who had had TV for at least three years spent slightly less time viewing than those for whom television was still a relative novelty. Viewing time was no greater in homes that had access to ITV as well as to the BBC, but program choices became more selective. Compared with the non-TV group, the viewers showed more ambition, self-confidence, and a more "middle-class" orientation to jobs and marriage.

In Maracaibo, Venezuela, a 1968 survey by Marta Colomina de Rivero among 1,000 families found that 54% of the children aged one to eight watch at least two soap operas a day on TV.

Irving Merrill, in a 700-household survey in Lansing, Michigan, in 1956, found no significant difference in viewing time between boys and girls. Average viewing per day rose from 1.8 hours among children aged four and five to about 2 hours among the children aged six to eight; it held at about the same level till age thirteen, and then dropped to 1.67 hours among children aged fourteen to eighteen. Merrill found some evidence of a novelty effect, but this was dissipated within about two and one-half years.

In 1961 the Japanese Ministry of Education in Tokyo conducted a survey of 327 children and found that while only 11% were watching television between the ages of one and two, 40% at the ages of two to three, and 71% at three to four, 96% were watching by the ages of four and five.

The tendency for viewing to drop as children move into adolescence has been found outside the United States. A 1964 survey in West Germany found that viewing daily or nearly every day was done by 40% of primary-school children, 30% of middle-school children, and 29% of those in upper schools.

A 1966 national Brand Rating Index survey also found younger U.S. teenagers watching more TV and listening to less radio than older ones.

A BBDO analysis in 1967 found teenagers more inclined than their elders to be samplers of new shows and also more likely to drop out of the audience.

Maxwell McCombs (1967) interviewed 816 undergraduate and graduate students at UCLA in the spring of 1967. Although this was a generation reared on television, he concluded that "they are clearly print-oriented." Over 20% reported that they never watch TV. Another 50% viewed only a few times a week or less. The viewing of newscasts and documentaries was higher among male than among female students, and this kind of information-seeking was higher among students who exhibited high political interest. It rose from 44% (in the past week) among freshmen to 55% among seniors.

Takeo Furu, after an exhaustive analysis of Japanese research on children's television viewing, concludes: "I think I have spent too much time on discussing the amount of viewing time and program preferences. I have attempted this kind of review: I selected valuable data from many complicated reports, and sometimes gave a statistical reexamination of them because I discovered that there were many reports in which the data did not support the conclusion."

(B)   Schramm, Lyle, and Parker found that children adapted their media habits at an early age to those of their families. Children whose parents were book readers or ETV viewers were the most likely to fall into these habits themselves. Watching of children's programs gave way during the school years to the viewing of children's variety and adventure shows, of Westerns, and eventually of situation comedies and other adult-oriented programs.

Steven Chaffee, Jack McLean, and Charles Atkin compared the television habits of parents and children and concluded that adolescents do not follow the patterns of their parents, although they tend to avoid the same kinds of programs their parents do.

Himmelweit reported that three-fourths of the programs children named as their favorites were actually adult shows, especially crime thrillers. A survey of 1,500 Ohio housewives by Harold Niven found that control over the set passed from children to parents as the evening progressed, but that children were responsible for many of the specific program selections that might not otherwise have been made.

(C)   A substantial volume of TV advertising continues to be directed at children, and TV has been
given credit for the gigantic expansion of the toy business during the 1960's. On a single Saturday in January, 1971, between 8:00 A.M. and 2:00 P.M., CBS
carried 126 different commercials interspersed in programming directed to children, according to *Advertising Age*. A 1967 Bruskin survey for ABC-TV, among
1,500 mothers of children aged four to twelve, found
that 94% named TV as their children's main source
of information about products and brands.

          Among 1,100 young people of the ages twelve
to seventeen interviewed by Scott Ward in Prince
Georges County, Maryland, criticism of TV advertising went up along with social class, as it does among
adults. Lower-class youngsters watched more TV and
were more favorable to the commercials. Paradoxically,
adolescents of high intelligence liked the commercials
more than less intelligent ones, and recalled them
better; in fact the ability to recall commercials was
linked to intelligence more than to the amount of
television viewing.

(D)   Paul Witty repeated his earlier studies among
200 Chicago-area children in 1963. He found that
about two-thirds of those in grades two through six
got at least occasional help from their parents in selecting programs; about half reported that their parents
limited the amount of TV viewing they were permitted.

(E)   Bradley Greenberg (and his associate Joseph
Dominick) queried 84 low-income Negro and 124
low-income white high-school students in Philadelphia
in 1968, as well as 98 middle-income high-school
students. About half the whites (of both income levels)
but only about a third of the Negroes, said their parents set rules on how late they could stay up to
watch TV.

(F)   One person in five interviewed for the Canadian

Broadcasting Corporation in 1963 felt that TV programs are harmful to children. In the United States, a 1966 poll for the National Association of Broadcasters found that 53% of the public thought TV had a good effect on children, overall, while 19% thought it had a harmful effect. In the same poll, 23% said TV kept children at home and out of trouble, 35% said violent programs increased juvenile delinquency, and 37% said TV exposed children to things that were bad for their morals.

Earl Barcus, in a small study of Boston children, found parental influence being exercised not merely through formal controls but through many subtle and informal communications: "Viewing with children, settlement of disputes over which programs to watch, and discussing program content or answering children's questions about the programs." Robert Blood's study of 100 families in Ann Arbor, Michigan, found that in lower-class households additional TV time was often used to reward good behavior, but that at all social levels there was a strong feeling that there were some programs that children should not watch.

Technology has placed new tools in the hands of less permissive parents. Sony Electronics has advertised a "Censor" to "screen out hate, guns, and violence," and to shield children "from the seamy side of life like a nanny. First you find out exactly what time the nice, educational, and funny programs are on. And exactly what time the mean, stupid, and bloody programs are on. Then you turn the built-in timer to turn the Sony Censor on when it's time for a good program. And to turn it off when it's time for a bad program."

(G)   Three out of five children interviewed by Witty in 1963 said their teachers made suggestions to them on what to view. About half admitted they frequently or occasionally studied while "watching" television. Witty concludes that book reading has increased "a little" since the advent of TV.

Schramm, Lyle, and Parker found no evidence that television improves school performance. Among first-grade children, those in Teletown had higher vocabulary scores than those in Radiotown, and the heavy TV viewers scored significantly higher. By the time children had reached the upper grades, however, this difference had faded.

Among tenth graders, high ability was strongly associated with light TV viewing and low intelligence with heavy viewing. (By contrast, among eighth-grade children daily newspapers were read by 65% of those with high mental ability but by only 30% of those with low intelligence.) Eleanor Maccoby compared children in television and nontelevision homes in 1950–51, and found that the former were more likely not to have done their homework.

In England, however, Himmelweit found that viewers and nonviewers spent the same amount of time on their homework and showed the same interest in their school subjects. Interestingly, individual children in the two groups were similarly rated by their teachers in terms of how well they concentrated on their studies and how tired they were in the morning. At the same time, half the teachers expressed the opinion that TV viewing in the evening left children tired and unable to concentrate the next day. Himmelweit concluded that television neither added nor detracted from general knowledge except in the case of young children who had not yet learned to read easily and who responded well to TV.

Irving Merrill found no difference in bedtime between children in TV and non-TV homes.

(H)		A variety of other studies have attempted to define and document the motivation and effects of TV viewing among children. Charles Winick, examining fan mail written by children, found that 88% of it was favorable in content and 70% of it involved some special request (for example, keeping a program on the air or rerunning a specific broadcast, changing its time, lengthening it, getting new performers, getting a photograph or a script). One 14 year old wrote: "I read with utter horror an announcement in the paper that my favorite program might go off. I am president of our school's fan club for the program. If the program leaves, we wouldn't have a club and there would be nothing to talk about in civics class on Tuesdays." Reuben Mehling found 91% of young Indiana children named television as the medium they would prefer to keep if they were limited to a single choice. In high school TV fell to a 56% share, while radio and print media became correspondingly more important. By college, TV was preferred by only 38% (McEvoy).

Schramm, Lyle, and Parker found that teen-agers were particularly resistant to the revelations of fakery in the quiz shows and "payola" for the disk jockeys on radio. Television's prestige diminished as children got older, while that of the newspaper rose. William S. Baxter, an Ohio University journalism professor, repeated in 1958 a study originally made in Des Moines, Iowa, in 1950 by Paul Lyness, among youngsters in the fifth, seventh, ninth, and eleventh grades of school. Between the two studies radio listening fell from 15 hours weekly to 9 hours, newspapers from 2 hours and 50 minutes to 2 hours and 30 minutes; magazines regularly read fell from 1.5 to 0.8, and comic books from about 5 to about 3 a month. Movie attendance dropped from once a week to once every three weeks.

Himmelweit, in England, concluded that television had a short-run negative effect on both movie-going and book reading, but that both these activities recovered with adolescence. Radio listening and the reading of comic books were sharply affected. While TV kept the family at home, it did not keep its members together in any binding sense, since viewing tended to get "more silent and personal" with the onset of adolescence. The TV viewers and the control groups showed no difference in their vision.

Among middle-school children in Japan, TV seemed to be responsible for an increased interest in self-improvement and career planning, while among children of primary-school age it fostered interest in entertainment and sports.

Just like radio and the movies, television helps to shape the perceptions that youngsters have of the world around them. Alberta Siegel exposed two groups of Pennsylvania schoolchildren to different versions of a radio show about taxi drivers and found that when they were later asked to complete a story about taxi drivers their earlier exposure was reflected in their accounts.

Melvin and Lois DeFleur conducted extensive interviews with 237 children and their mothers in a small Midwestern town of 35,000. They used cartoon-like representations of various occupations as stimuli to get children to report on role characteristics. The job descriptions tended to be stereotyped and "homogenized" in a way that was not true of occupations with which children were in firsthand personal contact.

Kent Geiger and Robert Sokol, comparing the viewing of commercial and educational TV among middle-class and working-class people, concluded that TV entertainment corresponded to the working-class need for immediate gratification rather than to the middle-class ideal of "deferred gratification." Testing this thesis, Schramm, Lyle, and Parker found that high use of TV was related to an orientation toward the present and toward fantasy, while low use of TV reflected an orientation to the future and a stronger sense of reality. They concluded that children used television as a stimulus for fantasy but that it was also a great device for learning, especially for incidental learning. The young child regards television as real, and only as children get older do they learn to "discount" the fictional element in what they see.

On most questions related to viewing habits and attitudes, Greenberg and Dominick found that social class seemed a more important determinant than race. Negro teenagers were more apt than whites to believe that TV depicted life "the way it is," but they were also most likely to say that they watched it because it excited them and kept their minds off other things.

Greenberg and Dominick also questioned 392 fourth- and fifth-grade children in East Cleveland, Ohio, in 1969, and matched Negroes and whites in three different occupational status groups. They found no differences by race or social position in the extent to which children talked about TV programs, though high-income white children were the most likely to say they watched TV for excitement, and poor Negro children were most convinced that television was true to life. (40% of the children said that they were sometimes punished by being denied the right to watch TV.)

Greenberg and Gordon conducted an experiment with 588 boys, some fifth-graders and some eighth-graders, using a sequence of violent and nonviolent TV scenes. Among younger boys from disadvantaged backgrounds the violence was more enjoyable and perceived as being more like "real life." Among the older boys, racial differences in the acceptability of violence seemed more important than social class differences. The violence was most acceptable to the most disadvantaged, though it was clearly recognized for what it was.

Gary Byrne, in a study of some 400 North Carolina schoolchildren, found Negro and white children about equally exposed to TV news, but since the Negro children were less often exposed to newspapers, the TV news loomed larger as an influence. Byrne concluded that the news on TV also made them more inclined to trust in governmental authority.

(I)   There continue to be striking instances of imitation by children of what they see on TV, and these cases are often cited as proof that televised scenes of aggressive or immoral behavior stimulate the young to behave in the same way. Takeo Furu reports that when television first appeared in Japan sets were installed in shrine compounds and the plazas in front of railway stations as well as in restaurants and coffee shops. "Riki (Rikidozan), a Japanese wrestler who always defeated the fierce foreign wrestlers, soon became a hero among children. The children would also attempt to imitate at their school playgrounds or parks the professional wrestlers they saw on television. But soon reports of children being seriously injured in this rough play began to appear in the newspapers, and professional wrestling on television became a target of criticism by both parents and educators. Finally, Riki himself went on the radio to warn children against playing at being wrestlers." Alberta Siegel reports on the case of a 12-year-old child who died in England, allegedly imitating his hero, Batman, in leaping from the roof of a shed. (But children are not the only ones to respond with imitations of what they see on TV. A 1966 NBC drama, "The Doomsday Flight," dealt with a bomb scare on a plane in flight and was shown in spite of complaints by the Air Lines Pilots Association. While the show was on the air, one airline received a bomb threat, and there were eight in the week after the broadcast, the same number as in the entire previous month.)

Violence in children's programming, and in adult programming exposed to children, continued to be a major target of TV's critics. Schramm, Lyle, and Parker, analyzing 100 hours of network TV during the "children's hours" in 1960, counted 12 murders,

16 major gunfights, and 103 other incidents of violence and mayhem, including a guillotining and a tidal wave. George Gerbner's more recent analyses, already cited, find a high level of violence in cartoon shows.

The very nature of the viewing process has been cited as a cause of violence. Dr. Lawrence J. Freedman of the Los Angeles Psychoanalytic Institute has blamed TV for much of the violence of "the first TV generation." His thesis is that television viewing makes children passive because it denies them normal outlets for aggressive energy that accumulates and finally explodes in destructive violence. Freedman believes that the content of the programming is actually irrelevant. "All television, except in small doses, feeds children ready-made fantasies at a time when fantasy-making and intellectual activity is crucial to their development. If a child watches enough television he will automatically become violent because he has nowhere else to go with his normal aggressive energy that he would be working off in creative activity . . . Many adolescents today take for granted that everything comes from the outside, that satisfactions come easily and can be enjoyed passively without taking others into consideration. These are attitudes that television encourages."

While these opinions have often been echoed it is hard to find solid evidence to back them up. Hilda Himmelweit noted a reduction in casual play with other children as TV imposed more rigid structure on a child's daily routine. She concluded from her massive research, however, that television did not make children more passive or less imaginative. In fact, it appeared to stimulate their reading interests, though it did not affect their visits to museums and galleries or their hobby activities.

Lyle and Hoffman also report that, among first-graders, the heavy viewers play less with other children.

Surveys conducted by NHK, the Japanese Broadcasting Corporation, in the late 1950's, found no difference between children in TV and non-TV households in the extent of outside activities or interests or on any other index of "passivity."

The limited data do not support the thesis that the passive nature of TV viewing is conducive to the expression of violence as a compensatory mechanism. Much more substantial evidence has accumulated, however, regarding the *direct* effects of exposure to television (with its substantial component of violent content) in arousing aggressive behavior. Such evidence comes both from large-scale survey comparisons of children in TV and non-TV situations (before television became universal) and from a variety of small-scale laboratory experiments. One of the largest of the comparative studies was that done by Schramm, Lyle, and Parker, who summarized their findings cautiously: "For some children, under some conditions, some television is harmful. For other children, under the same conditions, or for the same children under most conditions, it may be beneficial. For most children, under most conditions, most television is probably neither particularly harmful nor particularly beneficial."

Aggression levels among tenth graders in Radiotown and Teletown seemed about the same. Children in families with high levels of child-parent conflict tended to watch more television but to read fewer general and news magazines than did children with less family conflict. At the high social levels, high use of television seemed related to conflict and aggression; whereas at lower social levels it was associated with low conflict and aggression and was more of a direct response to the family environment. The authors comment: "The result of going to television fantasy, in a great proportion of the cases, may not be to reduce the level of tension in the real world, but only to change worlds. The child leaves the field where he finds violence and discontent."

Comparing viewers and controls in England, Himmelweit found no evidence that TV increased delinquency, aggressiveness, or maladjustment, though she acknowledges that it might precipitate antisocial behavior on the part of a child who was already disturbed. She concluded that the effect of violent programs was to counterbalance the discharge and arousal of aggressive impulses in real life.

Himmelweit also found that while fictional episodes of televised violence were sometimes frightening to children, they did not seem sensitive to real scenes of violence as shown in newsreels. Verbal aggression, particularly when it occurred in real-life broadcasts (among panelists or on sportscasts) was more disturbing than actual scenes of violence, though televised gun or swordplay and occasional fisticuffs at televised sporting events were frightening, too. Violent TV programs that were frightening to children on first exposure were no longer shocking to them after they became used to them.

It is interesting to review these observations in relation to children's reaction to what was perhaps the most intense, direct emotional experience of a major event by an entire population — the assassination of President Kennedy and its aftermath as mediated by television.

Roberta S. Sigel notes the "similarity of the Oswald-Ruby episode to those a child watches day after day on television, especially the favorite Western ... In the eyes of children, Oswald was clearly the bad guy of Dallas. Over and over they heard the Texas law-enforcement officials (replete with the same ten-gallon hats and boots children know so well) declare that they had enough incriminating evidence against

Oswald to ask for the death penalty and that they felt confident 'we will get it.' What then did Ruby do but gun down a man who by the standards of the Western deserved no better fate?" Sigel found children less upset than adults over Oswald's murder. More of them (19%) spontaneously expressed pleasure at his death than volunteered (16%) "we must not take the law into our own hands." Most children, however, recognized that Ruby still had to get a court trial and that Oswald, too, should have had one rather than mob justice. Younger and lower-class children were most likely of all to say they were glad to see Oswald shot. But although viewing increases as we go down the social scale, heavy viewers in *every* social class consistently outnumbered light viewers in their approval or unconcern about Oswald's murder, suggesting that TV operated independently as an influence on the moral standards of the juvenile audience.

The day is now past—in the United States at least—when comparisons of TV and non-TV groups can be made within the general population. Most of the significant recent research on the effects of TV violence comes from the tradition of experimental social psychology and is based on small and often atypical samples. A continuing theme in these studies has been the relationship between frustration and aggression. The effects of fictional violence within the media have been studied in relation to dispositions set off by other nonfictional experiences. Some of these studies suggested that media violence triggered a propensity to behave aggressively. For example, Leonard Berkowitz found that college students who had seen fight scenes from the film "The Champion" (in comparison with a control group) administered more "severe" (though actually fake) electric shocks to a "victim" who had previously insulted them, and who was actually a confederate of the experimenter.

Russell Geen also reports that aggression has the greatest likelihood of expression after the combination of exposure to filmed aggression and real stress. Berkowitz and Geen (1966) found that people were more apt to administer (fake) electric "shocks" to someone whose name resembled that of the victim in a boxing film they had seen earlier. (In yet another study in 1967, Berkowitz and Geen found that college students became less inhibited in their aggressive impulses after seeing a film of "justified aggression.")

Berkowitz (1964) concluded that the viewer of media violence may inhibit his aggressive impulses to avoid being punished for them. Berkowitz and his associates found that the catharsis effect was activated not by mere exposure to filmed violence but by subsequent punishment of the villain.

Albert Bandura found, in a series of studies, that nursery-school children showed more aggression toward a vinyl Bobo doll after they had been exposed to prior displays of aggressive behavior on the part of real adults, adults on film, and cartoon characters. When the children were shown scenes in which the aggressor was punished for his misdeeds, their level of subsequent aggressive behavior was less than that in a control group. These children, however, imitated the aggressive actions just as well as the others when they were specifically instructed to do so. This led Bandura to conclude that the techniques of aggression could be learned even when their display was discouraged.

But in another study in which they showed films of children playing with dogs to nursery schoolers, Bandura and Frances Menlove also found that media could be used to significantly reduce fear reactions. The children became less fearful of dogs than did those in a control group.

Other experiments (reported by William Catton)

conducted in 1961 by O. Ivar Lövass and by Paul Mussen and Eldred Rutherford similarly found that exposure to brief scenes of filmed aggression (including cartoons) resulted in greater displays of hostility afterwards.

Richard Walters, Edward Thomas, and William Ackers found that a group of hospital attendants displayed significantly greater willingness to "shock" a confederate of the experimenters after viewing a film of a knife fight than an equivalent group after viewing a neutral film. Berkowitz and Buck found that seeing a gun made experimental subjects more willing to administer a (fake) electric shock to others. Hartmann found aggression levels increased after exposure to a two-minute film.

David Hicks showed children aggressive models in a simulated TV show and found that they displayed more imitative aggression both immediately afterwards and also months later after a "refresher" of the original experiment. Hicks also observed that when a child had someone else watching along with him who was present later in the test situation, the observer's comments influenced the child's subsequent performance. This suggests that children are influenced not only by what they see but by the attitudes of their parents toward the programs.

A study of primary-school boys in Adelaide, Australia, by S. H. Lovibond found heavy TV viewing related to a preference for violent programming and to an admiration for the use of force. Boys (though not girls) studied by L. D. Eron watched more violent shows on television the more aggressive they were themselves. Lotte Bailyn found that preference for violent TV programs was associated with a high level of frustration and also with a tendency toward emotional disturbance. Maccoby, Levin, and Selya (1955) found that frustrated children remembered more aggressive media content than a nonfrustrated control group (though this was not confirmed in a subsequent study the following year).

James Halloran, R. L. Brown, and D. C. Chaney studied the television viewing habits of 281 young delinquents, aged 10–20, who were living at home on probation. This group was compared with two control groups of nondelinquent youngsters. The problem youngsters watched no more TV than the others, but the uses to which they put television were different. The delinquent boys showed far more interest in "exciting" programs and greater awareness of TV heroes. In short, the fantasy violence on TV seemed to go with the tendency to express violence in real life. An as yet uncompleted, continuing mail panel study of teen-age boys, conducted by John Robinson, is also turning up evidence that the amount of viewing of violent TV programming is linked to the incidence of aggressive behavior.

Not all the evidence has led to identical conclusions. Siegel (1956) found no difference in aggression levels among four- and five-year-old children after they watched violent cartoon films. A study in Sweden by Olaf Elthammar compared the reactions of delinquent and nondelinquent teen-agers in an experiment in which he showed them violent films. He found no difference in their aggressive reactions. In fact 80% of his subjects showed no "perceptible" reactions at all. Another study in Australia by R. J. Thomson produced no evidence that teen-agers exhibited psychopathic symptoms after viewing crime films.

In 1964, Ruth Hartley conducted an examination of some two dozen experiments reported in the recent psychological literature on the effects of televised violence upon children. While the conclusions of these studies generally supported the thesis that exposure to violent media content led to an increase in aggressive behavior on the part of the viewers,

Hartley was sharply critical of the research to date, both because of the small samples of subjects and because of what she considered the unwarranted extrapolation of the findings from the psychological laboratory to the real world. She criticized Bandura's studies of nursery-school children, arguing that "play behavior cannot serve as an accurate predictor of nonplay behavior." (This distinction between behavior in the laboratory and in real-life situations is supported in research by Willems and Rausch.)

Hartley summed up her analysis by saying: "It is impossible to predict accurately or even usefully from the results of the laboratory studies reviewed here to everyday viewing situations, partly because individual differences in response to the stimuli used were ignored in the reports. Additionally, the stimuli used were often vastly different from the materials of ordinary exposure in relation to several crucial elements .... The investigators who have linked the laboratory results with real-life events have done so by the device of using the same generalized label — e.g., 'aggression,' 'violence,' 'punitiveness' — to bracket quite different behavioral referents."

Hartley's critique was summarized by CBS's Joseph Klapper in 1969 for the National Commission on the Causes and Prevention of Violence, and presumably was still considered as a valid objection to the artificiality of the laboratory experiments. Members of the Commission retorted that TV could not have things both ways: they could not proclaim to advertisers that the medium had powerful effects and at the same time disclaim any harmful effects from the violence to which children were exposed.

The hearings held by the Violence Commission (headed by Milton Eisenhower) and the studies made for the Commission raised anew the perennial questions regarding the effects of televised violence. Another set of hearings held by a Senate Committee in 1969 led to the funding of a $1 million research program under the aegis of the National Institute of Mental Health, with a wide array of both field and laboratory studies conducted on a crash basis. At the same time, the television networks initiated new research programs. NBC, for example, set up a panel of 866 boys, aged 7 to 18, who with their parents were to be interviewed and tested repeatedly over a three-year period to determine whether viewing could be related to aggressive behavior.

In one of the N.I.M.H.-sponsored studies, Steven Chaffee and Jack McLeod studied aggressive behavior among two samples of children in the sixth to tenth years of school in Wisconsin and Maryland. They found aggressiveness to be correlated with the viewing of violence and, also, with the total amount of time spent viewing TV. The actual viewing of violence was associated with a favorable attitude toward violent programs and characters, but the preference for violent programs was only slightly related to aggressiveness. Children in "protective" family situations, where troublesome and challenging situations were discouraged, turned out to be heavy viewers, while children in more permissive family environments were less aggressive and watched less violent programming. This led to the conclusion that aggressive behavior reflected the family context in which television violence was viewed.

Other studies (made for N.I.M.H. by J. J. McIntyre and J. J. Teevan and by Jack McLeod, Charles Atkin, and Steven Chaffee) have also found a preference for violent programs to be associated with greater displays of aggression. A ten-year research on 400 children at three age levels, by M. M. Lefkowitz, L. D. Eron, and L. O. Walder, found that the amount of aggression displayed could be predicted better from the amount of TV violence watched in the third grade than by any other measure. A. Leifer and D. Roberts exposed children experimentally to TV programs that differed in the degree of their violent content. Subsequent responses on a test of aggression were associated with the amount of violence on the programs seen. R. M. Liebert and R. A. Baron exposed children aged between five and nine to one of two televised sequences: a violent program, "The Untouchables," or an active but nonaggressive sports show. Children exposed to the violence displayed more aggression afterwards. A. H. Stein, L. K. Friedrich, and F. Vondracek exposed 97 nursery-school children to programs with differing degrees of aggressive content, and concluded that children who were initially high in their aggressive impulses were particularly responsive to this type of stimulus.

Reviewing the experimental evidence for the Eisenhower Commission in 1969, Richard Goranson concluded that aggressive media content is more readily imitated in real life if it is presented in realistic rather than fantasy terms and if it resembles the real-life situation in which the effects on the viewer are subsequently measured. Goranson observes that a variety of experiments have revealed an immediate emotional response to shocking or violent scenes, "real" or filmed, but that this emotional response wears off with repeated exposure. This would seem to suggest that children become inured to TV violence merely because of its predictable and repetitive character.

The studies briefly noted here (which merely skim the voluminous experimental literature on aggression) reflect a considerable variety of research techniques as well as a wide range of subject populations. While their findings do not all mesh perfectly together, the weight of the evidence cited consistently supports the common-sense supposition that media violence is an irritant rather than a soothing influence on those exposed to it. An important exception to this conclusion must be taken very seriously because it is at variance with a number of the other experiments reported here:

Seymour Feshbach (1961) found that college students responded less aggressively to provocation after they had watched a film with brutal boxing scenes. In a subsequent series of studies, Feshbach and Robert Singer divided several hundred boarding-school boys — some in private schools and some in charitable institutions — into a group that could watch up to six hours of aggressive television programming a week for six weeks and a control group that watched the same amount of nonaggressive programs. They found no difference between the test and control groups among the private-school boys, but among the poor boys in "homes," the control group engaged in far more unprovoked aggressive behavior toward each other and toward property (though not toward authority figures). At the same time, they showed less fantasy aggression. Feshbach and Singer concluded that for these boys, who had fewer intellectual resources than their fellows in the private schools, television, with its usual component of violence, normally served as an outlet for aggressive impulses. When their viewing of aggressive programming was restricted, they lost a significant form of psychological support and became more aggressive as a result.

Berkowitz (1970), reviewing the evidence on the hypothesis that expression of hostility "clears the air," concludes that "the catharsis hypothesis blinds us to the important social principle that aggression is all too likely to lead to still more aggression."

Goranson suggests that what Feshbach interprets as catharsis is really the inhibiting effect of anxieties aroused by the violent episodes witnessed by the experimental subjects. He concludes wryly: "We would scarcely advocate that adolescents be shown libidinous films as a means of reducing sexual behavior, nor would we advise that a starving man observe the eating of a delicious meal in order to diminish his hunger pangs. Similarly, we should not expect that the out-pourings of violence in the mass media will have the effect of reducing aggressive behavior."

13. Frontiers of Television

(A)   In 1971, projection-television is still operational only for theatrical showings and has not yet arrived in the home.

(B)   The growth of color TV, already described in the Notes to Chapter 4, has followed predictions. By the beginning of 1971 there were nearly 32,000,000 color sets in the United States. Color has introduced a new dimension to the discussion of TV's sales effects. A 1966 study made by Ernest Dichter for Television Advertising Representatives found substantially more positive responses to color-TV commercials than to the same commercials in black and white. Color was seen as more "intimate," "active," "exciting," "near," "unique," "adventuresome," "real," "friendly," "modern," and "sophisticated." Its comparative appeal appeared to be greater the longer one had owned a color set.

(C)   By 1971 there were 93 million TV sets in use in the United States and another 180 million in 130 countries in the rest of the world (exclusive of China, North Korea, and North Vietnam). This included 28 million in the Soviet Union, 19 million in Japan (over 5 million with color TV), 16 million in Britain, 15.5 in West Germany, 5.3 million in East Germany, 10 million in France, 10 million in Italy, 7.7 million in Canada, 6.5 million in Brazil, and 4 million in Poland. (By contrast, India had only 21,000 sets; China a mere 300,000.) Over 10,000 TV stations were broadcasting to this vast audience, of which some 2,800 actually originated programs.

TABLE 120

TV Sets per 1000 Population

(Sources: 1970–71 TV Factbook and 1971 World Almanac)

Country	Sets/1000
United States	433
Canada	335
East Germany	311
Sweden	297
Great Britain	294
West Germany	269
Denmark	256
Australia	238
Japan	225
Netherlands	225
France	205
Belgium	194
Switzerland	184
Italy	166
Austria	154
Poland	107
Yugoslavia	72
Brazil	69
Mexico	52
Soviet Union	8

(D) As a means of mass instruction supplementing or anticipating the usual classroom experience, TV has clearly demonstrated its power to teach. A study among high-school students found that an audience participation program on the National Citizenship Test produced changes in information and attitudes that persisted after six months had passed.

"Sesame Street," a program directed at pre-schoolers and one of Public Television's notable successes, was the subject of a two-year study by Samuel Ball and Gerry Bogatz for the Educational Testing Service. They concluded in 1971 that three-year-old children who watched the instructional program regularly learned more from it than four- and five-year-old children who only watched it occasionally. The program used TV-commercial advertising techniques to pound away at the essentials of letter and number recognition. Although "Sesame Street" was acclaimed for its ability to help underprivileged children overcome the educational handicaps of their environment, its audience was proportionately smaller among those children than among youngsters in middle-class families.

Rural children whose performance in arithmetic fell below the national norm were brought up to the norm or even beyond it after exposure to closed-circuit TV instruction. But Godwin C. Chu and Wilbur Schramm, reviewing 421 comparative studies of televised and conventional instruction, found that in 308 cases there was no significant difference in their merits; in 63 cases the TV instruction was superior (especially at the lower levels); in 50 cases conventional teaching was better (especially at the college level). But Chu and Schramm point out that such comparisons are unrealistic, since televised instruction is normally used to supplement rather than to replace ordinary classroom teaching. The most effective use of televised instruction, they conclude, is when no feedback or discussion is necessary. In fact, television and film seem almost identical as instructional devices.

Research on the merits of televised teaching at the college level leads to somewhat qualified judgments of its effects. Studies of television instruction at the Pennsylvania State University in 1956–57 found that professors with experience in televised instruction preferred it to large classes, while those without such experience preferred the traditional classroom. Students also were predominantly favorable to television instruction, the most important reason being that the small TV room was more conducive to concentration than the large lecture hall. As the experiments progressed, students also came to hold the opinion that on television they had access to superior instructors.

Hope Klapper compared the achievements of four classes of a televised college course and found that performance was not affected by the absence of direct personal contact with the lecturer, though there was substantial variation in response to individual teachers. Bruce Westley and Lionel Barrow found that instructional television was significantly more effective in transmitting information than a radio version of the same program. This difference, however, disappeared after six weeks. Schramm and his associates concluded that while instructional television could be extremely effective, compared with traditional methods of education, its use should depend on the expense and suitability of adapting it to each individual educational problem. John V. Irwin and Arnold E. Aronson suggest on the basis of their experiments that students can play back verbal statements from a lecture better in a written examination than they can verbalize what they have seen in an instructional film.

About eight out of ten U.S. TV households are within receiving range of one or more of the 198 public or educational TV stations, and in about 20% of the homes public television is watched once a week or more often. In nineteen of the biggest cities, the American Research Bureau reported in 1970 that public-TV audiences grew from 4,214,000 people in 1966 to 7,369,000 in 1970.

Herman Land's analysis of TV audience found no evidence that viewing levels rose when educational television was introduced into a city.

A national coincidental-telephone survey in 1966, reported by Wilbur Schramm, found an estimated ¾ million people watching educational television. (This compared with some 66 million reported by Nielsen as viewing during the average evening minute.) Schramm found the average VHF station on ETV had a program rating of 1.3%, while the average UHF rating was 0.5%.

Are the ratings biased? An interesting experiment by Peter Fox compared the willingness of ETV viewers and nonviewers to cooperate with the standard approach used to recruit cooperators with the broadcast ratings services. The ETV viewers were above average in cooperativeness, thereby refuting the argument that television ratings are biased against cultural and educational programs.

The Carnegie Commission report on public broadcasting estimated that ETV had .4% the audience size of commercial television.

The social significance and impact of educational TV cannot be judged by the numerical size of its audiences, any more than the influence of a publication can be gauged by the size of its circulation. The creation of the Corporation for Public Broadcasting injected a vital, new creative force into TV programming, and the steady expansion of the public-television network will inevitably be reflected in a growing influence upon the nation's cultural and intellectual life.

Hugh Beville, Jr. of NBC conducted a study in Pittsburgh, which had a full-time VHF educational-TV station. Of those interviewed 76% agreed, "there ought to be more educational programs on television." An actual check by viewing diaries indicated that only 4% of those who wanted more ETV had viewed the ETV station in the course of the week. Beville concluded, "It is the heavy viewer of television who does most of the viewing of informational and cultural programming."

In 1959–60 Wilbur Schramm, Jack Lyle, and

Ithiel Pool conducted 30,000 telephone interviews and over 2,000 personal interviews in the areas of nine educational-television stations. (About a third of the broadcast time of these stations was devoted to school programming and two-thirds to more general programming.) The individual stations showed substantial differences in their abilities to attract viewers, and the typical "regular" viewer watched ETV for 1 hour to 1 hour and 20 minutes per week. The ETV viewers were of a higher income and better educated than the nonviewers; they were more readily characterized as active people, as "achievers," and as political liberals. They were much more heavily oriented to print, to high culture, and to information. In Boston, ETV viewing was high among Jews and low among Catholics, relative to their strength in the population. ETV viewing turned out to be characteristic of certain families; if parents watched it, the children did too. ETV viewers also were exceptionally selective in their general viewing habits.

Schramm, Lyle, and Pool found that, not only for ETV viewers but for nonviewers as well, two-thirds felt they learned things from watching TV. But the ETV viewers were better able to support their feeling with specific examples, especially with those of a cultural as well as of a political nature. It was precisely the people who most often gave cultural reasons who were the heaviest viewers of ETV. The ETV viewers evinced substantial satisfaction with the performance of their local educational stations, and the improvements they suggested tended to relate to specific program ideas rather than to changes in format or function. ETV viewers and nonviewers were remarkably similar in their notions of how ETV and commercial television could be described: "Commercial television is more fun and also apt to be more boring, and educational television is likely to be more useful and more informative." Maxwell E. McCombs, in a study of 200 viewers of an ETV station in California, found that information was more important than culture-seeking as a motivation for viewing.

Charles Winick interviewed 392 ETV viewers in a large Northeastern city and a matched sample of their non-ETV viewing next-door neighbors. He found that while the two groups were similar in income, the ETV viewers were better educated and in more specialized occupations. ETV viewing was more of a feminine than a masculine activity. The ETV viewers had acquired their sets an average of 2 years later than the non-ETV viewers, and their total use of the medium averaged 2.7 hours daily compared with 3.4 hours for the others. Only 37% of the ETV viewers had discussed a television program (any television program) with anyone outside the family in the previous 3 weeks. The corresponding figure for the nonviewers of ETV was 68%. Nonviewers described the ETV channel as "educational," while the viewers characterized it as "intellectual." The ETV viewers were people who were far less likely (33%) to say they got a "great deal of pleasure" out of TV, compared with their neighbors (80%). The ETV viewers were also more oriented to print and had higher levels of aspiration.

(E)   In five markets measured by the Nielsen Station Index, the UHF station reached half again as many households in the average week in the spring of 1968 as in the fall of 1966. But UHF continues to be TV's weak point. In 1971 there were 185 commercial and 111 noncommercial UHF stations. 43% of the TV stations in the top twenty markets were UHF stations in 1971, but these had only about a 6% share of the prime-time audience.

(F)   A variety of pay-TV systems have been suggested and used, involving the scrambling and unscrambling of messages placed on the air. The advent of cable TV made most of these technical alternatives obsolete. The unscrambling unit for on-air pay TV could be activated either by coins or by punch-cards inserted into a decoder hooked up between the TV set and the antenna.

In Etobicoke, Ontario, where Telemeter ran a pay-TV operation for a half-dozen years in the early 1960's, a survey among subscribers found that they reported reading more magazines and watching less regular television than they had done a year before. Most of their viewing continued to be on the regular, free channels. The absence of commercials was most often cited as the main virtue of pay TV.

A study of the pay-TV subscriber in four cities with pay-TV systems was made for CBS by Oxtoby-Smith and released in 1965. It showed that the subscribers were more active people than their neighbors: they entertained more, went out more, belonged to more organizations, and appeared to be more interested in cultural self-improvement. While they had hoped to get Broadway shows, dance recitals, and other cultural programs not ordinarily offered by commercial television, the subscribers found pay-TV's actual fare somewhat disappointing. They spent an average of something under $2 a week and were resistant to the automatic service charge. The absence of commercial interruptions seemed of less importance to them than the quality of the programming. The report was widely cited as evidence of pay television's economic non-viability, on the premise that a pay-TV system required a minimum expenditure of $175 a year from half the families in the service area. Since no more than a tiny fraction of the households in the areas served by these pioneer pay-TV systems were equipped to receive it, the question remained academic.

In a paper delivered before the American Economic Association in 1965, David Blank, the chief economist for CBS, expressed doubt that pay TV could generate substantial audiences for programs that differed in character from the standard entertainment offered by the commercial networks. Reviewing the experience to date of pay-TV experiments, Blank concluded that they had proved revenues insufficient to provide adequate self-support. In Etobicoke, with half the families on the wire, revenues were less than a $1 a week, and when the minimum was raised, only 15% of the families retained their subscriptions. In Los Angeles less than a third, and in San Francisco only a fifth, of the families in pay-TV areas chose to subscribe, and they spent little more than $1 a week. In Hartford, Connecticut, only 4% chose to subscribe, though revenues were about $2 a week.

Between 80% and 90% of the pay-TV viewing was of feature films not yet released to free TV. In Hartford, the highest percentage of viewing came for the boxing match between (the then) Cassius Clay and Sonny Liston. The lowest of 599 rated programs was a professorial talk show, "You and the Economy," which got one subscriber out of 4,717.

Blank took issue with the thesis advanced by another economist, Tibor Scitovsky, who argued that producers in a competitive market system tend "to play safe and not to risk imaginative innovations," in order to take advantage of the economies of scale inherent in mass production. Scitovsky felt that this philosophy could "lead to a serious misreading of the public taste and the imposition of a mythical majority taste that in fact few people have." Blank scoffed at the example Scitovsky cited to make his point: Detroit's insistence that the public wanted more powerful and larger cars, although competition from small foreign cars showed otherwise. Blank concluded, "Professor Scitovsky's view of the public desires, colored no doubt by his own attitude toward size and power of cars, has proved to be largely erroneous and any preference by the public for small cars has proved to be mostly a passing fancy." The passing of another half-dozen years has shown Scitovsky to be right after all, and has raised new questions about the finality of Blank's judgment about the inability of pay television to serve minority interests.

The heavyweight bout between Mohammed Ali and Joe Frazier in March, 1971, seen by two million fans over closed-circuit TV in movie theaters, yielded far greater revenues than commercial sponsorship could yield over free television accessible to a far wider audience. (Each of the boxers received a $2.5 million guarantee.) Although this was an extraordinary event that could hardly be duplicated every night, it did illustrate dramatically the possibility of making pay television an economically attractive proposition based on only a tiny minority of viewers, diverting talent away from commercial television.

The predictable growth of cable TV, with its ultimate conversion into a two-way system connected to a computerized billing facility, will make pay TV a more lively subject of discussion and experimentation in the years to come. Whether or not the growth of cable television is linked to a pay system, it will continue to provide viewers with an increased range of choices, but not all these choices will meet the tastes of the mass audience. In London, Ontario, in which eight out of ten homes had cable TV in 1971, a study by the Canadian Television Bureau found no viewing "of measurable proportions" for the locally programmed cable channel.

BIBLIOGRAPHY

Books

Advertising Research Foundation. *Recommended Standards for Radio and Television Program Audience Size Measurements.* New York: 1954.

Arnheim, Rudolf. *Radio.* London: Faber & Faber Ltd., 1936.

Bauchard, Philippe. *The Child Audience. A Report on Press, Film and Radio for Children.* Paris: UNESCO, 1952.

Berelson, Bernard R., Lazarsfeld, Paul F. and McPhee, William N. *Voting.* Chicago: University of Chicago Press, 1954.

Blumer, Herbert. *Movies and Conduct.* New York: Macmillan Company, 1933.

—— and Hauser, Philip. *Movies, Deliquency and Crime.* New York: Macmillan Company, 1933.

Cantril, Hadley, *The Invasion from Mars.* Princeton: Princeton University Press, 1940.

Crosby, John. *Out of the Blue.* New York: Simon and Schuster, 1952.

Dewhurst, J. F. and Associates. *America's Needs and Resources.* New York: Twentieth Century Fund, 1955.

Eisenberg, Azriel L. *Children and Radio Programs.* New York: Columbia University Press, 1936.

Elliott, William Y., (editor). *Television Impact on American Culture,* East Landing: Michigan State University Press, 1954.

Field, Harry and Lazarsfeld, Paul F. *The People Look at Radio.* Chapel Hill: University of North Carolina Press, 1946.

Forman, Henry James. *Our Movie-Made Children.* New York: Macmillan Company, 1933.

Gilbert, Eugene. "Advertising and Marketing to Young People," Pleasantville, New York: Printer's Ink Books, 1957.

Gorham, Maurice. *Broadcasting and Telecasting since 1900.* London: Andrews Dakers Ltd., 1952.

Head, Sydney W. *Broadcasting in America,* Boston: Houghton Mifflin, 1956.

Horton, Donald, Mauksch, Hans O. and Lang, Kurt. *Chicago Summer Television July 30-August 5, 1951.* Urbana: National Association of Educational Broadcasters, 1951.

Janowitz, Morris and Marvick, Dwaine. *Competitive Pressure and Democratic Consent,* Ann Arbor: Bureau of Government, Institute of Public Administration, University of Michigan, 1956.

Lazarsfeld, Paul F. *Radio and the Printed Page.* New York: Duell, Sloan and Pearce, Inc., 1940.

—— and Kendall, Patricia. *Radio Listening in America* New York: Prentice-Hall, 1948.

—— and Stanton, Frank N. *Communications Research, 1948-1949.* New York: Harper and Brothers, 1949.

—— and —— *Radio Research, 1941.* New York; Duell, Sloan and Pearce, Inc., 1941.

—— and —— *Radio Research, 1942-1943.* New York: Duell, Sloan and Pearce, Inc., 1944.

——, Berelson, Bernard R. and Gaudet, Hazel. *The People's Choice.* New York: Duell, Sloan and Pearce, Inc., 1944.

Manvell, Roger. "The Crowded Air," New York: Channel Press, 1953.

Marx, Herbert L., Jr. (ed.). *Television and Radio in American Life.* New York: H. W. Wilson Company, 1953.

Merton, Robert K. *Mass Persuasion: The Social Psychology of a War Bond Drive.* New York: Harper and Brothers, 1940.

Parker, Everett, Berry, David and Smythe, Dallas. *The Television-Radio Audience and Religion,* New York: Harper and Brothers, 1955.

Paulu, Burton, British Broadcasting. *Radio and Television in the United Kingdom,* Minneapolis: University of Minnesota Press, 1956.

Remmers, H. H., et al. *Four Years of New York Television,* 1951-1954, Urbana, Illinois: National Association of Educational Broadcasters, 1954.

Rose, Cornelia B., Jr. *National Policy for Radio Broadcasting.* New York: Harper and Brothers, 1940.

Seldes, Gilbert. *The Great Audience.* New York: The Viking Press, Inc., 1951.

——– *The Public Arts,* New York: Simon and Schuster, 1956.

Shayon, Robert Lewis. *Television and Our Children.* New York: Longmans, Green and Company, 1951.

Siepmann, Charles A. *Radio, Television and Society.* New York: Oxford University Press, 1950.

—— *Television and Education in the United States.* Paris: UNESCO, 1952.

Smythe, Dallas W. *New Haven Television, May 15-21, 1952.* Urbana: National Association of Educational Broadcasters, 1952.

—— *Three Years of New York Television—January 4-10, 1951, 1952, 1953.* Urbana: National Association of Educational Broadcasters, 1953.

—— and Campbell, Angus. *Los Angeles Television, May 23-29, 1951.* Urbana: National Association of Educational Broadcasters, 1951.

Turner. E. S. *The Shocking History of Advertising.* New York: E. P. Dutton, 1953.

United Nations Educational, Scientific and Cultural Organization. *Television: A World Survey.* Paris: 1953.

—— *Television: A World Survey.* Supplement 1955. Paris: 1955.

White, Llewellyn. *The American Radio.* Chicago: University of Chicago Press, 1947. *(The quotations on pp. 282, 302, 305, 308 and 309 are copyrighted by the University of Chicago Press.)*

Wylie, Max. *Clear Channels: Television and the American People.* New York: Funk and Wagnalls Company, 1955.

Articles

"Is Radio Overdoing Music-and-News Programming?" *Sponsor,* Vol. IX, No. 23, November 14, 1955. Pp. 32-33 & 144-45.

"What TV Is Doing to America," *U. S. News & World Report,* Vol. XXXIX, No. 10, September 2, 1955. Pp. 36-50.

Abrams, Mark. "Child Audiences for Television in Great Britain," *Journalism Quarterly,* Vol. XXXIII, No. 1, Winter, 1956. Pp. 35-41.

Adorno, T. W. "How To Look At Television," *Quarterly of Film, Radio and Television,* Vol. VII, No. 3, Spring, 1954.

(Alexander, Sidney S.) "CBS Says U. S. TV Limit Is 600 Healthy Stations," *Broadcasting-Telecasting,* Vol. XLIX, No. 16, October 17, 1955. Pp. 27-31.

Anders, Gunther. "The Phantom World of TV," *Dissent,* Vol. III, No. 1 (1956), pp. 14-24.

Baker, Kenneth. "An Analysis of Radio's Programming," in Paul F. Lazarsfeld's and Frank N. Stanton's *Communications Research, 1948-1949.* New York: Harper and Brothers, 1949. Pp. 51-72.

Bogart, Leo. "Fan Mail for the Philharmonic," *Public Opinion Quarterly,* Vol. XIII, No. 3, Fall, 1949. Pp. 423-34.

Bryson, Lyman. "Broadcasting," *American Scholar,* Vol. XX, Autumn, 1951. Pp. 221-24.

Campbell, Angus, Gurin, Gerald and Miller, Warren E. "Television and the Election," *Scientific American,* Vol. CXXCVIII, May, 1953. Pp. 46-48.

Carpenter, C. R. "Psychological Research Using Television," *The American Psychologist,* Vol. X, No. 10, October, 1955. Pp. 606-10.

Clarke, Alfred C. "The Use of Leisure and its Relation to Levels of Occupational Prestige," *American Sociological Review,* Vol. XXI, No. 3, June, 1956. Pp. 301-07.

Coffin, Thomas E. "Television's Effect on Leisure-Time Activities," *Journal of Applied Psychology,* Vol. XXXII, 1949. Pp. 550-58.

——— "Television's Impact on Society," *The American Psychologist,* Vol. X, No. 10, October, 1955. Pp. 630-41.

Cousins, Norman, "The Time Trap," *Saturday Review,* Vol. XXXII, No. 52, December 24, 1949. P. 20.

Dunham, Franklin. "A New Road to the Abundant Life: A Survey of Educational Television," *The American Psychologist,* Vol. X, No. 10, October, 1955. Pp. 615-17.

Faulkner, Nancy. "The State of Educational Television," *Senior Scholastic,* Vol. LXIV, No. 13, May 5, 1954. P. 37-T.

Freidson, Eliot. "The Relation of the Social Situation of Contact to the Media in Mass Communication," *Public Opinion Quarterly,* Vol. XVII, No. 2, Summer, 1954. Pp. 230-38.

Geiger, Theodor. "A Radio Test of Musical Taste," *Public Opinion Quarterly,* Vol. XIV, No. 3, Fall, 1950. Pp. 452-60.

Haskins, Jack B. and Jones, Robert L. "Trends in Newspaper Reading: Comic Strips, 1949-54," *Journalism Quarterly,* Vol. XXXII, No. 4, 1955. Pp. 422-33.

Hazard, Leland. "Educational Television," *The Atlantic Monthly,* Vol. CXCVI, No. 5, November, 1955. Pp. 61-64.

Head, Sydney W. "Content Analysis of Television Drama Programs," *The Quarterly of Film, Radio and Television,* Vol. IX, No. 2, Winter, 1954. Pp. 175-194.

Herzog, Herta. "Why Did People Believe in the 'Invasion From Mars'," in Paul F. Lazarsfeld's and Morris Rosenberg's *The Language of Social Research.* Glencoe: Free Press, 1954. Pp. 420-28.

Kaiser, Walter H. "TV and Reading; Report No. 1," *Library Journal,* Vol. LXXVI, February 15, 1951. Pp. 348-50.

———— "TV and Reading; Report No. 2," *Library Journal,* Vol. LXXVII, February 15, 1952. Pp. 309-16.

Kelly, George A. "Television and the Teacher," *The American Psychologist,* Vol. X, No. 10, October, 1955. Pp. 590-92.

Kintner, Robert E. "Television and Radio—Today and Tomorrow," *Television Digest,* Special Report, November 5, 1955.

Lazarsfeld, Paul F. "Why Is So Little Known About the Effects of TV and What Can Be Done About It," *Public Opinion Quarterly,* Vol. XIX, No. 3, Fall, 1955. Pp. 243-51.

———— and Dinerman, Helen. "Research for Action," in Paul F. Lazarsfeld's and Frank N. Stanton's *Communications Research, 1948-1949.* New York: Harper and Brothers, 1949. Pp. 73-106.

Levin, Harvey J. "Competition Among Mass Media and the Public Interest," *Public Opinion Quarterly,* Vol. XVII, No. 1, Spring, 1954. Pp. 62-79.

Maccoby, Eleanor. "Why Do Children Watch Television?", *Public Opinion Quarterly,* Vol. XVIII, No. 3, Fall, 1954. Pp. 239-44.

McDonagh, Edward C. "Television and the Family," *Sociology and Social Research,* Vol. XXXV, No. 2, November-December, 1950. Pp. 113-22.

McGinnis, W. G. "Now It's Television," *The Journal of Education,* Vol. CXXXIII, May, 1950. P. 152.

(McPhee, William N. and Meyersohn, Rolf.) "Broadcast Evolution: From Radio to Radio," *Broadcasting-Telecasting,* January 23, 1956. Pp. 78-80.

———— "Radio and the Fight for Time," *Broadcasting-Telecasting,* January 16, 1956. Pp. 84-86.

Meerloo, Joost A. M. "Television Addiction and Reactive Apathy," *The Journal of Nervous and Mental Disease,* Vol. CXX, Nos. 3 & 4, September-October, 1954. Pp. 290-91.

Meyersohn, Rolf B. "Social Research in Television" in Bernard Rosenberg and David Manning White, *Mass Culture,* Glencoe, Free Press, 1957. Pp. 345-357.

Meyrowitz, E. L. and Fiske, Marjorie. "The Relative Preference of Low-Income Groups for Small Stations," *Journal of Applied Psychology.* Vol. XXIII, No. 1, February, 1939.

Paulu, Burton. "The Challenge of the 242 Channels," *Quarterly of Film, Radio and Television,* Vol. VII, No. 1, Fall, 1952. Pp. 1-12 and Vol. VII. No. 3, Winter, 1952. Pp. 140-149.

Riley, Matilda W. and John W. "A Sociological Approach to Communication Research," *Public Opinion Quarterly,* Fall, 1951. Pp. 445-60.

Sandage, C. H. "Measuring the Results," *Education on the Air.* Columbus: Ohio State University, 1952.

Seiler, James W. "Novelty Factor in Viewing: It's Myth, Research Shows," *Telecasting Yearbook-Marketbook,* 1955-56.

―――― "The ARB Story," *Television Age,* Vol. III, No. 4, November, 1955. Pp. 50 & 104.

Siepmann, Charles A. and Reisberg, Sidney. " 'To Secure These Rights': Coverage of a Radio Documentary," *Public Opinion Quarterly,* Vol. XII, No. 4, Winter, 1948-49. Pp. 649-58.

Simon, Herbert A. and Stern, Frederick. "The Effect of Television Upon Voting Behavior in Iowa in the 1952 Presidential Election," *The American Political Science Review,* Vol. XLIX, No. 2, June, 1955. Pp. 470-77.

Smythe, Dallas W. "A National Policy on Television?", *Public Opinion Quarterly,* Vol. XIV, No. 3, Fall, 1950. Pp. 461-74.

―――― "Reality As Presented by Television," *Public Opinion Quarterly,* Vol. XVIII, No. 2, Summer, 1954. Pp. 143-56.

――― "The Consumer's State in Radio and Television," *Quarterly of Film, Radio and Television,* Vol. VI, No. 2, Winter, 1951. Pp. 109-28.

――― "What Television Programming is Like," Vol. VI, No. 1, Fall, 1952. Pp. 25-31.

Stewart, David C. "School Telecasting—A Report," *The Journal of the AERT,* Vol. XV, No. 6, April, 1956. Pp. 10-14.

Stouffer, Samuel A. "The Effects of Radio Upon Newspaper Circulation," in Paul F. Lazarsfeld's *Radio and the Printed Page.* New York: Duell, Sloan and Pearce, Inc., 1940. Pp. 266-72.

Swanson, Charles E. and Jones, R. D. "Television Owning and Its Correlates," *Journal of Applied Psychology,* Vol. XXXV, No. 5, October, 1955. Pp. 352-57.

Tannenbaum, Percy H. "What Effect When TV Covers a Congressional Hearing?" *Journalism Quarterly,* Vol. XXXII, No. 4, 1955. Pp. 434-40.

Usher, Ann. "TV . . . Good or Bad for Your Children?", *Better Homes & Gardens,* Vol. XXXIII, No. 10, October, 1955. P. 145.

Warner, W. Lloyd and Henry, William E. "The Radio Daytime Serial: A Symbolic Analysis," *Genetic Psychology Monographs,* Vol. XXXVII, 1948. Pp. 3-71.

Wiebe, Gerhart D. "A New Dimension in Journalism," *Journalism Quarterly,* Vol. XXXI, No. 4, Fall, 1954. Pp. 411-20.

—— "Radio and Television: Looking Ahead 20 Years," *Journalism Quarterly,* Vol. XXXII, No. 1, Winter, 1955, Pp. 27-30.

Wischner, George J. and Scheier, Ivan H. "Some Thoughts on Television as an Educational Tool," *The American Psychologist,* Vol. X, No. 10, October, 1955. Pp. 611-14.

Witty, Paul. "Children and TV—A Fifth Report," *Elementary English,* October, 1954, Pp. 9.

——"Children's, Parents' and Teachers' Reactions to Television," *Elementary English,* Vol. XXVII, No. 6, October, 1950. Pp. 8.

Zajonc, Robert. "Some Effects of the 'Space' Serials," *Public Opinion Quarterly,* Vol. XVIII, No. 4, Winter, 1954-55. Pp. 367-74.

Miscellaneous

Radio and Television Today in SUCCESSFUL FARMING Homes. Iowa: Meredith Publishing Company, 1953.

Adams, J. Stacy. *A Selected Bibliography of Research in Television.* North Carolina: *North Carolina Educational Radio and Television Commission, the University of North Carolina, 1955.*

——— "An Exploratory Study of Viewers and Non-Viewers of Educational Television," Chapel Hill: Institute for Research in Social Science, University of North Carolina, 1956.

Advertest Research. *News Bulletin.* Number 2. New Jersey: 1954.

Advertising Research Foundation. *National Survey of Television Sets in U. S. Households—June, 1955.* New York: 1955.

—— Radio-TV Bibliography. New York: 1954.

American Broadcasting Company. *Eye vs. Ear.* New York: 1952.

—— *Millions of Numbers.* New York. (no date)

—— *The P's and Q's of V's and U's.* New York: 1953.

—— *What's Happened to Network Radio?* New York. (no date)

Audience Research, Inc. *Effect of Television on Motion Picture Attendance.* Princeton: 1950.

Batten, Barton, Durstine & Osborn, Inc. *What's Happening to Leisure Time in Television Homes?* New York: 1951.

Battin, T. C. *Television and Youth.* Washington: National Association of Radio-Television Broadcasters, 1954.

——— "The Use of the Diary Method Involving the Questionnaire-Interview Technique to Determine the Impact of Television on School Children in Regard to Viewing Habits and Formal and Informal Education." Unpublished Ph.D. dissertation, University of Michigan, 1951.

Beville, Hugh M., Jr. *Television Ratings.* New York: National Broadcasting Company, 1954.

Broadcast Advertising Bureau, Inc. *Listeners on Wheels.* New York: 1952.

——— *Radio Set Sales in "Mature" TV Markets.* New York: 1954.

——— *The Cumulative Audience of Women's Radio Programs.* New York: 1954.

Bureau of Advertising, American Newspaper Publishers' Association, *The Little Woman Who Wasn't There.* New York: 1956.

Carr, Constance (ed.). *Children and TV.* (Bulletin 93). Washington: Association for Childhood Education International, 1954.

Chicago Tribune. *A Study of Television Viewing in the Chicago Market.* Chicago: 1955.

Coffin, Thomas E. *Television's Effects on the Family's Activities.* Hempstead, New York: Hofstra College, 1948.

Columbia Broadcasting System. *Added Perspective on Television.* New York: 1950.

——— *Television Today.* New York: 1949.

——— *The Sound of Your Life.* New York: 1950.

Crosley Broadcasting Corporation. *The Influence of Television on the 1952 Election.* Cincinnati: 1952.

Cunningham and Walsh, Inc. *Videotown.* 8 Annual Reports. NewYork: 1948-1955.

Erwin, Wasey and Company. *Audience Reaction to Evening Television Programs.* New York: 1951.

Field, Mervin D. *"Free" versus "Fee" TV.* Release #200. California: The California Poll, 1955.

Fine, Bernard J. and Maccoby, Nathan. *Television and Family Life.* Boston: Boston University School of Public Relations and Communications, 1952. (mimeographed)

Goldberg, Melvin Arthur. "Politics and Television." Unpublished Master's thesis, Columbia University, 1949.

Gray, Barbara. "The Emotional and Social Effects of the Recreational Film on Adolescents of 13 to 14 in the West Bromwich (Birmingham) Area." A thesis submitted to the University of Birmingham, 1952.

C. E. Hooper, Inc. *Coincidental-Diary Method of Television Audience Measurement.* New York: 1953.

Johnson, Donald William. "The Effect of Television Set Ownership Upon Public Library Use." Unpublished Master's thesis, Graduate Library School, University of Chicago, 1954.

Jordan, Jerry N. *Television's Novelty Is Over. What Can You Expect Now? (5th Annual Report).* Washington: Radio-Electronics-Television Manufacturers Association, 1954.

———— *The Long-Range Effect of Television and Other Factors on Sports Attendance.* Washington: Radio-Television Manufacturers Association, 1950.

Jorgensen, Erling S. "The Relative Effectiveness of Three Methods of Television Newscasting," unpublished, *Doctoral Dissertation,* University of Michigan, 1955.

Koch, Freda Postle. *Children's Television Habits in the Columbus Ohio, Area.* Ohio: Television Committee, Franklin County, Ohio Section, White House Conference on Children and Youth, 1952.

Lawton, Sherman. *When TV Moves In.* University of Oklahoma Broadcasting Studies #41, 42, 45, 46, 54, 55. Norman: 1950. (mimeographed)

Maccoby, Eleanor. "The Effects of Emotional Arousal on Retention of Aggressive and Non-Aggressive Movie Content." 1955. (unpublished)

Magazine Advertising Bureau. *Television as an Advertising Medium.* New York: 1952.

McDonagh, Edward C., et al. *Television and the Family.* California: University of Southern California, 1950.

McGeehan, John R. and Maranville, Robert L. *Television: Impact and Reaction in Lexington, Kentucky.* Lexington: University of Kentucky, 1953.

John Meck Industries, Inc. *A Study of the Comparative Viewing Habits, Program Preferences and Effects of Television Among High-Income and Low-Income Families.* Plymouth, Indiana: 1950.

Meyersohn, Rolf. *Television Research: An Annotated Bibliography.* New York: Bureau of Applied Social Research, Columbia University. (no date)

Mutual Broadcasting System. *Radio . . . The Living Medium.* New York: 1954.

National Broadcasting Company. *Daylight Selling Time.* New York: 1953.

———— *Evening Radio.* New York: 1955.

———— *How Television Changes Strangers Into Customers.* New York: 1955.

———— *Model House with 117,000,000 Rooms.* New York: 1952.

———— *NBC Study of Radio's Effective Sales Power.* New York: 1952.

———— *Recent Candid Pictures of a Friend, Evening Radio.* New York: 1954.

———— *Summer Television Advertising.* New York: 1952.

———— *Television Today:* Its Impact on People and Products. New York: 1951-52.

———— *Television's Daytime Profile.* New York: 1954.

———— *The Hofstra Study: A Measure of TV Sales Effectiveness.* New York: 1950.

———— *Why Sales Come in Curves.* New York: 1954.

National Citizens Committee for Educational Television. *This Is Educational Television.* Washington: 1955.

National Council of the Churches of Christ in the United States of America, Central Department of Research and Survey. *Information Service,* Vol. XXXIII, No. 17, April 24, 1954.

A. C. Nielsen Company, *Radio '55.* New York: 1955.

Nielsen, Arthur C. *Radio and Television Audience Research.* Michigan: Bureau of Business Research, School of Business Administration, University of Michigan, 1953.

Paulu, Burton (ed.). *Radio-Television Bibliography.* Urbana: National Association of Educational Broadcasters, 1952.

Peerless, Helen Evelyn. "The Effect of Television on Reading." Unpublished thesis, 1955.

Alfred Politz Research, Inc. *National Survey of Radio and Television Sets Associated with U. S. Households.* New York: The Advertising Research Foundation, 1954.

——— *Radio Today.* New York: Henry I. Christal Company, Inc., 1955.

——— *The Importance of Radio in Television Areas Today.* New York: Henry I. Christal Company, Inc., 1953.

Pool, Ithiel de Sola. *TV and the Images of the Candidates in '52.* Cambridge, Massachusetts: 1955. (unpublished)

The Pulse, Inc. *Radio Listening in Metropolitan New York Among. Families with 1, 2, and 3 or More Radios.* New York: 1953.

Radio Advertising Bureau. *Radio and Single Working Women in Metropolitan Markets.* New York: 1955.

——— *Radio and Working Housewives in Metropolitan Markets.* New York: 1955.

——— *They All Have Radio.* New York: 1955.

——— *Why Are They Buying All Those New Radio Sets?* New York: 1955.

Radio-Television Manufacturers Association. *The Impact of TV Expansion.* Washington: 1951.

Ratner, Victor. *Intellectuals and the Popular Taste.* New York: 1955. (unpublished)

Remmers, H. H., Horton, R. E. and Mainer, R. E. *Attitudes of High School Students toward Certain Aspects of Television.* Indiana: Purdue University, 1953.

Richmond Times-Dispatch and The Richmond News Leader. *The Impact of Television on Newspaper Reading.* Virginia: 1955.

Ripley, Joseph M., Jr. *Levels of Attention of Women Listeners to Daytime and Evening Television Programs in Columbus, Ohio.* Ohio: Department of Speech, Ohio State University, 1955.

Rock, Robert T., Duva, James S. and Murray, John E. *A Study in Learning and Retention.* Port Washington, New York: U. S. Navy Special Devices Center. (no date)

———*The Comparative Effectiveness of Instruction by Television, Television Recordings, and Conventional Classroom Procedures.* Port Washington, New York: U.S. Navy Special Devices Center. (no date)

Sarnoff, David. *Comments of National Broadcasting Company, Inc. Before the Federal Communications Commission,* Washington, D. C., June 6, 1955.

Seibert, Joseph. *The Influence of Television on the Election of 1952.* Oxford, Ohio: Miami University. (no date)

(Sheatsley, Paul B. and Borsky, Paul N.). *The Effects of Television on College Football Attendance.* 6 Reports. Chicago: National Opinion Research Center, University of Chicago, 1950-1954.

W. R. Simmons & Associates, Research, Inc. *Television's Daytime Profile.* New York: National Broadcasting Company, 1954.

Sponsor Services, Inc. *All-Media Evaluation Study.* New York: 1954.

Stanton, Frank N. *Memory for Advertising Copy Presented Visually vs. Orally.* Ohio: Ohio State University, 1933.

Stewart, Raymond F. *The Social Impact of Television on Atlanta Households.* Atlanta: Division of Journalism, Emory University, 1952.

Stuit, Dewey B., et al. "An Experiment in Teaching," State University of Iowa, Iowa City, 1956 (mimeographed).

Sweetser, Frank L., Jr. *Grade School Families Meet Television.* Research Report #1. Massachusetts: Department of Sociology and Anthropology, Graduate School, Boston University, 1953.

Taylor, Ruth E. "The Influence of Television on Leisure-Time Activities." Unpublished Master's thesis, Northwestern University, 1949.

Teen-Age Survey Service. *Radio, Television, Music Report.* New York: 1955.

Television Bureau of Advertising, Inc. *Advertising's All-Purpose Working Tool.* New York: 1956.

—— *The Case of the Curious Quintiles.* New York: 1956.

TV Guide. *Sources of TV Program Information Study of 12 Markets.* New York: 1955.

U. S. Congress. Senate Committee on Interstate and Foreign Commerce. *Status of UHF and Multiple Ownership of TV Stations.* Hearings before the Subcommittee on Communications. 83d Congress, 2d Session. Washington: Government Printing Office, 1954.

—— Senate Committee on the Judiciary. *Television and Juvenile Delinquency.* Interim Report of the Subcommittee to investigate juvenile delinquency. 84th Congress, 1st Session. Washington: Government Printing Office, 1955.

U. S. Department of Commerce. *Business Service Bulletin.* No. 53. Washington: Government Printing Office, 1954.

—— *Television as an Advertising Medium.* Washington: Government Printing Office, 1949.

University of Wisconsin Television Laboratory. *Content Preferences in Television.* Research Bulletin No. 4. Wisconsin: 1955.

Van Volkenburg, J. L. *Television's Impact on American Business.* New York: Columbia Broadcasting System, 1952.

WCBS. *What Television Didn't Do to Radio in New York.* New York: 1950.

Whan, Forest L. *1954 Iowa Radio-Television Audience Survey.* Des Moines: Central Broadcasting Company, 1954.

—— *1955 Iowa Radio Audience Survey.* Des Moines: Central Broadcasting Company, 1955.

—— *The Kansas Radio-Television Audience of 1953.* Manhattan, Kansas: 1953.

Xavier University. *Of Children and Television.* Cincinnati: 1951.

Young and Rubicam, Inc. *Effect of Television on Other Activities.* New York: 1951.

(Zorbaugh, Harvey and Mills, C. Wright). *A Report on the Impact of Television in a Major Metropolitan Market.* New York: Puck, the Comic Weekly, 1952.

SUPPLEMENTAL BIBLIOGRAPHY

Books

Arons, Leon and May, Mark. *Television and Human Behavior.* New York: Appleton-Century-Crofts, 1963.

Bandura, Albert and Walters, Richard H. *Social Learning and Personality Development.* New York: Holt, Rinehart & Winston, 1963.

Bauer, Raymond A. and Greyser, Stephen A. *Advertising in America: The Consumer View.* Boston: Harvard Graduate School of Business Administration, 1968.

Baumol, William J. and Bowen, William G. *Performing Arts: The Economic Dilemma,* Twentieth Century Fund: New York, 1966.

Benton, Charles W., Howell, Wayne K., Oppenheimer, Hugh C., and Urrows, Henry H. *Television in Urban Education.* New York: Praeger Publishers, 1969.

Blumler, Jay G. and McQuail, Denis. *Television in Politics.* Chicago: University of Chicago Press, 1969.

Bogart, Leo. *Strategy in Advertising.* New York: Harcourt Brace Jovanovich, 1967.

Carnegie Commission on Educational Television. *Public Television: A Program for Action.* New York: Bantam Books, 1967.

Chester, Edward W. *Radio, Television and American Politics.* New York: Sheed & Ward, 1969.

Chu, Godwin C. and Schramm, Wilbur. *Learning from Television: What the Research Says.* Washington, D.C.: National Association of Educational Broadcasters, 1967.

Feshbach, Seymour M. and Singer, Robert D. *Television and Aggression.* San Francisco: Jossey-Bass, 1971.

Friendly, Fred W. *Due to Circumstances beyond Our Control.* New York: Random House, 1967.

Glick, Ira and Levy, Sidney. *Living with Television.* Chicago: Aldine Publishing Company, 1962.

Greenberg, Bradley S. and Dervin, Brenda. *Use of the Mass Media by the Urban Poor.* New York: Praeger Publishers, 1970.

Halloran, James D. *The Effects of Mass Communication with Special Reference to Television.* Leicester: Leicester University Press, 1964.

Halloran, James D., Brown, R. L. and Chaney, D. C. *Television and Delinquency.* Leicester: Leicester University Press, 1970.

Hansen, Donald A. and Parsons, J. Herschel. *Mass Communication: A Research Bibliography.* Santa Barbara: Glendessary, 1968.

Hero, Alfred O. *Mass Media and World Affairs.* Boston: World Peace Foundation, 1959.

Himmelweit, Hilda T., Oppenheim, A. N. and Vince, Pamela. *Television and the Child.* London: Oxford University Press, 1958.

Johnson, Nicholas. *How to Talk Back to Your Television Set.* Boston: Little, Brown and Company, 1970.

Johnson, William O., Jr. *Super Spectator and the Electric Lilliputians.* Boston: Little, Brown and Company, 1971.

Klapper, Joseph T. *The Effects of Mass Communication.* New York: The Free Press, 1960.

Lang, Kurt and Lang, Gladys Engel. *Politics & Television.* Chicago: Quadrangle Books, 1968.

Lang, Kurt and Lang, Gladys Engel. *Voting and Nonvoting.* Waltham: Blaisdell Publishing Co., 1968.

Larsen, Otto N. (editor). *Violence and the Mass Media.* New York: Harper & Row, 1968.

Maletzke, Gerhard. *Fernsehen im Leben der Jugend.* Hamburg: Hans Bredow Verlag, 1959.

———. *Psychologie der Massenkommunikation.* Hamburg: Hans Bredow Verlag, 1963.

Mendelsohn, Harold and Crespi, Irving. *Polls, Television and the New Politics.* Scranton: Chandler Publishing Co., 1970.

National Advisory Commission on Civil Disorders. *Report.* New York: Bantam Books, 1968.

Schramm, Wilbur (editor). *The Impact of Television.* Urbana: University of Illinois Press, 1960.

Schramm, Wilbur, Lyle, Jack and Parker, Edwin B. *Television in the Lives of Our Children,* Stanford: Stanford University Press, 1961.

Schramm, Wilbur, Lyle, Jack and de Sola Pool, Ithiel. *The People Look at Educational Television.* Stanford: Stanford University Press, 1963.

Schramm, Wilbur, Coombs, Phillip H., Jahnert, Friedrich and Lyle, Jack. *The New Media: Memo to Educational Planners.* Paris: International Institute for Educational Planning, 1966.

Silbermann, Alphons. *Bildschirm und Wirklichkeit.* Berlin: Verlag Ullstein, 1966.

Skornia, Harry. *Television and Society.* New York: McGraw-Hill, 1965.

Small, William. *To Kill a Messenger: Television News and the Real World.* New York: Hastings House, Publishers, 1970.

Sopkin, Charles. *Seven Glorious Days, Seven Fun-Filled Nights.* New York: Simon & Schuster, 1968

Steiner, Gary A. *The People Look at Television.* New York: Alfred A. Knopf, 1963.

Thomson, R. J. *Television-Crime-Drama: Its Impact on Children and Adolescents.* Melbourne: F. W. Cheshire Pty., 1959.

Trenaman, John and McQuail, Denis. *Television and the Political Image.* London: Methuen, 1961.

Articles

Abel, John. "Television and Children: A Selective Bibliography of Use and Effects," *Journal of Broadcasting,* Vol. XIII, 1968-69. Pp. 101-105.

Alper, S. William and Leidy, Thomas R. "The Impact of Information Transmission through Television," *Public Opinion Quarterly,* Vol. XXXIII, No. 4, Winter, 1969-70. Pp. 556-62.

Bailyn, Lotte. "Approaches to the Study of Television," *The Journal of Social Issues,* Vol. XVIII, No. 2, 1962.

———. "Mass Media and Children: A Study of Exposure Habits and Cognitive Effects," *Psychological Monographs,* Vol. LXXIII, 1959. Pp. 1-48.

Bandura, A., Ross, D. and Ross, S. "Transmission of Aggression through Imitation of Aggressive Models," *Journal of Abnormal and Social Psychology,* Vol. LXIII, 1961. Pp. 575-82.

———. "Imitation of Film-Mediated Aggressive Models," *Journal of Abnormal and Social Psychology,* Vol. LXVI, 1963. Pp. 3-11.

———. "Vicarious Reinforcement and Imitative Learning," *Journal of Abnormal and Social Psychology,* Vol. LXVII, 1963. Pp. 601-607.

Bandura, A. "Influence of Models' Reinforcement Contingent on the Acquisition of Imitative Responses," *Journal of Personality and Social Psychology,* Vol. I, 1965. Pp. 589-95.

Bandura, Albert and Menlove, Frances L. "Factors Determining Vicarious Extinction of Avoidance Behavior through Symbolic Modeling," *Journal of Personality and Social Psychology,* Vol. VIII, 1966. Pp. 99-108.

Barcus, F. Earle. "Parental Influence on Children's Television Viewing," *Television Quarterly,* Vol. VIII, 1969. Pp. 63-73.

Barnes, Arthur M. "Research in Radio and Television News, 1947-57," *Journalism Quarterly,* Summer, 1957. Pp. 323-30.

Belson, William A. "Effects of Television on the Interests and Initiative of Adult Viewers in Greater London," *British Journal of Psychology,* Vol. L, Part 2, May, 1959. Pp. 145-58.

———. "Television and the Other Mass Media," *Business Review,* April, 1961.

Berkowitz, Leonard. "The Effects of Observing Violence," *Scientific American,* Vol. CCX, February, 1964. Pp. 35-41.

———. "Some Aspects of Observed Aggression," *Journal of Personality and Social Psychology,* Vol. II, No. 3, 1965. Pp. 359-69.

———. "Experimental Investigations of Hostility Catharsis," *Journal of Consulting and Clinical Psychology,* Vol. XXXV, 1970. Pp. 1-7.

Berkowitz, Leonard and Rawling, Edna. "Effects of Film Violence on Inhibitions against Subsequent Aggression," *Journal of Abnormal and Social Psychology,* Vol. LXVI, 1963. Pp. 405-412.

Berkowitz, Leonard and Geen, Russell. "Name-mediated Aggressive Cue Properties," *Journal of Personality and Social Psychology,* Vol. XXIII, 1966. Pp. 456–65.

———. "Stimulus Qualities of the Target of Aggression: A Further Study," *Journal of Personality and Social Psychology,* Vol. V, 1967. Pp. 364–68.

Blood, Robert. "Social Class and Family Control of Television Viewing," *Merrill-Palmer Quarterly,* Vol. VII, No. 2, 1961. Pp. 205–22.

Bogart, Leo. "Newspapers in the Age of Television," *Daedalus,* Winter, 1963.

Byrne, Gary C. "Mass Media and Political Socialization of Children and Pre-Adults," *Journalism Quarterly,* 1966. Pp. 140–42.

Carey, James W. "Variations in Negro-White Television Preference," *Journal of Broadcasting,* Vol. X, No. 3, 1966. Pp. 199–211.

Carter, Richard F. and Greenberg, Bradley S. "Newspapers or Television: Which Do You Believe?" *Journalism Quarterly,* Vol. XLII, No. 1, 1965. Pp. 29–34.

Catton, William R., Jr. "Value Modification by Mass Media," in Robert K. Baker and Sandra J. Ball, *Violence and the Media,* Staff Report to the National Commission on the Causes and Prevention of Violence. Washington, 1970.

Chaffee, Steven, McLean, Jack and Atkin, Charles. "Parental Influences on Adolescent Media Use," *American Behavioral Scientist,* Vol. XIV, 1971. Pp. 16–34.

Chang, Lawrence K. H. and Lemert, James B. "The Invisible Newsman and Other Factors in Media Competition," *Journalism Quarterly,* Autumn, 1968. Pp. 436–44.

Crozier, Michel. "Télévision et Développement culturel," *Communications,* Vol. VII, 1966. Pp. 11–26.

DeFleur, Melvin L. "Occupational Roles As Portrayed on Television," *Public Opinion Quarterly,* Vol. XXXVII, No. 1, Spring, 1964. Pp. 57-64.

DeFleur, Melvin L. and Lois B. "The Relative Contribution of Television As a Learning Source for Children's Occupational Knowledge," *American Sociological Review,* Vol. XXXII, No. 5, October, 1967. Pp. 777–89.

Duma, Andrzej. "Television Audience in Rural Clubs," *Gazette,* Vol. XIII, No. 1, 1967. Pp. 47–60.

Eron, L. D. "Relationship of TV Viewing Habits and Aggressive Behavior in Children," *Journal of Abnormal and Social Psychology,* Vol. LXVII, No. 2, 1963. Pp. 193–96.

Feshbach, S. "The Stimulating Versus Cathartic Effects of Vicarious Aggressive Activity," *Journal of Abnormal and Social Psychology,* Vol. LXIII, 1961. Pp. 381–85.

Firsov, Boris. "Leningrad's TV Audience," *Soviet Press*, Vol. VI, No. 3. Pp. 1–21.

Fletcher, Alan. "Negro and White Children's Television Program Preferences," *Journal of Broadcasting*, Vol. XIII, No. 4, 1969. Pp. 359–66.

Fox, Peter D. "Television Ratings and Cultural Programs," *Industrial Management Review*, Vol. V, No. 1, Fall, 1963. Pp. 37–44.

Friedmann, Georges. "Télévision et démocratie culturelle," *Communications*, No. 10, 1967.

Fuchs, Douglas A. "Election Day Television and Western Voting," *Public Opinion Quarterly*, Vol. XXX, No. 2, Summer, 1966. P. 2.

———. "Election-Day Radio-Television and Western Voting," *Public Opinion Quarterly*, Vol. XXX, Summer, 1966. Pp. 226–36.

Furu, Takeo. "Research on 'Television and the Child' in Japan," *Studies of Broadcasting*, No. 3, March, 1965. P. 51.

Gans, Herbert J. "The Mass Media As an Educational Institution," *Television Quarterly*, Vol. VI, No. 2, Spring, 1967. Pp. 20–37.

Geen, R. G. "Effects of Frustration, Attack and Prior Training in Aggressiveness upon Aggressive Behavior," *Journal of Personality and Social Psychology*. Vol. IX, No. 4, 1968. Pp. 316–21.

Geiger, Kent and Sokol, Robert. "Social Norms in Television Watching," *American Journal of Sociology*, Vol. LXV, 1959. Pp. 174–81.

Gentile, Frank and Miller, S. M. "TV and Social Class," *Sociology and Social Research*, Vol. XLV, No. 3, April, 1961. Pp. 259–64.

Glucksmann, Andre. "Rapport sur les recherches concernant les effets sur la jeunesse des scènes de violence au cinéma et à la télévision," *Communications*, Vol. VII, 1966. Pp. 74–119.

Goodman, Paul. "The Social Perspective," in Stanley T. Donner, ed., *The Meaning of Commercial Television*, Austin: University of Texas Press, 1966. Pp. 69–83.

Goranson, Richard E. "A Review of Recent Literature on Psychological Effects of Media Portrayals of Violence," in Robert K. Baker and Sandra J. Ball, *Violence and the Media*, Staff Report to the National Commission on the Causes and Prevention of Violence. Washington, 1970.

Greenberg, Bradley S. "Diffusion of News about the Kennedy Assassination," in Bradley S. Greenberg and Edwin B. Parker, eds., *The Kennedy Assassination and the American Public*. Stanford: Stanford University Press, 1965. Pp. 89–98.

Greenstein, Fred I. "College Students' Reactions to the Assassination," in Bradley S. Greenberg and Edwin B. Parker, eds., *The Kennedy Assassination and the American Public*. Stanford: Stanford University Press, 1965. Pp. 220–39.

Harvey, Bill. "Nonresponse in TV Meter Panels," *Journal of Advertising Research*, Vol. VIII, No. 2, June, 1968. Pp. 24–27.

Hazard, William R. "Anxiety and Preference for Television Fantasy,"

Journalism Quarterly, Vol. XLIV, No. 3, Autumn, 1967. Pp. 461–69.

Hess, Robert D. and Goldman, Harriet. "Parents' Views of the Effects of Television on Their Children," *Child Development,* Vol. XXXIII, 1962. Pp. 411–26.

Hicks, David. "Imitation and Retention of Film-mediated Aggressive Peer and Adult Models," *Journal of Personality and Social Psychology,* Vol. II, No. 1, 1965. Pp. 97–100.

Katz, Elihu and Feldman, Jacob J. "The Debates in the Light of Research: A Survey of Surveys," in Sidney Kraus, ed., *The Great Debates.* Bloomington: Indiana University Press, 1962.

Kay, Herbert. "You Just Think You Know!" *TV Guide,* October 13, 1962.

Klapper, Hope Lunin. "Does Lack of Contact with the Lecturer Handicap Televised Instruction?" in Harvey Zorbaugh, special-issue ed., *Journal of Educational Sociology*—"Television and College Teaching," Vol. XXXI, No. 9, May, 1958.

Krugman, Herbert E. "Brain Wave Measures of Media Involvement," *Journal of Advertising Research,* Vol. XI, No. 1, February, 1971. Pp. 3–9.

Larsen, Otto, Gray, Louis and Fortis, J. Gerald. "Achieving Goals through Violence on Television," *Sociological Inquiry,* Vol. VIII, 1963. Pp. 18–196.

Littler, Ner. "A Psychiatrist Looks at Television and Violence," *Television Quarterly,* Vol. VIII, No. 4, Fall, 1969. Pp. 7–23.

Lövass, O. Ivar. "Effect of Exposure to Symbolic Aggression on Aggressive Behavior," *Child Development,* Vol. XXXII, 1961. Pp. 37–44.

Lovibond, S. H. "The Effects of Media Stressing Crime and Violence upon Children's Attitudes," *Social Problems,* Vol. XV, 1967. Pp. 91–100.

McCombs, Maxwell E. "Negro Use of Television and Newspapers for Political Information, 1952–64," *Journal of Broadcasting,* Vol. XII, No. 3, Summer, 1968. Pp. 261–66.

McEvoy, Poynter. "Media Habit Survey of Indiana Homes," *Journalism Quarterly,* Vol. XXXVI, Winter, 1959. Pp. 63–64.

McNelly, John T. and Deutschmann, Paul J. "Media Use and Socio-Economic Status in a Latin American Capital," *Gazette,* Vol. LX, No. 1, 1963. Pp. 1–15.

Mendelsohn, Harold. "Election-Day Broadcasts and Terminal Voting Decisions," *Public Opinion Quarterly,* Vol. XXX, No. 2, 1966. Pp. 212–25.

Merrill, Irving R. "Broadcast Viewing and Listening," *Public Opinion Quarterly,* Vol. XXV, No. 2, Summer, 1961. Pp. 263–76.

Mindak, William H. and Hurse, Gerald D. "Television's Functions on the Assassination Weekend," in Bradley S. Greenberg and Edwin B. Parker, eds., *The Kennedy Assassination and the American Public,*

Stanford: Stanford University Press, 1965. Pp. 130–41.

Mussen, Paul and Rutherford, Eldred. "Effects of Aggressive Cartoons on Children's Aggressive Play," *Journal of Abnormal and Social Psychology,* Vol. LXII, 1961. Pp. 461–64.

Niven, Harold. "Who in the Family Selects the TV Program?" *Journalism Quarterly,* Vol. XXXVII, No. 1. Pp. 110–11.

Okabe, Keizo. "Broadcasting Research in Post-War Japan," *Studies of Broadcasting,* No. 1, March, 1963.

Parker, Edwin B. "The Effects of Television on Public Library Circulation," *The Public Opinion Quarterly,* Vol. XXVII, No. 4, Winter, 1963. Pp. 578–89.

Pearlin, L. I. "Social and Personal Stress and Escape Television Viewing," *Public Opinion Quarterly,* Vol. XXIII, No. 2, 1959. Pp. 255–59.

Potter, David. "The Historical Perspective," in Stanley T. Donner, ed., *The Meaning of Commercial Television.* Austin: University of Texas Press, 1966. Pp. 51–68.

Riter, Charles B. "What Influences Purchases of Color Televisions?" *Journal of Retailing,* Winter, 1966–67. Pp. 25–64.

Robinson, John P. and Converse, Philip E. "The Impact of Television on Mass Media Usage: A Cross-National Comparison," *Transactions of the Sixth World Congress of Sociology,* International Sociological Association, 1970.

Robinson, John P. and Swinehart, James W. "World Affairs and the TV Audience," *Television Quarterly,* Vol. VII, No. 2, Spring, 1968. Pp. 40–59.

Sato, Tomoo. "Sociological Structure of 'Mass Leisure,'" *Studies of Broadcasting,* No. 3, March, 1965. P. 134.

Scanlon, T. Joseph. "Color Television: New Language?" *Journalism Quarterly,* Vol. XLIV, No. 2, Summer, 1967. Pp. 225–30.

Schaps, Eric and Guest, Lester. "Some Pros and Cons of Color TV," *Journal of Advertising Research,* Vol. VIII, No. 2, June, 1968. Pp. 28–39.

Schramm, Wilbur. "Communication in Crisis," in Bradley S. Greenberg and Edwin B. Parker, eds., *The Kennedy Assassination and the American Public.* Stanford: Stanford University Press, 1965. Pp. 1–25.

Sheatsley, Paul B. and Feldman, Jacob J. "A National Survey of Public Reactions and Behavior," in Bradley S. Greenberg and Edwin B. Parker, eds., *The Kennedy Assassination and the American Public.* Stanford: Stanford University Press, 1965. Pp. 149–77.

Siegel, A. E. "Film-mediated Fantasy Aggression and Strength of Aggressive Drive," *Child Development,* Vol. XXVII, 1956. Pp. 355–78.

———. "The Influence of Violence in the Mass Media upon Children's Role Expectations," *Child Development,* Vol. XXIX, 1968. Pp. 35–56.

———. "The Effects of Media Violence on Social Learning," in Robert

K. Baker and Sandra J. Ball, *Violence and the Media,* Staff Report to the National Commission on the Causes and Prevention of Violence. Washington, 1970.

Sigel, Roberta S. "Television and the Reactions of Schoolchildren to the Assassination," in Bradley S. Greenberg and Edwin B. Parker, eds., *The Kennedy Assassination and the American Public.* Stanford: Stanford University Press, 1965. Pp. 199–219.

Suchy, John T. "How Does Commercial Television Affect British Viewing?" *Journalism Quarterly,* Winter, 1958. Pp. 65–71.

Thayer, John R. "The Relationship of Various Audience Composition Factors to Television Program Types," *Journal of Broadcasting,* Vol. VII, No. 3, 1963. Pp. 217–25.

———. "How Parents Rate TV Shows," *Television Magazine,* November, 1957. Pp. 55–106.

Venkatesan, M. and Haaland, G. A. "Divided Attention and Television Commercials: An Experimental Study," *Journal of Marketing Research,* Vol. V, No. 2, May, 1968. Pp. 203–205.

Walters, Richard H., Thomas, Edward Llewllyn and Acker, C. William. "Enhancement of Punitive Behavior by Audio-Visual Displays," *Science,* Vol. CXXXVI, No. 3519, 1962. Pp. 872–73.

Wand, Barbara. "Television Viewing and Family Choice Differences," *Public Opinion Quarterly,* Vol. XXXII, No. 1, Spring, 1968. Pp. 84–94.

Winick, Charles. "Censor and Sensibility: A Content Analysis of the Television Censor's Comments," *Journal of Broadcasting,* Spring, 1961. Pp. 117–35.

———. "Children's Television Fan Mail," *Television Quarterly,* Vol. III, No. 1, Winter, 1964. Pp. 57–71.

———. "How People Perceive Educational Television," *Journal of Social Psychology,* Vol. LXV, 1965. Pp. 259–67.

Witty, Paul. "Studies of the Mass Media 1949–1965," *Science Education,* Vol. L, No. 2, March, 1966. Pp. 119–26.

Witty, Paul A., Kinsella, Paul and Coomer, Anne. "A Summary of Yearly Studies of Televiewing, 1949–1963," *Elementary English,* October, 1963. Pp. 590–97.

Yamamoto, Toru. "The Growth of Television in Japan," *Studies of Broadcasting,* No. 2, March, 1964. P. 81.

Miscellaneous

Atkin, Charles K., Murray, John P. and Nayman, Oguz B. (editors). *Television and Social Behavior: An Annotated Bibliography of Research Focusing on Television's Impact on Children.* U. S. Department of

Health, Education, and Welfare, National Institute of Mental Health, 1971.

Barrow, Lionel C., Jr. and Westley, Bruce H. *Television Effects: A Summary of the Literature and Proposed General Theory.* Madison: University of Wisconsin Laboratory Bulletin No. 9, 1958.

Blank, David M. "The Quest for Quantity and Diversity in Television Programming" (mimeographed), New York: Columbia Broadcasting System, 1965.

Bower, Robert T. "Television and the Public," unpublished manuscript, Bureau of Social Science Research, Inc., Washington, D.C., 1971.

British Broadcasting Corporation. "The Public and the Programmes," London, 1959.

Buchanan, Dodds. "Product Interest as a Determinant of Differential Levels of Recall between Magazine Advertisements and Television Commercials," Ph.D. Dissertation, Massachusetts Institute of Technology, 1963.

Chaffee, Steven H. and McLeod, Jack M. "Adolescents, Parents, and Television Violence," paper presented at American Psychological Association convention, Washington, D.C., September, 1971.

Coffin, Thomas E. and Tuchman, Sam. "The Influence of Television Election Broadcasts in a Close Election" (mimeographed), New York: National Broadcasting Company, 1969.

Cunningham and Walsh, Inc. "Television and the Political Candidate," New York, 1959.

Ehrenberg, Andrew S. C. and Haldane, I. R. "The News in May" (mimeographed), 1968.

Foote, Cone & Belding Advertising, Inc. *TV Commercials: Who Pays Attention?* Media Research Department, September, 1970.

Gerbner, George. *Violence in Television Drama: A Study of Trends and Symbolic Functions* (mimeographed). Philadelphia: The Annenberg School of Communications, University of Pennsylvania, 1970.

Martin Goldfarb Consultants. "The Media and the People," in Special Senate Committee on Mass Media, *Research Studies,* Vol. III, Ottawa, 1970.

Greenberg, Bradley S. and Gordon, Thomas F. "Social Class and Racial Differences in Children's Perceptions of Television Violence," Department of Communication, Michigan State University. Report on research conducted for National Institute of Mental Health.

Hartley, Ruth L. *The Impact of Viewing "Aggression": Studies and Problems of Extrapolation.* New York: Columbia Broadcasting System Office of Social Research, 1964.

House of Representatives, 88th Congress. "The Methodology Accuracy and Use of Ratings in Broadcasting," Hearings before a Subcommittee of the Committee on Interstate and Foreign Commerce, Washington, 1963.

Horton, Robert W. "To Pay or Not to Pay: A Report on Subscription Television," Santa Barbara: Center for the Study of Democratic Institutions, 1960.

Irwin, John V. and Aronson, Arnold E. "Television Teaching" (mimeographed), University of Wisconsin Television Laboratory, 1958.

Jones, Mary Gardiner. "The Cultural and Social Impact of Advertising on American Society" (mimeographed), Washington: Federal Trade Commission, 1969.

Katz Television. "Factors Affecting Ratings of Early Evening Local TV Newscasts—Based on Analysis of ARB Reports for Top 100 Markets."

Herman W. Land Associates, "Television and the Wired City," Washington, D.C.: National Association of Broadcasters, 1968.

Liebert, Robert M. and Baron, Robert A. "Short-term Effects of Televised Aggression on Children's Aggressive Behavior," paper presented at American Psychological Association convention, Washington, D.C., September, 1971.

Lyle, Jack and Hoffman, Heidi R. "Television in the Daily Lives of Children," paper presented at American Psychological Association convention, Washington, D.C., September, 1971.

Maccoby, Michael. "Biophilia-Necrophilia and Television," in Ralph L. Stavins, editor, *Television Today*, Washington, D.C.: Communication Service Corporation (for The Institute for Policy Studies), 1971. Pp. 289–91.

Mazo, Earl, Moos, Malcolm, Hoffman, Hallock and Wheeler, Harvey. "The Great Debates," Santa Barbara: Center for the Study of Democratic Institutions, 1962.

McCombs, Maxwell. "Educational Television: Information versus Culture" (mimeographed), 1967.

———. "Mass Communication on the Campus," UCLA Communications Board, August, 1967.

Meyersohn, Rolf. "Criticisms of Television Commercials: A Report on Public Attitudes" (mimeographed), New York: National Association of Broadcasters, 1964.

Oxtoby-Smith, Inc. "Consumer Response to Pay TV" (mimeographed), New York, 1965.

Pennsylvania State University, Division of Academic Research and Services, "An Investigation of Closed-Circuit Television for Teaching University Courses," University Park, 1958.

Pockrass, Robert Mandell. "Effects of Learning on Continuous and Interrupted Exhibition of Educational Television Programs" (mimeographed), Palo Alto: Stanford University, 1960.

Alfred Politz Media Studies. "Coincidental Recall of Television Viewing," July, 1966.

Rarick, Galen. "Newspaper Item Readership and Prior Exposure Via Electronic Media" (mimeographed), University of Oregon, 1966.

Robinson, John P. "Social Change as Measured by Time-Budgets" (mimeographed), University of Michigan, 1967.

————. "Television and Leisure Time: Yesterday, Today and (Maybe) Tomorrow" (mimeographed), University of Michigan, 1967.

Simmons, W. R. "Evaluating Television Measurement Systems," unpublished paper delivered before the 14th Annual Conference, Advertising Research Foundation, October, 1968.

Singer, Benjamin D. "Television and the Riots" (mimeographed), London (Ontario): University of Western Ontario, 1968.

Sparks, Kenneth R. (editor). "A Bibliography of Doctoral Dissertations in Television and Radio," Syracuse: The School of Journalism, Newhouse Communications Center, Syracuse University, 1962 and 1965.

Television Advertising Representatives, Inc. *Psy-Color-Gy: A Study of the Impact of Color Television,* New York, 1966.

Television Information Office. "Television in Government and Politics: A Bibliography," New York, 1962.

Thomson, Charles A. H. "Television, Politics, and Public Policy," Washington: Brookings Institution, 1958.

Ward, Scott. "Children, Adolescents and Television Advertising" (mimeographed), Cambridge: Harvard Business School, 1970.

Westley, Bruce H. and Barrow, Lionel C., Jr. "Exploring the News" (mimeographed), University of Wisconsin Television Laboratory, 1959.

Winick, Charles. "Taste and the Censor in Television," New York: The Fund for the Republic, Inc., 1959.

Daniel Yankelovich, Inc. "A Study Concerning the Effect of Length on the Communication Value of Television Commercials" (mimeographed), New York, 1967.

INDEX